THE POCKET BOOK OF

modern verse is an original anthology edited for students and lovers of poetry by Oscar Williams, editor of *Immortal Poems of the English Language* and of the famous "Little Treasury Series," published by Charles Scribner's Sons, and a well-known contemporary poet in his own right. It is the most comprehensive and representative anthology of modern verse ever made available at so low a price. More than 500 poems by more than 100 poets are included. A glance at the Index of Authors and Titles will quickly show the extraordinary depth and scope of this volume— truly an exciting and rewarding bargain for every poetry lover.

*   *   *

THE POCKET BOOK OF

modern verse was first published in 1954 in a CARDINAL GIANT edition. It was revised to include an even more generous representation of contemporary poetry in a WASHINGTON SQUARE PRESS edition.

OTHER

POETRY ANTHOLOGIES

Edited by

Oscar Williams

MASTER POEMS OF THE ENGLISH LANGUAGE

Over 100 famous poems, from Wyatt to Dylan Thomas, each accompanied by a critical essay by a distinguished poet or critic of our time—including essays by I. A. Richards, Robert Penn Warren, William Empson, Cleanth Brooks, Robert Graves and Lionel Trilling.

1092 pages   W1446/$1.45

IMMORTAL POEMS OF THE ENGLISH LANGUAGE

A classic collection of the best-known works of British and American poets from Chaucer to Dylan Thomas, presented in chronological order, and including many longer works in their entirety.

638 pages   47591/90c

THE NEW POCKET ANTHOLOGY OF AMERICAN VERSE

A superb collection of poetry from colonial times to the present, emphasizing the poetry of the twentieth century and including new and exciting works by the younger poets of today.

638 pages   47592/90c

THE POCKET BOOK OF
modern verse

· ·

ENGLISH AND AMERICAN POETRY OF
THE LAST HUNDRED YEARS FROM
WALT WHITMAN TO DYLAN THOMAS

REVISED EDITION

EDITED BY

oscar williams

WASHINGTON SQUARE PRESS, INC. • NEW YORK

THE POCKET BOOK OF MODERN VERSE

REVISED EDITION

A *Washington Square Press* edition
1st printing.....................February, 1954
20th printing....................February, 1969

WSP

L

Published by
Washington Square Press, Inc., 630 Fifth Avenue, New York, N.Y.

WASHINGTON SQUARE PRESS editions are distributed in the
U.S. by Simon & Schuster, Inc., 630 Fifth Avenue, New
York, N.Y. 10020 and in Canada by Simon & Schuster
of Canada, Ltd., Richmond Hill, Ontario, Canada.

Standard Book Number: 671-47593-2.
Copyright, 1954, ©, 1958, by Washington Square Press, Inc.
Printed in the U.S.A.

ACKNOWLEDGMENTS AND COPYRIGHT NOTICES

*Most of the poems in this anthology are protected by copyright, and may not
be reproduced in any form without the consent of the poets, their publishers,
or their agents. Since this page cannot legibly accommodate all the copyright
notices, the five pages following (pages v through ix) constitute an extension of
the copyright page. Thanks are due to the following poets, their representatives,
and publishers for permission to include certain poems in this anthology:*

APPLETON-CENTURY-CROFTS, Inc.—for "The Apple Barrel of Johnny Appleseed" from *Going to the Sun* by Vachel Lindsay, copyright, 1923, by D. Appleton &
Co.; reprinted by permission of the publishers, Appleton-Century-Crofts, Inc.

JOSEPH BENNETT—for his two poems: "Uptown Express" reprinted from *The
Hudson Review*, Summer 1953, copyright, 1953, by The Hudson Review, Inc.; "To
Eliza, etc." from *Decembrist*, copyright, 1951, by Joseph Bennett, published by
Clarke & Way.

BRANDT & BRANDT—for "The Return" from *Wine from These Grapes*, published
by Harper & Row, copyright, 1934, by Edna St. Vincent Millay; for "On Hearing a
Symphony of Beethoven," "Moriturus" & "Dirge Without Music" from *The Buck
in the Snow*, published by Harper & Row, copyright, 1928, by Edna St. Vincent
Millay; for "Recuerdo" from *A few Figs from Thistles*, published by Harper &
Row, copyright, 1919, 1947, by Edna St. Vincent Millay; for "And you as well must
die, beloved dust" from *Second April*, published by Harper & Row, copyright, 1920,
1948, by Edna St. Vincent Millay; for "What lips my lips have kissed" from *The
Harp-Weaver and Other Poems*, published by Harper & Row, copyright, 1920, 1948, by
Edna St. Vincent Millay; for "Love is not all: it is not meat nor drink" from *Fatal
Interview*, published by Harper & Row, copyright, 1931, by Edna St. Vincent Millay.

JONATHAN CAPE, Ltd.—for the selections by W. H. Davies from *Collected Poems*;
for the selection by Henry Reed from *A Map of Verona*; for "The Holy Office" by
James Joyce from *The Essential James Joyce*.

CHATTO & WINDUS—for the selections by Wilfred Owen from *The Poems of Wilfred Owen*; for the selections by William Empson; for the selection by Peter Quennell.

THE CLARENDON PRESS—for the selections by Robert Bridges reproduced from *The Poetical Works of Robert Bridges*, by permission of the publishers.

J. V. CUNNINGHAM—for the two "Epigrams" from *New Poems by American Poets*, copyright, 1953, by Ballantine Books, Inc.

CURTIS BROWN, Ltd.—for "The Shield of Achilles" by W. H. Auden, from *Poetry*, copyright, 1952, by Modern Poetry Association; for "The Diaspora" by W. H. Auden; both poems reprinted by permission of the author; for "Choosing a Mast" by Roy Campbell, from a book published by Faber & Faber, Ltd.

THE JOHN DAY CO., Inc.—for the selections from *Selected Verse* by John Manifold, copyright, 1946, by The John Day Co., Inc.

REUEL DENNEY—for "McSorley's Bar" from *The Connecticut River*, published by Yale University Press.

GENE DERWOOD—for the selections from *New Poems 1940*, copyright, 1941, by Yardstick Press, from *New Poems 1942*, copyright, 1942, by The Peter Pauper Press, from *New Poems 1943*, copyright, 1943, by Oscar Williams, from *New Poems 1944*, copyright, 1944, by Oscar Williams, from *Accent*, copyright, 1941, by *Accent*, from *The Penguin Book of Sonnets*, copyright, 1943, by Penguin Books, Inc., and from John Holmes' *A Little Treasury of Love Poems*, copyright, 1950, by Charles Scribner's Sons.

THE DIAL PRESS—for the poem "The Zebras" from *Adamaster* by Roy Campbell, reprinted by permission of The Dial Press, copyright, 1931, by The Dial Press, Inc.

DODD, MEAD & CO.—for the selections by Rupert Brooke reprinted by permission of Dodd, Mead & Co. from *The Collected Poems of Rupert Brooke*, copyright, 1915, by Dodd, Mead & Co., Inc.; and also by permission of Sidgwick & Jackson, Ltd., Publishers, and McClelland and Stewart, Ltd.

DOUBLEDAY & CO., Inc.—for the selections by Rudyard Kipling from *A Diversity of Creatures*, by Rudyard Kipling, copyright, 1917, by Rudyard Kipling, from *The Seven Seas* by Rudyard Kipling, from *The Five Nations*, by Rudyard Kipling, copyright, 1903, by Rudyard Kipling, and from *Departmental Ditties and Ballads and Barrack Room Ballads*, by Rudyard Kipling, all reprinted by permission of Mrs. George Bambridge and Doubleday & Co., Inc.; for the selections by Theodore Roethke from *The Waking: Poems 1933-1953* by Theodore Roethke, copyright, 1932, 1953, by Theodore Roethke, reprinted by permission of Doubleday & Co., Inc.; for the selection from *Aegean Island and Other Poems*, by Bernard Spencer, copyright, 1946, by Bernard Spencer, reprinted by permission of Doubleday & Co., Inc.

RICHARD EBERHART—for the selections by Richard Eberhart from *Reading the Spirit, Burr Oaks, Song and Idea*, all published by Oxford University Press; for "The Noble Man" from *The Kenyon Review*, copyright, 1953, by Kenyon College; for "The Horse Chestnut Tree" from *Wake 10*, copyright, 1951, by Wake Editions, Inc.

FABER & FABER, Ltd.—for the selections by W. H. Auden, Louis MacNeice, Stephen Spender from the respective books by these authors; for the selections from *Collected Poems 1921-1951* by Edwin Muir; for the selections from *The Lady with the Unicorn* and *Ballad of the Mari Lwyd* by Vernon Watkins; for the selections from *Eros in Dogma* by George Barker.

FARRAR, STRAUS & YOUNG, Inc.—for the selections by W. R. Rodgers, from *Europa and the Bull*, copyright, 1952, by W. R. Rodgers, published by Farrar, Straus & Young, Inc.

ROY FULLER—for the poem "Meditation."

FUNK & WAGNALLS CO.—for the selection by Léonie Adams from *Poems: A Selection*, by permission of Funk & Wagnalls Co., New York, Publishers, copyright, 1954, by Léonie Adams.

DAVID GASCOYNE—for his poem "September Sun: 1947" from *A Vagrant and Other Poems*, published by John Lehmann.

HARCOURT, BRACE & WORLD, Inc.—for "i sing of Olaf" and "somewhere i have never travelled," copyright, 1931, 1959, by E. E. Cummings, reprinted from *Poems 1923-1954* by E. E. Cummings, by permission of Harcourt, Brace & World,

A. P. WATT & SON—for the selections by Robert Graves, from *Collected Poems (1914-1947)*, by permission of the author; for the selections by W. B. Yeats from *The Collected Poems of W. B. Yeats*, by permission of Mrs. W. B. Yeats and The Macmillan Co. of Canada; for the selections by Rudyard Kipling from *A Diversity of Creatures*, *The Seven Seas* and *Barrack Room Ballads*, by permission of Mrs. George Bambridge and The Macmillan Co. of Canada.

RICHARD WILBUR—for "Beasts" from *Bottegha Oscure* and *The Hudson Review*, Winter 1953, copyright, 1953, by The Hudson Review, Inc.; for "A Black November Turkey" from *The New Yorker*, copyright, 1953, by The New Yorker Magazine, Inc.

YALE UNIVERSITY PRESS—for "Dictum: For a Masque of Deluge" from *The Mask of Janus*, by W. S. Merwin, copyright, 1952, by Yale University.

ACKNOWLEDGMENTS FOR ADDITIONAL SELECTIONS IN THIS REVISED EDITION

The editor is deeply grateful to the following poets and publishers for permission:
ROY BASLER—for his poem "Exodus" first published in *The Silver Treasury of Light Verse*, copyright, 1957, by Oscar Williams; CHATTO & WINDUS—for "A Space in the Air" from *The Peaceable Kingdom* by Jon Silkin, copyright reserved; FREDERICK MORTIMER CLAPP—for three poems, copyright, 1958, by Frederick Mortimer Clapp; EDWIN DENBY—for two poems from *In Public, In Private*, copyright, 1948, by Edwin Denby; HOWARD GRIFFIN—for his poem first published in *The Criterion Book of Modern American Verse* edited by W. H. Auden, copyright, 1956, by Criterion Books, Inc.; GROVE PRESS—for "A Ballad of the Good Lord Nelson" from *Selected Poems* by Lawrence Durrell, copyright, 1956, by Lawrence Durrell; also for "To the Harbormaster" and "Poem" from *Meditations in an Emergency* by Frank O'Hara, copyright, 1957, by Frank O'Hara; THE HAND AND FLOWER PRESS, Aldington, Kent, England—for the two poems by Charles Causley from *Survivor's Leave*; HARPER & BROTHERS—for the three poems by Ted Hughes from *The Hawk in the Rain*, copyright, 1956, 1957, by Ted Hughes; EDWIN HONIG —for his poem "The Gazabos" first published in *The Nation*; HOUGHTON MIFFLIN CO.—for the poem "Old Inn on the Eastern Shore" from *Water Ouzel and Other Poems* by William H. Matchett; GALWAY KINNELL—for the revised version of his poem; PETER LEVI, S.J.—for the poem "From the Sixteenth Floor" by Richard Selig first published here; and to Miss Mary Buckley and Mr. John Hughes for their kindness in bringing the attention of the editor to this poem; LITTLE, BROWN & CO. and THE ATLANTIC MONTHLY PRESS—for "The Goose Fish" from *The Salt Gardens* by Howard Nemerov, copyright, 1950, 1951, 1952, 1953, 1954, 1955, by Howard Nemerov; THE MACMILLAN CO.—for "Notes on a Girl" from *For Some Stringed Instrument* by Peter Kane Dufault, copyright, 1954, 1955, 1956, 1957, by Peter Kane Dufault; also for "Samuel Sewall" from *A Summoning of Stones* by Anthony Hecht, copyright, 1948, 1949, 1950, 1951, 1952, 1953, 1954, by Anthony E. Hecht; Acknowledgments are due to THE MARVELL PRESS for permission to reprint "Next, Please" from *Less Deceived* by Philip Larkin; A. J. M. SMITH—for two poems from *A Sort of Ecstasy*, Ryerson Press and Michigan State College Press, copyright, 1954, by Michigan State College Press; W. D. SNODGRASS—for his poem "April Inventory" first published in *The Hudson Review*; JOHN THOMPSON, JR.— for his poem "A Love for Patsy" first published in *The Kenyon Review*; OSCAR WILLIAMS—for "Shelter" and "Third Madrigal" by Gene Derwood from *The Poems of Gene Derwood* published by Clarke & Way, copyright, 1955, by Oscar Williams; also for "Song" by Esther Mathews, copyright, 1938, by *Poetry* (Chicago); YALE UNIVERSITY PRESS—for "December: Of Aphrodite" from *The Dancing Bears* by W. S. Merwin, copyright, 1954, by Yale University Press.

EDITOR'S NOTE

The editor deeply regrets the omission of the poems of T. S. Eliot from this collection. Harcourt, Brace & Company have refused permission. In a letter dated November 4, 1953 Miss Catherine McCarthy of the Permissions Department writes, "The decision is not to permit the quotation of any of Mr. Eliot's verse in paperbound anthologies hereafter." See Publisher's Note, page 639.

contents

14 • contents

preface

Poetry is the natural language of lovers, whether they are entranced by a human being or anything else, quick, strange, familiar or odd, whether they love the creatures of life or life itself. Poetry is essential to all who feel, or are curious; it is a consolation to grief and a delight to speculation. Whenever an intensification of life occurs in that reading animal, man, he turns to poetry. The poet articulates what the reader experiences and exclaims.

And in poetry, as in ordinary speech, the right and best utterance for living readers is made in contemporary idiom. Everyone who is sensitive enough to seek and recognize the adventures of a day or of a lifetime needs at hand a compact and comprehensive collection of modern poetry in a format not too expensive to be dog-eared to pieces. It is to fill that need that *The Pocket Book of Modern Verse* is offered. It is the first all-modern anthology of such scope and size to be published since cheap paper editions have been available.

The collection is drawn from the work of the century from 1855 to the present. It begins with selections from *Leaves of Grass,* by Walt Whitman, which made 1855 auspicious, and made American poetry a peer of English literature. In this monumental work, modern poetry, both English and American, with its incessant experimentation in form, subject matter and vocabulary, may be said to have been initiated. When *Leaves of Grass* appeared Emily Dickinson was twenty-five and already writing her poems; Gerard Manley Hopkins was eleven but destined to complete his life's great work during the next thirty-four years. These two forerunners of modern poetry were unknown, and remained unheard in the latter half of the nineteenth century, Whitman was heard but unaccepted. Tennyson and Browning, however, were well-established poets in 1855. Although they continued to write after that year, they are so certainly Victorian that their work has been omitted herein. Certain poets of the latter nineteenth century, such as the Rossettis, Dowson, etc. have been sparingly included in spite of their Victorian flavor. Matthew Arnold, famous in his own day, still speaks satisfyingly in ours: his *Dover Beach,* with its prophetic insight of the human dilemma in latter day war, stirs a living generation still stranded on that uneasy shore. Thomas Hardy's astringent sadness bridges well the gap between his vision and W. H. Auden's *September 1, 1939.*

But the greater portion of this collection is devoted to the work of poets of the twentieth century, a lion's share of the space going to both older and younger poets now living, and writing.

It is astonishing to note the rapid maturing of American poetry, in this comparatively brief period of literary history, the number of major figures who have profoundly affected the writing of all poets, in English or other tongues. Whitman with his free (one is tempted to say liberated) verse, Emily Dickinson with her sparkingly specific imagery, Robert Frost with his homespun intelligence re-forming a classic philosophical content, Wallace Stevens and John Crowe Ransom bringing back a scholarly majesty to verse that had grown too easy, romantic and small.

British poetry too has seemed to gush forth with a renewed tensity of passion and sensitive understanding of the predicament of man, W. B. Yeats troubling his spirit into greatness, W. H. Auden reviving discarded forms and adorning them with the latest argot and vernacular, Dylan Thomas and George Barker swinging again to exciting romanticism but weighting it with a tragic quality that brings its own good order, and so on through the honor list not bettered by any century of the past, if we except Shakespeare's.

The Victorians were, on the whole, sure and optimistic about society, when they were gloomy it was in a nice, personal way with ruins, moonlight and early death for some person, somehow all nobly resolved with faith and a sigh. But in *Dover Beach* we begin to see concern of a social kind, for all mankind. Dylan Thomas' *A Refusal to Mourn* etc. and Yeats' *Second Coming* show the chaos and terror of a world. Modern poetry is of necessity war poetry, persistent and attentive to every pressure and shudder that occurs in crowds, or in individual man. The nightmares of the mind that breed war are forced to exhibit themselves through the compassionate lens of poetry. This nervous exposure, like technical innovation, is peculiar to the writing of our century. In former centuries war poetry was not about war at all; it was epic; it was about the hero. Today it is real and as useful in disclosing the cause of our war disease as the papers of the psychiatrists. But modern poetry speaks for us, the patients, and is therefore valuable. We live now, in terror or in faith, with cringing or with grandeur, and the poets speak with our voices. The poem is a way to emotional health.

It is always good to read poetry, it is better to read that which has been made out of our own lives, i.e., contemporary, modern poetry. This book contains over five hundred poems from the last hundred years, and almost all of them, especially those written in the last fifty years, can help in resolving our own dilemmas, in this year of time, as we read and experience them again and again.

—OSCAR WILLIAMS

THE POCKET BOOK OF

modern verse

. . . .

ONE'S-SELF I SING

One's-self I sing, a simple separate person,
Yet utter the word Democratic, the word En-Masse.

Of physiology from top to toe I sing,
Not physiognomy alone nor brain alone is worthy for the
        Muse, I say the Form complete is worthier far,
The Female equally with the Male I sing.

Of Life immense in passion, pulse, and power,
Cheerful, for freest action form'd under the laws divine,
The Modern Man I sing.

BEGINNING MY STUDIES

Beginning my studies the first step pleas'd me so much,
The mere fact consciousness, these forms, the power of motion,
The least insect or animal, the senses, eyesight, love,
The first step I say awed me and pleas'd me so much,
I have hardly gone and hardly wish'd to go any farther,
But stop and loiter all the time to sing it in ecstatic songs.

SHUT NOT YOUR DOORS

Shut not your doors to me proud libraries,
For that which was lacking on all your well-fill'd shelves, yet
        needed most, I bring,
Forth from the war emerging, a book I have made,
The words of my book nothing, the drift of it every thing,
A book separate, not link'd with the rest nor felt by the
        intellect,
But you ye untold latencies will thrill to every page.

THERE WAS A CHILD WENT FORTH

There was a child went forth every day,
And the first object he look'd upon, that object he became,
And that object became part of him for the day or a certain
    part of the day,
Or for many years or stretching cycles of years.

The early lilacs became part of this child,
And grass and white and red morning-glories, and white and
    red clover, and the song of the phœbe-bird,
And the Third-month lambs and the sow's pink-faint litter,
    and the mare's foal and the cow's calf,
And the noisy brood of the barnyard or by the mire of the
    pond-side,
And the fish suspending themselves so curiously below there,
    and the beautiful curious liquid,
And the water-plants with their graceful flat heads, all became
    part of him.
The field-sprouts of Fourth-month and Fifth-month became
    part of him,
Winter-grain sprouts and those of the light-yellow corn, and
    the esculent roots of the garden,
And the apple-trees cover'd with blossoms and the fruit after-
    ward, and wood-berries, and the commonest weeds by
    the road,
And the old drunkard staggering home from the outhouse of
    the tavern whence he had lately risen,
And the schoolmistress that pass'd on her way to the school,
And the friendly boys that pass'd, and the quarrelsome boys,
And the tidy and fresh-cheek'd girls, and the barefoot Negro
    boy and girl,
And all the changes of city and country wherever he went.

His own parents, he that had father'd him and she that had
    conceiv'd him in her womb and birth'd him,
They gave this child more of themselves than that,

They gave him afterward every day, they became part of him.

The mother at home quietly placing the dishes on the supper-
table,
The mother with mild words, clean her cap and gown, a whole-
some odor falling off her person and clothes as she walks
by,
The father, strong, self-sufficient, manly, mean, anger'd, unjust,
The blow, the quick loud word, the tight bargain, the crafty
lure,
The family usages, the language, the company, the furniture,
the yearning and swelling heart,
Affection that will not be gainsay'd, the sense of what is real,
the thought if after all it should prove unreal,
The doubts of day-time and the doubts of night-time, the curious whether and how,
Whether that which appears so is so, or is it all flashes and
specks?
Men and women crowding fast in the streets, if they are not
flashes and specks what are they?
The streets themselves and the façades of houses, and goods in
the windows,
Vehicles, teams, the heavy-plank'd wharves, the huge crossing
at the ferries,
The village of the highland seen from afar at sunset, the river
between,
Shadows, aureola and mist, the light falling on roofs and gables
of white or brown two miles off,
The schooner near by sleepily dropping down the tide, the little boat slack-tow'd astern,
The hurrying tumbling waves, quick-broken crests, slapping,
The strata of color'd clouds, the long bar of maroon-tint away
solitary by itself, the spread of purity it lies motionless in,
The horizon's edge, the flying sea-crow, the fragrance of salt
marsh and shore mud,
These became part of that child who went forth every day, and
who now goes, and will always go forth every day.

A HAND-MIRROR

Hold it up sternly—see this it sends back, (who is it? is it you?)
Outside fair costume, within ashes and filth,
No more a flashing eye, no more a sonorous voice or springy
    step,
Now some slave's eye, voice, hands, step,
A drunkard's breath, unwholesome eater's face, venerealee's
    flesh,
Lungs rotting away piecemeal, stomach sour and cankerous,
Joints rheumatic, bowels clogged with abomination,
Blood circulating dark and poisonous streams,
Words babble, hearing and touch callous,
No brain, no heart left, no magnetism of sex;
Such from one look in this looking-glass ere you go hence,
Such a result so soon—and from such a beginning!

WHEN I HEARD THE LEARN'D ASTRONOMER

When I heard the learn'd astronomer,
When the proofs, the figures, were ranged in columns before
    me,
When I was shown the charts and diagrams, to add, divide,
    and measure them,
When I sitting heard the astronomer where he lectured with
    much applause in the lecture-room,
How soon unaccountable I became tired and sick,
Till rising and gliding out I wander'd off by myself,
In the mystical moist night-air, and from time to time,
Look'd up in perfect silence at the stars.

I SIT AND LOOK OUT

I sit and look out upon all the sorrows of the world, and upon
    all oppression and shame,
I hear secret convulsive sobs from young men at anguish with
    themselves, remorseful after deeds done,

I see in low life the mother misused by her children, dying,
    neglected, gaunt, desperate,
I see the wife misused by her husband, I see the treacherous
    seducer of young women,
I mark the ranklings of jealousy and unrequited love attempted
    to be hid, I see these sights on the earth,
I see the workings of battle, pestilence, tyranny, I see martyrs
    and prisoners,
I observe a famine at sea, I observe the sailors casting lots who
    shall be kill'd to preserve the lives of the rest,
I observe the slights and degradations cast by arrogant persons
    upon laborers, the poor, and upon Negroes, and the like;
All these—all the meanness and agony without end I sitting
    look out upon,
See, hear, and am silent.

I CELEBRATE MYSELF

I celebrate myself, and sing myself,
And what I assume you shall assume,
For every atom belonging to me as good belongs to you.

I loafe and invite my soul,
I lean and loafe at my ease observing a spear of summer grass.

My tongue, every atom of my blood, form'd from this soil,
    this air,
Born here of parents born here from parents the same, and
    their parents the same,
I, now thirty-seven years old in perfect health begin,
Hoping to cease not till death.

Creeds and schools in abeyance,
Retiring back a while sufficed at what they are, but never
    forgotten,
I harbor for good or bad, I permit to speak at every hazard,
Nature without check with original energy.

From Song of Myself

ANIMALS

I think I could turn and live with animals, they are so placid
  and self-contained;
I stand and look at them long and long.
They do not sweat and whine about their condition;
They do not lie awake in the dark and weep for their sins;
They do not make me sick discussing their duty to God;
Not one is dissatisfied—not one is demented with the mania of
  owning things;
Not one kneels to another, nor to his kind that lived thousands
  of years ago;
Not one is respectable or industrious over the whole earth.

From *Song of Myself*

GRASS

A child said *What is the grass?* fetching it to me with full
  hands;
How could I answer the child? I do not know what it is any
  more than he.

I guess it must be the flag of my disposition, out of hopeful
  green stuff woven.
Or I guess it is the handkerchief of the Lord,
A scented gift and remembrancer designedly dropt,
Bearing the owner's name some way in the corners, that we
  may see and remark, and say *Whose?*
Or I guess the grass is itself a child, the produced babe of the
  vegetation.
Or I guess it is a uniform hieroglyphic,
And it means, Sprouting alike in broad zones and narrow
  zones,
Growing among black folks as among white,
Kanuck, Tuckahoe, Congressman, Cuff, I give them the same,
  I receive them the same.
And now it seems to me the beautiful uncut hair of graves.

Tenderly will I use you curling grass,
It may be you transpire from the breasts of young men,
It may be if I had known them I would have loved them,
It may be you are from old people, or from offspring taken
    soon out of their mother's laps,
And here you are the mother's laps.

This grass is very dark to be from the white heads of old
    mothers,
Darker than the colorless beards of old men,
Dark to come from under the faint red roofs of mouths.

O I perceive after all so many uttering tongues,
And I perceive they do not come from the roofs of mouths for
    nothing.
I wish I could translate the hints about the dead young men
    and women,
And the hints about old men and mothers, and the off-spring
    taken soon out of their laps.

What do you think has become of the young and old men?
And what do you think has become of the women and chil-
    dren?

They are alive and well somewhere,
The smallest sprout shows there is really no death,
And if ever there was it led forward life, and does not wait at
    the end to arrest it,
And ceas'd the moment life appear'd.
All goes onward and outward, nothing collapses,
And to die is different from what any one supposed, and
    luckier.

From *Song of Myself*

A HUB FOR THE UNIVERSE

I have said that the soul is not more than the body,
And I have said that the body is not more than the soul,

And nothing, not God, is greater to one than one's self is,
And whoever walks a furlong without sympathy walks to his
    own funeral drest in his shroud,
And I or you pocketless of a dime may purchase the pick of
    the earth,
And to glance with an eye or show a bean in its pod confounds
    the learning of all times,
And there is no trade or employment but the young man fol-
    lowing it may become a hero,
And there is no object so soft but it makes a hub for the
    wheeled universe.

From Song of Myself

MY BARBARIC YAWP

The spotted hawk swoops by and accuses me, he complains
    of my gab and my loitering.
I too am not a bit tamed, I too am untranslatable,
I sound my barbaric yawp over the roofs of the world.

The last scud of day holds back for me,
It flings my likeness after the rest and true as any on the
    shadow'd wilds,
It coaxes me to the vapor and the dusk.

I depart as air, I shake my white locks at the runaway sun,
I effuse my flesh in eddies, and drift it in lacy jags.
I bequeath myself to the dirt to grow from the grass I love,
If you want me again look for me under your boot-soles.

You will hardly know what I am or what I mean,
But I shall be good health to you nevertheless,
And filter and fibre your blood.

Failing to fetch me at first keep encouraged,
Missing me one place search another,
I stop somewhere waiting for you.

From Song of Myself

I SAW IN LOUISIANA A LIVE-OAK GROWING

I saw in Louisiana a live-oak growing,
All alone stood it, and the moss hung down from the branches;
Without any companion it grew there, uttering joyous leaves
    of dark green,
And its look, rude, unbending, lusty, made me think of myself;
But I wonder'd how it could utter joyous leaves, standing alone
    there, without its friend, its lover near—for I knew I could
    not;
And I broke off a twig with a certain number of leaves upon it,
    and twined around it a little moss,
And brought it away—and I have placed it in sight in my room;
It is not needed to remind me as of my own dear friends,
(For I believe lately I think of little else than of them:)
Yet it remains to me a curious token—it makes me think of
    manly love;
For all that, and though the live-oak glistens there in Louisi-
    ana, solitary, in a wide flat space,
Uttering joyous leaves all its life, without a friend, a lover,
    near,
I know very well I could not.

TO THINK OF TIME

I

To think of time—of all that retrospection,
To think of to-day, and the ages continued henceforward.
Have you guess'd you yourself would not continue?
Have you dreaded these earth-beetles?
Have you fear'd the future would be nothing to you?
Is to-day nothing? is the beginningless past nothing?
If the future is nothing they are just as surely nothing.
To think that the sun rose in the east—that men and women
    were flexible, real, alive—that everything was alive,
To think that you and I did not see, feel, think, nor bear our
    part,
To think that we are now here and bear our part.

II

Not a day passes, not a minute or second without an accouche-
   ment,
Not a day passes, not a minute or second without a corpse.
The dull nights go over and the dull days also,
The soreness of lying so much in bed goes over,
The physician after long putting off gives the silent and ter-
   rible look for an answer,
The children come hurried and weeping, and the brothers and
   sisters are sent for,
Medicines stand unused on the shelf, (the camphor-smell has
   long pervaded the rooms,)
The faithful hand of the living does not desert the hand of the
   dying,
The twitching lips press lightly on the forehead of the dying,
The breath ceases and the pulse of the heart ceases,
The corpse stretches on the bed and the living look upon it,
It is palpable as the living are palpable.
The living look upon the corpse with their eyesight,
But without eyesight lingers a different living and looks curi-
   ously on the corpse.

III

To think the thought of death merged in the thought of ma-
   terials,
To think of all these wonders of city and country, and others
   taking great interest in them, and we taking no interest in
   them.
To think how eager we are in building our houses,
To think others shall be just as eager, and we quite indifferent.
(I see one building the house that serves him a few years, or
   seventy or eighty years at most,
I see one building the house that serves him longer than that.)
Slow-moving and black lines creep over the whole earth—they
   never cease—they are the burial lines,
He that was President was buried, and he that is now Presi-
   dent shall surely be buried.

IV

A reminiscence of the vulgar fate,
A frequent sample of the life and death of workmen,
Each after his kind.
Cold dash of waves at the ferry-wharf, posh and ice in the
river, half-frozen mud in the streets,
A gray discouraged sky overhead, the short last daylight of
December,
A hearse and stages, the funeral of an old Broadway stage-
driver, the cortege mostly drivers.
Steady the trot to the cemetery, duly rattles the death-bell,
The gate is pass'd, the new-dug grave is halted at, the living
alight, the hearse uncloses,
The coffin is pass'd out, lower'd and settled, the whip is laid
on the coffin, the earth is swiftly shovel'd in,
The mound above is flatted with the spades—silence,
A minute—no one moves or speaks—it is done,
He is decently put away—is there any thing more?
He was a good fellow, free-mouth'd, quick-temper'd, not bad-
looking,
Ready with life or death for a friend, fond of women, gambled,
ate hearty, drank hearty,
Had known what it was to be flush, grew low-spirited toward
the last, sicken'd, was help'd by a contribution,
Died, aged forty-one years—and that was his funeral.
Thumb extended, finger uplifted, apron, cape, gloves, strap,
wet-weather clothes, whip carefully chosen,
Boss, spotter, starter, hostler, somebody loafing on you, you
loafing on somebody, headway, man before and man behind,
Good day's work, bad day's work, pet stock, mean stock, first
out, last out, turning-in at night,
To think that these are so much and so nigh to other drivers,
and he there takes no interest in them.

O CAPTAIN! MY CAPTAIN!

O Captain! my Captain! our fearful trip is done,
The ship has weather'd every rack, the prize we sought is won,
The port is near, the bells I hear, the people all exulting,
While follow eyes the steady keel, the vessel grim and daring;
      But O heart! heart! heart!
        O the bleeding drops of red,
          Where on the deck my Captain lies,
          Fallen cold and dead.

O Captain! my Captain! rise up and hear the bells;
Rise up—for you the flag is flung—for you the bugle trills,
For you bouquets and ribbon'd wreaths—for you the shores
    a-crowding,
For you they call, the swaying mass, their eager faces turning;
      Here Captain! dear father!
        The arm beneath your head!
          It is some dream that on the deck,
          You've fallen cold and dead.

My Captain does not answer, his lips are pale and still,
My father does not feel my arm, he has no pulse nor will.
The ship is anchor'd safe and sound, its voyage closed and
    done,
From fearful trip the victor ship comes in with object won;
      Exult O shores, and ring O bells!
        But I with mournful tread,
          Walk the deck my Captain lies,
          Fallen cold and dead.

WHEN LILACS LAST IN THE DOORYARD BLOOM'D

I

When lilacs last in the dooryard bloom'd
And the great star early droop'd in the western sky in the
    night,
I mourn'd, and yet shall mourn with ever-returning spring.

Ever-returning spring, trinity sure to me you bring,
Lilac blooming perennial and drooping star in the west,
And thought of him I love.

II

O powerful western fallen star!
O shades of night—O moody, tearful night!
O great star disappear'd—O the black murk that hides the star!
O cruel hands that hold me powerless—O helpless soul of me!
O harsh surrounding cloud that will not free my soul.

III

In the dooryard fronting an old farm-house near the white-
    wash'd palings,
Stands the lilac-bush tall-growing with heart-shaped leaves of
    rich green,
With many a pointed blossom rising delicate, with the per-
    fume strong I love,
With every leaf a miracle—and from this bush in the dooryard,
With delicate-color'd blossom and heart-shaped leaves of rich
    green,
A sprig with its flower I break.

IV

In the swamp in secluded recesses,
A shy and hidden bird is warbling a song.
Solitary the thrush,
The hermit withdrawn to himself, avoiding the settlements,
Sings by himself a song.
Song of the bleeding throat,
Death's outlet song of life, (for well dear brother I know,
If thou wast not granted to sing thou would'st surely die.)

V

Over the breast of the spring, the land, amid cities,
Amid lanes and through old woods, where lately the violets
    peep'd from the ground, spotting the gray debris,
Amid the grass in the fields each side of the lanes, passing the
    endless grass,

Passing the yellow-spear'd wheat, every grain from its shroud
    in the dark-brown fields uprisen,
Passing the apple-tree blows of white and pink in the orchards,
Carrying a corpse to where it shall rest in the grave,
Night and day journeys a coffin.

VI

Coffin that passes through lanes and streets,
Through day and night with the great cloud darkening the
    land,
With the pomp of the inloop'd flags with the cities draped in
    black,
With the show of the States themselves as of crape-veil'd
    women standing,
With processions long and winding and the flambeaus of the
    night,
With the countless torches lit, with the silent sea of faces and
    the unbared heads,
With the waiting depot, the arriving coffin, and the sombre
    faces,
With dirges through the night, with the thousand voices rising
    strong and solemn,
With all the mournful voices of the dirges pour'd around the
    coffin,
The dim-lit churches and the shuddering organs—where amid
    these you journey,
With the tolling tolling bells' perpetual clang,
Here, coffin that slowly passes,
I give you my sprig of lilac.

VII

(Nor for you, for one alone,
Blossoms and branches green to coffins all I bring,
For fresh as the morning, thus would I chant a song for you
    O sane and sacred death.
All over bouquets of roses,
O death, I cover you over with roses and early lilies,
But mostly and now the lilac that blooms the first,

Copious I break, I break the sprigs from the bushes,
With loaded arms I come, pouring for you,
For you and the coffins all of you O death.)

VIII

O western orb sailing the heaven,
Now I know what you must have meant as a month since I
walk'd,
As I walk'd in silence the transparent shadowy night,
As I saw you had something to tell as you bent to me night
after night,
As you drooped from the sky low down as if to my side, (while
the other stars all look'd on,)
As we wander'd together the solemn night, (for something
I know not what kept me from sleep,)
As the night advanced, and I saw on the rim of the west how
full you were of woe,
As I stood on the rising ground in the breeze in the cool
transparent night,
As I watch'd where you pass'd and was lost in the netherward
black of the night,
As my soul in its trouble dissatisfied sank, as where you, sad
orb,
Concluded, dropt in the night, and was gone.

IX

Sing on there in the swamp,
O singer bashful and tender, I hear your notes, I hear your call,
I hear, I come presently, I understand you,
But a moment I linger, for the lustrous star has detain'd me,
The star my departing comrade holds and detains me.

X

O how shall I warble myself for the dead one there I loved?
And how shall I deck my song for the large sweet soul that
has gone?
And what shall my perfume be for the grave of him I love?

Sea-winds blown from east and west,
Blown from the Eastern sea and blown from the Western
    sea, till there on the prairies meeting,
These and with these and the breath of my chant,
I'll perfume the grave of him I love.

XI

O what shall I hang on the chamber walls?
And what shall the pictures be that I hang on the walls,
To adorn the burial-house of him I love?

Pictures of growing spring and farms and homes,
With the Fourth-month eve at sundown, and the gray smoke
    lucid and bright,
With floods of the yellow gold of the gorgeous, indolent, sink-
    ing·sun, burning, expanding the air,
With the fresh sweet herbage under foot, and the pale green
    leaves of the trees prolific,
In the distance the flowing glaze, the breast of the river, with
    a wind-dapple here and there,
With ranging hills on the banks, with many a line against the
    sky, and shadows,
And the city at hand with dwellings so dense, and stacks of
    chimneys,
And all the scenes of life and the workshops, and the workmen
    homeward returning.

XII

Lo, body and soul—this land,
My own Manhattan with spires, and the sparkling and hurry-
    ing tides, and the ships,
The varied and ample land, the South and the North in the
    light, Ohio's shores and flashing Missouri,
And ever the far-spreading prairies cover'd with grass and
    corn.

Lo, the most excellent sun so calm and haughty,
The violet and purple morn with just-felt breezes,

The gentle soft-born measureless light,
The miracle spreading bathing all, the fulfill'd noon,
The coming eve delicious, the welcome night and the stars,
Over my cities shining all, enveloping man and land.

XIII

Sing on, sing on you gray-brown bird,
Sing from the swamps, the recesses, pour your chant from the
    bushes,
Limitless out of the dusk, out of the cedars and pines.

Sing on dearest brother, warble your reedy song,
Loud human song, with voice of uttermost woe.
O liquid and free and tender!
O wild and loose to my soul—O wondrous singer!
You only I hear—yet the star holds me, (but will soon depart,)
Yet the lilac with mastering odor holds me.

XIV

Now while I sat in the day and look'd forth,
In the close of the day with its light and the fields of spring,
    and the farmers preparing their crops,
In the large unconscious scenery of my land with its lakes and
    forests,
In the heavenly aerial beauty, (after the perturb'd winds and
    the storms,)
Under the arching heavens of the afternoon swift passing, and
    the voices of children and women,
The many-moving sea-tides, and I saw the ships how they
    sail'd,
And the summer approaching with richness, and the fields all
    busy with labor,
And the infinite separate houses, how they all went on, each
    with its meals and minutia of daily usages,
And the streets how their throbbings throbb'd, and the cities
    pent—lo, then and there,
Falling upon them all and among them all, enveloping me with
    the rest,

Appear'd the cloud, appear'd the long black trail,
And I knew death, its thought, and the sacred knowledge of
    death.

Then with the knowledge of death as walking one side of me,
And the thought of death close-walking the other side of me,
And I in the middle as with companions, and as holding the
    hands of companions,
I fled forth to the hiding receiving night that talks not,
Down to the shores of the water, the path by the swamp in the
    dimness,
To the solemn shadowy cedars and ghostly pines so still.
And the singer so shy to the rest receiv'd me,
The gray-brown bird I know receiv'd us comrades three,
And he sang the carol of death, and a verse for him I love.
From deep secluded recesses,
From the fragrant cedars and the ghostly pines so still,
Came the carol of the bird.
And the charm of the carol rapt me,
As I held as if by their hands my comrades in the night,
And the voice of my spirit tallied the song of the bird.

Come lovely and soothing death,
Undulate round the world, serenely arriving, arriving,
In the day, in the night, to all, to each,
Sooner or later delicate death.
Prais'd be the fathomless universe,
For life and joy, and for objects and knowledge curious,
And for love, sweet love—but praise! praise! praise!
For the sure-enwinding arms of cool-enfolding death.
Dark mother always gliding near with soft feet,
Have none chanted for thee a chant of fullest welcome?
Then I chant it for thee, I glorify thee above all,
I bring thee a song that when thou must indeed come, come
    unfalteringly.
Approach strong deliveress,
When it is so, when thou hast taken them I joyously sing the
    dead,

Lost in the loving floating ocean of thee,
Laved in the flood by thy bliss O death.
From me to thee glad serenades,
Dances for thee I propose saluting thee, adornments and feast-
*   ings for thee,*
And the sights of the open landscape and the high-spread sky
*   are fitting,*
And life and the fields, and the huge and thoughtful night.
The night in silence under many a star,
The ocean shore and the husky whispering wave whose voice
*   I know,*
And the soul turning to thee O vast and well-veil'd death,
And the body gratefully nestling close to thee.
Over the tree-tops I float thee a song,
Over the rising and sinking waves, over the myriad fields and
*   the prairies wide,*
Over the dense-pack'd cities all and the teeming wharves and
*   ways,*
I float this carol with joy, with joy to thee O death.

XV

To the tally of my soul,
Loud and strong kept up the gray-brown bird,
With pure deliberate notes spreading filling the night.
Loud in the pines and cedars dim,
Clear in the freshness moist and the swamp-perfume,
And I with my comrades there in the night.
While my sight that was bound in my eyes unclosed,
As to long panoramas of visions.

And I saw askant the armies,
I saw as in noiseless dreams hundreds of battle-flags,
Borne through the smoke of the battles and pierc'd with
    missiles I saw them,
And carried hither and yon through the smoke, and torn and
    bloody,
And at last but a few shreds left on the staffs, (and all in
    silence,)
And the staffs all splinter'd and broken.

I saw battle-corpses, myriads of them,
And the white skeletons of young men, I saw them,
I saw the debris and debris of all the slain soldiers of the war,
But I saw they were not as was thought,
They themselves were fully at rest, they suffer'd not,
The living remain'd and suffer'd, the mother suffer'd,
And the wife and the child and the musing comrade suffer'd,
And the armies that remain'd suffer'd.

XVI

Passing the visions, passing the night,
Passing, unloosing the hold of my comrades' hands,
Passing the song of the hermit bird and the tallying song of my
     soul,
Victorious song, death's outlet song, yet varying ever-altering
     song,
As low and wailing, yet clear the notes, rising and falling,
     flooding the night,

Sadly sinking and fainting, as warning and warning, and yet
     again bursting with joy,
Covering the earth and filling the spread of the heaven,
As that powerful psalm in the night I heard from recesses,
Passing, I leave thee lilac with heart-shaped leaves,
I leave thee there in the door-yard, blooming, returning with
     spring.
I cease from my song for thee,
From my gaze on thee in the west, fronting the west, com-
     muning with thee,
O comrade lustrous with silver face in the night.

Yet each to keep and all, retrievements out of the night,
The song, the wondrous chant of the gray-brown bird,
And the tallying chant, the echo arous'd in my soul,
With the lustrous and drooping star with the countenance full
     of woe,
With the holders holding my hand nearing the call of the bird,

Comrades mme and I in the midst, and their memory ever to
keep, for the dead I loved so well,
For the sweetest, wisest soul of all my days and lands—and this
for his dear sake,
Lilac and star and bird twined with the chant of my soul,
There in the fragrant pines and the cedars dusk and dim.

ABOARD AT A SHIP'S HELM

Aboard at a ship's helm,
A young steersman steering with care.
Through fog on a sea-coast dolefully ringing,
An ocean-bell—O a warning bell, rock'd by the waves.
O you give good notice indeed, you bell by the sea-reefs ring-
ing,
Ringing, ringing, to warn the ship from its wreck-place.

For as on the alert O steersman, you mind the loud admoni-
tion,
The bows turn, the freighted ship tacking speeds away under
her gray sails,
The beautiful and noble ship with all her precious wealth
speeds away gayly and safe.
But O the ship, the immortal ship! O ship aboard the ship!
Ship of the body, ship of the soul, voyaging, voyaging, voyaging.

ON THE BEACH AT NIGHT

On the beach at night,
Stands a child with her father,
Watching the east, the autumn sky.
Up through the darkness,
While ravening clouds, the burial clouds, in black masses
spreading,
Lower sullen and fast athwart and down the sky,
Amid a transparent clear belt of ether yet left in the east,
Ascends large and calm the lord-star Jupiter,
And nigh at hand, only a very little above,

Swim the delicate sisters the Pleiades.
From the beach the child holding the hand of her father,
Those burial clouds that lower victorious soon to devour all,
Watching, silently weeps.

Weep not, child,
Weep not, my darling,
With these kisses let me remove your tears,
The ravening clouds shall not long be victorious,
They shall not long possess the sky, they devour the stars only
    in apparition,
Jupiter shall emerge, be patient, watch again another night,
    the Pleiades shall emerge,
They are immortal, all those stars both silvery and golden shall
    shine out again,
The great stars and the little ones shall shine out again, they
    endure,
The vast immortal suns and the long-enduring pensive moons
    shall again shine.

Then dearest child mournest thou only for Jupiter?
Considerest thou alone the burial of the stars?
Something there is,
(With my lips soothing thee, adding I whisper,
I give thee the first suggestion, the problem and indirection,)
Something there is more immortal even than the stars,
(Many the burials, many the days and nights, passing away,)
Something that shall endure longer even than lustrous Jupiter,
Longer than sun or any revolving satellite,
Or the radiant sisters the Pleiades.

A NOISELESS PATIENT SPIDER

A noiseless patient spider,
I mark'd where on a little promontory it stood isolated,
Mark'd how to explore the vacant vast surrounding,
It launched forth filament, filament, filament, out of itself,
Ever unreeling them, ever tirelessly speeding them.

And you O my soul where you stand,
Surrounded, detached, in measureless oceans of space,
Ceaselessly musing, venturing, throwing, seeking the spheres
    to connect them,
Till the bridge you will need be form'd, till the ductile anchor
    hold,
Till the gossamer thread you fling catch somewhere, O my
    soul.

FACES

I

Sauntering the pavement or riding the country by-road, lo,
    such faces!
Faces of friendship, precision, caution, suavity, ideality,
The spiritual-prescient face, the always welcome common
    benevolent face,
The face of the singing of music, the grand faces of natural
    lawyers and judges broad at the back-top,
The faces of hunters and fishers bulged at the brows, the
    shaved blanch'd faces of orthodox citizens,
The pure, extravagant, yearning, questioning artist's face,
The ugly face of some beautiful soul, the handsome detested
    or despised face,
The sacred faces of infants, the illuminated face of the mother
    of many children,

The face of an amour, the face of veneration,
The face as of a dream, the face of an immobile rock,
The face withdrawn of its good and bad, a castrated face,
A wild hawk, his wings clipp'd by the clipper,
A stallion that yielded at last to the thongs and knife of the
    gelder.

Sauntering the pavement thus, or crossing the ceaseless ferry,
    faces and faces and faces,
I see them and complain not, and am content with all.

II

Do you suppose I could be content with all if I thought them
their own finalè?

This now is too lamentable a face for a man,
Some abject louse asking leave to be, cringing for it,
Some milk-nosed maggot blessing what lets it wrig to its hole.

This face is a dog's snout sniffing for garbage,
Snakes nest in that mouth, I hear the sibilant threat.

This face is a haze more chill than the arctic sea,
Its sleepy and wabbling icebergs crunch as they go.

This is a face of bitter herbs, this an emetic, they need no
label,
And more of the drug-shelf, laudanum, caoutchouc, or hog's-
lard.

This face is an epilepsy, its wordless tongue gives out the
unearthly cry,
Its veins down the neck distend, its eyes roll till they show
nothing but their whites,
Its teeth grit, the palms of the hands are cut by the turn'd-in
nails,
The man falls struggling and foaming to the ground, while he
speculates well.

This face is bitten by vermin and worms,
And this is some murderer's knife with a half-pull'd scabbard.

This face owes to the sexton his dismalest fee,
An unceasing death-bell tolls there.

III

Features of my equals would you trick me with your creas'd
and cadaverous march?
Well, you cannot trick me.

I see your rounded never-erased flow,
I see 'neath the rims of your haggard and mean disguises.

Splay and twist as you like, poke with the tangling fores of
fishes or rats,
You'll be unmuzzled, you certainly will.

I saw the face of the most smear'd and slobbering idiot they
had at the asylum,
And I knew for my consolation what they knew not,
I knew of the agents that emptied and broke my brother,
The same wait to clear the rubbish from the fallen tenement,
And I shall look again in a score or two of ages,
And I shall meet the real landlord perfect and unharm'd,
every inch as good as myself.

IV

The Lord advances, and yet advances,
Always the shadow in front, always the reach'd hand bringing
up the laggards.

Out of this face emerge banners and horses—O superb! I see
what is coming,
I see the high pioneer-caps, see staves of runners clearing the
way,
I hear the victorious drums.

This face is a life-boat,
This is the face commanding and bearded, it asks no odds of
the rest,
This face is flavor'd fruit ready for eating,
This face of a healthy honest boy is the programme of all good.

These faces bear testimony slumbering or awake,
They show their descent from the Master himself.

Of the word I have spoken I except not one—red, white, black,
are all deific,

In each house is the ovum, it comes forth after a thousand years.

Spots or cracks at the windows do not disturb me,
Tall and sufficient stand behind and make signs to me,
I read the promise and patiently wait.
This is a full-grown lily's face,
She speaks to the limber-hipp'd man near the garden pickets,
Come here she blushingly cries, *Come nigh to me limber-hipp'd man,*
Stand at my side till I lean as high as I can upon you,
Fill me with albescent honey, bend down to me,
Rub to me with your chafing beard, rub to my breast and shoulders.

v

The old face of the mother of many children,
Whist! I am fully content.
Lull'd and late is the smoke of the First-day morning,
It hangs low over the rows of trees by the fences,
It hangs thin by the sassafras and wild-cherry and cat-brier under them.
I saw the rich ladies in full dress at the soiree,
I heard what the singers were singing so long,
Heard who sprang in crimson youth from the white froth and the water-blue.
Behold a woman!
She looks out from her quaker cap, her face is clearer and more beautiful than the sky.
She sits in an armchair under the shaded porch of the farm-house,
The sun just shines on her old white head.
Her ample gown is of cream-hued linen,
Her grandsons raised the flax, and her grand-daughters spin it with the distaff and the wheel.
The melodious character of the earth,
The finish beyond which philosophy cannot go and does not wish to go,
The justified mother of men.

Carry me when you go forth over land or sea;
For thus merely touching you is enough, is best,
And thus touching you would I silently sleep and be carried
  eternally.

But these leaves conning you con at peril,
For these leaves and me you will not understand,
They will elude you at first and still more afterward, I will
  certainly elude you,
Even while you should think you had unquestionably caught
  me, behold!
Already you see I have escaped from you.

For it is not for what I have put into it that I have written this
  book,
Nor is it by reading it you will acquire it,
Nor do those know me best who admire me and vauntingly
  praise me,
Nor will the candidates for my love (unless at most a very
  few) prove victorious,
Nor will my poems do good only, they will do just as much
  evil, perhaps more,
For all is useless without that which you may guess at many
  times and not hit, that which I hinted at;
Therefore release me and depart on your way.

RESPONDEZ!

Respondez! Respondez!
(The war is completed—the price is paid—the title is settled
  beyond recall;)
Let every one answer! let those who sleep be waked! let none
  evade!
Must we still go on with our affectations and sneaking?
Let me bring this to a close—I pronounce openly for a new
  distribution of roles;
Let that which stood in front go behind! and let that which
  was behind advance to the front and speak;

Let murderers, bigots, fools, unclean persons, offer new propositions!

Let the old propositions be postponed!

Let faces and theories be turn'd inside out! let meanings be freely criminal, as well as results!

Let there be no suggestion above the suggestion of drudgery!

Let none be pointed toward his destination! (Say! do you know your destination?)

Let men and women be mock'd with bodies and mock'd with Souls!

Let the love that waits in them, wait! let it die, or pass still-born to other spheres!

Let the sympathy that waits in every man, wait! or let it also pass, a dwarf, to other spheres!

Let contradictions prevail! let one thing contradict another! and let one line of my poems contradict another!

Let the people sprawl with yearning, aimless hands! let their tongues be broken! let their eyes be discouraged! let none descend into their hearts with the fresh lusciousness of love!

(Stifled, O days! O lands! in every public & private corruption!

Smother'd in thievery, impotence, shamelessness, mountain-high;

Brazen effrontery, scheming, rolling like ocean's waves around and upon you, O my days! my lands!

For not even those thunderstorms, nor fiercest lightnings of the war, have purified the atmosphere;)

—Let the theory of America still be management, caste, comparison! (Say! what other theory would you?)

Let them that distrust birth and death still lead the rest! (Say! why shall they not lead you?)

Let the crust of hell be neared and trod on! let the days be darker than the nights! let slumber bring less slumber than waking time brings!

Let the world never appear to him or her for whom it was all made!

Let the heart of the young man still exile itself from the heart of the old man! and let the heart of the old man be exiled from that of the young man!

Let the sun and moon go! let scenery take the applause of the audience! let there be apathy under the stars!

Let freedom prove no man's inalienable right! every one who can tyrannize, let him tyrannize to his satisfaction!

Let none but infidels be countenanced!

Let the eminence of meanness, treachery, sarcasm, hate, greed, indecency, impotence, lust, be taken for granted above all! let writers, judges, governments, households, religions, philosophies, take such for granted above all!

Let the worst men beget children out of the worst women!

Let the priest still play at immortality!

Let death be inaugurated!

Let nothing remain but the ashes of teachers, artists, moralists, lawyers, and learn'd and polite persons!

Let him who is without my poems be assassinated!

Let the cow, the horse, the camel, the garden-bee—let the mud-fish, the lobster, the mussel, eel, the stingray, and the grunting pig-fish—let these, and the like of these, be put on a perfect equality with man and woman!

Let churches accommodate serpents, vermin, and the corpses of those who have died of the most filthy diseases!

Let marriage slip down among fools, and be for none but fools!

Let men among themselves talk and think forever obscenely of women! and let women among themselves talk and think obscenely of men!

Let us all, without missing one, be exposed in public, naked, monthly, at the peril of our lives! let our bodies be freely handled and examined by whoever chooses!

Let nothing but copies at second hand be permitted to exist upon the earth!

Let the earth desert God, nor let there ever henceforth be mention'd the name of God!

Let there be no God!

Let there be money, business, imports, exports, custom, authority, precedents, pallor, dyspepsia, smut, ignorance, unbelief!

Let judges and criminals be transposed! let the prison-keepers be put in prison! let those that were prisoners take the keys!

(Say! why might they not just as well be transposed?)
Let the slaves be masters! let the masters become slaves!
Let the reformers descend from the stands where they are forever bawling! let an idiot or insane person appear on each
of the stands!
Let the Asiatic, the African, the European, the American, and
the Australian, go armed against the murderous stealthiness
of each other! let them sleep armed! let none believe in
good will!
Let there be no unfashionable wisdom! let such be scorn'd and
derided off from the earth!
Let a floating cloud in the sky—let a wave of the sea—let growing mint, spinach, onions, tomatoes—let these be exhibited
as shows, at a great price for admission!
Let all the men of These States stand aside for a few smouch-
ers! let the few seize on what they choose! let the rest
gawk, giggle, starve, obey!
Let shadows be furnish'd with genitals! let substances be deprived of their genitals!
Let there be wealthy and immense cities—but still through any
of them, not a single poet, savior, knower, lover!
Let the infidels of These States laugh all faith away!
If one man be found who has faith, let the rest set upon him!
Let them affright faith! let them destroy the power of breed-
ing faith!
Let the she-harlots and the he-harlots be prudent! let them
dance on, while seeming lasts! (O seeming! seeming! seem-
ing!)
Let the preachers recite creeds! let them still teach only what
they have been taught!
Let insanity still have charge of sanity!
Let books take the place of trees, animals, rivers, clouds!
Let the daub'd portraits of heroes supersede heroes!
Let the manhood of man never take steps after itself!
Let it take steps after eunuchs, and after consumptive and
genteel persons!
Let the white person again tread the black person under his
heel! (Say! which is trodden under heel, after all?)

Let the reflections of the things of the world be studied in
    mirrors! let the things themselves still continue unstudied!
Let a man seek pleasure everywhere except in himself!
Let a woman seek happiness everywhere except in herself!
(What real happiness have you had one single hour through
    your whole life?)
Let the limited years of life do nothing for the limitless years
    of death! (What do you suppose death will do, then?)

POETS TO COME

Poets to come! orators, singers, musicians to come!
Not to-day is to justify me and answer what I am for,
But you, a new brood, native, athletic, continental, greater
    than before known,
Arouse! for you must justify me.

I myself but write one or two indicative words for the future,
I but advance a moment only to wheel and hurry back in the
    darkness.

I am a man who, sauntering along without fully stopping,
    turns a casual look upon you and then averts his face,
Leaving it to you to prove and define it,
Expecting the main things from you.

I HEAR IT WAS CHARGED AGAINST ME

I hear it was charged against me that I sought to destroy in-
    stitutions.
But really I am neither for nor against institutions.
(What indeed have I in common with them? or what with the
    destruction of them?)
Only I will establish in the Mannahatta and in every city of
    these States inland and seaboard,
And in the fields and woods, and above every keel little or
    large that dents the water,
Without edifices or rules or trustees or any argument,
The institution of the dear love of comrades.

THIS COMPOST

I

Something startles me where I thought I was safest;
I withdraw from the still woods I loved;
I will not go now on the pastures to walk;
I will not strip the clothes from my body to meet my lover the
    sea;
I will not touch my flesh to the earth, as to other flesh, to
    renew me.

O how can it be that the ground does not sicken?
How can you be alive, you growths of spring?
How can you furnish health, you blood of herbs, roots, or-
    chards, grain?
Are they not continually putting distemper'd corpses within
    you?
Is not every continent work'd over and over with sour dead?

Where have you disposed of their carcasses?
Those drunkards and gluttons of so many generations;
Where have you drawn off all the foul liquid and meat?
I do not see any of it upon you to-day—or perhaps I am de-
    ceiv'd;
I will run a furrow with my plough—I will press my spade
    through the sod, and turn it up underneath;
I am sure I shall expose some of the foul meat.

II

Behold this compost! behold it well!
Perhaps every mite has once form'd part of a sick person—Yet
    behold!
The grass of spring covers the prairies,
The bean bursts noiselessly through the mould in the garden,
The delicate spear of the onion pierces upward,
The apple-buds cluster together on the apple-branches,
The resurrection of the wheat appears with pale visage out of
    its graves,
The tinge awakes over the willow-tree and the mulberry-tree,

The he-birds carol mornings and evenings, while the she-birds
    sit on their nests,
The young of poultry break through the hatch'd eggs,
The new-born of animals appear—the calf is dropt from the
    cow, the colt from the mare,
Out of its little hill faithfully rise the potato's dark green leaves,
Out of its hill rises the yellow maize-stalk—the lilacs bloom in
    the door-yards;
The summer growth is innocent and disdainful above all those
    strata of sour dead.

What chemistry!
That the winds are really not infectious,
That this is no cheat, this transparent green-wash of the sea,
    which is so amorous after me,
That it is safe to allow it to lick my naked body all over with
    its tongues,
That it will not endanger me with the fevers that have de-
    posited themselves in it,
That all is clean, forever and forever.
That the cool drink from the well tastes so good,
That blackberries are so flavorous and juicy,
That the fruits of the apple-orchard, and of the orange-orchard
    —that melons, grapes, peaches, plums, will none of them
    poison me,
That when I recline on the grass I do not catch any disease,
Though probably every spear of grass rises out of what was
    once a catching disease.

III

Now I am terrified at the Earth! it is that calm and patient,
It grows such sweet things out of such corruptions,
It turns harmless and stainless on its axis, with such endless
    successions of diseas'd corpses,
It distills such exquisite winds out of such infused fetor,
It renews with such unwitting looks, its prodigal, annual,
    sumptuous crops,
It gives such divine materials to men, and accepts such leav-
    ings from them at last.

CROSSING BROOKLYN FERRY

I

Flood-tide below me! I see you face to face!
Clouds of the west—sun there half an hour high—I see you also
    face to face.

Crowds of men and women attired in the usual costumes, how
    curious you are to me!
On the ferry-boats the hundreds and hundreds that cross, re-
    turning home, are more curious to me than you suppose,
And you that shall cross from shore to shore years hence are
    more to me, and more in my meditations, than you might
    suppose.

II

The impalpable sustenance of me from all things at all hours
    of the day,
The simple, compact, well-join'd scheme, myself disintegrated,
    every one disintegrated yet part of the scheme,
The similitudes of the past and those of the future,
The glories strung like beads on my smallest sights and hear-
    ings, on the walk in the street and the passage over the
    river,
The current rushing so swiftly and swimming with me far
    away,
The others that are to follow me, the ties between me and
    them,
The certainty of others, the life, love, sight, hearing of others.

Others will enter the gates of the ferry and cross from shore to
    shore,
Others will watch the run of the flood-tide,
Others will see the shipping of Manhattan north and west, and
    the heights of Brooklyn to the south and east,
Others will see the islands large and small;
Fifty years hence, others will see them as they cross, the sun
    half an hour high,

A hundred years hence, or ever so many hundred years hence,
    others will see them,
Will enjoy the sunset, the pouring-in of the flood-tide, the fall-
    ing-back to the sea of the ebb-tide.

III

It avails not, time nor place—distance avails not,
I am with you, you men and women of a generation, or ever
    so many generations hence,
Just as you feel when you look on the river and sky, so I felt,
Just as any of you is one of a living crowd, I was one of a
    crowd,
Just as you are refresh'd by the gladness of the river and the
    bright flow, I was refresh'd,
Just as you stand and lean on the rail, yet hurry with the swift
    current, I stood yet was hurried,
Just as you look on the numberless masts of ships and the
    thick-stemm'd pipes of steamboats, I look'd.

I too many and many a time cross'd the river of old,
Watched the Twelfth-month sea-gulls, saw them high in the
    air floating with motionless wings, oscillating their bodies,
Saw how the glistening yellow lit up parts of their bodies and
    left the rest in strong shadow,
Saw the slow-wheeling circles and the gradual edging toward
    the south,
Saw the reflection of the summer sky in the water,
Had my eyes dazzled by the shimmering track of beams,
Look'd at the fine centrifugal spokes of light round the shape
    of my head in the sunlit water,
Look'd on the haze on the hills southward and southwestward,
Look'd on the vapor as it flew in fleeces tinged with violet,
Look'd toward the lower bay to notice the vessels arriving,
Saw their approach, saw aboard those that were near me,
Saw the white sails of schooners and sloops, saw the ships at
    anchor,
The sailors at work in the rigging or out astride the spars,

The round masts, the swinging motion of the hulls, the slender
    serpentine pennants,
The large and small steamers in motion, the pilots in their
    pilot-houses,
The white wake left by the passage, the quick tremulous whirl
    of the wheels,
The flags of all nations, the falling of them at sunset,
The scalloped-edged waves in the twilight, the ladled cups, the
    frolicsome crests and glistening,
The stretch afar growing dimmer and dimmer, the gray
    walls of the granite storehouses by the docks,
On the river the shadowy group, the big steam-tug closely
    flank'd on each side by the barges, the hay-boat, the be-
    lated lighter,
On the neighboring shore the fires from the foundry chimneys
    burning high and glaringly into the night,
Casting their flicker of black contrasted with wild red and yel-
    low light over the tops of houses, and down into the clefts
    of streets.

IV

These and all else were to me the same as they are to you,
I loved well those cities, loved well the stately and rapid river,
The men and women I saw were all near to me,
Others the same—others who look back on me because I
    look'd forward to them,
(The time will come, though I stop here to-day and to-night.)

V

What is it then between us?
What is the count of the scores or hundreds of years between
    us?

Whatever it is, it avails not—distance avails not, and place
    avails not,
I too lived, Brooklyn of ample hills was mine,
I too walk'd the streets of Manhattan island, and bathed in
    the waters around it,

I too felt the curious abrupt questionings stir within me.
In the day among crowds of people sometimes they came
  upon me,
In my walks home late at night or as I lay in my bed they
  came upon me,
I too had been struck from the float forever held in solution,
I too had receiv'd identity by my body,
That I was I knew was of my body, and what I should be I
  knew I should be of my body.

VI

It is not upon you alone the dark patches fall,
The dark threw its patches down upon me also,
The best I had done seem'd to me blank and suspicious,
My great thoughts as I supposed them, were they not in
  reality meagre?
Nor is it you alone who know what it is to be evil,
I am he who knew what it was to be evil,
I too knitted the old knot of contrariety,
Blabb'd, blush'd, resented, lied, stole, grudg'd,
Had guile, anger, lust, hot wishes I dared not speak,
Was wayward, vain, greedy, shallow, sly, cowardly, malignant,
The wolf, the snake, the hog, not wanting in me,
The cheating look, the frivolous word, the adulterous wish,
  not wanting,
Refusals, hates, postponements, meanness, laziness, none of
  these wanting,
Was one with the rest, the days and haps of the rest,
Was call'd by my nighest name by clear loud voices of young
  men as they saw me approaching or passing,
Felt their arms on my neck as I stood, or the negligent leaning
  of their flesh against me as I sat,
Saw many I loved in the street or ferry-boat or public as-
  sembly, yet never told them a word,
Lived the same life with the rest, the same old laughing,
  gnawing, sleeping,
Play'd the part that still looks back on the actor or actress,

The same old role, the role that is what we make it, as great
   as we like,
Or as small as we like, or both great and small.

VII

Closer yet I approach you,
What thought you have of me now, I had as much of you
   —I laid in my stores in advance,
I consider'd long and seriously of you before you were born.

Who was to know what should come home to me?
Who knows but I am enjoying this?
Who knows, for all the distance, but I am as good as looking
   at you now, for all you cannot see me?

VIII

Ah, what can ever be more stately and admirable to me than
   mast-hemm'd Manhattan?
River and sunset and scallop-edg'd waves of flood-tide?
The sea-gulls oscillating their bodies, the hay-boat in the
   twilight, and the belated lighter?
What gods can exceed these that clasp me by the hand, and
   with voices I love call me promptly and loudly by my
   nighest name as I approach?

What is more subtle than this which ties me to the woman
   or man that looks in my face?
Which fuses me into you now, and pours my meaning into
   you?

We understand then do we not?
What I promis'd without mentioning it, have you not accepted?
What the study could not teach—what the preaching could
   not accomplish is accomplish'd, is it not?

IX

Flow on, river! flow with the flood-tide, and ebb with the ebb-tide!

Frolic on, crested and scallop-edg'd waves!

Gorgeous clouds of the sunset! drench with your splendor me, or the men and women generations after me!

Cross from shore to shore, countless crowds of passengers!

Stand up, tall masts of Mannahatta! stand up, beautiful hills of Brooklyn!

Throb, baffled and curious brain! throw out questions and answers!

Suspend here and everywhere, eternal float of solution!

Gaze, loving and thirsting eyes, in the house or street or public assembly!

Sound out, voices of young men! loudly and musically call me by my nighest name!

Live, old life! play the part that looks back on the actor or actress!

Play the old role, the role that is great or small according as one makes it!

Consider, you who peruse me, whether I may not in unknown ways be looking upon you;

Be firm, rail over the river, to support those who lean idly, yet haste with the hasting current;

Fly on, sea-birds! fly sideways, or wheel in large circles high in the air;

Receive the summer sky, you water, and faithfully hold it till all downcast eyes have time to take it from you!

Diverge, fine spokes of light, from the shape of my head, or any one's head, in the sunlit water!

Come on, ships from the lower bay! pass up or down, white-sail'd schooners, sloops, lighters!

Flaunt away, flags of all nations! be duly lower'd at sunset!

Burn high your fires, foundry chimneys! cast black shadows at nightfall! cast red and yellow light over the tops of the houses!

Appearances, now or henceforth, indicate what you are,
You necessary film, continue to envelop the soul,
About my body for me, and your body for you, be hung our
    divinest aromas,
Thrive, cities—bring your freight, bring your shows, ample
    and sufficient rivers,
Expand, being than which none else is perhaps more spiritual,
Keep your places, objects than which none else is more lasting.

You have waited, you always wait, you dumb, beautiful
    ministers,
We receive you with free sense at last, and are insatiate
    henceforward,
Not you any more shall be able to foil us, or withhold your-
    selves from us,
We use you, and do not cast you aside—we plant you per-
    manently within us,
We fathom you not—we love you—there is perfection in you
    also,
You furnish your parts toward eternity,
Great or small, you furnish your parts toward the soul.

THE LAST INVOCATION

At the last, tenderly,
From the walls of the powerful fortress'd house,
From the clasp of the knitted locks, from the keep of the
    well-closed doors,
Let me be wafted.
Let me glide noiselessly forth;
With the key of softness unlock the locks—with a whisper,
Set ope the doors O soul.
Tenderly—be not impatient,
(Strong is your hold O mortal flesh,
Strong is your hold O love.)

herman melville

THE MARCH INTO VIRGINIA

(July 1861)

Did all the lets and bars appear
   To every just or larger end,
Whence should come the trust and cheer?
   Youth must its ignorant impulse lend—
Age finds place in the rear.
   All wars are boyish, and are fought by boys,
The champions and enthusiasts of the state:
     Turbid ardours and vain joys
       Not barrenly abate—
     Stimulants to the power mature,
       Preparatives of fate.

Who here forecasteth the event?
What heart but spurns at precedent
And warnings of the wise,
Contemned foreclosures of surprise?
The banners play, the bugles call,
The air is blue and prodigal.
   No berrying party, pleasure-wooed,
No picnic party in the May,
Ever went less loth than they
   Into that leafy neighborhood.
In Bacchic glee they file toward Fate,
Moloch's uninitiate;
Expectancy, and glad surmise
Of battle's unknown mysteries.
All they feel is this: 'tis glory,
A rapture sharp, though transitory,
Yet lasting in belaurelled story.
So they gaily go to fight,
Chatting left and laughing right.
But some who this blithe mood present,

As on it lightsome files they fare,
Shall die experienced ere three days are spent—
    Perish, enlightened by the volleyed glare;
Or shame survive, and like to adamant,
    The throe of Second Manassas share.

THE BERG

A Dream

I saw a ship of martial build
(Her standards set, her brave apparel on)
Directed as by madness mere
Against a stolid iceberg steer,
Nor budge it, though the infatuate ship went down.
The impact made huge ice-cubes fall
Sullen, in tons that crashed the deck;
But that one avalanche was all—
No other movement save the foundering wreck.

Along the spurs of ridges pale,
Not any slenderest shaft and frail,
A prism over glass-green gorges lone,
Toppled; nor lace of traceries fine,
Nor pendant drops in grot or mine
Were jarred, when the stunned ship went down.
Nor sole the gulls in cloud that wheeled
Circling one snow-flanked peak afar,

But nearer fowl the floes that skimmed
And crystal beaches, felt no jar.
No thrill transmitted stirred the lock
Of jack-straw needle-ice at base;
Towers undermined by waves—the block
Atilt impending—kept their place.
Seals, dozing sleek on sliddery ledges
Slipt never, when by loftier edges
Through very inertia overthrown,
The impetuous ship in bafflement went down.

Hard Berg (methought), so cold, so vast,
With mortal damps self-overcast;
Exhaling still thy dankish breath—
Adrift dissolving, bound for death;
Though lumpish thou, a lumbering one—
A lumbering lubbard, loitering slow,
Impingers rue thee and go down,
Sounding thy precipice below,
Nor stir the slimy slug that sprawls
Along thy dead indifference of walls.

matthew arnold

DOVER BEACH

The sea is calm to-night.
The tide is full, the moon lies fair
Upon the straits;—on the French coast the light
Gleams and is gone; the cliffs of England stand
Glimmering and vast, out in the tranquil bay.

Come to the window, sweet is the night-air!
Only, from the long line of spray
Where the sea meets the moon-blanch'd land,
Listen! you hear the grating roar
Of pebbles which the waves draw back, and fling,
At their return, up the high strand.
Begin, and cease, and then again begin,
With tremulous cadence slow, and bring
The eternal note of sadness in.

Sophocles long ago
Heard it on the Ægean, and it brought
Into his mind the turbid ebb and flow,
Of human misery; we
Find also in the sound a thought,
Hearing it by this distant northern sea.

The Sea of Faith
Was once, too, at the full, and round earth's shore
Lay like the folds of a bright girdle furl'd.
But now I only hear
Its melancholy, long, withdrawing roar,
Retreating, to the breath
Of the night-wind, down the vast edges drear
And naked shingles of the world.

Ah, love, let us be true
To one another! for the world, which seems
To lie before us like a land of dreams,
So various, so beautiful, so new,
Hath really neither joy, nor love, nor light,
Nor certitude, nor peace, nor help for pain;
And we are here as on a darkling plain
Swept with confused alarms of struggle and flight,
Where ignorant armies clash by night.

sir w. s. gilbert

NIGHTMARE

When you're lying awake with a dismal headache, and repose
is taboo'd by anxiety,
I conceive you may use any language you choose to indulge
in, without impropriety;
For your brain is on fire—the bedclothes conspire of usual
slumber to plunder you:
First your counterpane goes, and uncovers your toes, and your
sheet slips demurely from under you;
Then the blanketing tickles—you feel like mixed pickles—so
terribly sharp is the pricking,
And you're hot, and you're cross, and you tumble and toss till
there's nothing 'twixt you and the ticking.

Then the bedclothes all creep to the ground in a heap, and
you pick 'em all up in a tangle;

Next your pillow resigns and politely declines to remain at its
usual angle!

Well, you get some repose in the form of a doze, with hot eyeballs and head ever aching,

But your slumbering teems with such horrible dreams that
you'd very much better be waking;

For you dream you are crossing the Channel, and tossing
about in a steamer from Harwich—

Which is something between a large bathing machine and a
very small second-class carriage—

And you're giving a treat (penny ice and cold meat) to a
party of friends and relations—

They're a ravenous horde—and they all came on board at
Sloane Square and South Kensington Stations.

And bound on that journey you find your attorney (who
started that morning from Devon);

He's a bit undersized, and you don't feel surprised when he
tells you he's only eleven.

Well, you're driving like mad with this singular lad (by-the-
bye the ship's now a four-wheeler),

And you're playing round games, and he calls you bad names
when you tell him that 'ties pay the dealer';

But this you can't stand, so you throw up your hand, and you
find you're as cold as an icicle,

In your shirt and your socks (the black silk with gold clocks),
crossing Salisbury Plain on a bicycle:

And he and the crew are on bicycles too—which they've somehow or other invested in—

And he's telling the tars, all the particu*lars* of a company he's
interested in—

It's a scheme of devices, to get at low prices, all goods from
cough mixtures to cables

(Which tickled the sailors) by treating retailers, as though
they were all vege*ta*bles—

You get a good spadesman to plant a small tradesman, (first
take off his boots with a boot-tree),

And his legs will take root, and his fingers will shoot, and
  they'll blossom and bud like a fruit-tree—
From the greengrocer tree you gets grapes and green pea,
  cauliflower, pineapple, and cranberries,
While the pastrycook plant, cherry brandy will grant, apple
  puffs, and three-corners, and banberries—
The shares are a penny, and ever so many are taken by Roths-
  child and Baring,
And just as a few are allotted to you, you awake with a shudder despairing—
You're a regular wreck, with a crick in your neck, and no wonder you snore, for your head's on the floor, and you've
  needles and pins from your soles to your shins, and your
  flesh is a-creep for your left leg's asleep, and you've cramp
  in your toes, and a fly on your nose, and some fluff in your
  lung, and a feverish tongue, and a thirst that's intense, and
  a general sense that you haven't been sleeping in clover;
But the darkness has passed, and it's daylight at last, and the
  night has been long—ditto ditto my song—and thank goodness they're both of them over!

From *Iolanthe*

SIR JOSEPH'S SONG

When I was a lad I served a term
As office boy to an Attorney's firm.
I cleaned the windows and I swept the floor,
And I polished up the handle of the big front door.
  I polished up that handle so carefullee
  That now I am the Ruler of the Queen's Navee!

As office boy I made such a mark
That they gave me the post of a junior clerk.
I served the writs with a smile so bland,
And I copied all the letters in a big round hand—
  I copied all the letters in a hand so free,
  That now I am the Ruler of the Queen's Navee!

In serving writs I made such a name
That an articled clerk I soon became;
I wore clean collars and a brand new suit
For the pass examination at the Institute,
    And that pass examination did so well for me,
      That now I am the Ruler of the Queen's Navee!

Of legal knowledge I acquired such a grip
That they took me into the partnership.
And that junior partnership, I ween,
Was the only ship that I ever had seen.
    But that kind of ship so suited me,
      That now I am the Ruler of the Queen's Navee!

I grew so rich that I was sent
By a pocket borough into Parliament.
I always voted at my party's call,
And I never thought of thinking for myself at all.
    I thought so little, they rewarded me
      By making me the Ruler of the Queen's Navee!

Now Landsmen all, whoever you may be,
If you want to rise to the top of the tree,
If your soul isn't fettered to an office stool,
Be careful to be guided by this golden rule—
    Stick close to your desks and never go to sea,
      And you all may be Rulers of the Queen's Navee!

From H.M.S. Pinafore

BUNTHORNE'S SONG

If you're anxious for to shine in the high aesthetic line as a
    man of culture rare,
You must get up all the germs of the transcendental terms,
    and plant them everywhere.
You must lie upon the daisies and discourse in novel phrases
    of your complicated state of mind,

The matter doesn't matter if it's only idle chatter of a tran-
    scendental kind.
  And every one will say,
  As you walk your mystic way,
'If this young man expresses himself in terms too deep for *me*,
'Why, what a very singularly deep young man this deep young
    man must be!'

Be eloquent in praise of the very dull old days which have
    long since passed away,
And convince 'em, if you can, that the reign of good Queen
    Anne was Culture's palmiest day.
Of course you will pooh-pooh whatever's fresh and new, and
    declare it's crude and mean,
For Art stopped short in the cultivated court of the Empress
    Josephine.
  And everyone will say,
  As you walk your mystic way,
'If that's not good enough for him which is good enough for
    me,
Why, what a very cultivated kind of youth this kind of youth
    must be!'

Then a sentimental passion of a vegetable fashion must excite
    your languid spleen,
An attachment *à la Plato* for a bashful young potato, or a not-
    too-French French bean!
Though the Philistines may jostle, you will rank as an apostle
    in the high aesthetic band,
If you walk down Piccadilly with a poppy or a lily in your
    mediaeval hand.
  And everyone will say,
  As you walk your flowery way,
'If he's content with a vegetable love which would certainly
    not suit *me*,
Why, what a most particularly pure young man this pure
    young man must be!'

From *Patience*

KO-KO'S SONG

As some day it may happen that a victim must be found, I've
    got a little list—I've got a little list
Of society offenders who might well be underground,
    And who never would be missed—who never would be
    missed!
There's the pestilential nuisances who write for autographs—
All people who have flabby hands and irritating laughs—
All children who are up in dates, and floor you with 'em flat—
All persons who in shaking hands, shake hands with you like
    that—
And all third persons who on spoiling *tête-à-têtes* insist—
    They'd none of 'em be missed—they'd none of 'em be
    missed!

Chorus.   He's got 'em on the list—he's got 'em on the list;
    And they'll none of 'em be missed—they'll none of 'em be
    missed.

There's the nigger serenader, and the others of his race,
    And the piano-organist—I've got him on the list!
And the people who eat peppermint and puff it in your face,
    They never would be missed—they never would be missed!
Then the idiot who praises, with enthusiastic tone,
All centuries but this, and every country but his own;
And the lady from the provinces, who dresses like a guy,
And who 'doesn't think she waltzes, but would rather like to
    try';
And that singular anomaly, the lady novelist—
    I don't think she'd be missed—I'm *sure* she'd not be missed!

Chorus.   He's got her on the list—he's got her on the list;
    And I don't think she'll be missed—I'm sure she'll not be
    missed!

And that *Nisi Prius* nuisance, who just now is rather rife,
    That judicial humourist—I've got *him* on the list!

All funny fellows, comic men, and clowns of private life—
    They'd none of 'em be missed—they'd none of 'em be missed.
And apologetic statesmen of a compromising kind,
Such as—What d'ye call him—Thing'em-bob, and likewise—
    Nevermind,
And 'St—'st—'st—and What's-his-name, and also You-know-
    who—
The task of filling up the blanks I'd rather leave to *you*.
But it really doesn't matter whom you put upon the list,
    For they'd none of 'em be missed—they'd none of 'em be
    missed!

Chorus.   *You may put 'em on the list—you may put 'em on*
    the list,
    And they'll none of 'em be missed—they'll none of 'em be
    missed!

From *The Mikado*

THE MIKADO'S SONG

A more humane Mikado never
    Did in Japan exist,
        To nobody second,
        I'm certainly reckoned
A true philanthropist.
It is my very humane endeavour
    To make, to some extent,
        Each evil liver
        A running river
Of harmless merriment.

My object all sublime
I shall achieve in time—
To let the punishment fit the crime—
    The punishment fit the crime;
And make each prisoner pent
Unwillingly represent
A source of innocent merriment!
    Of innocent merriment!

All prosy dull society sinners,
   Who chatter and bleat and bore,
      Are sent to hear sermons
      From mystical Germans
   Who preach from ten till four.
The amateur tenor, whose vocal villainies
   All desire to shirk,
      Shall, during off-hours,
      Exhibit his powers,
To Madame Tussaud's waxwork.

The lady who dyes a chemical yellow
   Or stains her gray hair puce,
      Or pinches her figger,
      Is blacked like a nigger
With permanent walnut juice.
The idiot who, in railway carriages,
   Scribbles on window-panes,
      We only suffer
      To ride on a buffer
In Parliamentary trains.

    My object all sublime, etc.

The advertising quack who wearies
   With tales of countless cures,
      His teeth, I've enacted,
      Shall all be extracted
By terrified amateurs.
The music-hall singer attends a series
   Of masses and fugues and "ops"
      By Bach, interwoven
      With Spohr and Beethoven,
At classical Monday Pops.

The billiard sharp whom any one catches,
   His doom's extremely hard—
      He's made to dwell—
      In a dungeon cell

On a spot that's always barred.
And there he plays extravagant matches
    In fitless finger-stalls
        On a cloth untrue,
        With a twisted cue
    And elliptical billiard balls!
        My object all sublime, etc.

From *The Mikado*

TIT WILLOW

On a tree by a river a little tom-tit
        Sang 'Willow, titwillow, titwillow!'
And I said to him, 'Dicky-bird, why do you sit
        Singing "Willow, titwillow, titwillow"?
Is it weakness of intellect, birdie?' I cried,
'Or a rather tough worm in your little inside?'
With a shake of his poor little head he replied,
        'Oh, willow, titwillow, titwillow!'

He slapped at his chest, as he sat on that bough,
        Singing 'Willow, titwillow, titwillow!'
And a cold perspiration bespangled his brow,
        'Oh, willow, titwillow, titwillow!'
He sobbed and he sighed, and a gurgle he gave,
Then he threw himself into the billowy wave,
And an echo arose from the suicide's grave—
        'Oh, willow, titwillow, titwillow!'

Now, I feel just as sure as I'm sure that my name
        Isn't Willow, titwillow, titwillow,
That 'twas blighted affection that made him exclaim,
        'Oh, willow, titwillow, titwillow!'
And if you remain callous and obdurate, I
Shall perish as he did, and you will know why,
Though I probably shall not exclaim as I die,
        'Oh, willow, titwillow, titwillow!'

From *The Mikado*

dante gabriel rossetti

A SUPERSCRIPTION

Look in my face; my name is Might-have-been;
I am also called No-more, Too-late, Farewell;
Unto thine ear I hold the dead-sea-shell
Cast up thy Life's foam-fretted feet between;
Unto thine eyes the glass where that is seen
Which had Life's form and Love's, but by my spell
Is now a shaken shadow intolerable,
Of ultimate things unuttered the frail screen.
Mark me, how still I am! But should there dart
One moment through thy soul the soft surprise
Of that winged Peace which lulls the breath of sighs,—
Then shalt thou see me smile, and turn apart
Thy visage to mine ambush at thy heart
Sleepless with cold commemorative eyes.

christina rossetti

ECHO

Come to me in the silence of the night;
  Come in the speaking silence of a dream;
Come with soft rounded cheeks and eyes as bright
    As sunlight on a stream;
      Come back in tears,
O memory, hope, love of finished years.

O dream how sweet, too sweet, too bitter sweet,
  Whose wakening should have been in Paradise,
Where souls brimful of love abide and meet;
    Where thirsty longing eyes
      Watch the slow door
That opening, letting in, lets out no more.

Yet come to me in dreams, that I may live
   My very life again though cold in death:
Come back to me in dreams, that I may give
   Pulse for pulse, breath for breath:
     Speak low, lean low,
As long ago, my love, how long ago!

AMOR MUNDI

'Oh, where are you going with your lovelocks flowing,
   On the west wind blowing along this valley track?'
'The downhill path is easy, come with me an' it please ye,
   We shall escape the uphill by never turning back.'

So they two went together in glowing August weather,
   The honey-breathing heather lay to their left and right;
And dear she was to doat on, her swift feet seemed to float on
   The air like soft twin pigeons too sportive to alight.

'Oh, what is that in heaven where grey cloudflakes are seven,
   Where blackest clouds hang riven just at the rainy skirt?'
'Oh, that's a meteor sent us, a message dumb, portentous,
   An undecipher'd solemn signal of help or hurt.'

'Oh, what is that glides quickly where velvet flowers grow
    thickly,
   Their scent comes rich and sickly?' 'A scaled and hooded
    worm.'
'Oh, what's that in the hollow, so pale I quake to follow?'
   'Oh, that's a thin dead body which waits the eternal term.'

'Turn again, O my sweetest,—turn again, false and fleetest:
   This beaten way thou beatest I fear is hell's own track.'
'Nay, too steep for hill-mounting; nay, too late for cost count-
    ing:
   This downhill path is easy, but there's no turning back.'

WHEN I AM DEAD, MY DEAREST

When I am dead, my dearest,
  Sing no sad songs for me;
Plant thou no roses at my head,
  Nor shady cypress tree:
Be the green grass above me
  With showers and dewdrops wet;
And if thou wilt, remember,
  And if thou wilt, forget.

I shall not see the shadows,
  I shall not feel the rain;
I shall not hear the nightingale
  Sing on, as if in pain;
And dreaming through the twilight
  That doth not rise nor set,
Haply I may remember,
  And haply may forget.

emily dickinson

THIS IS MY LETTER TO THE WORLD

This is my letter to the world,
  That never wrote to me,—
The simple news that Nature told,
  With tender majesty.

Her message is committed
  To hands I cannot see;
For love of her, sweet countrymen,
  Judge tenderly of me!

SUCCESS IS COUNTED SWEETEST

Success is counted sweetest
By those who ne'er succeed.
To comprehend a nectar
Requires sorest need.

Not one of all the purple host
Who took the flag to-day
Can tell the definition,
So clear, of victory,

As he, defeated, dying,
On whose forbidden ear
The distant strains of triumph
Break, agonized and clear.

THE HEART ASKS PLEASURE FIRST

The heart asks pleasure first,
And then, excuse from pain;
And then, those little anodynes
That deaden suffering;

And then, to go to sleep;
And then, if it should be
The will of its Inquisitor,
The liberty to die.

MUCH MADNESS IS DIVINEST SENSE

Much madness is divinest sense
To a discerning eye;
Much sense the starkest madness.
'T is the majority
In this, as all, prevails.
Assent, and you are sane;
Demur,—you're straightway dangerous,
And handled with a chain.

THE SOUL SELECTS HER OWN SOCIETY

The soul selects her own society,
Then shuts the door;
On her divine majority
Obtrude no more.

Unmoved, she notes the chariot's pausing
At her low gate;
Unmoved, an emperor is kneeling
Upon her mat.

I've known her from an ample nation
Choose one;
Then close the valves of her attention
Like stone.

I NEVER SAW A MOOR

I never saw a moor,
I never saw the sea;
Yet know I how the heather looks,
And what a wave must be.

I never spoke with God,
Nor visited in heaven;
Yet certain am I of the spot
As if the chart were given.

I YEARS HAD BEEN FROM HOME

I years had been from home,
And now, before the door
I dared not open, lest a face
I never saw before

Stare vacant into mine
And ask my business there.

My business,—just a life I left,
Was such still dwelling there?

I fumbled at my nerve,
I scanned the windows near;
The silence like an ocean rolled,
And broke against my ear.

I laughed a wooden laugh
That I could fear a door,
Who danger and the dead had faced,
But never quaked before.

I fitted to the latch
My hand, with trembling care,
Lest back the awful door should spring,
And leave me standing there.

I moved my fingers off
As cautiously as glass,
And held my ears, and like a thief
Fled gasping from the house.

MY LIFE CLOSED TWICE BEFORE ITS CLOSE

My life closed twice before its close;
    It yet remains to see
If Immortality unveil
    A third event to me,

So huge, so hopeless to conceive,
    As these that twice befell.
Parting is all we know of heaven,
    And all we need of hell.

I FELT A CLEAVAGE IN MY MIND

I felt a cleavage in my mind
   As if my brain had split;
I tried to match it, seam by seam,
   But could not make them fit.

The thought behind I strove to join
   Unto the thought before,
But sequence ravelled out of reach
   Like balls upon a floor.

THE BRAIN IS WIDER THAN THE SKY

The brain is wider than the sky,
   For, put them side by side,
The one the other will include
   With ease, and you beside.

The brain is deeper than the sea,
   For, hold them, blue to blue,
The one the other will absorb,
   As sponges, buckets do.

The brain is just the weight of God,
   For, lift them, pound for pound,
And they will differ, if they do,
   As syllable from sound.

I HAD BEEN HUNGRY

I had been hungry all the years;
My noon had come to dine;
I, trembling, drew the table near,
And touched the curious wine.

'Twas this on tables I had seen,
When turning, hungry, lone,

I looked in windows, for the wealth
I could not hope to own.

I did not know the ample bread;
'Twas so unlike the crumb
The birds and I had often shared
In Nature's dining-room.

The plenty hurt me, 'twas so new,—
Myself felt ill and odd,
As berry of a mountain bush
Transplanted to the road.

Nor was I hungry; so I found
That hunger was a way
Of persons outside windows,
The entering takes away.

BEFORE I GOT MY EYE PUT OUT

Before I got my eye put out,
I liked as well to see
As other creatures that have eyes,
And know no other way.

But were it told to me, to-day,
That I might have the sky
For mine, I tell you that my heart
Would split, for size of me.

The meadows mine, the mountains mine,—
All forests, stintless stars,
As much of noon as I could take
Between my finite eyes.

The motions of the dipping birds,
The lightning's jointed road,

For mine to look at when I liked—
The news would strike me dead!

So, safer, guess, with just my soul
Upon the window-pane
Where other creatures put their eyes,
Incautious of the sun.

I TASTE A LIQUOR NEVER BREWED

I taste a liquor never brewed,
From tankards scooped in pearl;
Not all the vats upon the Rhine
Yield such an alcohol!

Inebriate of air am I,
And debauchee of dew,
Reeling, through endless summer days,
From inns of molten blue.

When landlords turn the drunken bee
Out of the foxglove's door,
When butterflies renounce their drams,
I shall but drink the more!

Till seraphs swing their snowy hats,
And saints to windows run,
To see the little tippler
Leaning against the sun!

HOPE IS THE THING WITH FEATHERS

Hope is the thing with feathers
That perches in the soul,
And sings the tune without the words,
And never stops at all.

And sweetest in the gale is heard;
And sore must be the storm
That could abash the little bird
That kept so many warm.

I've heard it in the chillest land,
And on the strangest sea;
Yet, never, in extremity,
It asked a crumb of me.

I LIKE TO SEE IT LAP THE MILES

I like to see it lap the miles,
And lick the valleys up,
And stop to feed itself at tanks;
And then, prodigious, step

Around a pile of mountains,
And, supercilious, peer
In shanties by the sides of roads;
And then a quarry pare

To fit its sides, and crawl between,
Complaining all the while
In horrid, hooting stanza;
Then chase itself down hill

And neigh like Boanerges;
Then, punctual as a star,
Stop—docile and omnipotent—
At its own stable door.

A BIRD CAME DOWN THE WALK

A bird came down the walk:
He did not know I saw;
He bit an angle-worm in halves
And ate the fellow, raw.

And then he drank a dew
From a convenient grass,
And then hopped sidewise to the wall
To let a beetle pass.

He glanced with rapid eyes
That hurried all abroad,—
They looked like frightened beads, I thought
He stirred his velvet head

Like one in danger; cautious,
I offered him a crumb,
And he unrolled his feathers
And rowed him softer home

Than oars divide the ocean,
Too silver for a seam,
Or butterflies, off banks of noon,
Leap, plashless, as they swim.

A NARROW FELLOW IN THE GRASS

A narrow fellow in the grass
Occasionally rides;
You may have met him,—did
    you not?
His notice sudden is.

The grass divides as with a
    comb,
A spotted shaft is seen;
And then it closes at your feet
And opens further on.

He likes a boggy acre,
A floor too cool for corn.
Yet when a child, & barefoot,
I more than once, at morn,

Have passed, I thought, a
    whip-lash
Unbraiding in the sun,—
When, stooping to secure it,
It wrinkled, and was gone.

Several of nature's people
I know, and they know me;
I feel for them a transport
Of cordiality;

But never met this fellow,
Attended or alone,
Without a tighter breathing,
And zero at the bone.

THERE CAME A WIND LIKE A BUGLE

There came a wind like a bugle;
It quivered through the grass,
And a green chill upon the heat
So ominous did pass
We barred the windows and the doors
As from an emerald ghost;
The doom's electric moccasin
That very instant passed.
On a strange mob of panting trees,
And fences fled away,
And rivers where the houses ran
The living looked that day.
The bell within the steeple wild
The flying tidings whirled.
How much can come
And much can go
And yet abide the world!

BESIDES THE AUTUMN POETS SING

Besides the autumn poets sing,
A few prosaic days
A little this side of the snow
And that side of the haze.

A few incisive mornings,
A few ascetic eves,—
Gone Mr. Bryant's golden-rod,
And Mr. Thomson's sheaves.

Still is the bustle in the brook,
Sealed are the spicy valves;
Mesmeric fingers softly touch
The eyes of many elves.

Perhaps a squirrel may remain,
My sentiments to share.
Grant me, O Lord, a sunny mind,
Thy windy will to bear!

THE SKY IS LOW, THE CLOUDS ARE MEAN

The sky is low, the clouds are mean,
A travelling flake of snow
Across a barn or through a rut
Debates if it will go.

A narrow wind complains all day
How some one treated him;
Nature, like us, is sometimes caught
Without her diadem.

THERE'S A CERTAIN SLANT OF LIGHT

There's a certain slant of light,
On winter afternoons,
That oppresses, like the weight
Of cathedral tunes.

Heavenly hurt it gives us;
We can find no scar,
But internal difference
Where the meanings are.

None may teach it anything,
'T is the seal, despair,—
An imperial affliction
Sent us of the air.

When it comes, the landscape listens,
Shadows hold their breath;
When it goes, 't is like the distance
On the look of death.

BECAUSE I COULD NOT STOP FOR DEATH

Because I could not stop for Death,
He kindly stopped for me;
The carriage held but just ourselves
And Immortality.

We slowly drove, he knew no haste,
And I had put away
My labor, and my leisure too,
For his civility.

We passed the school where children played
At wrestling in a ring;
We passed the fields of gazing grain,
We passed the setting sun.

We paused before a house that seemed
A swelling of the ground;
The roof was scarcely visible,
The cornice but a mound.

Since then 't is centuries; but each
Feels shorter than the day
I first surmised the horses' heads
Were toward eternity.

I FELT A FUNERAL IN MY BRAIN

I felt a funeral in my brain,
    And mourners, to and fro,
Kept treading, treading, till it seemed
    That sense was breaking through.

And when they all were seated,
    A service like a drum
Kept beating, beating, till I thought
    My mind was going numb.

And then I heard them lift a box,
   And creak across my soul
With those same boots of lead, again.
   Then space began to toll

As all the heavens were a bell,
   And Being but an ear,
And I and silence some strange race,
   Wrecked, solitary, here.

I HEARD A FLY BUZZ WHEN I DIED

I heard a fly buzz when I died;
The stillness in the room
Was like the stillness in the air
Between the heaves of storm.

The eyes around had wrung them dry,
And breaths were gathering firm
For that last onset, when the king
Be witnessed in the room.

I willed my keepsakes, signed away
What portion of me be
Assignable—and then it was
There interposed a fly,

With blue, uncertain, stumbling buzz,
Between the light and me;
And then the windows failed, and then
I could not see to see.

A LIGHT EXISTS IN SPRING

A light exists in spring
   Not present on the year
At any other period.
   When March is scarcely here

A color stands abroad
  On solitary hills
That science cannot overtake,
  But human nature *feels*.

It waits upon the lawn;
  It shows the furthest tree
Upon the furthest slope we
    know;
  It almost speaks to me.

Then, as horizons step,
  Or noons report away,
Without the formula of
    sound,
  It passes, and we stay:

A quality of loss
  Affecting our content,
As trade had suddenly
    encroached
  Upon a sacrament.

SAFE IN THEIR ALABASTER CHAMBERS

Safe in their alabaster chambers,
Untouched by morning and untouched by noon,
Sleep the meek members of the resurrection,
Rafter of satin, and roof of stone.

Light laughs the breeze in her castle of sunshine;
Babbles the bee in a stolid ear;
Pipe the sweet birds in ignorant cadence,—
Ah, what sagacity perished here!

Grand go the years in the crescent above them;
Worlds scoop their arcs, and firmaments row,
Diadems drop and Doges surrender,
Soundless as dots on a disk of snow.

AFTER GREAT PAIN A FORMAL FEELING COMES

After great pain a formal feeling comes—
The nerves sit ceremonious like tombs;
The stiff Heart questions—was it He that bore?
And yesterday—or centuries before?

The feet mechanical
Go round a wooden way
Of ground or air or Ought, regardless grown,
A quartz contentment like a stone.

This is the hour of lead
Remembered if outlived,
As freezing persons recollect the snow—
First chill, then stupor, then the letting go.

lewis carroll

JABBERWOCKY

'Twas brillig, and the slithy toves
  Did gyre and gimble in the wabe:
All mimsy were the borogoves,
  And the mome raths outgrabe.

'Beware the Jabberwock, my son!
  The jaws that bite, the claws that catch!
Beware the Jubjub bird, and shun
  The frumious Bandersnatch!'

He took his vorpal sword in hand;
  Long time the manxome foe he sought—
So rested he by the Tumtum tree,
  And stood awhile in thought.

And, as in uffish thought he stood,
   The Jabberwock, with eyes of flame,
Came whiffling through the tulgey wood,
   And burbled as it came!

One, two! One, two! And through and through
   The vorpal blade went snicker-snack!
He left it dead, and with its head
   He went galumphing back.

'And hast thou slain the Jabberwock?
   Come to my arms, my beamish boy!
O frabjous day! Callooh, Callay!'
   He chorted in his joy.

'Twas brillig, and the slithy toves
   Did gyre and gimble in the wabe:
All mimsy were the borogoves,
   And the mome raths outgrabe.

THE WALRUS AND THE CARPENTER

The sun was shining on the sea,
   Shining with all his might:
He did his very best to make
   The billows smooth and bright—
And this was odd, because it was
   The middle of the night.

The moon was shining sulkily,
   Because she thought the sun
Had got no business to be there
   After the day was done—
'It's very rude of him,' she said,
   'To come and spoil the fun!'

The sea was wet as wet could be,
   The sands were dry as dry.

You could not see a cloud, because
  No cloud was in the sky:
No birds were flying overhead—
  There were no birds to fly.

The Walrus and the Carpenter
  Were walking close at hand:
They wept like anything to see
  Such quantities of sand:
'If this were only cleared away,'
  They said, 'it *would* be grand!'

'If seven maids with seven mops
  Swept it for half a year,
Do you suppose,' the Walrus said,
  'That they could get it clear?'
'I doubt it,' said the Carpenter,
  And shed a bitter tear.

'O oysters, come and walk with us!'
  The Walrus did beseech.
'A pleasant walk, a pleasant talk,
  Along the briny beach:
We cannot do with more than four,
  To give a hand to each.'

The eldest Oyster looked at him,
  But never a word he said:
The eldest Oyster winked his eye,
  And shook his heavy head—
Meaning to say he did not choose
  To leave the oyster-bed.

But four young Oysters hurried up,
  All eager for the treat:
Their coats were brushed, their faces washed,
  Their shoes were clean and neat—

And this was odd, because, you know,
    They hadn't any feet.

Four other Oysters followed them,
    And yet another four;
And thick and fast they came at last,
    And more, and more, and more—
All hopping through the frothy waves,
    And scrambling to the shore.

The Walrus and the Carpenter
    Walked on a mile or so,
And then they rested on a rock
    Conveniently low:
And all the little Oysters stood
    And waited in a row.

'The time has come,' the Walrus said,
    'To talk of many things:
Of shoes—and ships—and sealing wax—
    Of cabbages—and kings—
And why the sea is boiling hot—
    And whether pigs have wings.'

'But wait a bit,' the Oysters cried,
    'Before we have our chat;
For some of us are out of breath,
    And all of us are fat!'
'No hurry!' said the Carpenter.
    They thanked him much for that.

'A loaf of bread,' the Walrus said,
    'Is what we chiefly need:
Pepper and vinegar besides
    Are very good indeed—
Now, if you're ready, Oysters dear,
    We can begin to feed.'

'But not on us!' the Oysters cried,
    Turning a little blue.

'After such kindness, that would be
    A dismal thing to do!'
'The night is fine,' the Walrus said.
    'Do you admire the view?'

'It was so kind of you to come!
    And you are very nice!'
The Carpenter said nothing but
    'Cut us another slice.
I wish you were not quite so deaf—
    I've had to ask you twice!'

'It seems a shame,' the Walrus said,
    'To play them such a trick.
After we've brought them out so far,
    And made them trot so quick!'
The Carpenter said nothing but
    'The butter's spread too thick!'

'I weep for you,' the Walrus said:
    'I deeply sympathize.'
With sobs and tears he sorted out
    Those of the largest size,
Holding his pocket-handkerchief
    Before his streaming eyes.

'O Oysters,' said the Carpenter.
    'You've had a pleasant run!
Shall we be trotting home again?'
    But answer came there none—
And this was scarcely odd, because
    They'd eaten every one.

FATHER WILLIAM

'You are old, Father William,' the young man said,
  'And your hair has become very white;
And yet you incessantly stand on your head—
  Do you think, at your age, it is right?'

'In my youth,' Father William replied to his son,
  'I feared it might injure the brain;
But, now that I'm perfectly sure I have none,
  Why, I do it again and again.'

'You are old,' said the youth, 'as I mentioned before,
  And have grown most uncommonly fat;
Yet you turned a back-somersault in at the door—
  Pray, what is the reason of that?'

'In my youth,' said the sage, as he shook his gray locks,
  'I kept all my limbs very supple
By the use of this ointment—one shilling the box—
  Allow me to sell you a couple?'

'You are old,' said the youth, 'and your jaws are too weak
  For anything tougher than suet;
Yet you finished the goose, with the bones and the beak—
  Pray, how did you manage to do it?'

'In my youth,' said his father, 'I took to the law,
  And argued each case with my wife;
And the muscular strength which it gave to my jaw,
  Has lasted the rest of my life.'

'You are old,' said the youth, 'one would hardly suppose
  That your eye was as steady as ever;
Yet you balanced an eel on the end of your nose—
  What made you so awfully clever?'

'I have answered three questions, and that is enough,'
  Said his father; 'don't give yourself airs!
Do you think I can listen all day to such stuff?
  Be off, or I'll kick you downstairs.'

oscar wilde

IN READING GAOL BY READING TOWN

In Reading gaol by Reading town
  There is a pit of shame,
And in it lies a wretched man
  Eaten by teeth of flame,
In a burning winding-sheet he lies,
  And his grave has got no name.

And there, till Christ call forth the dead,
  In silence let him lie:
No need to waste the foolish tear,
  Or heave the windy sigh:
The man had killed the thing he loved,
  And so he had to die.

And all men kill the thing they love,
  By all let this be heard,
Some do it with a bitter look,
  Some with a flattering word,
The coward does it with a kiss,
  The brave man with a sword!

From The Ballad of Reading Gaol

lionel johnson

THE DARK ANGEL

Dark Angel, with thine aching lust
To rid the world of penitence:
Malicious Angel, who still dost
My soul such subtile violence!

Because of thee, no thought, no thing
Abides for me undesecrate:

Dark Angel, ever on the wing,
Who never reachest me too late!

When music sounds, then changest thou
Its silvery to a sultry fire:
Nor will thine envious heart allow
Delight untortured by desire.

Through thee, the gracious Muses turn
To Furies, O mine Enemy!
And all the things of beauty burn
With flames of evil ecstasy.

Because of thee, the land of dreams
Becomes a gathering-place of fears:
Until tormented slumber seems
One vehemence of useless tears.

When sunlight glows upon the flowers,
Or ripples down the dancing sea:
Thou, with thy troop of passionate powers,
Beleaguerest, bewilderest me.

Within the breath of autumn woods,
Within the winter silences:
Thy venomous spirit stirs and broods,
O master of impieties!

The ardour of red flame is thine,
And thine the steely soul of ice:
Thou poisonest the fair design
Of nature, with unfair device.

Apples of ashes, golden bright;
Waters of bitterness, how sweet!
O banquet of a foul delight,
Prepared by thee, dark Paraclete.

Thou art the whisper in the gloom,
The hinting tone, the haunting laugh:
Thou art the adorner of my tomb,
The minstrel of mine epitaph.

I fight thee, in the Holy Name!
Yet, what thou dost, is what God saith:
Tempter! should I escape thy flame,
Thou wilt have helped my soul from Death:

The second Death, that never dies,
That cannot die, when time is dead:
Live Death, wherein the lost soul cries,
Eternally uncomforted.

Dark Angel, with thine aching lust!
Of two defeats, of two despairs:
Less dread, a change to drifting dust,
Than thine eternity of cares.

Do what thou wilt, thou shalt not so,
Dark Angel! triumph over me:
Lonely, unto the Lone I go;
Divine, to the Divinity.

ernest dowson

NON SUM QUALIS ERAM BONAE SUB REGNO CYNARAE

Last night, ah, yesternight, betwixt her lips and mine
There fell thy shadow, Cynara! thy breath was shed
Upon my soul between the kisses and the wine;
And I was desolate and sick of an old passion,
    Yea, I was desolate and bowed my head:
I have been faithful to thee, Cynara! in my fashion.

All night upon mine heart I felt her warm heart beat,
Night-long within mine arms in love and sleep she lay;

Surely the kisses of her bought red mouth were sweet;
But I was desolate and sick of an old passion,
    When I awoke and found the dawn was gray:
I have been faithful to thee, Cynara! in my fashion.

I have forgot much, Cynara! gone with the wind,
Flung roses, roses riotously with the throng,
Dancing, to put thy pale, lost lilies out of mind;
But I was desolate and sick of an old passion,
    Yea, all the time, because the dance was long:
I have been faithful to thee, Cynara! in my fashion.

I cried for madder music and for stronger wine,
But when the feast is finished and the lamps expire,
Then falls thy shadow, Cynara! the night is thine;
And I am desolate and sick of an old passion,
    Yea hungry for the lips of my desire:
I have been faithful to thee, Cynara! in my fashion.

algernon charles swinburne

BEFORE THE BEGINNING OF YEARS

Before the beginning of years
    There came to the making of man
Time, with a gift of tears;
    Grief, with a glass that ran;
Pleasure, with pain for leaven;
    Summer, with flowers that fell;
Remembrance fallen from heaven,
    And madness risen from hell;
Strength without hands to smite;
    Love that endures for a breath;
Night, the shadow of light,
    And life, the shadow of death.

And the high gods took in hand
  Fire, and the falling of tears,
And a measure of sliding sand
  From under the feet of the years;
And froth and drift of the sea;
  And dust of the labouring earth;
And bodies of things to be
  In the houses of death and of birth;
And wrought with weeping and laughter,
  And fashion'd with loathing and love,
With life before and after
  And death beneath and above,
For a day and a night and a morrow,
  That his strength might endure for a span
With travail and heavy sorrow,
  The holy spirit of man.

From the winds of the north and the south
  They gather'd as unto strife;
They breathed upon his mouth,
  They filled his body with life;
Eyesight and speech they wrought
  For the veils of the soul therein,
A time for labour and thought,
  A time to serve and to sin;
They gave him light in his ways,
  And love, and a space for delight,
And beauty and length of days,
  And night, and sleep in the night.
His speech is a burning fire;
  With his lips he travaileth;
In his heart is a blind desire,
  In his eyes foreknowledge of death;
He weaves, and is clothed with derision;
  Sows, and he shall not reap;
His life is a watch or a vision
  Between a sleep and a sleep.

CHORUS

When the hounds of spring are on winter's traces,
 The mother of months in meadow or plain
Fills the shadows and windy places
 With lisp of leaves and ripple of rain;
And the brown bright nightingale amorous
Is half assuaged for Itylus,
For the Thracian ships and the foreign faces,
 The tongueless vigil, and all the pain.

Come with bows bent and with emptying of quivers,
 Maiden most perfect, lady of light,
With a noise of winds and many rivers,
 With a clamour of waters, and with might;
Bind on thy sandals, O thou most fleet,
Over the splendour and speed of thy feet;
For the faint east quickens, the wan west shivers,
 Round the feet of the day and the feet of the night.

Where shall we find her, how shall we sing to her,
 Fold our hands round her knees, and cling?
O that man's heart were as fire and could spring to her,
 Fire, or the strength of the streams that spring!
For the stars and the winds are unto her
As raiment, as songs of the harp-player;
For the risen stars and the fallen cling to her,
 And the southwest-wind and the west-wind sing.

For winter's rains and ruins are over,
 And all the season of snows and sins;
The days dividing lover and lover,
 The light that loses, the night that wins;
And time remembered is grief forgotten,
And frosts are slain and flowers begotten,
And in green underwood and cover
 Blossom by blossom the spring begins.

The full streams feed on a flower of rushes,
　　Ripe grasses trammel a travelling foot,
The faint fresh flame of the young year flushes
　　From leaf to flower and flower to fruit;
And fruit and leaf are as gold and fire,
And the oat is heard above the lyre,
And the hoofèd heel of a satyr crushes
　　The chestnut-husk at the chestnut-root.

And Pan by noon and Bacchus by night,
　　Fleeter of foot than the fleet-foot kid,
Follows with dancing and fills with delight
　　The Mænad and the Bassarid;
And soft as lips that laugh and hide
The laughing leaves of the trees divide,
And screen from seeing and leave in sight
　　The god pursuing, the maiden hid.

The ivy falls with the Bacchanal's hair
　　Over her eyebrows hiding her eyes;
The wild vine slipping down leaves bare
　　Her bright breast shortening into sighs;
The wild vine slips with the weight of its leaves,
But the berried ivy catches and cleaves
To the limbs that glitter, the feet that scare
　　The wolf that follows, the fawn that flies.

From *Atalanta in Calydon*

A LEAVE-TAKING

Let us go hence, my songs; she will not hear.
Let us go hence together without fear;
Keep silence now, for singing-time is over,
And over all things and all things dear.
She loves not you nor me as all we love her.
Yea, though we sang as angels in her ear,
　　　　She would not hear.

Let us rise up and part; she will not know.
Let us go seaward as the great winds go,
Full of blown sand and foam; what help is here?
There is no help, for all these things are so,
And all the world is bitter as a tear.
And how these things are, though ye strove to show,
      She would not know.

Let us go home and hence; she will not weep,
We gave love many dreams and days to keep,
Flowers without scent, and fruits that would not grow,
Saying, 'If thou wilt, thrust in thy sickle and reap.'
All is reaped now; no grass is left to mow;
And we that sowed, though all we fell on sleep,
      She would not weep.

Let us go hence and rest; she will not love.
She shall not hear us if we sing hereof,
Nor see love's ways, how sore they are and steep.
Come hence, let be, lie still; it is enough.
Love is a barren sea, bitter and deep;
And though she saw all heaven in flower above,
      She would not love.

Let us give up, go down; she will not care.
Though all the stars made gold of all the air,
And the sea moving saw before it move
One moon-flower making all the foam-flowers fair;
Though all those waves went over us, and drove
Deep down the stifling lips and drowning hair,
      She would not care.

Let us go hence, go hence; she will not see.
Sing all once more together: surely she,
She too, remembering days and words that were,
Will turn a little toward us, sighing; but we,
We are hence, we are gone, as though we had not been there.
Nay, and though all men seeing had pity on me,
      She would not see.

EROTION

Sweet for a little even to fear, and sweet
O love, to lay down fear at loves's fair feet;
Shall not some fiery memory of his breath
Lie sweet on lips that touch the lips of death?
You leave me not; yet, if thou wilt, be free;
Love me no more, but love my love of thee,
Love where thou wilt, and live thy life; and I,
One thing I can, and one love cannot—die.
Pass from me; yet thine arms, thine eyes, thine hair,
Feed my desire and deaden my despair.
Yet once more ere time change us, ere my cheek
Whiten, ere hope be dumb or sorrow speak,
Yet once more ere thou hate me, one full kiss;
Keep other hours for others, save me this.
Yea, and I will not (if it please thee) weep,
Lest thou be sad; I will but sigh, and sleep.
Sweet, does death hurt? thou canst not do me wrong:
I shall not lack thee, as I loved thee, long.
Hast thou not given me above all that live
Joy, and a little sorrow shalt not give?
What even though fairer fingers of strange girls
Pass nestling through thy beautiful boy's curls
As mine did, or those curled lithe lips of thine
Meet theirs as these, all theirs come after mine;
And though I were not, though I be not, best,
I have loved and love thee more than all the rest.
O love, O lover, loose or hold me fast,
I had thee first, whoever had thee last;
Fairer or not, what need I know, what care?
To thy fair bud my blossom once seemed fair.
Why am I fair at all before thee, why
At all desired? seeing thou art fair, not I.
I shall be glad of thee, O fairest head,
Alive, alone, without thee, with thee, dead:
I shall remember while the light lives yet,
And in the night-time I shall not forget.

Thou (as thou wilt) thou leave me ere life leave,
I will not, for thy love I will not grieve;
Not as they use who love not more than I,
Who love not as I love thee though I die;
And though thy lips, once mine, be oftener prest
To many another brow and balmier breast,
And sweeter arms, or sweeter to thy mind,
Lull thee or lure, more fond thou wilt not find.

STAGE LOVE

When the game began between them for a jest,
He played king and she played queen to match the best;
Laughter soft as tears, and tears that turned to laughter,
These were things she sought for years and sorrowed after.

Pleasure with dry lips, and pain that walks by night;
All the sting and all the stain of long delight;
These were things she knew not of, that knew not of her,
When she played at half a love with half a lover.

Time was chorus, gave them cues to laugh or cry;
They would kill, befool, amuse him, let him die;
Set him webs to weave to-day and break to-morrow,
Till he died for good in play, and rose in sorrow.

What the years mean; how time dies and is not slain;
How love grows and laughs and cries and wanes again;
These were things she came to know, and take their measure,
When the play was played out so for one man's pleasure.

james thomson

AS I CAME THROUGH THE DESERT

As I came through the desert thus it was,
As I came through the desert: All was black,
In heaven no single star, on earth no track;
A brooding hush without a stir or note,
The air so thick it clotted in my throat;
And thus for hours; then some enormous things
Swooped past with savage cries and clanking wings:
       But I strode on austere;
       No hope could have no fear.

As I came through the desert thus it was,
As I came through the desert: Eyes of fire
Glared at me throbbing with a starved desire;
The hoarse and heavy and carnivorous breath
Was hot upon me from deep jaws of death;
Sharp claws, swift talons, fleshless fingers cold
Plucked at me from the bushes, tried to hold:
       But I strode on austere;
       No hope could have no fear.

As I came through the desert thus it was,
As I came through the desert: Lo you, there,
That hillock burning with a brazen glare;
Those myriad dusky flames with points a-glow
Which writhed and hissed and darted to and fro;
A Sabbath of the Serpents, heaped pell-mell
For Devil's roll-call and some *fête* of Hell:
       Yet I strode on austere;
       No hope could have no fear.

As I came through the desert thus it was,
As I came through the desert: Meteors ran
And crossed their javelins on the black sky-span;

The zenith opened to a gulf of flame,
The dreadful thunderbolts jarred earth's fixed frame;
The ground all heaved in waves of fire that surged
And weltered round me sole there unsubmerged:
>Yet I strode on austere;
>No hope could have no fear.

As I came through the desert thus it was,
As I came through the desert: Air once more,
And I was close upon a wild sea-shore;
Enormous cliffs arose on either hand,
The deep tide thundered up a league-broad strand;
White foambelts seethed there, wan spray swept and flew;
The sky broke, moon and stars and clouds and blue:
>And I strode on austere;
>No hope could have no fear.

As I came through the desert thus it was,
As I came through the desert: On the left
The sun arose and crowned a broad crag-cleft;
There stopped and burned out black, except a rim,
A bleeding eyeless socket, red and dim;
Whereon the moon fell suddenly south-west,
And stood above the right-hand cliffs at rest:
>Still I strode on austere;
>No hope could have no fear.

As I came through the desert thus it was,
As I came through the desert: From the right
A shape came slowly with a ruddy light;
A woman with a red lamp in her hand,
Bareheaded and barefooted on that strand;
O desolation moving with such grace!
O anguish with such beauty in thy face!
>I fell as on my bier,
>Hope travailed with such fear.

As I came through the desert thus it was,
As I came through the desert: I was twain,

Two selves distinct that cannot join again;
One stood apart and knew but could not stir,
And watched the other stark in swoon and her;
And she came on, and never turned aside,
Between such sun and moon and roaring tide:
      And as she came more near
      My soul grew mad with fear.

As I came through the desert thus it was,
As I came through the desert: Hell is mild
And piteous matched with that accursèd wild;
A large black sign was on her breast that bowed,
A broad black band ran down her snow-white shroud;
That lamp she held was her own burning heart,
Whose blood-drops trickled step by step apart:
      The mystery was clear;
      Mad rage had swallowed fear.

As I came through the desert thus it was,
As I came through the desert: By the sea
She knelt and bent above that senseless me;
Those lamp-drops fell upon my white brow there,
She tried to cleanse them with her tears and hair;
She murmured words of pity, love, and woe,
She heeded not the level rushing flow:
      And mad with rage and fear,
      I stood stonebound so near.

As I came through the desert thus it was,
As I came through the desert: When the tide
Swept up to her there kneeling by my side,
She clasped that corpse-like me, and they were borne
Away, and this vile me was left forlorn;
I know the whole sea cannot quench that heart,
Or cleanse that brow, or wash those two apart:
      They love; their doom is drear,
      Yet they nor hope nor fear;
      But I, what do I here?

From *The City of Dreadful Night*

coventry patmore

TO THE BODY

Creation's and Creator's crowning good;
Wall of infinitude;
Foundation of the sky,
In Heaven forecast
And long'd for from eternity,
Though laid the last;
Reverberating dome,
Of music cunningly built home
Against the void and indolent disgrace
Of unresponsive space;
Little, sequester'd pleasure-house
For God and for His Spouse;
Elaborately, yea, past conceiving, fair,
Since, from the graced decorum of the hair,
Ev'n to the tingling, sweet
Soles of the simple, earth-confiding feet,
And from the inmost heart
Outwards unto the thin
Silk curtains of the skin,
Every least part astonish'd hears
And sweet replies to some like region of the spheres;
Form'd for a dignity prophets but darkly name,
Lest shameless men cry "Shame!"
So rich with wealth conceal'd
That Heaven and Hell fight chiefly for this field;
Clinging to everything that pleases thee
With indefectible fidelity;
Alas, so true
To all thy friendships that no grace
Thee from thy sin can wholly disembrace;
Which thus 'bides with thee as the Jebusite,
That, maugre all God's promises could do,
The chosen People never conquer'd quite,

Who therefore lived with them,
And that by formal truce and as of right,
In metropolitan Jerusalem.
For which false fealty
Thou needs must, for a season, lie
In the grave's arms, foul and unshriven,
Albeit, in Heaven,
Thy crimson-throbbing Glow
Into its old abode aye pants to go,
And does with envy see
Enoch, Elijah, and the Lady, she
Who left the lilies in her body's lieu.
O, if the pleasures I have known in thee
But my poor faith's poor first-fruits be,
What quintessential, keen, ethereal bliss
Then shall be his
Who has thy birth-time's consecrating dew
For death's sweet chrism retain'd,
Quick, tender, virginal, and unprofaned!

george meredith

LUCIFER IN STARLIGHT

On a starred night Prince Lucifer uprose.
Tired of his dark dominion swung the fiend
Above the rolling ball in cloud part screened,
Where sinners hugged their specter of repose.
Poor prey to his hot fit of pride were those.
And now upon his western wing he leaned,
Now his huge bulk o'er Afric's sands careened,
Now the black planet shadowed Arctic snows.
Soaring through wider zones that pricked his scars
With memory of the old revolt from Awe,
He reached a middle height, and at the stars,
Which are the brain of heaven, he looked, and sank.
Around the ancient track marched, rank on rank,
The army of unalterable law.

THUS PITEOUSLY LOVE CLOSED

Thus piteously Love closed what he begat:
The union of this ever-diverse pair!
These two were rapid falcons in a snare,
Condemned to do the flitting of the bat.
Lovers beneath the singing sky of May,
They wandered once; clear as the dew on flowers:
But they fed not on the advancing hours:
Their hearts held cravings for the buried day.
Then each applied to each that fatal knife,
Deep questioning, which probes to endless dole.

Ah, what a dusty answer gets the soul
When hot for certainties in this our life!—
In tragic hints here see what evermore
Moves dark as yonder midnight ocean's force,
Thundering like ramping hosts of warrior horse,
To throw that faint thin line upon the shore!

sidney lanier

BALLAD OF TREES AND THE MASTER

Into the woods my Master went,
Clean forspent, forspent.
Into the woods my Master came,
Forspent with love and shame.
But the olives they were not blind to Him,
The little gray leaves were kind to Him:
The thorn-tree had a mind to Him
When into the woods He came.

Out of the woods my Master went,
And he was well content.

Out of the woods my Master came,
Content with death and shame.
When Death and Shame would woo Him last,
From under the trees they drew Him last:
'Twas on a tree they slew Him—last
When out of the woods He came.

william ernest henley

INVICTUS

Out of the night that covers me,
    Black as the Pit from pole to pole,
I thank whatever gods may be
    For my unconquerable soul.

In the fell clutch of circumstance
    I have not winced nor cried aloud.
Under the bludgeonings of chance
    My head is bloody, but unbowed.

Beyond this place of wrath and tears
    Looms but the horror of the shade,
And yet the menace of the years
    Finds, and shall find me, unafraid.

It matters not how strait the gate,
    How charged with punishments the scroll,
I am the master of my fate:
    I am the captain of my soul.

francis thompson

THE HOUND OF HEAVEN

I fled Him, down the nights and down the days;
   I fled Him, down the arches of the years;
I fled Him, down the labyrinthine ways
   Of my own mind; and in the mist of tears
I hid from Him, and under running laughter.
         Up vistaed hopes I sped;
         And shot, precipitated,
Adown Titanic glooms of chasmèd fears,
  From those strong Feet that followed, followed after.
       But with unhurrying chase,
       And unperturbèd pace,
   Deliberate speed, majestic instancy,
     They beat—and a Voice beat
     More instant than the Feet—
  "All things betray thee, who betrayest Me."
    I pleaded, outlaw-wise,
By many a hearted casement, curtained red,
  Trellised with intertwining charities;
(For, though I knew His love Who followèd,
     Yet was I sore adread
Lest, having Him, I must have naught beside);
But, if one little casement parted wide,
  The gust of His approach would clash it to.
  Fear wist not to evade, as Love wist to pursue.
Across the margent of the world I fled,
  And troubled the gold gateways of the stars,
  Smiting for shelter on their clangèd bars;
    Fretted to dulcet jars
And silvern chatter the pale ports o' the moon.
I said to Dawn: Be sudden—to Eve: Be soon;
  With thy young skiey blossoms heap me over
    From this tremendous Lover—
Float thy vague veil about me, lest He see!
  I tempted all His servitors, but to find

My own betrayal in their constancy,
In faith to Him their fickleness to me,
   Their traitorous trueness, and their loyal deceit.
To all swift things for swiftness did I sue;
   Clung to the whistling mane of every wind.
       But whether they swept, smoothly fleet,
      The long savannahs of the blue;
         Or whether, Thunder-driven,
         They clanged his chariot 'thwart a heaven
Plashy with flying lightnings round the spurn o' their feet:—
   Fear wist not to evade as Love wist to pursue.
        Still with unhurrying chase,
       And unperturbèd pace,
     Deliberate speed, majestic instancy,
        Came on the following Feet,
        And a Voice above their beat—
   "Naught shelters thee, who wilt not shelter Me."

I sought no more that after which I strayed
        In face of man or maid;
But still within the little children's eyes
       Seems something, something that replies,
They at least are for me, surely for me!
I turned me to them very wistfully;
But just as their young eyes grew sudden fair
       With dawning answers there,
Their angel plucked them from me by the hair.
"Come then, ye other children, Nature's—share
With me" (said I) "your delicate fellowship;
      Let me greet you lip to lip,
      Let me twine with your caresses, Wantoning
      With our Lady-Mother's vagrant tresses,
       Banqueting
      With her in her wind-walled palace,
      Underneath her azured daïs,
      Quaffing, as your taintless way is,
       From a chalice
Lucent-weeping out of the dayspring." So it was done:

I in their delicate fellowship was one—
Drew the bolt of Nature's secrecies.
      I knew all the swift importings
      On the willful face of skies;
      I knew how the clouds arise
      Spumèd of the wild sea-snortings;
        All that's born or dies
      Rose and drooped with; made them shapers
Of mine own moods, or wailful or divine;
      With them joyed and was bereaven.
      I was heavy with the even,
      When she lit her glimmering tapers
      Round the day's dead sanctities.
      I laughed in the morning's eyes.
I triumphed and I saddened with all weather,
      Heaven and I wept together,
And its sweet tears were salt with mortal mine.

Against the red throb of its sunset-heart
      I laid my own to beat,
      And share commingling heat;
But not by that, by that, was eased my human smart.
In vain my tears were wet on Heaven's grey cheek.
For ah! we know not what each other says,
      These things and I; in sound *I* speak—
Their sound is but their stir, they speak by silences.
Nature, poor stepdame, cannot slake my drouth;
      Let her, if she would owe me,
Drop yon blue bosom-veil of sky, and show me
      The breasts o' her tenderness:
Never did any milk of hers once bless
      My thirsting mouth.
      Nigh and nigh draws the chase,
      With unperturbèd pace,
    Deliberate speed, majestic instancy;
      And past those noisèd Feet
      A Voice comes yet more fleet—
    "Lo! naught contents thee, who content'st not Me."

Naked I wait Thy love's uplifted stroke!
My harness piece by piece Thou hast hewn from me,
      And smitten me to my knee;
    I am defenceless utterly.
    I slept, methinks, and woke,
And, slowly gazing, find me stripped in sleep.
In the rash lustihead of my young powers,
    I shook the pillaring hours
And pulled my life upon me; grimed with smears,
I stand amid the dust o' the mounded years—
My mangled youth lies dead beneath the heap,
My days have crackled and gone up in smoke,
Have puffed and burst as sun-starts on a stream.

      Yea, faileth now even dream
The dreamer, and the lute the lutanist;
Even the linked fantasies, in whose blossomy twist
I swung the earth a trinket at my wrist,
Are yielding; cords of all too weak account
For earth with heavy griefs so overplussed.
      Ah! is Thy love indeed
A weed, albeit an amaranthine weed,
Suffering no flowers except its own to mount?
      Ah! must—
      Designer infinite!—
Ah, must Thou char the wood ere Thou canst limn with it?
My freshness spent its wavering shower i' the dust;
And now my heart is as a broken fount,
Wherein tear-drippings stagnate, spilt down ever
      From the dank thoughts that shiver
Upon the sightful branches of my mind.
      Such is; what is to be?
The pulp so bitter, how shall taste the rind?
I dimly guess what Time in mists confounds;
Yet ever and anon a trumpet sounds
From the hid battlements of Eternity;
Those shaken mists a space unsettle, then
Round the half-glimpsèd turrets slowly wash again.

But not ere him who summoneth
I first have seen, enwound
With glooming robes purpureal, cypress-crowned;
His name I know, and what his trumpet saith.
Whether man's heart or life it be which yields
Thee harvest, must Thy harvest-fields
Be dunged with rotten death?

Now of that long pursuit
Comes at hand the bruit;
That Voice is round me like a bursting sea:
"And is thy earth so marred,
Shattered in shard on shard?
Lo, all things fly thee, for thou fliest Me!
Strange, piteous, futile thing!
Wherefore should any set thee love apart?
Seeing none but I made much of naught" (He said),
"And human love needs human meriting:
How hast thou merited—
Of all man's clotted clay the dingiest clot?
Alack, thou knowest not
How little worthy of any love thou art!
Whom wilt thou find to love ignoble thee
Save Me, save only Me?
All which I took from thee I did but take,
Not for thy harms,
But just that thou might'st seek it in My arms.
All which thy child's mistake
Fancies as lost, I have stored for thee at home:
Rise, clasp My hand, and come!"

Halts by me that footfall:
Is my gloom, after all,
Shade of His hand, outstretched caressingly?
"Ah, fondest, blindest, weakest,
I am He Whom thou seekest!
Thou dravest love from thee, who dravest Me."

thomas hardy

THE DARKLING THRUSH

I leant upon a coppice gate
    When Frost was spectre-gray,
And Winter's dregs made desolate
    The weakening eye of day.
The tangled bine-stems scored the sky
    Like strings of broken lyres,
And all mankind that haunted nigh
    Had sought their household fires.

The land's sharp features seemed to be
    The Century's corpse outleant,
His crypt the cloudy canopy,
    The wind his death-lament.
The ancient pulse of germ and birth
    Was shrunken hard and dry,
And every spirit upon earth
    Seemed fervourless as I.

At once a voice arose among
    The bleak twigs overhead
In a full-hearted evensong
    Of joy illimited;
An aged thrush, frail, gaunt, and small,
    In blast-beruffled plume,
Had chosen thus to fling his soul
    Upon the growing gloom.

So little cause for carolings
    Of such ecstatic sound
Was written on terrestrial things
    Afar or nigh around,

That I could think there trembled through
   His happy good-night air
Some blessed Hope, whereof he knew
   And I was unaware.
December 1900.

TO AN UNBORN PAUPER CHILD

Breathe not, hid Heart: cease silently,
And though thy birth-hour beckons thee,
   Sleep the long sleep:
   The Doomsters heap
Travails and teens around us here,
And Time-wraiths turn our songsingings to fear.

Hark, how the people surge and sigh,
And laughters fail, and greetings die:
   Hopes dwindle; yea,
   Faiths waste away,
Affections and enthusiasms numb;
Thou canst not mend these things if thou dost come.

Had I the ear of wombèd souls
Ere their terrestrial chart unrolls,
   And thou wert free
   To cease, or be,
Then would I tell thee all I know,
And put it to thee: Wilt thou take Life so?

Vain vow! No hint of mine may hence
To theeward fly: to thy locked sense
   Explain none can
   Life's pending plan:
Thou wilt thy ignorant entry make
Though skies spout fire and blood and nations quake.

Fain would I, dear, find some shut plot
Of earth's wide wold for thee, where not

One tear, one qualm,
Should break the calm.
But I am weak as thou and bare;
No man can change the common lot to rare.

Must come and bide. And such are we—
Unreasoning, sanguine, visionary—
That I can hope
Health, love, friends, scope
In full for thee; can dream thou wilt find
Joys seldom yet attained by humankind!

THE LAST CHRYSANTHEMUM

Why should this flower delay so long
To show its tremulous plumes?
Now is the time of plaintive robin-song,
When flowers are in their tombs.

Through the slow summer, when the sun
Called to each frond and whorl
That all he could for flowers was being done,
Why did it not uncurl?

It must have felt that fervid call
Although it took no heed,
Waking but now, when leaves like corpses fall,
And saps all retrocede.

Too late its beauty, lonely thing,
The season's shine is spent,
Nothing remains for it but shivering
In tempests turbulent.

Had it a reason for delay,
Dreaming in witlessness
That for a bloom so delicately gay
Winter would stay its stress?

—I talk as if the thing were born
　　With sense to work its mind;
Yet it is but one mask of many worn
　　By the Great Face behind.

THE RUINED MAID

'O 'melia, my dear, this does everything crown!
Who could have supposed I should meet you in Town?
And whence such fair garments, such prosperi-ty?'—
'O didn't you know I'd been ruined?' said she.

—'You left us in tatters, without shoes or socks,
Tired of digging potatoes, and spudding up docks;
And now you've gay bracelets and bright feathers three!'—
'Yes: that's how we dress when we're ruined,' said she.

—'At home in the barton you said "thee" and "thou,"
And "thik oon," and "theäs oon," and "t'other"; but now
Your talking quite fits 'ee for high compa-ny!'—
'Some polish is gained with one's ruin,' said she.

—'Your hands were like paws then, your face blue and bleak
But now I'm bewitched by your delicate cheek,
And your little gloves fit as on any la-dy!'—
'We never do work when we're ruined,' said she.

—'You used to call home-life a hag-ridden dream.
And you'd sigh, and you'd sock; but at present you seem
To know not of megrims or melancho-ly!'—
'True. One's pretty lively when ruined,' said she.

—'I wish I had feathers, a fine sweeping gown,
And a delicate face, and could strut about Town!'—
'My dear—a raw country girl, such as you be,
Cannot quite expect that. You ain't ruined,' said she.

IN TENEBRIS

I

"Percussus sum sicut foenum, et aruit cor meum."—Ps. ci.

Wintertime nighs;
But my bereavement-pain
It cannot bring again:
    Twice no one dies.

Leaves freeze to dun;
But friends can not turn cold
This season as of old
    For him with none.

Flower-petals flee;
But, since it once hath been,
No more that severing scene
    Can harrow me.

Tempests may scath;
But love can not make smart
Again this year his heart
    Who no heart hath.

Birds faint in dread:
I shall not lose old strength
In the lone frost's black length:
    Strength long since fled!

Black is night's cope;
But death will not appal
One who, past doubtings all,
    Waits in unhope.

II

"Considerabam ad dexteram, et videbam; et non erat qui cognosceret me. . . . Non est qui requirat animam meam."—Ps. cxli.

When the clouds' swoln bosoms echo back the shouts of the
    many and strong
That things are all as they best may be, save a few to be right
    ere long,
And my eyes have not the vision in them to discern what to
    these is so clear,
The blot seems straightway in me alone; one better he were
    not here.

The stout upstanders say, All's well with us: ruers have nought
    to rue!
And what the potent say so oft, can it fail to be somewhat true?

Breezily go they, breezily come; their dust smokes around their
    career,
Till I think I am one born out of due time, who has no calling
    here.

Their dawns bring lusty joys, it seems; their evenings all that
    is sweet;
Our times are blessed times, they cry: Life shapes it as is most
    meet,
And nothing is much the matter; there are many smiles to a
    tear;
Then what is the matter is I, I say. Why should such an one
    be here? . . .

Let him in whose ears the low-voiced Best is killed by the
    clash of the First,
Who holds that if way to the Better there be, it exacts a full
    look at the Worst,
Who feels that delight is a delicate growth cramped by crook-
    edness, custom, and fear,
Get him up and be gone as one shaped awry; he disturbs the
    order here.

III

*"Heu mihi, quia incolatus meus prolongatus est! Habitavi cum
habitantibus Cedar; multum incola fuit anima mea."—Ps. cxix.*

There have been times when I well might have passed and the
    ending have come—
Points in my path when the dark might have stolen on me, art-
    less, unrueing—
Ere I had learnt that the world was a welter of futile doing:
Such had been times when I well might have passed, and the
    ending have come!

Say, on the noon when the half-sunny hours told that April
    was nigh,

And I upgathered and cast forth the snow from the crocus-
    border,
Fashioned and furbished the soil into a summer-seeming order,
Glowing in gladsome faith that I quickened the year thereby.

Or on that loneliest of eves when afar and benighted we stood,
She who upheld me and I, in the midmost of Egdon together,
Confident I in her watching and ward through the blackening
    heather,
Deeming her matchless in might and with measureless scope
    endued.

Or on that winter-wild night when, reclined by the chimney-
    nook quoin,
Slowly a drowse overgat me, the smallest and feeblest of folk
    there,
Weak from my baptism of pain; when at times and anon I
    awoke there—
Heard of a world wheeling on, with no listing or longing to
    join.

Even then! while unweeting that vision could vex or that
    knowledge could numb,
That sweets to the mouth in the belly are bitter, and tart, and
    untoward,
Then, on some dim-coloured scene should my briefly raised
    curtain have lowered,
Then might the Voice that is law have said "Cease!" and the
    ending have come.

THE SOULS OF THE SLAIN

The thick lids of Night closed upon me
        Alone at the Bill
        Of the Isle by the Race [1]—
Many-caverned, bald, wrinkled of face—
And with darkness and silence the spirit was on me
        To brood and be still.

[1] The "Race" is the turbulent sea-area off the Bill of Portland, where
contrary tides meet.

No wind fanned the flats of the ocean,
    Or promontory sides,
    Or the ooze by the strand,
Or the bent-bearded slope of the land,
Whose base took its rest amid everlong motion
    Of criss-crossing tides.

Soon from out of the Southward seemed nearing
    A whirr, as of wings
    Waved by mighty-vanned flies,
Or by night-moths of measureless size,
And in softness and smoothness well-nigh beyond hearing
    Of corporal things.

And they bore to the bluff, and alighted—
    A dim-discerned train
    Of sprites without mould,
Frameless souls none might touch or might hold—
On the ledge by the turreted lantern, far-sighted
    By men of the main.

And I heard them say 'Home!' and I knew them
    For souls of the felled
    On the earth's nether bord
Under Capricorn, whither they'd warred,
And I neared in my awe, and gave heedfulness to them
    With breathings inheld.

Then, it seemed, there approached from the northward
    A senior soul-flame
    Of the like filmy hue:
And he met them and spake: 'Is it you,
O my men?' Said they, 'Aye! We bear homeward and
        hearthward
    To feast on our fame!"

'I've flown there before you,' he said then:
     'Your households are well;
      But—your kin linger less
  On your glory and war-mightiness
Than on dearer things.'—'Dearer?' cried these from the
      dead then,
     'Of what do they tell?'

'Some mothers muse sadly, and murmur
     Your doings as boys—
     Recall the quaint ways
  Of your babyhood's innocent days.
Some pray that, ere dying, your faith had grown firmer,
     And higher your joys.

'A father broods: 'Would I had set him
     To some humble trade,
     And so slacked his high fire,
  And his passionate martial desire;
And told him no stories to woo him and whet him
     To this dire crusade!'

'And, General, how hold out our sweethearts,
     Sworn loyal as doves?'
    —'Many mourn; many think
  It is not unattractive to prink
Them in sables for heroes. Some fickle and fleet hearts
     Have found them new loves.'

'And our wives?' quoth another resignedly,
     'Dwell they on our deeds?'
    —'Deeds of home; that live yet
  Fresh as new—deeds of fondness or fret;
Ancient words that were kindly expressed or unkindly,
     These, these have their heeds.'

—'Alas! then it seems that our glory
  Weighs less in their thought
  Than our old homely acts,
And the long-ago commonplace facts
Of our lives—held by us as scarce part of our story,
  And rated as nought!'

Then bitterly some: 'Was it wise now
  To raise the tomb-door
  For such knowledge? Away!'
But the rest: 'Fame we prized till to-day;
Yet that hearts keep us green for old kindness we prize now
  A thousand times more!'

Thus speaking, the trooped apparitions
  Began to disband
  And resolve them in two:
Those whose record was lovely and true
Bore to northward for home: those of bitter traditions
  Again left the land,

And, towering to seaward in legions,
  They paused at a spot
  Overbending the Race—
That engulphing, ghast, sinister place—
Whither headlong they plunged, to the fathomless regions
  Of myriads forgot.

And the spirits of those who were homing
  Passed on, rushingly,
  Like the Pentecost Wind;
And the whirr of their wayfaring thinned
And surceased on the sky, and but left in the gloaming
  Sea-mutterings and me.

December 1899.

THE OXEN

Christmas Eve, and twelve of the clock.
  'Now they are all on their knees,'
An elder said as we sat in a flock
  By the embers in hearthside ease.

We pictured the meek mild creatures where
  They dwelt in their strawy pen,
Nor did it occur to one of us there
  To doubt they were kneeling then.

So fair a fancy few would weave
  In these years! Yet, I feel,
If someone said on Christmas Eve,
  'Come; see the oxen kneel,

'In the lonely barton by yonder coomb
  Our childhood used to know,'
I should go with him in the gloom,
  Hoping it might be so.

THE MAN HE KILLED

'Had he and I but met
  By some old ancient inn,
We should have sat us down to wet
  Right many a nipperkin!

'But ranged as infantry,
  And staring face to face,
I shot at him as he at me,
  And killed him in his place.

'I shot him dead because—
  Because he was my foe,
Just so: my foe of course he was;
  That's clear enough; although

'He thought he'd 'list, perhaps,
Off-hand like—just as I—
Was out of work—had sold his traps—
No other reason why.

'Yes; quaint and curious war is!
You shoot a fellow down
You'd treat if met where any bar is,
Or help to half-a-crown.'

UNDER THE WATERFALL

'Whenever I plunge my arm, like this,
In a basin of water, I never miss
The sweet sharp sense of a fugitive day
Fetched back from its thickening shroud of gray.
          Hence the only prime
          And real love-rhyme
          That I know by heart,
          And that leaves no smart,
Is the purl of a little valley fall
About three spans wide and two spans tall
Over a table of solid rock,
And into a scoop of the self-same block;
The purl of a runlet that never ceases
In stir of kingdoms, in wars, in peaces;
With a hollow boiling voice it speaks
And has spoken since hills were turfless peaks.'

'And why gives this the only prime
Idea to you of a real love-rhyme?
And why does plunging your arm in a bowl
Full of spring water, bring throbs to your soul?'

'Well, under the fall, in a crease of the stone,
Though where precisely none ever has known,
Jammed darkly, nothing to show how prized,
And by now with its smoothness opalized,

Is a drinking-glass:
For, down that pass
My lover and I
Walked under a sky
Of blue with a leaf-wove awning of green,
In the burn of August, to paint the scene,
And we placed our basket of fruit and wine
By the runlet's rim, where we sat to dine;
And when we had drunk from the glass together,
Arched by the oak-copse from the weather,
I held the vessel to rinse in the fall,
Where it slipped, and sank, and was past recall,
Though we stooped and plumbed the little abyss
With long bared arms.   There the glass still is.
And, as said, if I thrust my arm below
Cold water in basin or bowl, a throe
From the past awakens a sense of that time,
And the glass we used, and the cascade's rhyme.
The basin seems the pool, and its edge
The hard smooth face of the brook-side ledge,
And the leafy pattern of china-ware
The hanging plants that were bathing there.
'By night, by day, when it shines or lours,
There lies intact that chalice of ours,
And its presence adds to the rhyme of love
Persistently sung by the fall above.
No lip has touched it since his and mine
In turns therefrom sipped lovers' wine.'

THE GOING

Why did you give no hint that night
That quickly, as if indifferent quite,
You would close your term here, up and be gone
        Where I could not follow
        With wing of swallow
To gain one glimpse of you ever anon!

Never to bid good-bye,
Or lip me the softest call,
Or utter a wish for a word, while I
Saw morning harden upon the wall,
Unmoved, unknowing
That your great going
Had place that moment, and altered all.

Why do you make me leave the house
And think for a breath it is you I see
At the end of the alley of bending boughs
Where so often at dusk you used to be;
Till in darkening dankness
The yawning blankness
Of the perspective sickens me!

You were she who abode
By those red-veined rocks far West,
You were the swan-necked one who rode
Along the beetling Beeny Crest,
And, reining nigh me,
Would muse and eye me,
While Life unrolled us its very best.

Why, then, latterly did we not speak,
Did we not think of those days long dead,
And ere your vanishing strive to seek
That time's renewal? We might have said,
'In this bright spring weather
We'll visit together
Those places that once we visited.'

Well, Well! All's past amend,
Unchangeable. It must go.
I seem but a dead man held on end
To sink down soon. . . . O you could not know
That such swift fleeing
No soul foreseeing—
Not even I—would undo me so!

IN TIME OF 'THE BREAKING OF NATIONS'

Only a man harrowing clods
   In a slow silent walk
With an old horse that stumbles and nods
   Half asleep as they stalk.

Only thin smoke without flame
   From the heaps of couch-grass;
Yet this will go onward the same
   Though Dynasties pass.

Yonder a maid and her wight
   Come whispering by:
War's annals will fade into night
   Ere their story die.

AFTERWARDS

When the Present has latched its postern behind my tremulous
    stay,
   And the May month flaps its glad green leaves like wings,
Delicate-filmed as new-spun silk, will the neighbours say,
   'He was a man who used to notice such things'?

If it be in the dusk when, like an eyelid's soundless blink,
   The dewfall-hawk comes crossing the shades to alight
Upon the wind-warped upland thorn, a gazer may think,
   'To him this must have been a familiar sight.'

If I pass during some nocturnal blackness, mothy and warm,
   When the hedgehog travels furtively over the lawn,
One may say, 'He strove that such innocent creatures should
    come to no harm,
   But he could do little for them; and now he is gone.'

If, when hearing that I have been stilled at last, they stand at
    the door,
   Watching the full-starred heavens that winter sees,

Will this thought rise on those who will meet my face no more,
  'He was one who had an eye for such mysteries'?

And will any say when my bell of quittance is heard in the
    gloom,
  And a crossing breeze cuts a pause in its outrollings,
Till they rise again, as they were a new bell's boom,
  'He hears it not now, but used to notice such things'?

NO BUYERS: A STREET SCENE

A load of brushes and baskets and cradles and chairs
    Labours along the street in the rain:
With it a man, a woman, a pony with whiteybrown hairs.—
  The man foots in front of the horse with a shambling sway
    At a slower tread than a funeral train,
  While to a dirge-like tune he chants his wares,
  Swinging a Turk's-head brush (in a drum-major's way
    When the bandsmen march and play).

A yard from the back of the man is the whiteybrown pony's
    nose:
He mirrors his master in every item of pace and pose:
  He stops when the man stops, without being told,
  And seems to be eased by a pause; too plainly he's old,
    Indeed, not strength enough shows
    To steer the disjointed waggon straight,
  Which wriggles left and right in a rambling line,
  Deflected thus by its own warp and weight,
  And pushing the pony with it in each incline.

  The woman walks on the pavement verge,
    Parallel to the man:
She wears an apron white and wide in span,
And carries a like Turk's-head, but more in nursing-wise:
  Now and then she joins in his dirge,
  But as if her thoughts were on distant things.
  The rain clams her apron till it clings.—
So, step by step, they move with their merchandize,
    And nobody buys.

CHANNEL FIRING

That night your great guns, unawares,
Shook all our coffins as we lay,
And broke the chancel window-squares,
We thought it was the Judgment-day

And sat upright.   While drearisome
Arose the howl of wakened hounds:
The mouse let fall the altar-crumb,
The worms drew back into the mounds,

The glebe cow drooled.   Till God called, 'No;
It's gunnery practice out at sea
Just as before you went below;
The world is as it used to be:

'All nations striving strong to make
Red war yet redder.   Mad as hatters
They do no more for Christés sake
Than you who are helpless in such matters.

'That this is not the judgment-hour
For some of them's a blessed thing,
For if it were they'd have to scour
Hell's floor for so much threatening. . . .

'Ha, ha.   It will be warmer when
I blow the trumpet (if indeed
I ever do; for you are men,
And rest eternal sorely need).'

So down we lay again. 'I wonder,
Will the world ever saner be,'
Said one, 'than when He sent us under
In our indifferent century!'

And many a skeleton shook his head.
'Instead of preaching forty year,'

My neighbour Parson Thirdly said,
'I wish I had stuck to pipes and beer.'

Again the guns disturbed the hour,
Roaring their readiness to avenge,
As far inland as Stourton Tower,
And Camelot, and starlit Stonehenge.

THE CONVERGENCE OF THE TWAIN

(Lines on the loss of the "Titanic")

In a solitude of the sea
Deep from human vanity,
And the Pride of Life that planned her, stilly couches she.

Steel chambers, late the pyres
Of her salamandrine fires,
Cold currents thrid, and turn to rhythmic tidal lyres.

Over the mirrors meant
To glass the opulent
The sea-worm crawls—grotesque, slimed, dumb, indifferent.

Jewels in joy designed
To ravish the sensuous mind
Lie lightless, all their sparkles bleared and black and blind.

Dim moon-eyed fishes near
Gaze at the gilded gear
And query: 'What does this vaingloriousness down here?' . . .

Well: while was fashioning
This creature of cleaving wing,
The Immanent Will that stirs and urges everything

Prepared a sinister mate
For her—so gaily great—
A Shape of Ice, for the time far and dissociate.

And as the smart ship grew
In stature, grace, and hue,
In shadowy silent distance grew the Iceberg too.

Alien they seemed to be:
No mortal eye could see
The intimate welding of their later history.

Or sign that they were bent
By paths coincident
On being anon twin halves of one august event,

Till the Spinner of the Years
Said 'Now!'   And each one hears,
And consummation comes, and jars two hemispheres.

gerard manley hopkins

GOD'S GRANDEUR

The world is charged with the grandeur of God.
It will flame out, like shining from shook foil;
It gathers to a greatness, like the ooze of oil
Crushed. Why do men then now not reck his rod?
Generations have trod, have trod, have trod;
And all is seared with trade; bleared, smeared with toil;
And wears man's smudge and shares man's smell: the soil
Is bare now, nor can foot feel, being shod.
And for all this, nature is never spent;
There lives the dearest freshness deep down things;
And though the last lights off the black West went
Oh, morning, at the brown brink eastward, springs—
Because the Holy Ghost over the bent
World broods with warm breast and with ah! bright wings.

SPRING AND FALL: TO A YOUNG CHILD

Márgarét, are you gríeving
Over Goldengrove unleaving?
Leáves, líke the things of man, you
With your fresh thoughts care for, can you?
Ah! ás the heart grows older
It will come to such sights colder
By and by, nor spare a sigh
Though worlds of wanwood leafmeal lie;
And yet you wíll weep and know why.
Now no matter, child, the name:
Sórrow's spríngs áre the same.
Nor mouth had, no nor mind, expressed
What heart heard of, ghost guessed:
It ís the blight man was born for,
It is Margaret you mourn for.

THE CANDLE INDOORS

Some candle clear burns somewhere I come by.
I muse at how its being puts blissful back
With yellowy moisture mild night's blear-all black,
Or to-fro tender trambeams truckle at the eye.
By that window what task what fingers ply,
I plot wondering, a-wanting, just for lack
Of answer the eagerer a-wanting Jessy or Jack
There, God to aggrándize, God to glorify.—

Come you indoors, come home; your fading fire
Mend first and vital candle in close heart's vault:
You there are master, do your own desire;
What hinders? Are you beam-blind, yet to a fault
In a neighbour deft-handed? Are you that liar
And, cast by conscience out, spendsavour salt?

PIED BEAUTY

Glory be to God for dappled things—
   For skies of couple-colour as a brindled cow;
     For rose-moles all in stipple upon trout that swim;
Fresh-firecoal chestnut-falls; finches wings;
   Landscape plotted and pieced—fold, fallow, and plough;
     And áll trádes, their gear and tackle and trim.

All things, counter, original, spare, strange;
   Whatever is fickle, freckled (who knows how?)
     With swift, slow; sweet, sour; adazzle, dim;
He father's-forth whose beauty is past change:
              Praise him.

THAT NATURE IS A HERACLITEAN FIRE AND OF THE COMFORT
OF THE RESURRECTION

Cloud-puffball, torn tufts, tossed pillows flaunt forth, then
   chevy on an air-
built thoroughfare: heaven-roysterers, in gay-gangs they
   throng; they glitter in marches.
Down roughcast, down dazzling whitewash, wherever an elm
   arches,
Shivelights and shadowtackle in long lashes lace, lance, and
   pair.
Delightfully the bright wind boisterous ropes, wrestles, beats
   earth bare
Of yestertempest's creases; in pool and rut peel parches
Squandering ooze to squeezed dough, crust, dust; stanches,
   starches
Squadroned masks and manmarks treadmire toil there
Footfretted in it.   Million-fuelèd, nature's bonfire burns on.
But quench her bonniest, dearest to her, her clearest-selvèd
   spark
Man, how fast his firedint, his mark on mind, is gone!
Both are in an unfathomable, all is in an enormous dark

Drowned. O pity and indignation! Manshape, that shone
Sheer off, disseveral, a star, death blots black out; nor mark
                    Is any of him at all so stark
But vastness blurs and time beats level. Enough! the Resur-
    rection,
A heart's-clarion! Away grief's gasping, joyless days, dejection.
                    Across my foundering deck shone
A beacon, an eternal beam. Flesh fade, and mortal trash
Fall to the residuary worm; world's wildfire, leave but ash:
                    In a flash, at a trumpet crash,
I am all at once what Christ is, since he was what I am, and
This Jack, joke, poor potsherd, patch, matchwood, immortal
    diamond,
                    Is immortal diamond.

CARRION COMFORT

Not, I'll not, carrion comfort, despair, not feast on thee;
Not untwist—slack they may be—these last strands of man
In me ór, most weary, cry *I can no more.* I can;
Can something, hope, wish day come, not choose not to be.
But ah, but O thou terrible, why wouldst thou rude on me
Thy wring-world right foot rock? lay a lionlimb against me?
    scan
With darksome devouring eyes my bruisèd bones? and fan,
O in turns of tempest, me heaped there; me frantic to avoid
    thee and flee?
Why? That my chaff might fly; my grain lie, sheer and clear.
Nay in all that toil, that coil, since (seems) I kissed the rod,
Hand rather, my heart lo! lapped strength, stole joy, would
    laugh, chéer.
Cheer whom though? the hero whose heaven-handling flung
    me, fóot tród
Me? or me that fought him? O which one? is it each one? That
    night, that year
Of now done darkness I wretch lay wrestling with (my God!)
    my God.

I WAKE AND FEEL THE FELL OF DARK

I wake and feel the fell of dark, not day.
What hours, O what black hoürs we have spent
This night! what sights you, heart, saw; ways you went!
And more must, in yet longer light's delay.
With witness I speak this. But where I say
Hours I mean years, mean life. And my lament
Is cries countless, cries like dead letters sent
To dearest him that lives alas! away.

I am gall, I am heartburn. God's most deep decree
Bitter would have me taste: my taste was me;
Bones built in me, flesh filled, blood brimmed the curse.
Selfyeast of spirit a dull dough sours. I see
The lost are like this, and their scourge to be
As I am mine, their sweating selves; but worse.

NO WORST, THERE IS NONE

No worst, there is none. Pitched past pitch of grief,
More pangs will, schooled at forepangs, wilder wring.
Comforter, where, where is your comforting?
Mary, mother of us, where is your relief?
My cries heave, herds-long; huddle in a man, a chief
Woe, world-sorrow; on an age-old anvil wince and sing—
Then lull, then leave off. Fury had shrieked 'No ling-
ering! Let me be fell: force I must be brief.'

O the mind, mind has mountains; cliffs of fall
Frightful, sheer, no-man-fathomed. Hold them cheap
May who ne'er hung there. Nor does long our small
Durance deal with that steep or deep. Here! creep,
Wretch, under a comfort serves in a whirlwind: all
Life death does end and each day dies with sleep.

THE SEA AND THE SKYLARK

On ear and ear two noises too old to end
Trench — right, the tide that ramps against the shore;
With a flood or a fall, low lull-off or all roar,
Frequenting there while moon shall wear and wend.
Left hand, off land, I hear the lark ascend,
His rash-fresh re-winded new-skeinèd score
In crisps of curl off wild winch whirl, and pour
And pelt music, till none's to spill nor spend.

How these two shame this shallow and frail town!
How ring right out our sordid turbid time,
Being pure!   We, life's pride and cared-for crown,
Have lost that cheer and charm of earth's past prime:
Our make and making break, are breaking, down
To man's last dust, drain fast towards man's first slime.

THE STARLIGHT NIGHT

Look at the stars! look, look up at the skies!
O look at all the fire-folk sitting in the air!
The bright boroughs, the circle-citadels there!
Down in dim woods the diamond delves! the elves'-eyes!
The gray lawns cold where gold, where quickgold lies!
Wind-beat whitebeam! airy abeles set on a flare!
Flake-doves sent floating forth at a farmyard scare!
Ah, well! it is all a purchase, all is a prize.

Buy then! bid then!—What?—Prayer, patience, alms, vows.
Look, look: a May-mess, like on orchard boughs!
Look! March-bloom, like on mealed-with-yellow sallows!
These are indeed the barn; withindoors house
The shocks. This piece-bright paling shuts the spouse
Christ home, Christ and his mother and all his hallows.

HURRAHING IN HARVEST

Summer ends now; now, barbarous in beauty, the stooks arise
Around; up above, what wind-walks! what lovely behaviour
Of silk-sack clouds! has wilder, wilful-wavier
Meal-drift moulded ever and melted across skies?
I walk, I lift up, I lift up heart, eyes,
Down all that glory in the heavens to glean our Saviour;
And, éyes, heárt, what looks, what lips yet gave you a
Rapturous love's greeting of realer, of rounder replies?

And the azurous hung hills are his world-wielding shoulder
Majestic—as a stallion stalwart, very-violet-sweet!—
These things, these things were here and but the beholder
Wanting; which two when they once meet,
The heart rears wings bold and bolder
And hurls for him, O half hurls earth for him off under his feet.

THE WINDHOVER

To Christ our Lord

I caught this morning morning's minion, king-
dom of daylight's dauphin, dapple-dawn-drawn Falcon, in his
   riding
Of the rolling level underneath him steady air, and striding
High there, how he rung upon the rein of a wimpling wing
In his ecstasy! then off, off forth on swing,
As a skate's heel sweeps smooth on a bow-bend: the hurl and
   gliding
Rebuffed the big wind. My heart in hiding
Stirred for a bird,—the achieve of, the mastery of the thing!

Brute beauty and valour and act, oh, air, pride, plume, here
Buckle! AND the fire that breaks from thee then, a billion
Times told lovelier, more dangerous, O my chevalier!
No wonder of it: shéer plód makes plough down sillion
Shine, and blue-bleak embers, ah my dear,
Fall, gall themselves, and gash gold-vermilion.

THE CAGED SKYLARK

As a dare-gale skylark scanted in a dull cage
Man's mounting spirit in his bone-house, mean house, dwells—
That bird beyond the remembering his free fells;
This in drudgery, day-labouring-out life's age.

Though aloft on turf or perch or poor low stage,
Both sing sometímes the sweetest, sweetest spells,
Yet both droop deadly sómetimes in their cells
Or wring their barriers in bursts of fear or rage.

Not that the sweet-fowl, song-fowl, needs no rest—
Why, hear him, hear him babble and drop down to his nest,
But his own nest, wild nest, no prison.

Man's spirit will be flesh-bound when found at best,
But uncumbered: meadow-down is not distressed
For a rainbow footing it nor he for his bónes rísen.

FELIX RANDAL

Felix Randal the farrier, O he is dead then? my duty all
ended,
Who have watched his mould of man, big-boned and hardy-
handsome
Pining, pining, till time when reason rambled in it and some
Fatal four disorders, fleshed there, all contended?

Sickness broke him. Impatient he cursed at first, but mended
Being anointed and all; though a heavenlier heart began some
Months earlier, since I had our sweet reprieve and ransom
Tendered to him. Ah well, God rest him all road ever he
offended!

This seeing the sick endears them to us, us too it endears.
My tongue had taught thee comfort, touch had quenched
thy tears,
Thy tears that touched my heart, child, Felix, poor Felix Randal;

How far from then forethought of, all thy more boisterous
years,
When thou at the random grim forge, powerful amidst peers,
Didst fettle for the great grey drayhorse his bright and battering sandal!

INVERSNAID

This darksome burn, horseback brown,
His rollrock highroad roaring down,
In coop and in comb the fleece of his foam
Flutes and low to the lake falls home.

A windpuff-bonnet of fawn-froth
Turns and twindles over the broth
Of a pool so pitchblack, fell-frowning,
It rounds and rounds Despair to drowning.

Degged with dew, dappled with dew
Are the groins of the braes that the brook treads through,
Wiry heathpacks, flitches of fern,
And the beadbonny ash that sits over the burn.

What would the world be, once bereft
Of wet and of wildness? Let them be left,
O let them be left, wildness and wet;
Long live the weeds and the wilderness yet.

IN THE VALLEY OF THE ELWY

I remember a house where all were good
To me, God knows, deserving no such thing:
Comforting smell breathed at very entering,
Fetched fresh, as I suppose, off some sweet wood.
That cordial air made those kind people a hood
All over, as a bevy of eggs the mothering wing
Will, or mild nights the new morsels of spring:
Why, it seemed of course; seemed of right it should.
Lovely the woods, waters, meadows, combes, vales,
All the air things wear that build this world of Wales;
Only the inmate does not correspond:
God, lover of souls, swaying considerate scales,
Complete thy creature dear O where it fails,
Being mighty a master, being a father and fond.

THOU ART INDEED JUST, LORD

Justus quidem tu es, Domine, si disputem tecum: verumta-
nen justa loquar ad te: Quare via impiorum prosperatur? etc.

Thou art indeed just, Lord, if I contend
With thee; but, sir, so what I plead is just.
Why do sinners' ways prosper? and why must
Disappointment all I endeavour end?
Wert thou my enemy, O thou my friend,
How wouldst thou worse, I wonder, than thou dost
Defeat, thwart me? Oh, the sots and thralls of lust
Do in spare hours more thrive than I that spend,
Sir, life upon thy cause. See, banks and brakes
Now, leavèd how thick! lacèd they are again
With fretty chervil, look, and fresh wind shakes
Them; birds build—but not I build; no, but strain,
Time's eunuch, and not breed one work that wakes.
Mine, O thou lord of life, send my roots rain.

THE HABIT OF PERFECTION

Elected Silence, sing to me
And beat upon my whorlèd ear,
Pipe me to pastures still and be
The music that I care to hear.

Shape nothing, lips; be lovely-dumb:
It is the shut, the curfew sent
From there where all surrenders come
Which only makes you eloquent.

Be shellèd, eyes, with double dark
And find the uncreated light:
This ruck and reel which you remark
Coils, keeps, and teases simple sight.

Palate, the hutch of tasty lust,
Desire not to be rinsed with wine:

The can must be so sweet, the crust
So fresh that come in fasts divine!

Nostrils, your careless breath that spend
Upon the stir and keep of pride,
What relish shall the censers send
Along the sanctuary side!

O feel-of-primrose hands, O feet
That want the yield of plushy sward,
But you shall walk the golden street
And you unhouse and house the Lord.

And, Poverty, be thou the bride
And now the marriage feast begun,
And lily-coloured clothes provide
Your spouse not laboured-at nor spun.

THE LEADEN ECHO AND THE GOLDEN ECHO

(Maidens' Song from St. Winefred's Well)

THE LEADEN ECHO

How to kéep—is there any any, is there none such, nowhere
   known some, bow or brooch or braid or brace, láce, latch
   or catch or key to keep
Back beauty, keep it, beauty, beauty, beauty, . . . from vanish-
   ing away?
O is there no frowning of these wrinkles, rankèd wrinkles
   deep,
Dówn? no waving off of these most mournful messengers, still
   messengers, sad and stealing messengers of grey?
No there's none, there's none, O no there's none,
Nor can you long be, what you now are, called fair,
Do what you may do, what, do what you may,
And wisdom is early to despair:
Be beginning; since, no, nothing can be done to keep at bay
Age and age's evils, hoar hair,
Ruck and wrinkle, drooping, dying, death's worst, winding
   sheets, tombs and worms and tumbling to decay;

So be beginning, be beginning to despair.
O there's none; no no no there's none:
Be beginning to despair, to despair,
Despair, despair, despair, despair.

THE GOLDEN ECHO

 Spare!
There is one, yes I have one (Hush there!);
Only not within seeing of the sun,
Not within the singeing of the strong sun,
Tall sun's tingeing, or treacherous the tainting of the earth's
 air,
Somewhere elsewhere there is ah well where! one,
One. Yes I can tell such a key, I do know such a place,
Where whatever's prized and passes of us, everything that's
 fresh and fast flying of us, seems to us sweet of us and
 swiftly away with, done away with, undone,
Undone, done with, soon done with, and yet dearly and dan-
 gerously sweet
Of us, the wimpled-water-dimpled, not-by-morning-matchèd
 face,
The flower of beauty, fleece of beauty, too too apt to, ah! to
 fleet,
Never fleets móre, fastened with the tenderest truth
To its own best being and its loveliness of youth: it is an ever-
 lastingness of, O it is an all youth!
Come then, your ways and airs and looks, locks, maiden gear,
 gallantry and gaiety and grace,
Winning ways, airs innocent, maiden manners, sweet looks,
 loose locks, long locks, lovelocks, gaygear, going gallant,
 girlgrace—
Resign them, sign them, seal them, send them, motion them
 with breath,
And with sighs soaring, soaring síghs deliver
Them; beauty-in-the-ghost, deliver it, early now, long before
 death
Give beauty back, beauty, beauty, beauty, back to God,
 beauty's self and beauty's giver.

See; not a hair is, not an eyelash, not the least lash lost; every
    hair
Is, hair of the head, numbered.
Nay, what we had lighthanded left in surly the mere mould
Will have waked and have waxed and have walked with the
    wind whatwhile we slept,
This side, that side hurling a heavyheaded hundredfold
Whatwhile we, while we slumbered.
O then, weary then why should we tread? O why are we so
    haggard at the heart, so care-coiled, care-killed, so fagged,
    so fashed, so cogged, so cumbered,
When the thing we freely fórfeit is kept with fonder a care,
Fonder a care kept than we could have kept it, kept
Far with fonder a care (and we, we should have lost it) finer,
    fonder
A care kept.—Where kept? Do but tell us where kept, where.—
Yonder.—What high as that! We follow, now we follow.
    —Yonder, yes yonder, yonder,
Yonder.

robert bridges

A PASSER-BY

Whither, O splendid ship, thy white sails crowding,
    Leaning across the bosom of the urgent West
That fearest nor sea rising, nor sky clouding,
    Whither away, fair rover, and what thy quest?
    Ah! soon, when Winter has all our vales opprest,
When skies are cold and misty, and hail is hurling,
    Wilt thou glide on the blue Pacific, or rest
In a summer haven asleep, thy white sails furling.

I there before thee, in the country that well thou knowest,
    Already arrived am inhaling the odorous air:
I watch thee enter unerringly where thou goest,
    And anchor queen of the strange shipping there,

Thy sails for awnings spread, thy masts bare:
Nor is aught from the foaming reef to the snow-capped, grandest
   Peak, that is over the feathery palms more fair
Than thou, so upright, so stately, and still thou standest.

And yet, O splendid ship, unhailed and nameless,
   I know not if, aiming a fancy, I rightly divine
That thou hast a purpose joyful, a courage blameless,
   Thy port assured in a happier land than mine.
   But for all I have given thee, beauty enough is thine,
As thou, aslant with trim tackle and shrouding,
   From the proud nostril curve of a prow's line
In the offing scatterest foam, thy white sails crowding.

NIGHTINGALES

Beautiful must be the mountains whence ye come,
And bright in the fruitful valleys the streams wherefrom
         Ye learn your song:
Where are those starry woods? O might I wander there,
   Among the flowers, which in that heavenly air
         Bloom the year long!

Nay, barren are those mountains and spent the streams:
Our song is the voice of desire, that haunts our dreams,
         A throe of the heart,
Whose pining visions dim, forbidden hopes profound,
   No dying cadence nor long sigh can sound,
         For all our art.

Alone, aloud in the raptured ear of men
We pour our dark nocturnal secret; and then,
         As night is withdrawn
From these sweet-springing meads and bursting boughs of May,
   Dream, while the innumerable choir of day
         Welcome the dawn.

LOW BAROMETER

The south-wind strengthens to a gale,
Across the moon the clouds fly fast,
The house is smitten as with a flail,
The chimney shudders to the blast.

On such a night, when Air has loosed
Its guardian grasp on blood and brain,
Old terrors then of god or ghost
Creep from their caves to life again;

And Reason kens he herits in
A haunted house. Tenants unknown
Assert their squalid lease of sin
With earlier title than his own.

Unbodied presences, the pack'd
Pollution and remorse of Time,
Slipp'd from oblivion reënact
The horrors of unhouseld crime.

Some men would quell the thing with prayer
Whose sightless footsteps pad the floor,
Whose fearful trespass mounts the stair
Or bursts the lock'd forbidden door.

Some have seen corpses long interr'd
Escape from hallowing control,
Pale charnel forms—nay ev'n have heard
The shrilling of a troubled soul,

That wanders till the dawn hath cross'd
The dolorous dark, or Earth hath wound
Closer her storm-spredd cloke, and thrust
The baleful phantoms under ground.

EROS

Why hast thou nothing in thy face?
Thou idol of the human race,
Thou tyrant of the human heart,
The flower of lovely youth that art;
Yea, and that standest in thy youth
An image of eternal Truth,
With thy exuberant flesh so fair,
That only Pheidias might compare,
Ere from his chaste marmoreal form
Time had decayed the colours warm;
Like to his gods in thy proud dress,
Thy starry sheen of nakedness.

Surely thy body is thy mind,
For in thy face is nought to find,
Only thy soft unchristen'd smile,
That shadows neither love nor guile,
But shameless will and power immense,
In secret sensuous innocence.

O king of joy, what is thy thought?
I dream thou knowest it is nought,
And wouldst in darkness come, but thou
Makest the light where'er thou go.
Ah yet no victim of thy grace,
None who e'er long'd for thy embrace,
Hath cared to look upon thy face.

JOHANNES MILTON, SENEX
Scazons

Since I believe in God the Father Almighty,
Man's Maker and Judge, Overruler of Fortune,
'Twere strange should I praise anything and refuse Him praise,
Should love the creature forgetting the Créator,
Nor unto Him ^v in suff'ring and sorrow turn me:
Nay how could I withdraw from ^v His embracing?

But since that I have seen not, and cannot know Him,
Nor in my earthly temple apprehend rightly
His wisdom and the heav'nly purpose eternal;
Therefore will I be bound to no studied system
Nor argument, nor with delusion enslave me,
Nor seek to pleáse Him in any foolish invention,
Which my spirit within me, that loveth beauty
And hateth evil, hath reprov'd as unworthy:

But I cherish my freedom in loving service,
Gratefully adoring for delight beyond asking
Or thinking, and in hours of anguish and darkness
Confiding always on ⱽHis excellent greatness.

NOEL: CHRISTMAS EVE, 1913

Pax hominibus bonae voluntatis

A frosty Christmas Eve
  when the stars were
    shining
Fared I forth alone
  where westward falls the
    hill,
And from many a village
  in the water'd valley
Distant music reach'd me
  peals of bells aringing:
The constellated sounds
  ran sprinkling on earth's
    floor
As the dark vault above
  with stars was spangled
    o'er.

Then sped my thoughts to
  keep that first Christmas of
    all

When the shepherds watch-
  ing by the folds ere the
    dawn
Heard music in the fields
  and marveling could not
    tell
Whether it were angels
  or the bright stars singing.

Now blessed be the tow'rs
  that crown England so fair
That stand up strong in
  prayer unto God for our
    souls:
Blessed be their founders
  (said I) an' our country
    folk
Who are ringing for Christ
  in the belfries to-night
With arms lifted to clutch

the rattling ropes that race
Into the dark above
   and the mad romping din.

But to me heard afar
   it was starry music
Angels' song, comforting
   as the comfort of Christ

When he spake tenderly
   to his sorrowful flock:
The old words came to me
   by the riches of time
Mellow'd and transfigured
   as I stood on the hill
Heark'ning in the aspect
   of th'eternal silence.

THE PSALM

While Northward the hot sun was sinking o'er the trees
as we sat pleasantly talking in the meadow,
the swell of a rich music suddenly on our ears
gush'd thru' the wide-flung doors, where village-folk in church
stood to their evening psalm praising God together—
and when it came to cloze, paused, and broke forth anew.

A great Huguenot psalm it trod forth on the air
with full slow notes moving as a goddess stepping
through the responsive figures of a stately dance
conscious of beauty and of her fair-flowing array
in the severe perfection of an habitual grace,
then stooping to its cloze, paused to dance forth anew;

To unfold its bud of melody everlastingly
fresh as in springtime when, four centuries agone,
it wing'd the souls of martyrs on their way to heav'n
chain'd at the barbarous stake, mid the burning faggots
standing with tongues cut out, all singing in the flames—
O evermore, sweet Psalm, shalt thou break forth anew.

Thou, when in France that self-idolatrous idol reign'd
that starv'd his folk to fatten his priests and concubines,

thou wast the unconquerable paean of resolute men
who fell in coward massacre or with Freedom fled
from the palatial horror into far lands away,
and England learnt to voice thy deathless strain anew.

Ah! they endured beyond worst pangs of fire and steel
torturings invisible of tenderness and untold;
No Muse may name them, nay, no man will whisper them;
sitting alone he dare not think of them—and wail
of babes and mothers' wail flouted in ribald song.
Draw to thy cloze, sweet Psalm, pause and break forth anew!

Thy minstrels were no more, yet thy triumphing plaint
haunted their homes, as once in a deserted house
in Orthes, as 'twas told, the madden'd soldiery
burst in and search'd but found nor living man nor maid
only the sound flow'd round them and desisted not
but when it wound to cloze, paused, and broke forth anew.

And oft again in some lone valley of the Cevennes
where unabsolvèd crime yet calleth plagues on France
thy heavenly voice would lure the bloodhounds on, astray,
hunting their fancied prey afar in the dark night
and with its ghostly music mock'd their oaths and knives.
O evermore great Psalm spring forth! spring forth anew!

john davidson

THIRTY BOB A WEEK

I couldn't touch a step and turn a screw,
    And set the blooming world a-work for me,
Like such as cut their teeth—I hope, like you—
    On the handle of a skeleton gold key;
I cut mine on a leek, which I eat it every week:
    I'm a clerk at thirty bob as you can see.

But I don't allow it's luck and all a toss;
  There's no such thing as being starred and crossed;
It's just the power of some to be a boss,
  And the bally power of others to be bossed:
I face the music, sir; you bet I ain't a cur;
  Strike me lucky if I don't believe I'm lost!

For like a mole I journey in the dark,
  A-travelling along the underground
From my Pillar'd Halls and broad Suburban Park,
  To come the daily dull official round;
And home again at night with my pipe all alight,
  A-scheming how to count ten bob a pound.

And it's often very cold and very wet,
  And my missis stitches towels for a hunks;
And the Pillar'd Halls is half of it to let—
  Three rooms about the size of travelling trunks.
And we cough, my wife and I, to dislocate a sigh,
  When the noisy little kids are in their bunks.

But you never hear her do a growl or whine,
  For she's made of flint and roses, very odd;
And I've got to cut my meaning rather fine,
  Or I'd blubber, for I'm made of greens and sod:
So p'r'aps we are in Hell for all that I can tell,
  And lost and damn'd and served up hot to God.

I ain't blaspheming, Mr. Silver-tongue;
  I'm saying things a bit beyond your art:
Of all the rummy starts you ever sprung,
  Thirty bob a week's the rummiest start!
With your science and your books and your the'ries about
    spooks,
  Did you ever hear of looking in your heart?

I didn't mean your pocket, Mr., no:
  I mean that having children and a wife,
With thirty bob on which to come and go,

Isn't dancing to the tabor and the fife:
When it doesn't make you drink, by Heaven! it makes you
     think,
     And notice curious items about life.

I step into my heart and there I meet
     A god-almighty devil singing small,
Who would like to shout and whistle in the street,
     And squelch the passers flat against the wall;
If the whole world was a cake he had the power to take,
     He would take it, ask for more, and eat it all.

And I meet a sort of simpleton beside,
     The kind that life is always giving beans;
With thirty bob a week to keep a bride
     He fell in love and married in his teens:
At thirty bob he stuck; but he knows it isn't luck:
     He knows the seas are deeper than tureens.

And the god-almighty devil and the fool
     That meet me in the High Street on the strike,
When I walk about my heart a-gathering wool,
     Are my good and evil angels if you like.
And both of them together in every kind of weather
     Ride me like a double-seated bike.

That's rough a bit and needs its meaning curled.
     But I have a high old hot un in my mind—
A most engrugious notion of the world,
     That leaves your lightning 'rithmetic behind:
I give it at a glance when I say "There ain't no chance,
     Nor nothing of the lucky-lottery kind."

And it's this way I make it out to be:
     No fathers, mothers, countries, climates—none;
Not Adam was responsible for me,
     Nor society, nor systems, nary one:
A little sleeping seed, I woke—I did, indeed—
     A million years before the blooming sun.

I woke because I thought the time had come;
    Beyond my will there was no other cause;
And every where I found myself at home,
    Because I chose to be the thing I was;
And in what ever shape of mollusc or of ape
    I always went according to the laws.

I was the love that chose my mother out;
    I joined two lives and from the union burst;
My weakness and my strength without a doubt
    Are mine alone for ever from the first:
It's just the very same with a difference in the name
    As "Thy will be done." You say it if you durst!

They say it daily up and down the land
    As easy as you take a drink, it's true;
But the difficultest go to understand,
    And the difficultest job a man can do,
Is to come it brave and meek with thirty bob a week,
    And feel that that's the proper thing for you.

It's a naked child against a hungry wolf;
    It's playing bowls upon a splitting wreck;
It's walking on a string across a gulf
    With millstones fore-and-aft about your neck;
But the thing is daily done by many and many a one;
    And we fall, face forward, fighting, on the deck.

A RUNNABLE STAG

When the pods went pop on the broom, green broom,
    And apples began to be golden-skinn'd,
We harbour'd a stag in the Priory coomb,
    And we feather'd his trail up-wind, up-wind,
    We feather'd his trail up-wind—
        A stag of warrant, a stag, a stag,
        A runnable stag, a kingly crop,

Brow, bay and tray and three on top,
A stag, a runnable stag.

Then the huntsman's horn rang yap, yap, yap,
And 'Forwards' we heard the harbourer shout;
But 'twas only a brocket that broke a gap
In the beechen underwood, driven out,
From the underwood antler'd out
By warrant and might of the stag, the stag,
The runnable stag, whose lordly mind
Was bent on sleep, though beam'd and tined
He stood, a runnable stag.

So we tufted the covert till afternoon
With Tinkerman's Pup and Bell-of-the-North;
And hunters were sulky and hounds out of tune
Before we tufted the right stag forth,
Before we tufted him forth,
The stag of warrant, the wily stag,
The runnable stag with his kingly crop,
Brow, bay and tray and three on top,
The royal and runnable stag.

It was Bell-of-the-North and Tinkerman's Pup
That stuck to the scent till the copse was drawn.
'Tally ho! tally ho!' and the hunt was up,
The tufters whipp'd and the pack laid on,
The resolute pack laid on,
And the stag of warrant away at last,
The runnable stag, the same, the same,
His hoofs on fire, his horns like flame,
A stag, a runnable stag.

'Let your gelding be: if you check or chide
He stumbles at once and you're out of the hunt;
For three hundred gentlemen, able to ride,
On hunters accustom'd to bear the brunt,

Accustom'd to bear the brunt,
   Are after the runnable stag, the stag,
   The runnable stag with his kingly crop,
   Brow, bay and tray and three on top,
   The right, the runnable stag.'

By perilous paths in coomb and dell,
   The heather, the rocks, and the river-bed,
The pace grew hot, for the scent lay well,
   And a runnable stag goes right ahead,
   The quarry went right ahead—
      Ahead, ahead, and fast and far;
      His antler'd crest, his cloven hoof,
      Brow, bay and tray and three aloof,
      The stag, the runnable stag.

For a matter of twenty miles and more,
   By the densest hedge and the highest wall,
Through herds of bullocks he baffled the lore
   Of harbourer, huntsman, hounds and all,
   Of harbourer, hounds and all—
      The stag of warrant, the wily stag,
      For twenty miles, and five and five,
      He ran, and he never was caught alive,
      This stag, this runnable stag.

When he turn'd at bay in the leafy gloom,
   In the emerald gloom where the brook ran deep
He heard in the distance the rollers boom,
   And he saw in a vision of peaceful sleep,
   A stag of warrant, a stag, a stag,
      A runnable stag in a jewell'd bed,
      Under the sheltering ocean dead,
      A stag, a runnable stag.

So a fateful hope lit up his eye,
   And he open'd his nostrils wide again,

And he toss'd his branching antlers high
 As he headed the hunt down the Charlock glen
 As he raced down the echoing glen—
  For five miles more, the stag, the stag,
  For twenty miles, and five and five,
  Not to be caught now, dead or alive,
  The stag, the runnable stag.

Three hundred gentlemen, able to ride,
 Three hundred horses as gallant and free,
Beheld him escape on the evening tide,
 Far out till he sank in the Severn Sea,
 Till he sank in the depths of the sea—
  The stag, the buoyant stag, the stag
  That slept at last in a jewell'd bed
  Under the sheltering ocean spread,
  The stag, the runnable stag.

a. e. housman

LOVELIEST OF TREES, THE CHERRY NOW

Loveliest of trees, the cherry now
Is hung with bloom along the bough,
And stands about the woodland ride
Wearing white for Eastertide.

Now, of my threescore years and ten,
Twenty will not come again,
And take from seventy springs a score,
It only leaves me fifty more.

And since to look at things in bloom
Fifty springs are little room,
About the woodlands I will go
To see the cherry hung with snow.

REVEILLE

Wake: the silver dusk returning
　　Up the beach of darkness brims,
And the ship of sunrise burning
　　Strands upon the eastern rims.

Wake: the vaulted shadow shatters,
　　Trampled to the floor it spanned,
And the tent of night in tatters
　　Straws the sky-pavilioned land.

Up, lad, up, 'tis late for lying:
　　Hear the drums of morning play;
Hark, the empty highways crying
　　'Who'll beyond the hills away?'

Towns and countries woo together,
　　Forelands beacon, belfries call;
Never lad that trod on leather
　　Lived to feast his heart with all.

Up, lad: thews that lie and cumber
　　Sunlit pallets never thrive;
Morns abed and daylight slumber
　　Were not meant for man alive.

Clay lies still, but blood's a rover;
　　Breath's a ware that will not keep.
Up, lad: when the journey's over
　　There'll be time enough to sleep.

WHEN I WAS ONE-AND-TWENTY

When I was one-and-twenty
　　I heard a wise man say,
'Give crowns and pounds and guineas
　　But not your heart away;

Give pearls away and rubies
　But keep your fancy free.'
But I was one-and-twenty,
　No use to talk to me.

When I was one-and-twenty
　I heard him say again,
'The heart out of the bosom
　Was never given in vain;
'Tis paid with sighs a plenty
　And sold for endless rue.'
And I am two-and-twenty,
　And oh, 'tis true, 'tis true.

OH, WHEN I WAS IN LOVE WITH YOU

Oh, when I was in love with you,
　Then I was clean and brave,
And miles around the wonder grew
　How well did I behave.

And now the fancy passes by,
　And nothing will remain,
And miles around they'll say that I
　Am quite myself again.

WITH RUE MY HEART IS LADEN

With rue my heart is laden
　For golden friends I had,
For many a rose-lipt maiden
　And many a lightfoot lad.

By brooks too broad for leaping
　The lightfoot boys are laid;
The rose-lipt girls are sleeping
　In fields where roses fade.

TO AN ATHLETE DYING YOUNG

The time you won your town the race
We chaired you through the market-place;
Man and boy stood cheering by,
And home we brought you shoulder-high.

To-day, the road all runners come,
Shoulder-high we bring you home,
And set you at your threshold down,
Townsman of a stiller town.

Smart lad, to slip betimes away
From fields where glory does not stay
And early though the laurel grows
It withers quicker than the rose.

Eyes the shady night has shut
Cannot see the record cut,
And silence sounds no worse than cheers
After earth has stopped the ears:

Now you will not swell the rout
Of lads that wore their honours out,
Runners whom renown outran
And the name died before the man.

So set, before its echoes fade,
The fleet foot on the sill of shade,
And hold to the low lintel up
The still-defended challenge-cup.

And round that early-laurelled head
Will flock to gaze the strengthless dead,
And find unwithered on its curls
The garland briefer than a girl's.

INTO MY HEART

Into my heart an air that kills
    From yon far country blows:
What are those blue remembered hills,
    What spires, what farms are those?

That is the land of lost content,
    I see it shining plain,
The happy highways where I went
    And cannot come again.

ON WENLOCK EDGE THE WOOD'S IN TROUBLE

On Wenlock Edge the wood's in trouble;
His forest fleece the Wrekin heaves;
The gale, it plies the saplings double,
And thick on Severn snow the leaves.

'Twould blow like this through holt and hanger
When Uricon the city stood;
'Tis the old wind in the old anger,
But then it threshed another wood.

Then, 'twas before my time, the Roman
At yonder heaving hill would stare;
The blood that warms an English yeoman,
The thoughts that hurt him, they were there.

There, like the wind through woods in riot,
Through him the gale of life blew high;
The tree of man was never quiet:
Then 'twas the Roman, now 'tis I.

The gale, it plies the saplings double,
It blows so hard, 'twill soon be gone:
Today the Roman and his trouble
Are ashes under Uricon.

TERENCE, THIS IS STUPID STUFF

'Terence, this is stupid stuff:
You eat your victuals fast enough;
There can't be much amiss, 'tis clear,
To see the rate you drink your beer.
But oh, good Lord, the verse you make,
It gives a chap the belly-ache.
The cow, the old cow, she is dead;
It sleeps well, the horned head:
We poor lads, 'tis our turn now
To hear such tunes as killed the cow.
Pretty friendship 'tis to rhyme
Your friends to death before their time
Moping melancholy mad:
Come, pipe a tune to dance to, lad.'

Why, if 'tis dancing you would be,
There's brisker pipes than poetry.
Say, for what were hop-yards meant,
Or why was Burton built on Trent?
Oh many a peer of England brews
Livelier liquor than the Muse,
And malt does more than Milton can
To justify God's ways to man.
Ale, man, ale's the stuff to drink
For fellows whom it hurts to think:
Look into the pewter pot
To see the world as the world's not.
And faith, 'tis pleasant till 'tis past:
The mischief is that 'twill not last.
Oh I have been to Ludlow fair
And left my necktie God knows where,
And carried half-way home, or near,
Pints and quarts of Ludlow beer:
Then the world seemed none so bad,
And I myself a sterling lad;
And down in lovely muck I've lain,

Happy till I woke again.
Then I saw the morning sky:
Heigho, the tale was all a lie;
The world, it was the old world yet,
I was I, my things were wet,
And nothing now remained to do
But begin the game anew.

Therefore, since the world has still
Much good, but much less good than ill,
And while the sun and moon endure
Luck's a chance, but trouble's sure,
I'd face it as a wise man would,
And train for ill and not for good.
'Tis true, the stuff I bring for sale
Is not so brisk a brew as ale:
Out of a stem that scored the hand
I wrung it in a weary land.
But take it: if the smack is sour,
The better for the embittered hour;
It should do good to heart and head
When your soul is in my soul's stead;
And I will friend you, if I may,
In the dark and cloudy day.

There was a king reigned in the East:
There, when kings will sit to feast,
They get their fill before they think
With poisoned meat and poisoned drink.
He gathered all that springs to birth
From the many-venomed earth;
First a little, thence to more,
He sampled all her killing store;
And easy, smiling, seasoned sound,
Sate the king when healths went round.
They put arsenic in his meat
And stared aghast to watch him eat;
They poured strychnine in his cup

And shook to see him drink it up:
They shook, they stared as white's their shirt:
Them it was their poison hurt.
—I tell the tale that I heard told.
Mithridates, he died old.

BREDON HILL

In summertime on Bredon
  The bells they sound so clear;
Round both the shires they ring them
  In steeples far and near,
  A happy noise to hear.

Here of a Sunday morning
  My love and I would lie,
And see the coloured counties,
  And hear the larks so high
  About us in the sky.

The bells would ring to call her
  In valleys miles away:
'Come all to church, good people;
  Good people, come and pray.'
  But here my love would stay.

And I would turn and answer
  Among the springing thyme,
'Oh, peal upon our wedding,
  And we will hear the chime,
  And come to church in time.'

But when the snows at Christmas
  On Bredon top were strown,
My love rose up so early
  And stole out unbeknown
  And went to church alone.

They tolled the one bell only,
  Groom there was none to see,
The mourners followed after,
  And so to church went she,
  And would not wait for me.

The bells they sound on Bredon,
  And still the steeples hum.
'Come all to church, good people,'—
  Oh, noisy bells, be dumb;
  I hear you, I will come.

THE LADS IN THEIR HUNDREDS

The lads in their hundreds to Ludlow come in for the fair,
  There's men from the barn and the forge and the mill and
    the fold,
The lads for the girls and the lads for the liquor are there,
  And there with the rest are the lads that will never be old.

There's chaps from the town and the field and the till and the
    cart,
  And many to count are the stalwart, and many the brave,
And many the handsome of face and the handsome of heart,
  And few that will carry their looks or their truth to the
    grave.

I wish one could know them, I wish there were tokens to tell
The fortunate fellows that now you can never discern;
And then one could talk with them friendly and wish them
    farewell
  And watch them depart on the way that they will not return.

But now you may stare as you like and there's nothing to scan;
  And brushing your elbow unguessed-at and not to be told
They carry back bright to the coiner the mintage of man,
  The lads that will die in their glory and never be old.

OH SEE HOW THICK THE GOLDCUP FLOWERS

Oh see how thick the goldcup flowers
    Are lying in field and lane,
With dandelions to tell the hours
    That never are told again.
Oh may I squire you round the meads
    And pick you posies gay?
—'T will do no harm to take my arm.
    'You may, young man, you may.'

Ah, spring was sent for lass and lad,
    'Tis now the blood runs gold,
And man and maid had best be glad
    Before the world is old.
What flowers to-day may flower to-morrow,
    But never as good as new.
—Suppose I wound my arm right round—
    ' 'Tis true, young man, 'tis true.'

Some lads there are, 'tis shame to say,
    That only court to thieve,
And once they bear the bloom away
    'Tis little enough they leave.
Then keep your heart for men like me
    And safe from trustless chaps.
My love is true and all for you.
    'Perhaps, young man, perhaps.'

Oh, look in my eyes then, can you doubt?
    —Why, 'tis a mile from town.
How green the grass is all about!
    We might as well sit down.
—Ah, life, what is it but a flower?
    Why must true lovers sigh?
Be kind, have pity, my own, my pretty,—
    'Good-bye, young man, good-bye.'

THE IMMORTAL PART

When I meet the morning beam
Or lay me down at night to dream,
I hear my bones within me say,
'Another night, another day.

'When shall this slough of sense be cast,
This dust of thoughts be laid at last,
The man of flesh and soul be slain
And the man of bone remain?

'This tongue that talks, these lungs that shout,
These thews that hustle us about,
This brain that fills the skull with schemes,
And its humming hive of dreams,—

'These to-day are proud in power
And lord it in their little hour:
The immortal bones obey control
Of dying flesh and dying soul.

' 'Tis long till eve and morn are gone:
Slow the endless night comes on,
And late to fulness grows the birth
That shall last as long as earth.

'Wanderers eastward, wanderers west,
Know you why you cannot rest?
'Tis that every mother's son
Travails with a skeleton.

'Lie down in the bed of dust;
Bear the fruit that bear you must;
Bring the eternal seed to light,
And morn is all the same as night.

'Rest you so from trouble sore,
Fear the heat o' the sun no more,

Nor the snowing winter wild,
Now you labour not with child.

'Empty vessel, garment cast,
We that wore you long shall last.
—Another night, another day.'
So my bones within me say.

Therefore they shall do my will
To-day while I am master still,
And flesh and soul, now both are strong,
Shall hale the sullen slaves along,

Before this fire of sense decay,
This smoke of thought blow clean away,
And leave with ancient night alone
The stedfast and enduring bone.

OTHERS, I AM NOT THE FIRST

Others, I am not the first,
Have willed more mischief than they durst:
If in the breathless night I too
Shiver now, 'tis nothing new.

More than I, if truth were told,
Have stood and sweated hot and cold,
And through their veins in ice and fire
Fear contended with desire.

Agued once like me were they,
But I like them shall win my way
Lastly to the bed of mould
Where there's neither heat nor cold.

But from my grave across my brow
Plays no wind of healing now,

And fire and ice within me fight
Beneath the suffocating night.

YOU SMILE UPON YOUR FRIEND TO-DAY

You smile upon your friend to-day,
    To-day his ills are over;
You hearken to the lover's say,
    And happy is the lover.

'Tis late to hearken, late to smile,
    But better late than never:
I shall have lived a little while
    Before I die for ever.

I HOED AND TRENCHED AND WEEDED

I hoed and trenched and weeded,
    And took the flowers to fair:
I brought them home unheeded;
    The hue was not the wear.

So up and down I sow them
    For lads like me to find,
When I shall lie below them,
    A dead man out of mind.

Some seed the birds devour,
    And some the season mars,
But here and there will flower
    The solitary stars,

And fields will yearly bear them
    As light-leaved spring comes on,
And luckless lads will wear them
    When I am dead and gone.

william butler yeats

WHEN YOU ARE OLD

When you are old and grey and full of sleep,
And nodding by the fire, take down this book,
And slowly read, and dream of the soft look
Your eyes had once, and of their shadows deep;

How many loved your moments of glad grace,
And loved your beauty with love false or true,
But one man loved the pilgrim soul in you,
And loved the sorrows of your changing face;

And bending down beside the glowing bars,
Murmur, a little sadly, how Love fled
And paced upon the mountains overhead
And hid his face amid a crowd of stars.

THE LAKE ISLE OF INNISFREE

I will arise and go now, and go to Innisfree,
And a small cabin build there, of clay and wattles made:
Nine bean-rows will I have there, a hive for the honey-bee,
And live alone in the bee-loud glade.

And I shall have some peace there, for peace comes dropping
    slow,
Dropping from the veils of the morning to where the cricket
    sings;
There midnight's all a glimmer, and noon a purple glow,
And evening full of linnet's wings.

I will arise and go now, for always night and day
I hear lake water lapping with low sounds by the shore;
While I stand on the roadway, or on the pavements grey,
I hear it in the deep heart's core.

TO A SHADE

If you have revisited the town, thin Shade,
Whether to look upon your monument
(I wonder if the builder has been paid)
Or happier-thoughted when the day is spent
To drink of that salt breath out of the sea
When grey gulls flit about instead of men,
And the gaunt houses put on majesty:
Let these content you and be gone again;
For they are at their old tricks yet.

                          A man
Of your own passionate serving kind who had brought
In his full hands what, had they only known,
Had given their children's children loftier thought,
Sweeter emotion, working in their veins
Like gentle blood, has been driven from the place,
And insult heaped upon him for his pains,
And for his open-handedness, disgrace;
Your enemy, an old foul mouth, had set
The pack upon him.

                     Go, unquiet wanderer,
And gather the Glasnevin coverlet
About your head till the dust stops your ear,
The time for you to taste of that salt breath
And listen at the corners has not come;
You had enough of sorrow before death—
Away, away! You are safer in the tomb.

September 29, 1913

A BRONZE HEAD

Here at right of the entrance this bronze head,
Human, superhuman, a bird's round eye,
Everything else withered and mummy-dead.
What great tomb-haunter sweeps the distant sky
(Something may linger there though all else die;)

And finds there nothing to make its terror less
Hysterica passio ot its own emptiness?

No dark tomb-haunter once; her form all full
As though with magnanimity of light,
Yet a most gentle woman; who can tell
Which of her forms has shown her substance right?
Or maybe substance can be composite,
Profound McTaggart thought so, and in a breath
A mouthful held the extreme of life and death.

But even at the starting-post, all sleek and new,
I saw the wildness in her and I thought
A vision of terror that it must live through
Had shattered her soul. Propinquity had brought
Imagination to that pitch where it casts out
All that is not itself: I had grown wild
And wandered murmuring everywhere, 'My child, my child!'

Or else I thought her supernatural;
As though a sterner eye looked through her eye
On this foul world in its decline and fall;
On gangling stocks grown great, great stocks run dry,
Ancestral pearls all pitched into a sty,
Heroic reverie mocked by clown and knave,
And wondered what was left for massacre to save.

LAPIS LAZULI

I have heard that hysterical women say
They are sick of the palette and fiddle-bow,
Of poets that are always gay,
For everybody knows or else should know
That if nothing drastic is done
Aeroplane and Zeppelin will come out,
Pitch like King Billy bomb-balls in
Until the town lie beaten flat.

All perform their tragic play,
There struts Hamlet, there is Lear,
That's Ophelia, that Cordelia;
Yet they, should the last scene be there,
The great stage curtain about to drop,
If worthy their prominent part in the play,
Do not break up their lines to weep.
They know that Hamlet and Lear are gay;
Gaiety transfiguring all that dread.
All men have aimed at, found and lost;
Black out; Heaven blazing into the head:
Tragedy wrought to its uttermost.
Though Hamlet rambles and Lear rages,
And all the drop-scenes drop at once
Upon a hundred thousand stages,
It cannot grow by an inch or an ounce.

On their own feet they came, or on shipboard,
Camel-back, horse-back, ass-back, mule-back,
Old civilisations put to the sword.
Then they and their wisdom went to rack:
No handiwork of Callimachus,
Who handled marble as if it were bronze,
Made draperies that seemed to rise
When sea-wind swept the corner, stands;
His long lamp-chimney shaped like the stem
Of a slender palm, stood but a day;
All things fall and are built again,
And those that build them again are gay.

Two Chinamen, behind them a third,
Are carved in lapis lazuli,
Over them flies a long-legged bird,
A symbol of longevity;
The third, doubtless a serving-man,
Carries a musical instrument.

Every discoloration of the stone,
Every accidental crack or dent,

Seems a water-course or an avalanche,
Or lofty slope where it still snows
Though doubtless plum or cherry-branch
Sweetens the little half-way house
Those Chinamen climb towards, and I
Delight to imagine them seated there;
There, on the mountain and the sky,
On all the tragic scene they stare.
One asks for mournful melodies;
Accomplished fingers begin to play.
Their eyes mid many wrinkles, their eyes,
Their ancient, glittering eyes, are gay.

NEWS FOR THE DELPHIC ORACLE

I

There all the golden codgers lay,
There the silver dew,
And the great water sighed for love,
And the wind sighed too.
Man-picker Niamh leant and sighed
By Oisin on the grass;
There sighed amid his choir of love
Tall Pythagoras.
Plotinus came and looked about,
The salt-flakes on his breast,
And having stretched and yawned awhile
Lay sighing like the rest.

II

Straddling each a dolphin's back
And steadied by a fin,
Those Innocents re-live their death,
Their wounds open again.
The ecstatic waters laugh because
Their cries are sweet and strange,
Through their ancestral patterns dance,

And the brute dolphins plunge
Until, in some cliff-sheltered bay
Where wades the choir of love
Proffering its sacred laurel crowns,
They pitch their burdens off.

III

Slim adolescence that a nymph has stripped,
Peleus on Thetis stares.
Her limbs are delicate as an eyelid,
Love has blinded him with tears;
But Thetis' belly listens.
Down the mountain walls
From where Pan's cavern is
Intolerable music falls.
Foul goat-head, brutal arm appear,
Belly, shoulder, bum,
Flash fishlike; nymphs and satyrs
Copulate in the foam.

NINETEEN HUNDRED AND NINETEEN

I

Many ingenious lovely things are gone
That seemed sheer miracle to the multitude,
Protected from the circle of the moon
That pitches common things about. There stood
Amid the ornamental bronze and stone
An ancient image made of olive wood—
And gone are Phidias' famous ivories
And all the golden grasshoppers and bees.

We too had many pretty toys when young;
A law indifferent to blame or praise,
To bribe or threat; habits that made old wrong
Melt down, as it were wax in the sun's rays;
Public opinion ripening for so long

We thought it would outlive all future days.
O what fine thought we had because we thought
That the worst rogues and rascals had died out.

All teeth were drawn, all ancient tricks unlearned,
And a great army but a showy thing;
What matter that no cannon had been turned
Into a ploughshare? Parliament and king
Thought that unless a little powder burned
The trumpeters might burst with trumpeting
And yet it lack all glory; and perchance
The guardsmen's drowsy chargers would not prance.

Now days are dragon-ridden, the nightmare
Rides upon sleep: a drunken soldiery
Can leave the mother, murdered at her door,
To crawl in her own blood, and go scot-free;
The night can sweat with terror as before
We pieced our thoughts into philosophy,
And planned to bring the world under a rule,
Who are but weasels fighting in a hole.

He who can read the signs nor sink unmanned
Into the half-deceit of some intoxicant
From shallow wits; who knows no work can stand,
Whether health, wealth or peace of mind were spent
On master-work of intellect or hand,
No honour leave its mighty monument,
Has but one comfort left: all triumph would
But break upon his ghostly solitude.

But is there any comfort to be found?
Man is in love and loves what vanishes,
What more is there to say? That country round
None dared admit, if such a thought were his,
Incendiary or bigot could be found
To burn that stump on the Acropolis,
Or break in bits the famous ivories
Or traffic in the grasshoppers or bees.

II

When Loie Fuller's Chinese dancers enwound
A shining web, a floating ribbon of cloth,
It seemed that a dragon of air
Had fallen among dancers, had whirled them round
Or hurried them off on its own furious path;
So the Platonic Year
Whirls out new right and wrong,
Whirls in the old instead;
All men are dancers and their tread
Goes to the barbarous clangour of a gong.

III

Some moralist or mythological poet
Compares the solitary soul to a swan;
I am satisfied with that,
Satisfied if a troubled mirror show it,
Before that brief gleam of its life be gone,
An image of its state;
The wings half spread for flight,
The breast thrust out in pride
Whether to play, or to ride
Those winds that clamour of approaching night.

A man in his own secret meditation
Is lost amid the labyrinth that he has made
In art or politics;
Some Platonist affirms that in the station
Where we should cast off body and trade
The ancient habit sticks,
And that if our works could
But vanish with our breath
That were a lucky death,
For triumph can but mar our solitude.

The swan has leaped into the desolate heaven:
That image can bring wildness, bring a rage

To end all things, to end
What my laborious life imagined, even
The half-imagined, the half-written page;
O but we dreamed to mend
What ever mischief seemed
To afflict mankind, but now
That winds of winter blow
Learn that we were crack-pated when we dreamed.

IV

We, who seven years ago
Talked of honour and of truth,
Shriek with pleasure if we show
The weasel's twist, the weasel's tooth.

V

Come let us mock at the great
That had such burdens on the mind
And toiled so hard and late
To leave some monument behind,
Nor thought of the levelling wind.

Come let us mock at the wise;
With all those calendars whereon
They fixed old aching eyes,
They never saw how seasons run,
And now but gape at the sun.

Come let us mock at the good
That fancied goodness might be gay,
And sick of solitude
Might proclaim a holiday:
Wind shrieked—and where are they?

Mock mockers after that
That would not lift a hand maybe
To help good, wise or great
To bar that foul storm out, for we
Traffic in mockery.

VI

Violence upon the roads: violence of horses;
Some few have handsome riders, are garlanded
On delicate sensitive ear or tossing mane,
But wearied running round and round in their courses
All break and vanish, and evil gathers head:
Herodias' daughters have returned again,
A sudden blast of dusty wind and after
Thunder of feet, tumult of images,
Their purpose in the labyrinth of the wind;
And should some crazy hand dare touch a daughter
All turn with amorous cries, or angry cries,
According to the wind, for all are blind.
But now wind drops, dust settles; thereupon
There lurches past, his great eyes without thought
Under the shadow of stupid straw-pale locks,
That insolent fiend Robert Artisson
To whom the love-lorn Lady Kyteler brought
Bronzed peacock feathers, red combs of her cocks.

A PRAYER FOR MY DAUGHTER

Once more the storm is howling, and half hid
Under this cradle-hood and coverlid
My child sleeps on. There is no obstacle
But Gregory's wood and one bare hill
Whereby the haystack- and roof-levelling wind,
Bred on the Atlantic, can be stayed;
And for an hour I have walked and prayed
Because of the great gloom that is in my mind.

I have walked and prayed for this young child an hour
And heard the sea-wind scream upon the tower,
And under the arches of the bridge, and scream
In the elms above the flooded stream;
Imagining in excited reverie

That the future years had come,
Dancing to a frenzied drum,
Out of the murderous innocence of the sea.

May she be granted beauty and yet not
Beauty to make a stranger's eye distraught,
Or hers before a looking-glass, for such,
Being made beautiful overmuch,
Consider beauty a sufficient end,
Lose natural kindness and maybe
The heart-revealing intimacy
That chooses right, and never find a friend.

Helen being chosen found life flat and dull
And later had much trouble from a fool,
While that great Queen, that rose out of the spray,
Being fatherless could have her way
Yet chose a bandy-leggèd smith for man.
It's certain that fine women eat
A crazy salad with their meat
Whereby the Horn of Plenty is undone.

In courtesy I'd have her chiefly learned;
Hearts are not had as a gift but hearts are earned
By those that are not entirely beautiful;
Yet many, that have played the fool
For beauty's very self, has charm made wise,
And many a poor man that has roved,
Loved and thought himself beloved,
From a glad kindness cannot take his eyes.

May she become a flourishing hidden tree
That all her thoughts may like the linnet be,
And have no business but dispensing round
Their magnanimities of sound,
Nor but in merriment begin a chase,
Nor but in merriment a quarrel.

O may she live like some green laurel
Rooted in one dear perpetual place.

My mind, because the minds that I have loved,
The sort of beauty that I have approved,
Prosper but little, has dried up of late,
Yet knows that to be choked with hate
May well be of all evil chances chief.
If there's no hatred in a mind
Assault and battery of the wind
Can never tear the linnet from the leaf.

An intellectual hatred is the worst,
So let her think opinions are accursed.
Have I not seen the loveliest woman born
Out of the mouth of Plenty's horn,
Because of her opinionated mind
Barter that horn and every good
By quiet natures understood
For an old bellows full of angry wind?

Considering that, all hatred driven hence,
The soul recovers radical innocence
And learns at last that it is self-delighting,
Self-appeasing, self-affrighting,
And that its own sweet will is Heaven's will;
She can, though every face should scowl
And every windy quarter howl
Or every bellows burst, be happy still.

And may her bridegroom bring her to a house
Where all's accustomed, ceremonious;
For arrogance and hatred are the wares
Peddled in the thoroughfares.
How but in custom and in ceremony
Are innocence and beauty born?
Ceremony's a name for the rich horn,
And custom for the spreading laurel tree.
        June 1919

THE SECOND COMING

Turning and turning in the widening gyre
The falcon cannot hear the falconer;
Things fall apart; the centre cannot hold;
Mere anarchy is loosed upon the world,
The blood-dimmed tide is loosed, and everywhere
The ceremony of innocence is drowned;
The best lack all conviction, while the worst
Are full of passionate intensity.

Surely some revelation is at hand;
Surely the Second Coming is at hand.
The Second Coming! Hardly are those words out
When a vast image out of *Spiritus Mundi*
Troubles my sight: somewhere in sands of the desert
A shape with lion body and the head of a man,
A gaze blank and pitiless as the sun,
Is moving its slow thighs, while all about it
Reel shadows of the indignant desert birds.
The darkness drops again; but now I know
That twenty centuries of stony sleep
Were vexed to nightmare by a rocking cradle,
And what rough beast, its hour come round at last,
Slouches towards Bethlehem to be born?

A DIALOGUE OF SELF AND SOUL

I

MY SOUL. I summon to the winding ancient stair;
Set all your mind upon the steep ascent,
Upon the broken, crumbling battlement,
Upon the breathless starlit air,
Upon the star that marks the hidden pole;
Fix every wandering thought upon
That quarter where all thought is done:
Who can distinguish darkness from the soul?

MY SELF. The consecrated blade upon my knees
    Is Sato's ancient blade, still as it was,
    Still razor-keen, still like a looking-glass
    Unspotted by the centuries;
    That flowering, silken, old embroidery, torn
    From some court-lady's dress and round
    The wooden scabbard bound and wound,
    Can, tattered, still protect, faded adorn.

MY SOUL. Why should the imagination of a man
    Long past his prime remember things that are
    Emblematical of love and war?
    Think of ancestral night that can,
    If but imagination scorn the earth
    And intellect its wandering
    To this and that and t' other thing,
    Deliver from the crime of death and birth.

MY SELF. Montashigi, third of his family, fashioned it
    Five hundred years ago, about it lie
    Flowers from I know not what embroidery—
    Heart's purple—and all these I set
    For emblems of the day against the tower
    Emblematical of the night,
    And claim as by a soldier's right
    A charter to commit the crime once more.

MY SOUL. Such fullness in that quarter overflows
    And falls into the basin of the mind
    That man is stricken deaf and dumb and blind,
    For intellect no longer knows
    Is from the *Ought*, or *Knower* from the *Known*—
    That is to say, ascends to Heaven;
    Only the dead can be forgiven;
    But when I think of that my tongue's a stone.

II

MY SELF. A living man is blind and drinks his drop.
What matter if the ditches are impure?
What matter if I live it all once more?
Endure that toil of growing up;
The ignominy of boyhood; the distress
Of boyhood changing into man;
The unfinished man and his pain
Brought face to face with his own clumsiness;

The finished man among his enemies?—
How in the name of Heaven can he escape
That defiling and disfigured shape
The mirror of malicious eyes
Casts upon his eyes until at last
He thinks that shape must be his shape?
And what's the good of an escape
If honour find him in the wintry blast?

I am content to live it all again
And yet again, if it be life to pitch
Into the frog-spawn of a blind man's ditch,
A blind man battering blind men;
Or into that most fecund ditch of all,
The folly that man does
Or must suffer, if he woos
A proud woman not kindred of his soul.

I am content to follow to its source,
Every event in action or in thought;
Measure the lot; forgive myself the lot!
When such as I cast out remorse
So great a sweetness flows into the breast
We must laugh and we must sing,
We are blest by everything,
Everything we look upon is blest.

SAILING TO BYZANTIUM

That is no country for old men. The young
In one another's arms, birds in the trees,
—Those dying generations—at their song,
The salmon-falls, the mackerel-crowded seas,
Fish, flesh, or fowl, commend all summer long
Whatever is begotten, born, and dies.
Caught in that sensual music all neglect
Monuments of unageing intellect.

An aged man is but a paltry thing,
A tattered coat upon a stick, unless
Soul clap its hands and sing, and louder sing
For every tatter in its mortal dress,
Nor is there singing school but studying
Monuments of its own magnificence;
And therefore I have sailed the seas and come
To the holy city of Byzantium.

O sages standing in God's holy fire
As in the gold mosaic of a wall,
Come from the holy fire, perne in a gyre,
And be the singing-masters of my soul.
Consume my heart away; sick with desire
And fastened to a dying animal
It knows not what it is; and gather me
Into the artifice of eternity.

Once out of nature I shall never take
My bodily form from any natural thing,
But such a form as Grecian goldsmiths make
Of hammered gold and gold enamelling
To keep a drowsy Emperor awake;
Or set upon a golden bough to sing
To lords and ladies of Byzantium
Of what is past, or passing, or to come.

THE TOWER

I

What shall I do with this absurdity—
O heart, O troubled heart—this caricature,
Decrepit age that has been tied to me
As to a dog's tail?
                Never had I more
Excited, passionate, fantastical
Imagination, nor an ear and eye
That more expected the impossible—
No, not in boyhood when with rod and fly,
Or the humbler worm, I climbed Ben Bulben's back
And had the livelong summer day to spend.
It seems that I must bid the Muse go pack,
Choose Plato and Plotinus for a friend
Until imagination, ear and eye,
Can be content with argument and deal
In abstract things; or be derided by
A sort of battered kettle at the heel.

II

I pace upon the battlements and stare
On the foundations of a house, or where
Tree, like a sooty finger, starts from the earth;
And send imagination forth
Under the day's declining beam, and call
Images and memories
From ruin or from ancient trees,
For I would ask a question of them all.

Beyond that ridge lived Mrs. French, and once
When every silver candlestick or sconce
Lit up the dark mahogany and the wine,
A serving-man, that could divine
That most respected lady's every wish,
Ran and with the garden shears
Clipped an insolent farmer's ears
And brought them in a little covered dish.

Some few remembered still when I was young
A peasant girl commended by a song,
Who'd lived somewhere upon that rocky place,
And praised the colour of her face,
And had the greater joy in praising her,
Remembering that, if walked she there,
Farmers jostled at the fair
So great a glory did the song confer.

And certain men, being maddened by those rhymes,
Or else by toasting her a score of times,
Rose from the table and declared it right
To test their fancy by their sight;
But they mistook the brightness of the moon
For the prosaic light of day—
Music had driven their wits astray—
And one was drowned in the great bog of Cloone.

Strange, but the man who made the song was blind;
Yet, now I have considered it, I find
That nothing strange; the tragedy began
With Homer that was a blind man,
And Helen has all living hearts betrayed.
O may the moon and sunlight seem
One inextricable beam,
For if I triumph I must make men mad.

And I myself created Hanrahan
And drove him drunk or sober through the dawn
From somewhere in the neighbouring cottages.
Caught by an old man's juggleries
He stumbled, tumbled, fumbled to and fro
And had but broken knees for hire
And horrible splendour of desire;
I thought it all out twenty years ago:

Good fellows shuffled cards in an old bawn;
And when that ancient ruffian's turn was on

He so bewitched the cards under his thumb
That all but the one card became
A pack of hounds and not a pack of cards,
And that he changed into a hare.
Hanrahan rose in frenzy there
And followed up those baying creatures towards—

O towards I have forgotten what—enough!
I must recall a man that neither love
Nor music nor an enemy's clipped ear
Could, he was so harried, cheer;
A figure that has grown so fabulous
There's not a neighbour left to say
When he finished his dog's day:
An ancient bankrupt master of this house.

Before that ruin came, for centuries,
Rough men-at-arms, cross-gartered to the knees
Or shod in iron, climbed the narrow stairs,
And certain men-at-arms there were
Whose images, in the Great Memory stored,
Come with loud cry and panting breast
To break upon a sleeper's rest
While their great wooden dice beat on the board.

As I would question all, come all who can;
Come old, necessitous, half-mounted man;
And bring beauty's blind rambling celebrant;
The red man the juggler sent
Through God-forsaken meadows; Mrs. French,
Gifted with so fine an ear;
The man drowned in a bog's mire,
When mocking muses chose the country wench.

Did all old men and women, rich and poor,
Who trod upon these rocks or passed this door,
Whether in public or in secret rage
As I do now against old age?

But I have found an answer in those eyes
That are impatient to be gone;
Go therefore; but leave Hanrahan,
For I need all his mighty memories.

Old lecher with a love on every wind,
Bring up out of that deep considering mind
All that you have discovered in the grave,
For it is certain that you have
Reckoned up every unforeknown, unseeing
Plunge, lured by a softening eye,
Or by a touch or a sigh,
Into the labyrinth of another's being;

Does the imagination dwell the most
Upon a woman won or woman lost?
If on the lost, admit you turned aside
From a great labyrinth out of pride,
Cowardice, some silly over-subtle thought
Or anything called conscience once;
And that if memory recur, the sun's
Under eclipse and the day blotted out.

III

It is time that I wrote my will;
I choose upstanding men
That climb the streams until
The fountain leap, and at dawn
Drop their cast at the side
Of dripping stone; I declare
They shall inherit my pride,
The pride of people that were
Bound neither to Cause nor to State,
Neither to slaves that were spat on,
Nor to the tyrants that spat,
The people of Burke and Grattan
That gave, though free to refuse—
Pride, like that of the morn,

When the headlong light is loose,
Or that of the fabulous horn,
Or that of the sudden shower
When all streams are dry,
Or that of the hour
When the swan must fix his eye
Upon a fading gleam,
Float out upon a long
Last reach of glittering stream
And there sing his last song.
And I declare my faith:
I mock Plotinus' thought
And cry in Plato's teeth,
Death and life were not
Till man made up the whole,
Made lock, stock and barrel
Out of his bitter soul,
Aye, sun and moon and star, all,
And further add to that
That, being dead, we rise,
Dream and so create
Translunar Paradise.
I have prepared my peace
With learned Italian things
And the proud stones of Greece,
Poet's imaginings
And memories of love,
Memories of the words of women,
All those things whereof
Man makes a superhuman
Mirror-resembling dream.

As at the loophole there
The daws chatter and scream,
And drop twigs layer upon layer.
When they have mounted up,
The mother bird will rest

On their hollow top,
And so warm her wild nest.

I leave both faith and pride
To young upstanding men
Climbing the mountain side,
That under bursting dawn
They may drop a fly;
Being of that metal made
Till it was broken by
This sedentary trade.

Now shall I make my soul,
Compelling it to study
In a learned school
Till the wreck of body,
Slow decay of blood,
Testy delirium
Or dull decrepitude,
Or what worse evil come—
The death of friends, or death
Of every brilliant eye
That made a catch in the breath—
Seem but the clouds of the sky
When the horizon fades;
Or a bird's sleepy cry
Among the deepening shades.

JOHN KINSELLA'S LAMENT FOR MRS. MARY MOORE

A bloody and a sudden end,
    Gunshot or a noose,
For death who takes what man would keep,
    Leaves what man would lose.

He might have had my sister,
    My cousins by the score,
But nothing satisfied the fool
    But my dear Mary Moore,
None other knows what pleasures man
    At table or in bed.
What shall I do for pretty girls
    Now my old bawd is dead?

Though stiff to strike a bargain,
    Like an old Jew man,
Her bargain struck we laughed and talked
    And emptied many a can;
And O! but she had stories,
    Though not for the priest's ear,
To keep the soul of man alive,
    Banish age and care,
And being old she put a skin
    On everything she said.
What shall I do for pretty girls
    Now my old bawd is dead?

The priests have got a book that says
    But for Adam's sin
Eden's Garden would be there
    And I there within.
No expectation fails there,
    No pleasing habit ends,
No man grows old, no girl grows cold,
    But friends walk by friends.
Who quarrels over halfpennies
    That plucks the trees for bread?
What shall I do for pretty girls
    Now my old bawd is dead?

CRAZY JANE TALKS WITH THE BISHOP

I met the Bishop on the road
And much said he and I.
'Those breasts are flat and fallen now,
Those veins must soon be dry;
Live in a heavenly mansion,
Not in some foul sty.'

'Fair and foul are near of kin,
And fair needs foul,' I cried.
'My friends are gone, but that's a truth
Nor grave nor bed denied,
Learned in bodily lowliness
And in the heart's pride.

'A woman can be proud and stiff
When on love intent;
But Love has pitched his mansion in
The place of excrement;
For nothing can be sole or whole
That has not been rent.'

POLITICS

*"In our time the destiny of man presents its meaning in
political terms."* —THOMAS MANN

How can I, that girl standing there,
My attention fix
On Roman or on Russian
Or on Spanish politics?
Yet here's a travelled man that knows
What he talks about,
And there's a politician
That has read and thought,
And maybe what they say is true
Of war and war's alarms,
But O that I were young again
And held her in my arms!

THE THREE BUSHES

(An incident from the 'Historia mei Temporis' of the Abbe Michel de Bourdeille)

Said lady once to lover,
'None can rely upon
A love that lacks its proper food;
And if your love were gone
How could you sing those songs of love?
I should be blamed, young man.'
                    O my dear, O my dear.

'Have no lit candles in your room,'
That lovely lady said,
'That I at midnight by the clock
May creep into your bed,
For if I saw myself creep in
I think I should drop dead.'
                    O my dear, O my dear.

'I love a man in secret,
Dear chambermaid,' said she.
'I know that I must drop down dead
If he stop loving me,
Yet what could I but drop down dead
If I lost my chastity?'
                    O my dear, O my dear.

'So you must lie beside him
And let him think me there,
And maybe we are all the same
Where no candles are,
And maybe we are all the same
That strip the body bare.'
                    O my dear, O my dear.

But no dogs barked, and midnights chimed,
And through the chime she'd say,

'That was a lucky thought of mine,
My lover looked so gay';
But heaved a sigh if the chambermaid
Looked half asleep all day.
                    O my dear, O my dear.

'No, not another song,' said he,
'Because my lady came
A year ago for the first time
At midnight to my room,
And I must lie between the sheets
When the clock begins to chime.'
                    O my dear, O my dear.

'A laughing, crying, sacred song,
A leching song,' they said.
Did ever men hear such a song?
No, but that day they did.
Did ever man ride such a race?
No, not until he rode.
                    O my dear, O my dear.

But when his horse had put its hoof
Into a rabbit-hole
He dropped upon his head and died.
His lady saw it all
And dropped and died thereon, for she
Loved him with her soul.
                    O my dear, O my dear.

The chambermaid lived long, and took
Their graves into her charge,
And there two bushes planted
That when they had grown large
Seemed sprung from but a single root
So did their roses merge.
                    O my dear, O my dear.

When she was old and dying,
The priest came where she was;
She made a full confession.
Long looked he in her face,
And O he was a good man
And understood her case.
                O my dear, O my dear.

He bade them take and bury her
Beside her lady's man,
And set a rose-tree on her grave,
And now none living can,
When they have plucked a rose there,
Know where its roots began.
                O my dear, O my dear.

rudyard kipling

REBIRTH

If any God should say
        'I will restore
The world her yesterday
        Whole as before
My Judgment blasted it'—who would not lift
Heart, eye, and hand in passion o'er the gift?

If any God should will
        To wipe from mind
The memory of this ill
        Which is mankind
In soul and substance now—who would not bless
Even to tears His loving-tenderness?

If any God should give
        Us leave to fly
These present deaths we live,

And safely die
In those lost lives we lived ere we were born—
What man but would not laugh the excuse to scorn?

For we are what we are—
So broke to blood
And the strict works of war—
So long subdued
To sacrifice, that threadbare Death commands
Hardly observance at our busier hands.

Yet we were what we were,
And, fashioned so,
It pleases us to stare
At the far show
Of unbelievable years and shapes that flit;
In our own likeness, on the edge of it.

SESTINA OF THE TRAMP-ROYAL

Speakin' in general, I 'ave tried 'em all—
The 'appy roads that take you o'er the world.
Speakin' in general, I 'ave found them good
For such as cannot use one bed too long,
But must get 'ence, the same as I 'ave done,
An' go observin' matters till they die.

What do it matter where or 'ow we die,
So long as we've our 'ealth to watch it all—
The different ways that different things are done,
An' men an' women lovin' in this world;
Takin' our chances as they come along,
An' when they ain't, pretendin' they are good?

In cash or credit—no, it aren't no good;
You 'ave to 'ave the 'abit or you'd die,
Unless you lived your life but one day long,

Nor didn't prophesy nor fret at all,
But drew your tucker some'ow from the world,
An' never bothered what you might ha' done.

But, Gawd, what things are they I 'aven't done!
I've turned my 'and to most, an' turned it good,
In various situations round the world—
For 'im that doth not work must surely die;
But that's no reason man should labor all
'Is life on one same shift—life's none so long.

Therefore, from job to job I've moved along.
Pay couldn't 'old me when my time was done,
For something in my 'ead upset it all,
Till I 'ad dropped whatever 't was for good,
An' out at sea, be'eld the dock-lights die,
An' met my mate—the wind that tramps the world!

It's like a book, I think, this bloomin' world,
Which you can read and care for just so long,
But presently you feel that you will die
Unless you get the page you're readin' done,
An' turn another—likely not so good;
But what you're after is to turn 'em all.

Gawd bless this world! Whatever she 'ath done—
Excep' when awful long—I've found it good.
So write, before I die, ' 'E liked it all!'

DANNY DEEVER

'What are the bugles blowin' for?' said Files-on-Parade.
'To turn you out, to turn you out,' the Color-Sergeant said.
'What makes you look so white, so white?' said Files-on-Parade.
'I'm dreadin' what I've got to watch,' the Color-Sergeant said.
   For they're hangin' Danny Deever, you can hear the Dead
   March play,

The regiment's in 'ollow square—they're hangin' him to-day;
They've taken of his buttons off an' cut his stripes away,
An' they're hangin' Danny Deever in the mornin'.

'What makes the rear-rank breathe so 'ard?' said Files-on-
    Parade.
'It's bitter cold, it's bitter cold,' the Color-Sergeant said.
'What makes that front-rank man fall down?' said Files-on-
    Parade.
'A touch o' sun, a touch o' sun,' the Color-Sergeant said.
    They are hangin' Danny Deever, they are marchin' of 'im
      round,
    They 'ave 'alted Danny Deever by 'is coffin on the ground;
    An' 'e'll swing in 'arf a minute for a sneakin' shootin'
      hound—
    O they're hangin' Danny Deever in the mornin'!

' 'Is cot was right-'and cot to mine,' said Files-on-Parade.
' 'E's sleepin' out an' far to-night,' the Color-Sergeant said.
'I've drunk 'is beer a score o' times,' said Files-on-Parade.
' 'E's drinkin' bitter beer alone,' the Color-Sergeant said.
    They are hangin' Danny Deever, you must mark 'im to 'is
      place,
    For 'e shot a comrade sleepin'—you must look 'im in the
      face;
    Nine 'undred of 'is county an' the regiment's disgrace,
    While they're hangin' Danny Deever in the mornin'.

'What's that so black agin the sun?' said Files-on-Parade.
'It's Danny fightin' 'ard for life,' the Color-Sergeant said.
'What's that that whimpers over'ead?' said Files-on-Parade.
'It's Danny's soul that's passin' now,' the Color-Sergeant said.
    For they're done with Danny Deever, you can 'ear the
      quickstep play,
    The Regiment's in column, an' they're marchin' us away;
    Ho! the young recruits are shakin', an' they'll want their
      beer to-day,
    After hangin' Danny Deever in the mornin'.

RECESSIONAL

God of our fathers, known of old,
    Lord of our far-flung battle-line,
Beneath whose awful hand we hold
    Dominion over palm and pine—
Lord God of Hosts, be with us yet,
Lest we forget—lest we forget!

The tumult and the shouting dies;
    The captains and the kings depart:
Still stands Thine ancient sacrifice,
    An humble and a contrite heart.
Lord God of Hosts, be with us yet,
Lest we forget—lest we forget!

Far-called, our navies melt away;
    On dune and headland sinks the fire:
Lo, all our pomp of yesterday
    Is one with Nineveh and Tyre!
Judge of the Nations, spare us yet,
Lest we forget—lest we forget!

If, drunk with sight of power, we loose
    Wild tongues that have not Thee in awe,
Such boastings as the Gentiles use,
    Or lesser breeds without the Law—
Lord God of Hosts, be with us yet,
Lest we forget—lest we forget!

For heathen heart that puts her trust
    In reeking tube and iron shard,
All valiant dust that builds on dust,
    And, guarding, calls not Thee to guard,
For frantic boast and foolish word—
Thy Mercy on Thy People, Lord!

WHEN EARTH'S LAST PICTURE IS PAINTED

When Earth's last picture is painted and the tubes are twisted
and dried,
When the oldest colors have faded, and the youngest critic has
died,
We shall rest, and, faith, we shall need it—lie down for an æon
or two,
Till the Master of All Good Workmen shall put us to work
anew.

And those that were good shall be happy: they shall sit in a
golden chair;
They shall splash at a ten-league canvas with brushes of
comets' hair.
They shall find real saints to draw from—Magdalene, Peter,
and Paul;
They shall work for an age at a sitting and never be tired at
all!

And only the Master shall praise us, and only the Master shall
blame;
And no one shall work for money, and no one shall work for
fame,
But each for the joy of the working, and each, in his separate
star,
Shall draw the Thing as he sees It for the God of Things as
They are!

MANDALAY

By the old Moulmein Pagoda, lookin' lazy at the sea,
There's a Burma girl a-settin', and I know she thinks o' me;
For the wind is in the palm-trees, and the temple-bells they
say:
'Come you back, you British soldier; come you back to Man-
dalay!'

Come you back to Mandalay,
Where the old Flotilla lay:
Can't you 'ear their paddles chunkin' from Rangoon to
  Mandalay?
On the road to Mandalay,
Where the flyin'-fishes play,
An' the dawn comes up like thunder outer China 'crost
  the Bay!

'Er petticoat was yaller an' 'er little cap was green,
An' 'er name was Supi-yaw-lat—jes' the same as Theebaw's
  Queen,
An' I seed her first a-smokin' of a whackin' white cheroot,
An' a-wastin' Christian kisses on an 'eathen idol's foot:
  Bloomin' idol made o' mud—
  Wot they called the Great Gawd Budd—
  Plucky lot she cared for idols when I kissed 'er where she
    stud!
  On the road to Mandalay ...

When the mist was on the rice-fields an' the sun was droppin'
  slow,
She'd git 'er little banjo an' she'd sing 'Kulla-lo-lo!'
With 'er arm upon my shoulder an' 'er cheek agin my cheek
We useter watch the steamers an' the *hathis* pilin' teak.
  Elephints a'pilin' teak
  In the sludgy, squdgy creek,
  Where the silence 'ung that 'eavy you was 'arf afraid to
    speak!
  On the road to Mandalay ...

But that's all shove be'ind me—long ago an' fur away,
An' there ain't no 'busses runnin' from the Bank to Mandalay;
An' I'm learnin' 'ere in London what the ten-year soldier tells:
'If you've 'eard the East a-callin', you won't never 'eed naught
  else.'
  No! you won't 'eed nothin' else
  But them spicy garlic smells,

L

An' the sunshine an' the palm-trees an' the tinkly-temple-bells;
    On the road to Mandalay . . .

I am sick o' wastin' leather on these gritty pavin'-stones,
An' the blasted English drizzle wakes the fever in my bones;
Tho' I walks with fifty 'ousemaids outer Chelsea to the Strand,
An' they talks a lot o' lovin', but wot do they understand?
        Beefy face an' grubby 'and—
        Law! wot do they understand?
I've a neater, sweeter maiden in a cleaner, greener land!
    On the road to Mandalay . . .

Ship me somewheres east of Suez, where the best is like the
    worst
Where there aren't no Ten Commandments an' a man can
    raise a thirst;
For the temple-bells are callin', an' it's there that I would be—
By the old Moulmein Pagoda, looking lazy at the sea;
        On the road to Mandalay,
        Where the old Flotilla lay,
        With our sick beneath the awnings when we went to
            Mandalay!
        O the road to Mandalay,
        Where the flyin'-fishes play,
        An' the dawn comes up like thunder outer China 'crost
            the Bay!

edwin markham

THE MAN WITH THE HOE

God made man in His own image
In the image of God He made him.—GENESIS

Bowed by the weight of centuries he leans
Upon his hoe and gazes on the ground,
The emptiness of ages in his face,
And on his back the burden of the world.

Who made him dead to rapture and despair,
A thing that grieves not and that never hopes,
Stolid and stunned, a brother to the ox?
Who loosened and let down this brutal jaw?
Whose was the hand that slanted back this brow?
Whose breath blew out the light within this brain?

Is this the Thing the Lord God made and gave
To have dominion over sea and land;
To trace the stars and search the heavens for power;
To feel the passion of Eternity?
Is this the dream He dreamed who shaped the suns
And markt their ways upon the ancient deep?
Down all the caverns of Hell to their last gulf
There is no shape more terrible than this—
More tongued with censure of the world's blind greed—
More filled with signs and portents for the soul—
More packt with danger to the universe.

What gulfs between him and the seraphim!
Slave of the wheel of labor, what to him
Are Plato and the swing of Pleiades?
What the long reaches of the peaks of song,
The rife of dawn, the reddening of the rose?
Through this dread shape the suffering ages look;
Time's tragedy is in that aching stoop;
Through this dread shape humanity betrayed,
Plundered, profaned and disinherited,
Cries protest to the Powers that made the world,
A protest that is also prophecy.

O masters, lords and rulers in all lands,
Is this the handiwork you give to God,
This monstrous thing distorted and soul-quencht?
How will you ever straighten up this shape;
Touch it again with immortality;
Give back the upward looking and the light;
Rebuild in it the music and the dream;

Make right the immemorial infamies,
Perfidious wrongs, immedicable woes?

O masters, lords and rulers in all lands,
How will the future reckon with this Man?
How answer his brute question in that hour
When whirlwinds of rebellion shake all shores?
How will it be with kingdoms and with kings—
With those who shaped him to the thing he is—
When this dumb Terror shall rise to judge the world,
After the silence of the centuries?

edgar lee masters

FIDDLER JONES

The earth keeps some vibration going
There in your heart, and that is you.
And if the people find you can fiddle,
Why, fiddle you must, for all your life.
What do you see, a harvest of clover?
Or a meadow to walk through to the river?
The wind's in the corn; you rub your hands
For beeves hereafter ready for market;
Or else you hear the rustle of skirts
Like the girls when dancing at Little Grove.
To Cooney Potter a pillar of dust
Or whirling leaves meant ruinous drouth;
They looked to me like Red-Head Sammy
Stepping it off, to 'Toor-a-Loor.'
How could I till my forty acres
Not to speak of getting more,
With a medley of horns, bassoons and piccolos
Stirred in my brain by crows and robins
And the creak of a wind-mill—only these?
And I never started to plow in my life
That some one did not stop in the road

And take me away to a dance or picnic.
I ended up with forty acres;
I ended up with a broken fiddle—
And a broken laugh, and a thousand memories,
And not a single regret.

CARL HAMBLIN

The press of the Spoon River *Clarion* was wrecked,
And I was tarred and feathered,
For publishing this on the day the Anarchists were hanged in
    Chicago:
"I saw a beautiful woman with bandaged eyes
Standing on the steps of a marble temple.
Great multitudes passed in front of her,
Lifting their faces to her imploringly.
In her left hand she held a sword.
She was brandishing the sword,
Sometimes striking a child, again a laborer,
Again a slinking woman, again a lunatic.
In her right hand she held a scale;
Into the scale pieces of gold were tossed
By those who dodged the strokes of the sword.
A man in a black gown read from a manuscript:
'She is no respecter of persons.'
Then a youth wearing a red cap
Leaped to her side and snatched away the bandage.
And lo, the lashes had been eaten away
From the oozy eye-lids;
The eye-balls were seared with a milky mucus;
The madness of a dying soul
Was written on her face—
But the multitude saw why she wore the bandage."

THE VILLAGE ATHEIST

Ye young debaters over the doctrine
Of the soul's immortality,
I who lie here was the village atheist,
Talkative, contentious, versed in the arguments
Of the infidels.
But through a long sickness
Coughing myself to death
I read the *Upanishads* and the poetry of Jesus.
And they lighted a torch of hope and intuition
And desire which the Shadow,
Leading me swiftly through the caverns of darkness,
Could not extinguish.
Listen to me, ye who live in the senses
And think through the senses only:
Immortality is not a gift,
Immortality is an achievement;
And only those who strive mightily
Shall possess it.

edwin arlington robinson

THE DARK HILLS

Dark hills at evening in the west,
Where sunset hovers like a sound
Of golden horns that sang to rest
Old bones of warriors under ground,
Far now from all the bannered ways
Where flash the legions of the sun,
You fade—as if the last of days
Were fading, and all wars were done.

RICHARD CORY

Whenever Richard Cory went down town,
    We people on the pavement looked at him:
He was a gentleman from sole to crown,
    Clean favored, and imperially slim.

And he was always quietly arrayed,
    And he was always human when he talked;
But still he fluttered pulses when he said,
    "Good-morning," and he glittered when he walked.

And he was rich—yes, richer than a king,
    And admirably schooled in every grace:
In fine, we thought that he was everything
    To make us wish that we were in his place.

So on we worked, and waited for the light,
    And went without the meat, and cursed the bread;
And Richard Cory, one calm summer night,
    Went home and put a bullet through his head.

FOR A DEAD LADY

No more with overflowing light
Shall fill the eyes that now are faded,
Nor shall another's fringe with night
Their woman-hidden world as they did.
No more shall quiver down the days
The flowing wonder of her ways,
Whereof no language may requite
The shifting and the many-shaded.

The grace, divine, definitive,
Clings only as a faint forestalling;
The laugh that love could not forgive
Is hushed, and answers to no calling;
The forehead and the little ears
Have gone where Saturn keeps the years;

The breast where roses could not live
Has done with rising and with falling.

The beauty, shattered by the laws
That have creation in their keeping,
No longer trembles at applause,
Or over children that are sleeping;
And we who delve in beauty's lore
Know all that we have known before
Of what inexorable cause
Makes Time so vicious in his reaping.

MR. FLOOD'S PARTY

Old Eben Flood, climbing alone one night
Over the hill between the town below
And the forsaken upland hermitage
That held as much as he should ever know
On earth again of home, paused warily.
The road was his with not a native near;
And Eben, having leisure, said aloud,
For no man else in Tilbury Town to hear:

'Well, Mr. Flood, we have the harvest moon
Again, and we may not have many more;
The bird is on the wing, the poet says,
And you and I have said it here before.
Drink to the bird.' He raised up to the light
The jug that he had gone so far to fill,
And answered huskily: 'Well, Mr. Flood,
Since you propose it, I believe I will.'

Alone, as if enduring to the end
A valiant armor of scarred hopes outworn,
He stood there in the middle of the road
Like Roland's ghost winding a silent horn.
Below him, in the town among the trees,

Where friends of other days had honored him,
A phantom salutation of the dead
Rang thinly till old Eben's eyes were dim.

Then, as a mother lays her sleeping child
Down tenderly, fearing it may awake,
He set the jug down slowly at his feet
With trembling care, knowing that most things break;
And only when assured that on firm earth
It stood, as the uncertain lives of men
Assuredly did not, he paced away,
And with his hand extended paused again:

'Well, Mr. Flood, we have not met like this
In a long time; and many a change has come
To both of us, I fear, since last it was
We had a drop together. Welcome home!'
Convivially returning with himself,
Again he raised the jug up to the light;
And with an acquiescent quaver said:
'Well, Mr. Flood, if you insist, I might.

'Only a very little, Mr. Flood—
For auld lang syne. No more, sir; that will do.'
So, for the time, apparently it did,
And Eben evidently thought so too;
For soon amid the silver loneliness
Of night he lifted up his voice and sang,
Secure, with only two moons listening,
Until the whole harmonious landscape rang—

'For auld lang syne.' The weary throat gave out,
The last word wavered, and the song was done.
He raised again the jug regretfully
And shook his head, and was again alone.
There was not much that was ahead of him,
And there was nothing in the town below—
Where strangers would have shut the many doors
That many friends had opened long ago.

WALT WHITMAN

The master-songs are ended, and the man
That sang them is a name. And so is God
A name; and so is love, and life, and death,
And everything. But we, who are too blind
To read what we have written, or what faith
Has written for us, do not understand:
We only blink, and wonder.

Last night it was the song that was the man,
But now it is the man that is the song.
We do not hear him very much to-day:
His piercing and eternal cadence rings
Too pure for us—too powerfully pure,
Too lovingly triumphant, and too large;
But there are some that hear him, and they know
That he shall sing to-morrow for all men,
And that all time shall listen.

The master-songs are ended? Rather say
No songs are ended that are ever sung,
And that no names are dead names. When we write
Men's letters on proud marble or on sand,
We write them there forever.

CLIFF KLINGENHAGEN

Cliff Klingenhagen had me in to dine
With him one day; and after soup and meat,
And all the other things there were to eat,
Cliff took two glasses and filled one with wine
And one with wormwood. Then, without a sign
For me to choose at all, he took the draught
Of bitterness himself, and lightly quaffed
It off, and said the other one was mine.
And when I asked him what the deuce he meant
By doing that, he only looked at me

And grinned, and said it was a way of his.
And though I know the fellow, I have spent
Long time a-wondering when I shall be
As happy as Cliff Klingenhagen is.

REUBEN BRIGHT

Because he was a butcher and thereby
Did earn an honest living (and did right)
I would not have you think that Reuben Bright
Was any more a brute than you or I;
For when they told him that his wife must die,
He stared at them and shook with grief and fright,
And cried like a great baby half that night,
And made the women cry to see him cry.
And after she was dead, and he had paid
The singers and the sexton and the rest,
He packed a lot of things that she had made
Most mournfully away in an old chest
Of hers, and put some chopped-up cedar boughs
In with them, and tore down the slaughter-house.

CREDO

I cannot find my way: there is no star
In all the shrouded heavens anywhere;
And there is not a whisper in the air
Of any living voice but one so far
That I can hear it only as a bar
Of lost, imperial music, played when fair
And angel fingers wove, and unaware,
Dead leaves to garlands where no roses are.
No, there is not a glimmer, nor a call,
For one that welcomes, welcomes when he fears,
The black and awful chaos of the night;
But through it all,—above, beyond it all—
I know the far-sent message of the years,
I feel the coming glory of the Light!

LUKE HAVERGAL

Go to the western gate, Luke Havergal,
There where the vines cling crimson on the wall,
And in the twilight wait for what will come.
The leaves will whisper there of her, and some,
Like flying words, will strike you as they fall;
But go, and if you listen, she will call.
Go to the western gate, Luke Havergal—
Luke Havergal.

No, there is not a dawn in eastern skies
To rift the fiery night that's in your eyes;
But there, where western glooms are gathering,
The dark will end the dark, if anything:
God slays himself with every leaf that flies,
And hell is more than half of paradise.
No, there is not a dawn in eastern skies—
In eastern skies.

Out of a grave I come to tell you this,
Out of a grave I come to quench the kiss
That flames upon your forehead with a glow
That blinds you to the way that you must go.
Yes, there is yet one way to where she is,
Bitter, but one that faith may never miss.
Out of a grave I come to tell you this—
To tell you this.

There is the western gate, Luke Havergal,
There are the crimson leaves upon the wall.
Go, for the winds are tearing them away,—
Nor think to riddle the dead words they say,
Nor any more to feel them as they fall;
But go, and if you trust her she will call.
There is the western gate, Luke Havergal—
Luke Havergal.

stephen crane

I STOOD UPON A HIGH PLACE

I stood upon a high place,
And saw, below, many devils
Running, leaping,
And carousing in sin.
One looked up, grinning,
And said, "Comrade! Brother!"

A MAN SAW A BALL OF GOLD IN THE SKY

A man saw a ball of gold in the sky;
He climbed for it,
And eventually he achieved it—
It was clay.

Now this is the strange part:
When the man went to the earth
And looked again,
Lo, there was the ball of gold.
Now this is the strange part:
It was a ball of gold.
Ay, by the heavens, it was a ball of gold.

IT WAS WRONG TO DO THIS, SAID THE ANGEL

"It was wrong to do this," said the angel.
"You should live like a flower,
Holding malice like a puppy,
Waging war like a lambkin."

"Not so," quoth the man
Who had no fear of spirits;
"It is only wrong for angels
Who can live like flowers,
Holding malice like the puppies,
Waging war like the lambkins."

w. h. davies

LEISURE

What is this life, if, full of care,
We have no time to stand and stare,

No time to stand beneath the boughs
And stare as long as sheep or cows.

No time to see, when woods we pass,
Where squirrels hide their nuts in grass.

No time to see, in broad daylight,
Streams full of stars, like skies at night.

No time to turn at Beauty's glance,
And watch her feet, how they can dance.

No time to wait till her mouth can
Enrich that smile her eyes began.

A poor life this if, full of care,
We have no time to stand and stare.

THE WHITE MONSTER

Last night I saw the monster near; the big
White monster that was like a lazy slug,
That hovered in the air, not far away,
As quiet as the black hawk seen by day.
I saw it turn its body round about,
And look my way; I saw its big, fat snout
Turn straight towards my face, till I was one
In coldness with that statue made of stone,
The one-armed sailor seen upon my right—
With no more power than he to offer fight;
The great white monster slug that, even then,

Killed women, children, and defenceless men.
But soon its venom was discharged, and it,
Knowing it had no more the power to spit
Death on the most defenceless English folk,
Let out a large, thick cloud of its own smoke;
And when the smoke had cleared away from there,
I saw no sign of any monster near;
And nothing but the stars to give alarm—
That never did the earth a moment's harm.
Oh, it was strange to see a thing like jelly,
An ugly, boneless thing all back and belly,
Among the peaceful stars—that should have been
A mile deep in the sea, and never seen:
A big, fat, lazy slug that, even then,
Killed women, children, and defenceless men.

walter de la mare

THE BOTTLE

Of green and hexagonal glass,
　　With sharp, fluted sides—
Vaguely transparent these walls,
　　Wherein motionless hides
A simple so potent it can
　　To oblivion lull
The weary, the racked, the bereaved,
　　The miserable.

Flowers in silent desire
　　Their life-breath exhale—
Self-heal, hellebore, aconite,
　　Chamomile, dwale:
Sharing the same gentle heavens,
　　The sun's heat and light,
And, in the dust at their roots,
　　The same shallow night.

Each its own livelihood hath,
    Shape, pattern, hue;
Age on to age unto these
    Keeping steadfastly true;
And, musing amid them, there moves
    A stranger, named Man,
Who of their ichor distils
    What virtue he can;

Plucks them ere seed-time to blazon
His house with their radiant dyes;
Prisons their attar in wax;
Candies their petals; denies
Them freedom to breed in their wont;
Buds, fecundates, grafts them at will;
And with cunningest leechcraft compels
    Their good to his ill.

Intrigue fantastic as this
    Where shall we find?
Mute in their beauty they serve him,
    Body and mind.
And one—but a weed in his wheat—
Is the poppy—frail, pallid, whose juice
With its saplike and opiate fume
    Strange dreams will induce

Of wonder and horror. And none
    Can silence the soul,
Wearied of self and of life,
    Earth's darkness and dole,
More secretly, deeply. But finally?—
    Waste not thy breath;
The words that are scrawled on this phial
    Have for synonym, death—

Wicket out into the dark
    That swings but one way;

Infinite hush in an ocean of silence
    Aeons away—
Thou forsaken!—even thou!—
    The dread good-bye;
The abandoned, the thronged, the watched, the unshared—
    Awaiting me—I!

THE LISTENERS

'Is there anybody there?' said the Traveller,
    Knocking on the moonlit door;
And his horse in the silence champed the grasses
    Of the forest's ferny floor:
And a bird flew up out of the turret,
    Above the Traveller's head:
And he smote upon the door again a second time;
    'Is there anybody there?' he said.
But no one descended to the Traveller;
    No head from the leaf-fringed sill
Leaned over and looked into his grey eyes,
    Where he stood perplexed and still.
But only a host of phantom listeners
    That dwelt in the lone house then
Stood listening in the quiet of the moonlight
    To that voice from the world of men:
Stood thronging the faint moonbeams on the dark stair,
    That goes down to the empty hall,
Hearkening in an air stirred and shaken
    By the lonely Traveller's call.
And he felt in his heart their strangeness,
    Their stillness answering his cry,
While his horse moved, cropping the dark turf,
    'Neath the starred and leafy sky;
For he suddenly smote on the door, even
    Louder, and lifted his head:—
'Tell them I came, and no one answered,
    That I kept my word,' he said.
Never the least stir made the listeners,

Though every word he spake
Fell echoing through the shadowiness of the still house
    From the one man left awake:
Ay, they heard his foot upon the stirrup,
    And the sound of iron on stone,
And how the silence surged softly backward,
    When the plunging hoofs were gone.

SUNK LYONESSE

In sea-cold Lyonesse,
When the Sabbath eve shafts down
On the roofs, walls, belfries
Of the foundered town,
The Nereids pluck their lyres
Where the green translucency beats,
And with motionless eyes at gaze
Make minstrelsy in the streets.
And the ocean water stirs
In salt-worn casement and porch.
Plies the blunt-snouted fish
With fire in his skull for torch.
And the ringing wires resound;
And the unearthly lovely weep,
In lament of the music they make
In the sullen courts of sleep:
Whose marble flowers bloom for aye:
And—lapped by the moon-guiled tide—
Mock their carver with heart of stone,
Caged in his stone-ribbed side.

NIGHT

That shining moon—watched by that one faint star:
Sure now am I, beyond the fear of change,
The lovely in life is the familiar,
And only the lovelier for continuing strange.

THE CHILDREN OF STARE

Winter is fallen early
On the house of Stare,
Birds in reverberating flocks
Haunt its ancestral box;
Bright are the plenteous berries
In clusters in the air.

Still is the fountain's music,
The dark pool icy still,
Whereupon a small and sanguine sun
Floats in a mirror on,
Into a West of crimson,
From a South of daffodil.

'Tis strange to see young children
In such a wintry house;
Like rabbits' on the frozen snow
Their tell-tale footprints go;
Their laughter rings like timbrels
'Neath evening ominous:

Their small and heightened faces
Like wine-red winter buds;
Their frolic bodies gentle as
Flakes in the air that pass,
Frail as the twirling petal
From the briar of the woods.

Above them silence lours,
Still as an arctic sea;
Light fails; night falls; the wintry moon
Glitters; the crocus soon
Will open grey and distracted
On earth's austerity:

Thick mystery, wild peril,
Law like an iron rod:—

Yet sport they on in Spring's attire,
    Each with his tiny fire
    Blown to a core of ardour
    By the awful breath of God.

A PORTRAIT

Old: yet unchanged;—still pottering in his thoughts;
Still eagerly enslaved by books and print;
Less plagued, perhaps, by rigid musts and oughts,
But no less frantic in vain argument;

Still happy as a child, with its small toys,
Over his inkpot and his bits and pieces,—
Life's arduous, fragile and ingenuous joys,
Whose charm failed never—nay, it even increases!

Ev'n happier in watch of bird or flower,
Rainbow in heaven, or bud on thorny spray,
A star-strewn nightfall, and that heart-break hour
Of sleep-drowsed senses between dawn and day;

Loving the light—laved eyes in those wild hues!—
And dryad twilight, and the thronging dark;
A Crusoe ravished by mere solitude—
And silence—edged with music's faintest *Hark!*

And any chance-seen face whose loveliness
Hovers, a mystery, between dream and real;
Things usual yet miraculous that bless
And overwell a heart that still can feel;

Haunted by questions no man answered yet;
Pining to leap from A clean on to Z;
Absorbed by problems which the wise forget;
Avid for fantasy—yet how staid a head!

Senses at daggers with his intellect;
Quick, stupid; vain, retiring; ardent, cold;
Faithful and fickle; rash and circumspect;
And never yet at rest in any fold;

Punctual at meals; a spendthrift, close as Scot;
Rebellious, tractable, childish—long gone grey!
Impatient, volatile, tongue wearying not—
Loose, too; which, yet, thank heaven, was taught to pray;

'Childish' indeed!—a waif on shingle shelf
Fronting the rippled sands, the sun, the sea;
And nought but his marooned precarious self
For questing consciousness and will-to-be;

A feeble venturer—in a world so wide!
So rich in action, daring, cunning, strife!
You'd think, poor soul, he had taken Sloth for bride,—
Unless the imagined is the breath of life;

Unless to speculate bring virgin gold,
And *Let's-pretend* can range the seven seas,
And dreams are not mere tales by idiot told,
And tongueless truth may hide in fantasies;

Unless the alone may their own company find,
And churchyards harbour phantoms 'mid their bones,
And even a daisy may suffice a mind
Whose bindweed can redeem a heap of stones;

Too frail a basket for so many eggs—
Loose-woven: Gosling? cygnet? Laugh or weep?
Or is the cup at richest in its dregs?
The actual realest on the verge of sleep?

One yet how often the prey of doubt and fear,
Of bleak despondence, stark anxiety;

Ardent for what is neither now nor here,
An Orpheus fainting for Eurydice;

Not yet inert, but with a tortured breast
At hint of that bleak gulf—his last farewell;
Pining for peace, assurance, pause and rest,
Yet slave to what he loves past words to tell;

A foolish, fond old man, his bed-time nigh,
Who still at western window stays to win
A transient respite from the latening sky,
And scarce can bear it when the Sun goes in.

THE ROUND

I watched, upon a vase's rim,
An earwig—strayed from honeyed cell—
Circling a track once strange to him,
But now known far too well.

With vexed antennae, searching space,
And giddy grope to left and right,
On—and still on—he pressed apace,
Out of, and into, sight.

In circumambulation drear,
He neither wavered, paused nor stayed;
But now kind Providence drew near—
A slip of wood I laid

Across his track. He scaled its edge:
And soon was safely restored to where
A sappy, dew-bright, flowering hedge
Of dahlias greened the air.

Ay, and as apt may be my fate! . . . . .
Smiling, I turned to work again:
But shivered, where in shade I sate,
And idle did remain.

edward thomas

THE OWL

Down hill I came, hungry, and yet not starved;
Cold, yet had heat within me that was proof
Against the North wind; tired, yet so that rest
Had seemed the sweetest thing under a roof.

Then at the inn I had food, fire, and rest,
Knowing how hungry, cold, and tired was I.
All of the night was quite barred out except
An owl's cry, a most melancholy cry

Shaken out long and clear upon the hill,
No merry note, nor cause of merriment,
But one telling me plain what I escaped
And others could not, that night, as in I went.

And salted was my food, and my repose,
Salted and sobered, too, by the bird's voice
Speaking for all who lay under the stars,
Soldiers and poor, unable to rejoice.

james joyce

THE BALLAD OF PERSSE O'REILLY

Have you heard of one Humpty Dumpty
How he fell with a roll and a rumble
And curled up like Lord Olofa Crumple
By the butt of the Magazine Wall,
    (*Chorus*) Of the Magazine Wall,
          Hump, helmet and all?

He was one time our King of the Castle
Now he's kicked about like a rotten old parsnip.

And from Green street he'll be sent by order of his Worship
To the penal jail of Mountjoy
   (Chorus) To the jail of Mountjoy!
         Jail him and joy.

He was fafafather of all schemes for to bother us
Slow coaches and immaculate contraceptives for the populace,
Mare's milk for the sick, seven dry Sundays a week,
Openair love and religion's reform,
   (Chorus) And religious reform,
         Hideous in form.

Arrah, why, says you, couldn't he manage it?
I'll go bail, my fine dairyman darling,
Like the bumping bull of the Cassidys
All your butter is in your horns.
   (Chorus) His butter is in his horns.
         Butter his horns!

(Repeat) Hurrah there, Hosty, frosty Hosty, change that shirt
       on ye,
       Rhyme the rann, the king of all ranns!

       Balbaccio, balbuccio!
We had chaw chaw chops, chairs, chewing gum, the chicken-
    pox and china chambers
Universally provided by this soffsoaping salesman.
Small wonder He'll Cheat E'erawan our local lads nicknamed
    him
When Chimpden first took the floor
   (Chorus) With his bucketshop store
         Down Bargainweg, Lower.

So snug he was in his hotel premises sumptuous
But soon we'll bonfire all his trash, tricks and trumpery
And 'tis short till sheriff Clancy'll be winding up his unlimited
    company
With the bailiff's bom at the door,

(*Chorus*) Bimbam at the door.
　　　　Then he'll bum no more.

Sweet bad luck on the waves washed to our island
The hooker of that hammerfast viking
And Gall's curse on the day when Eblana bay
Saw his black and tan man-o'-war.
　　(*Chorus*) Saw his man-o'-war.
　　　　　　On the harbour bar.

Where from? roars Poolbeg. Cookingha'pence, he bawls Don-
　　nezmoi scampitle, wick an wipin'fampiny
Fingal Mac Oscar Onesine Bargearse Boniface
Thok's min gammelhole Norveegickers moniker
Og as ay are at gammelhore Norveegickers cod.
　　(*Chorus*) A Norwegian camel old cod.
　　　　　　He is, begod.

Lift it, Hosty, lift it, ye devil ye! up with the rann, the rhym-
　　ing rann!

It was during some fresh water garden pumping
Or, according to the *Nursing Mirror*, while admiring the
　　monkeys
That our heavyweight heathen Humpharey
Made bold a maid to woo
　　(*Chorus*) Woohoo, what'll she doo!
　　　　　　The general lost her maidenloo!

He ought to blush for himself, the old hayheaded philosopher,
For to go and shove himself that way on top of her.
Begob, he's the crux of the catalogue
Of our antediluvial zoo,
　　(*Chorus*) Messrs. Billing and Coo.
　　　　　　Noah's larks, good as noo.

He was joulting by Wellinton's monument
Our rotorious hippopopotamuns

When some bugger let down the backtrap of the omnibus
And he caught his death of fusiliers,
  (Chorus) With his rent in his rears.
        Give him six years.

'Tis sore pity for his innocent poor children
But look out for his missus legitimate!
When that frew gets a grip of old Earwicker
Won't there be earwigs on the green?
  (Chorus) Big earwigs on the green,
        The largest ever you seen.

Suffoclose! Shikespower! Seudodanto! Anonymoses!

Then we'll have a free trade Gaels' band and mass meeting
For to sod the brave son of Scandiknavery.
And we'll bury him down in Oxmanstown
Along with the devil and Danes,
  (Chorus) With the deaf and dumb Danes,
        And all their remains.

And not all the king's men nor his horses
Will resurrect his corpus
For there's no true spell in Connacht or hell
  (bis) That's able to raise a Cain.

                          From *Finnegan's Wake*

THE HOLY OFFICE

Myself unto myself will give
This name, Katharsis-Purgative.
I, who dishevelled ways forsook
To hold the poets' grammar-book,
Bringing to tavern and to brothel
The mind of witty Aristotle,
Lest bards in the attempt should err
Must here be my interpreter:

Wherefore receive now from my lip
Peripatetic scholarship.
To enter heaven, travel hell,
Be piteous or terrible
One positively needs the ease
Of plenary indulgences.
For every true-born mysticist
A Dante is, unprejudiced,
Who safe at ingle-nook, by proxy,
Hazards extremes of heterodoxy,
Like him who finds joy at a table
Pondering the uncomfortable.
Ruling one's life by common sense
How can one fail to be intense?
But I must not accounted be
One of that mumming company—
With him who hies him to appease
His giddy dames' frivolities
While they console him when he whinges
With gold-embroidered Celtic fringes—
Or him who sober all the day
Mixes a naggin in his play—
Or him whose conduct 'seems to own'
His preference for a man of 'tone'—
Or him who plays the ragged patch
To millionaires in Hazelpatch
But weeping after holy fast
Confesses all his pagan past—
Or him who will his hat unfix
Neither to malt nor crucifix
But show to all that poor-dressed be
His high Castilian courtesy—
Or him who loves his Master dear—
Or him who drinks his pint in fear—
Or him who once when snug abed
Saw Jesus Christ without his head
And tried so hard to win for us
The long-lost works of Aeschylus.

But all these men of whom I speak
Make me the sewer of their clique.
That they may dream their dreamy dreams
I carry off their filthy streams
For I can do those things for them
Through which I lost my diadem,
Those things for which Grandmother Church
Left me severely in the lurch.
Thus I relieve their timid arses,
Perform my office of Katharsis.
My scarlet leaves them white as wool:
Through me they purge a bellyful.
To sister mummers one and all
I act as vicar-general
And for each maiden, shy and nervous,
I do a similar kind service.
For I detect without surprise
That shadowy beauty in her eyes,
The 'dare not' of sweet maidenhood
That answers my corruptive 'would',
Whenever publicly we meet
She never seems to think of it;
At night when close in bed she lies
And feels my hand between her thighs
My little love in light attire
Knows the soft flame that is desire.
But Mammon places under ban
The uses of Leviathan
And that high spirit ever wars
On Mammon's countless servitors
Nor can they ever be exempt
From his taxation of contempt.
So distantly I turn to view
The shamblings of that motley crew,
Those souls that hate the strength that mine has
Steeled in the school of old Aquinas.
Where they have crouched and crawled and prayed
I stand, the self-doomed, unafraid,

Unfellowed, friendless and alone,
Indifferent as the herring-bone,
Firm as the mountain-ridges where
I flash my antlers on the air.
Let them continue as is meet
To adequate the balance-sheet.
Though they may labour to the grave
My spirit shall they never have
Nor make my soul with theirs as one
Till the Mahamanvantara be done:
And though they spurn me from their door
My soul shall spurn them evermore.

robert frost

NEITHER OUT FAR NOR IN DEEP

The people along the sand
All turn and look one way.
They turn their back on the land.
They look at the sea all day.

As long as it takes to pass
A ship keeps raising its hull;
The wetter ground like glass
Reflects a standing gull.

The land may vary more;
But wherever the truth may be—
The water comes ashore,
And the people look at the sea.

They cannot look out far.
They cannot look in deep.
But when was that ever a bar
To any watch they keep?

PROVIDE PROVIDE

The witch that came (the withered hag)
To wash the steps with pail and rag,
Was once the beauty Abishag,

The picture pride of Hollywood.
Too many fall from great and good
For you to doubt the likelihood.

Die early and avoid the fate.
Or if predestined to die late,
Make up your mind to die in state.

Make the whole stock exchange your own!
If need be occupy a throne,
Where nobody can call *you* crone.

Some have relied on what they knew;
Others on being simply true.
What worked for them might work for you.

No memory of having starred
Atones for later disregard,
Or keeps the end from being hard.

Better to go down dignified
With boughten friendship at your side
Than none at all. Provide, provide!

THE ONSET

Always the same, when on a fated night
At last the gathered snow lets down as white
As may be in dark woods, and with a song
It shall not make again all winter long
Of hissing on the yet uncovered ground,

I almost stumble looking up and round,
As one who overtaken by the end
Gives up his errand, and lets death descend
Upon him where he is, with nothing done
To evil, no important triumph won,
More than if life had never been begun.

Yet all the precedent is on my side:
I know that winter death has never tried
The earth but it has failed: the snow may heap
In long storms an undrifted four feet deep
As measured against maple, birch and oak,
It cannot check the peeper's silver croak;
And I shall see the snow all go down hill
In water of a slender April rill
That flashes tail through last year's withered brake
And dead weeds, like a disappearing snake.
Nothing will be left white but here a birch,
And there a clump of houses with a church.

DESIGN

I found a dimpled spider, fat and white,
On a white heal-all, holding up a moth
Like a white piece of rigid satin cloth—
Assorted characters of death and blight
Mixed ready to begin the morning right,
Like the ingredients of a witches' broth—
A snow-drop spider, a flower like froth,
And dead wings carried like a paper kite.
What had that flower to do with being white,
The wayside blue and innocent heal-all?
What brought the kindred spider to that height,
Then steered the white moth thither in the night?
What but design of darkness to appall?—
If design govern in a thing so small.

MENDING WALL

Something there is that doesn't love a wall,
That sends the frozen-ground-swell under it,
And spills the upper boulders in the sun;
And makes gaps even two can pass abreast.
The work of hunters is another thing:
I have come after them and made repair
Where they have left not one stone on a stone,
But they would have the rabbit out of hiding,
To please the yelping dogs. The gaps I mean,
No one has seen them made or heard them made,
But at spring mending-time we find them there.
I let my neighbour know beyond the hill;
And on a day we meet to walk the line
And set the wall between us once again.
We keep the wall between us as we go.
To each the boulders that have fallen to each.
And some are loaves and some so nearly balls
We have to use a spell to make them balance:
'Stay where you are until our backs are turned!'
We wear our fingers rough with handling them.
Oh, just another kind of out-door game,
One on a side. It comes to little more:
There where it is we do not need the wall:
He is all pine and I am apple orchard.
My apple trees will never get across
And eat the cones under his pines, I tell him.
He only says, 'Good fences make good neighbours.'
Spring is the mischief in me, and I wonder
If I could put a notion in his head:
'*Why* do they make good neighbours? Isn't it
Where there are cows? But here there are no cows.
Before I built a wall I'd ask to know
What I was walling in or walling out,
And to whom I was like to give offence.
Something there is that doesn't love a wall,
That wants it down.' I could say 'Elves' to him,

But it's not elves exactly, and I'd rather
He said it for himself. I see him there
Bringing a stone grasped firmly by the top
In each hand, like an old-stone savage armed.
He moves in darkness as it seems to me,
Not of woods only and the shade of trees.
He will not go behind his father's saying,
And he likes having thought of it so well
He says again, 'Good fences make good neighbours.'

THE ROAD NOT TAKEN

Two roads diverged in a yellow wood,
And sorry I could not travel both
And be one traveler, long I stood
And looked down one as far as I could
To where it bent in the undergrowth;

Then took the other, as just as fair,
And having perhaps the better claim,
Because it was grassy and wanted wear;
Though as for that the passing there
Had worn them really about the same,

And both that morning equally lay
In leaves no step had trodden black.
Oh, I kept the first for another day!
Yet knowing how way leads on to way,
I doubted if I should ever come back.

I shall be telling this with a sigh
Somewhere ages and ages hence:
Two roads diverged in a wood, and I—
I took the one less traveled by,
And that has made all the difference.

AFTER APPLE-PICKING

My long two-pointed ladder's sticking through a tree
Toward heaven still,
And there's a barrel that I didn't fill
Beside it, and there may be two or three
Apples I didn't pick upon some bough.
But I am done with apple-picking now.
Essence of winter sleep is on the night,
The scent of apples: I am drowsing off.
I cannot rub the strangeness from my sight
I got from looking through a pane of glass
I skimmed this morning from the drinking trough
And held against the world of hoary grass.
It melted, and I let it fall and break.
But I was well
Upon my way to sleep before it fell,
And I could tell
What form my dreaming was about to take.
Magnified apples appear and disappear
Stem end and blossom end,
And every fleck of russet showing clear.
My instep arch not only keeps the ache,
It keeps the pressure of a ladder-round.
I feel the ladder sway as the boughs bend.
And I keep hearing from the cellar bin
The rumbling sound
Of load on load of apples coming in.
For I have had too much
Of apple-picking: I am overtired
Of the great harvest I myself desired.
There were ten thousand thousand fruit to touch,
Cherish in hand, lift down, and not let fall.
For all
That struck the earth,
No matter if not bruised or spiked with stubble,
Went surely to the cider-apple heap
As of no worth.

One can see what will trouble
This sleep of mine, whatever sleep it is.
Were he not gone,
The woodchuck could say whether it's like his
Long sleep, as I describe its coming on,
Or just some human sleep.

TWO TRAMPS IN MUD TIME

Out of the mud two strangers came
And caught me splitting wood in the yard.
And one of them put me off my aim
By hailing cheerily "Hit them hard!"
I knew pretty well why he dropped behind
And let the other go on a way.
I knew pretty well what he had in mind:
He wanted to take my job for pay.

Good blocks of beech it was I split,
As large around as the chopping block;
And every piece I squarely hit
Fell splinterless as a cloven rock.
The blows that a life of self-control
Spares to strike for the common good
That day, giving a loose to my soul,
I spent on the unimportant wood.

The sun was warm but the wind was chill.
You know how it is with an April day
When the sun is out and the wind is still,
You're one month on in the middle of May.
But if you so much as dare to speak,
A cloud comes over the sunlit arch,
A wind comes off a frozen peak,
And you're two months back in the middle of March.

A bluebird comes tenderly up to alight
And fronts the wind to unruffle a plume
His song so pitched as not to excite
A single flower as yet to bloom.
It is snowing a flake: and he half knew
Winter was only playing possum.
Except in color he isn't blue,
But he wouldn't advise a thing to blossom.

The water for which we may have to look
In summertime with a witching-wand,
In every wheelrut's now a brook,
In every print of a hoof a pond.
Be glad of water, but don't forget
The lurking frost in the earth beneath
That will steal forth after the sun is set
And show on the water its crystal teeth.

The time when most I loved my task
These two must make me love it more
By coming with what they came to ask.
You'd think I never had felt before
The weight of an ax-head poised aloft,
The grip on earth of outspread feet,
The life of muscles rocking soft
And smooth and moist in vernal heat.

Out of the woods two hulking tramps
(From sleeping God knows where last night,
But not long since in the lumber camps).
They thought all chopping was theirs of right.
Men of the woods and lumberjacks,
They judged me by their appropriate tool.
Except as a fellow handled an ax,
They had no way of knowing a fool.

Nothing on either side was said.
They knew they had but to stay their stay

And all their logic would fill my head:
As that I had no right to play
With what was another man's work for gain.
My right might be love but theirs was need.
And where the two exist in twain
Theirs was the better right—agreed.

But yield who will to their separation,
My object in living is to unite
My avocation and my vocation
As my two eyes make one in sight.
Only where love and need are one,
And the work is play for mortal stakes,
Is the deed ever really done
For Heaven and the future's sakes.

STOPPING BY WOODS ON A SNOWY EVENING

Whose woods these are I think I know.
His house is in the village though;
He will not see me stopping here
To watch his woods fill up with snow.

My little horse must think it queer
To stop without a farmhouse near
Between the woods and frozen lake
The darkest evening of the year.

He gives his harness bells a shake
To ask if there is some mistake.
The only other sound's the sweep
Of easy wind and downy flake.

The woods are lovely, dark and deep.
But I have promises to keep,
And miles to go before I sleep,
And miles to go before I sleep.

MEETING AND PASSING

As I went down the hill along the wall
There was a gate I had leaned at for the view
And had just turned from when I first saw you
As you came up the hill. We met. But all
We did that day was mingle great and small
Footprints in summer dust as if we drew
The figure of our being less than two
But more than one as yet. Your parasol
Pointed the decimal off with one deep thrust.
And all the time we talked you seemed to see
Something down there to smile at in the dust.
(Oh, it was without prejudice to me!)
Afterward I went past what you had passed
Before we met and you what I had passed.

DIRECTIVE

Back out of all this now too much for us,
Back in a time made simple by the loss
Of detail, burned, dissolved, and broken off
Like graveyard marble sculpture in the weather,
There is a house that is no more a house
Upon a farm that is no more a farm
And in a town that is no more a town.
The road there, if you'll let a guide direct you
Who only has at heart your getting lost,
May seem as if it should have been a quarry—
Great monolithic knees the former town
Long since gave up pretence of keeping covered.
And there's a story in a book about it:
Besides the wear of iron wagon wheels
The ledges show lines ruled southeast northwest,
The chisel work of an enormous Glacier
That braced his feet against the Arctic Pole.
You must not mind a certain coolness from him

Still said to haunt this side of Panther Mountain.
Nor need you mind the serial ordeal
Of being watched from forty cellar holes
As if by eye pairs out of forty firkins.
As for the woods' excitement over you
That sends light rustle rushes to their leaves,
Charge that to upstart inexperience.
Where were they all not twenty years ago?
They think too much of having shaded out
A few old pecker-fretted apple trees.
Make yourself up a cheering song of how
Someone's road home from work this once was,
Who may be just ahead of you on foot
Or creaking with a buggy load of grain.
The height of the adventure is the height
Of country where two village cultures faded
Into each other. Both of them are lost.
And if you're lost enough to find yourself
By now, pull in your ladder road behind you
And put a sign up CLOSED to all but me.
Then make yourself at home. The only field
Now left's no bigger than a harness gall.
First there's the children's house of make believe,
Some shattered dishes underneath a pine,
The playthings in the playhouse of the children.
Weep for what little things could make them glad.
Then for the house that is no more a house,
But only a belilaced cellar hole,
Now slowly closing like a dent in dough.
This was no playhouse but a house in earnest.
Your destination and your destiny's
A brook that was the water of the house,
Cold as a spring as yet so near its source,
Too lofty and original to rage.
(We know the valley streams that when aroused
Will leave their tatters hung on barb and thorn.)
I have kept hidden in the instep arch
Of an old cedar at the waterside

A broken drinking goblet like the Grail
Under a spell so the wrong ones can't find it,
So can't get saved, as Saint Mark says they mustn't.
(I stole the goblet from the children's playhouse.)
Here are your waters and your watering place.
Drink and be whole again beyond confusion.

BIRCHES

When I see birches bend to left and right
Across the lines of straighter darker trees,
I like to think some boy's been swinging them.
But swinging doesn't bend them down to stay.
Ice-storms do that. Often you must have seen them
Loaded with ice a sunny winter morning
After a rain. They click upon themselves
As the breeze rises, and turn many-coloured
As the stir cracks and crazes their enamel.
Soon the sun's warmth makes them shed crystal shells
Shattering and avalanching on the snowcrust—
Such heaps of broken glass to sweep away
You'd think the inner dome of heaven had fallen.
They are dragged to the withered bracken by the load,
And they seem not to break; though once they are bowed
So low for long, they never right themselves:
You may see their trunks arching in the woods
Years afterwards, trailing their leaves on the ground
Like girls on hands and knees that throw their hair
Before them over their heads to dry in the sun.
But I was going to say when Truth broke in
With all her matter-of-fact about the ice-storm
(Now am I free to be poetical?)
I should prefer to have some boy bend them
As he went out and in to fetch the cows—
Some boy too far from town to learn baseball,
Whose only play was what he found himself,
Summer or winter, and could play alone.
One by one he subdued his father's trees

By riding them down over and over again
Until he took the stiffness out of them,
And not one but hung limp, not one was left
For him to conquer. He learned all there was
To learn about not launching out too soon
And so not carrying the tree away
Clear to the ground. He always kept his poise
To the top branches, climbing carefully
With the same pains you use to fill a cup
Up to the brim, and even above the brim.
Then he flung outward, feet first, with a swish,
Kicking his way down through the air to the ground.
So was I once myself a swinger of birches.
And so I dream of going back to be.
It's when I'm weary of considerations,
And life is too much like a pathless wood
Where your face burns and tickles with the cobwebs
Broken across it, and one eye is weeping
From a twig's having lashed it open,
I'd like to get away from earth a while
And then come back to it and begin over.
May no fate wilfully misunderstand me
And half grant what I wish and snatch me away
Not to return. Earth's the right place for love:
I don't know where it's likely to go better.
I'd like to go by climbing a high birch tree,
And climb black branches up a snow-white trunk
Toward heaven, till the tree could bear no more,
But dipped its top and set me down again.
That would be good both going and coming back.
One could do worse than be a swinger of birches.

A CONSIDERABLE SPECK

A speck that would have been beneath my sight
On any but a paper sheet so white
Set off across what I had written there.
And I had idly poised my pen in air
To stop it with a period of ink
When something strange about it made me think.
This was no dust speck by my breathing blown,
But unmistakably a living mite
With inclinations it could call its own.
It paused as with suspicion of my pen,
And then came racing wildly on again
To where my manuscript was not yet dry;
Then paused again and either drank or smelt—
With loathing, for again it turned to fly.
Plainly with an intelligence I dealt.
It seemed too tiny to have room for feet,
Yet must have had a set of them complete
To express how much it didn't want to die.
It ran with terror and with cunning crept.
It faltered; I could see it hesitate;
Then in the middle of the open sheet
Cower down in desperation to accept
Whatever I accorded it of fate.

I have none of the tenderer-than-thou
Collectivistic regimenting love
With which the modern world is being swept.
But this poor microscopic item now!
Since it was nothing I knew evil of
I let it lie there till I hope it slept.

I have a mind myself and recognize
Mind when I meet with it in any guise.
No one can know how glad I am to find
On any sheet the least display of mind.

THE GIFT OUTRIGHT

The land was ours before we were the land's.
She was our land more than a hundred years
Before we were her people. She was ours
In Massachusetts, in Virginia,
But we were England's, still colonials,
Possessing what we still were unpossessed by,
Possessed by what we now no more possessed.
Something we were withholding made us weak
Until we found out that it was ourselves
We were withholding from our land of living,
And forthwith found salvation in surrender.
Such as we were we gave ourselves outright
(The deed of gift was many deeds of war)
To the land vaguely realizing westward,
But still unstoried, artless, unenhanced,
Such as she was, such as she would become.

john masefield

THERE, ON THE DARKENED DEATHBED

There, on the darkened deathbed, dies the brain
That flared three several times in seventy years;
It cannot lift the silly hand again,
Nor speak, nor sing, it neither sees nor hears.
And muffled mourners put it in the ground
And then go home, and in the earth it lies,
Too dark for vision and too deep for sound,
The million cells that made a good man wise.
Yet for a few short years an influence stirs,
A sense or wraith or essence of him dead,
Which makes insensate things its ministers
To those beloved, his spirit's daily bread;
Then that, too, fades; in book or deed a spark
Lingers, then that, too, fades; then all is dark.

THE WEST WIND

It's a warm wind, the west wind, full of birds' cries;
I never hear the west wind but tears are in my eyes.
For it comes from the west lands, the old brown hills,
And April's in the west wind, and daffodils.

It's a fine land, the west land, for hearts as tired as mine,
Apple orchards blossom there, and the air's like wine.
There is cool green grass there, where men may lie at rest,
And the thrushes are in song there, fluting from the nest.

'Will ye not come home, brother? ye have been long away,
It's April, and blossom time, and white is the may;
And bright is the sun, brother, and warm is the rain,—
Will ye not come home, brother, home to us again?

'The young corn is green, brother, where the rabbits run,
It's blue sky, and white clouds, and warm rain and sun.
It's song to a man's soul, brother, fire to a man's brain,
To hear the wild bees and see the merry spring again.

'Larks are singing in the west, brother, above the green wheat,
So will ye not come home, brother, and rest your tired feet?
I've a balm for bruised hearts, brother, sleep for aching eyes,'
Says the warm wind, the west wind, full of birds' cries.

It's the white road westwards is the road I must tread
To the green grass, the cool grass, and rest for heart and head,
To the violets and the warm hearts and the thrushes' song,
In the fine land, the west land, the land where I belong.

AN OLD SONG RE-SUNG

I saw a ship a-sailing, a-sailing, a-sailing,
With emeralds and rubies and sapphires in her hold;
And a bosun in a blue coat bawling at the railing,
Piping through a silver call that had a chain of gold;
The summer wind was falling and the tall ship rolled.

I saw a ship a-steering, a-steering, a-steering,
With roses in red thread worked upon her sails;
With sacks of purple amethysts, the spoils of buccaneering,
Skins of musky yellow wine, and silks in bales,
Her merry men were cheering, hauling in the brails.

I saw a ship a-sinking, a-sinking, a-sinking,
With glittering sea-water splashing on her decks,
With seamen in her spirit-room singing songs and drinking,
Pulling claret bottles down, and knocking off the necks,
The broken glass was chinking as she sank among the wrecks.

NIGHT ON THE DOWNLAND

Night is on the downland, on the lonely moorland,
On the hills where the wind goes over sheep-bitten turf,
Where the bent grass beats upon the unplowed poorland
And the pine-woods roar like the surf.

Here the Roman lived on the wind-barren lonely,
Dark now and haunted by the moorland fowl;
None comes here now but the peewit only,
And moth-like death in the owl.

Beauty was here on this beetle-droning downland;
The thought of a Caesar in the purple came
From the palace by the Tiber in the Roman townland
To this wind-swept hill with no name.

Lonely Beauty came here and was here in sadness,
Brave as a thought on the frontier of the mind,
In the camp of the wild upon the march of madness,
The bright-eyed Queen of the Blind.

Now where Beauty was are the wind-withered gorses,
Moaning like old men in the hill-wind's blast;
The flying sky is dark with running horses,
And the night is full of the past.

THE PASSING STRANGE

Out of the earth to rest or range
Perpetual in perpetual change,
The unknown passing through the strange.

Water and saltness held together
To tread the dust and stand the weather,
And plow the field and stretch the tether,

To pass the wine-cup and be witty,
Water the sands and build the city,
Slaughter like devils and have pity,

Be red with rage and pale with lust,
Make beauty come, make peace, make trust,
Water and saltness mixed with dust;

Drive over earth, swim under sea,
Fly in the eagle's secrecy,
Guess where the hidden comets be;

Know all the deathy seeds that still
Queen Helen's beauty, Caesar's will,
And slay them even as they kill;

Fashion an altar for a rood,
Defile a continent with blood,
And watch a brother starve for food:

Love like a madman, shaking, blind,
Till self is burnt into a kind
Possession of another mind;

Brood upon beauty, till the grace
Of beauty with the holy face
Brings peace into the bitter place;

Prove in the lifeless granites, scan
The stars for hope, for guide, for plan;
Live as a woman or a man;

Fasten to lover or to friend,
Until the heart break at the end
The break of death that cannot mend:

Then to lie useless, helpless, still,
Down in the earth, in dark, to fill
The roots of grass or daffodil.

Down in the earth, in dark, alone,
A mockery of the ghost in bone,
The strangeness, passing the unknown.

Time will go by, that outlasts clocks,
Dawn in the thorps will rouse the cocks,
Sunset be glory on the rocks:

But it, the thing, will never heed
Even the rootling from the seed
Thrusting to suck it for its need.

Since moons decay and suns decline,
How else should end this life of mine?
Water and saltness are not wine.

But in the darkest hour of night,
When even the foxes peer for sight,
The byre-cock crows; he feels the light.

So, in this water mixed with dust,
The byre-cock spirit crows from trust
That death will change because it must.

For all things change: the darkness changes,
The wandering spirits change their ranges,
The corn is gathered to the granges.

The corn is sown again, it grows;
The stars burn out, the darkness goes;
The rhythms change, they do not close.

They change, and we, who pass like foam,
Like dust blown through the streets of Rome,
Change ever, too; we have no home,

Only a beauty, only a power,
Sad in the fruit, bright in the flower,
Endlessly erring for its hour,

But gathering as we stray, a sense
Of Life, so lovely and intense,
It lingers when we wander hence,

That those who follow feel behind
Their backs, when all before is blind,
Our joy, a rampart to the mind.

carl sandburg

LOST

Desolate and lone
All night long on the lake
Where fog trails and mist
  creeps,
The whistle of a boat

Calls and cries unendingly,
Like some lost child
In tears and trouble
Hunting the harbor's breast
And the harbor's eyes.

THEY HAVE YARNS

They have yarns
  Of a skyscraper so tall they had to put hinges
  On the two top stories so to let the moon go by,
  Of one corn crop in Missouri when the roots
  Went so deep and drew off so much water
  The Mississippi riverbed that year was dry,
  Of pancakes so thin they had only one side,
Of "a fog so thick we shingled the barn and six feet out on the
  fog,"
Of Pecos Pete straddling a cyclone in Texas and riding it to
  the west coast where "it rained out under him,"
Of the man who drove a swarm of bees across the Rocky
  Mountains and the Desert "and didn't lose a bee,"
Of a mountain railroad curve where the engineer in his cab
  can touch the caboose and spit in the conductor's eye,

Of the boy who climbed a cornstalk growing so fast he would
    have starved to death if they hadn't shot biscuits up
    to him,
Of the old man's whiskers: "When the wind was with him his
    whiskers arrived a day before he did,"
Of the hen laying a square egg and cackling, "Ouch!" and of
    hens laying eggs with the dates printed on them,
Of the ship captain's shadow: it froze to the deck one cold
    winter night,
Of mutineers on that same ship put to chipping rust with
    rubber hammers,
Of the sheep counter who was fast and accurate: "I just count
    their feet and divide by four,"
Of the man so tall he must climb a ladder to shave himself,
Of the runt so teeny-weeny it takes two men and a boy to
    see him,
Of mosquitoes: one can kill a dog, two of them a man,
Of a cyclone that sucked cookstoves out of the kitchen, up the
    chimney flue, and on to the next town,
Of the same cyclone picking up wagon-tracks in Nebraska
    and dropping them over in the Dakotas,
Of the hook-and-eye snake unlocking itself into forty pieces,
    each piece two inches long, then in nine seconds flat
    snapping itself together again,
Of the watch swallowed by the cow—when they butchered her
    a year later the watch was running and had the correct
    time,
Of horned snakes, hoop snakes that roll themselves where they
    want to go, and rattlesnakes carrying bells instead of
    rattles on their tails,
Of the herd of cattle in California getting lost in a giant red-
    wood tree that had hollowed out,
Of the man who killed a snake by putting its tail in its mouth
    so it swallowed itself,
Of railroad trains whizzing along so fast they reach the station
    before the whistle,
Of pigs so thin the farmer had to tie knots in their tails to keep
    them from crawling through the cracks in their pens,

Of Paul Bunyan's big blue ox, Babe, measuring between the
    eyes forty-two ax-handles and a plug of Star tobacco
    exactly,
Of John Henry's hammer and the curve of its swing and his
    singing of it as "a rainbow round my shoulder."
        "Do tell!"
        "I want to know!"
        "You don't say so!"
        "For the land's sake!"
        "Gosh all fish-hooks!"
        "Tell me some more.
        I don't believe a word you say
        but I love to listen
        to your sweet harmonica
        to your chin-music.
        Your fish stories hang together
        when they're just a pack of lies:
        you ought to have a leather medal:
        you ought to have a statue
        carved of butter: you deserve
        a large bouquet of turnips."
    "Yessir," the traveler drawled,
"Away out there in the petrified forest
everything goes on the same as usual.
The petrified birds sit in their petrified nests
and hatch their petrified young from petrified eggs."
A high pressure salesman jumped off the Brooklyn Bridge and
    was saved by a policeman. But it didn't take him long to
    sell the idea to the policeman. So together they jumped
    off the bridge.
One of the oil men in heaven started a rumor of a gusher
    down in hell. All the other oil men left in a hurry for hell.
    As he gets to thinking about the rumor he had started he
    says to himself there might be something in it after all.
    So he leaves for hell in a hurry.
"The number 42 will win this raffle, that's my number." And
    when he won they asked him whether he guessed the
    number or had a system. He said he had a system. "I took

up the old family album and there on page 7 was my
grandfather and grandmother both on page 7. I said to
myself this is easy for 7 times 7 is the number that will
win and 7 times 7 is 42."

Once a shipwrecked sailor caught hold of a stateroom door
and floated for hours till friendly hands from out of
the darkness threw him a rope. And he called across the
night, "What country is this?" and hearing voices answer,
"New Jersey," he took a fresh hold on the floating stateroom door and called back half-wearily, "I guess I'll float
a little farther."

An Ohio man bundled up the tin roof of a summer kitchen
and sent it to a motor car maker with a complaint of his
car not giving service. In three weeks a new car arrived
for him and a letter: "We regret delay in shipment but
your car was received in a very bad order."

A Dakota cousin of this Ohio man sent six years of tin can
accumulations to the same works, asking them to over-
haul his car. Two weeks later came a rebuilt car, five old
tin cans, and a letter: "We are also forwarding you five
parts not necessary in our new model."

Thus fantasies heard at filling stations in the midwest. Another
relates to a Missouri mule who took aim with his heels at
an automobile rattling by. The car turned a somersault,
lit next a fence, ran right along through a cornfield till it
came to a gate, moved onto the road and went on its way
as though nothing had happened. The mule heehawed
with desolation, "What's the use?"

Another tells of a farmer and his family stalled on a railroad
crossing, how they jumped out in time to see a limited
express knock it into flinders, the farmer calling, "Well, I
always did say that car was no shucks in a real pinch."

When the Masonic Temple in Chicago was the tallest building
in the United States west of New York, two men who
would cheat the eyes out of you if you gave 'em a chance,
took an Iowa farmer to the top of the building and asked
him, "How is this for high?" They told him that for $25
they would go down in the basement and turn the build-

ing around on its turn-table for him while he stood on the roof and saw how this seventh wonder of the world worked. He handed them $25. They went. He waited. They never came back.

This is told in Chicago as a folk tale, the same as the legend of Mrs. O'Leary's cow kicking over the barn lamp that started the Chicago fire, when the Georgia visitor, Robert Toombs, telegraphed an Atlanta crony, "Chicago is on fire, the whole city burning down, God be praised!"

Nor is the prize sleeper Rip Van Winkle and his scolding wife forgotten, nor the headless horseman scooting through Sleepy Hollow

Nor the sunken treasure-ships in coves and harbors, the hideouts of gold and silver sought by Coronado, nor the Flying Dutchman rounding the Cape doomed to nevermore pound his ear nor ever again take a snooze for himself

Nor the sailor's caretaker Mother Carey seeing to it that every seafaring man in the afterworld has a seabird to bring him news of ships and women, an albatross for the admiral, a gull for the deckhand

Nor the sailor with a sweetheart in every port of the world, nor the ships that set out with flying colors and all the promises you could ask, the ships never heard of again

Nor Jim Liverpool, the riverman who could jump across any river and back without touching land he was that quick on his feet

Nor Mike Fink along the Ohio and the Mississippi, half wild horse and half cock-eyed alligator, the rest of him snags and snapping turtle. "I can out-run, out-jump, out-shoot, out-brag, out-drink, and out-fight, rough and tumble, no holts barred, any man on both sides of the river from Pittsburgh to New Orleans and back again to St. Louis. My trigger finger itches and I want to go redhot. War, famine and bloodshed put flesh on my bones, and hardship's my daily bread."

Nor the man so lean he threw no shadow: six rattlesnakes struck at him at one time and every one missed him.

From *The People, Yes*

vachel lindsay

THE EAGLE THAT IS FORGOTTEN
(John P. Altgeld, b. December 30, 1847; d. March 12, 1902)

Sleep softly . . . eagle forgotten . . . under the stone.
Time has its way with you there, and the clay has its own.

'We have buried him now,' thought your foes, and in secret
rejoiced.
They made a brave show of their mourning, their hatred un-
voiced.
They had snarled at you, barked at you, foamed at you day
after day.
Now you were ended. They praised you, . . . and laid you
away.

The others that mourned you in silence and terror and truth,
The widow bereft of her crust, and the boy without youth,
The mocked and the scorned and the wounded, the lame and
the poor
That should have remembered forever, . . . remember no more.

Where are those lovers of yours, on what name do they call
The lost, that in armies wept over your funeral pall?
They call on the names of a hundred high-valiant ones,
A hundred white eagles have risen the sons of your sons,
The zeal in their wings is a zeal that your dreaming began
The valor that wore out your soul in the service of man.

Sleep softly, . . . eagle forgotten, . . . under the stone,
Time has its way with you there and the clay has its own.
Sleep on, O brave-hearted, O wise man, that kindled the
flame—
To live in mankind is far more than to live in a name,
To live in mankind, far, far more . . . than to live in a name.

THE CONGO

(A Study of the Negro Race)

I—THEIR BASIC SAVAGERY

Fat black bucks in a wine-barrel room,
Barrel-house kings, with feet unstable,
Sagged and reeled and pounded on the table,
Pounded on the table,
Beat an empty barrel with the handle of a broom,
Hard as they were able,
Boom, boom, Boom,
With a silk umbrella and the handle of a broom,
Boomlay, boomlay, boomlay, Boom.

A deep rolling bass

Then I had religion, Then I had a vision.
I could not turn from their revel in derision.
Then I saw the Congo, creeping through the
black,
Cutting through the jungle with a golden
track.

More deliberate. Solemnly chanted

Then along that riverbank
A thousand miles
Tattooed cannibals danced in files;
Then I heard the boom of the blood-lust son
And a thigh-bone beating on a tin-pan gong.
And "blood!" screamed the whistles and the fifes
of the warriors,
"Blood!" screamed the skull-faced, lean witch-
doctors;
"Whirl ye the deadly voo-doo rattle,
Harry the uplands,
Steal all the cattle,
Rattle-rattle, rattle-rattle, Bing!
Boomlay, boomlay, boomlay, Boom!"

A rapidly piling climax of speed and racket

A roaring, epic, rag-time tune
From the mouth of the Congo
To the Mountains of the Moon.
Death is an Elephant,
Torch-eyed and horrible.

With a philosophic pause

Shrilly and with a heavily accented metre

Foam-flanked and terrible.
BOOM, steal the pygmies,
BOOM, kill the Arabs,
BOOM, kill the white men,
HOO, HOO, HOO.

Like the wind in the chimney

Listen to the yell of Leopold's ghost
Burning in Hell for his hand-maimed host.
Hear how the demons chuckle and yell
Cutting his hands off down in Hell.
Listen to the creepy proclamation,
Blown through the lairs of the forest-nation,
Blown past the white-ants' hill of clay,
Blown past the marsh where the butterflies play:—
"Be careful what you do,

All the O sounds very golden. Heavy accents very heavy. Light accents very light. Last line whispered

Or Mumbo-Jumbo, god of the Congo,
And all of the other
Gods of the Congo,
Mumbo-Jumbo will hoo-doo you,
Mumbo-Jumbo will hoo-doo you,
Mumbo-Jumbo will hoo-doo you."

II—THEIR IRREPRESSIBLE HIGH SPIRITS

Wild crap-shooters with a whoop and a call

Rather shrill and high

Danced the juba in their gambling-hall,
And laughed fit to kill, and shook the town,
And guyed the policemen and laughed them down
With a boomlay, boomlay, boomlay, BOOM.
THEN I SAW THE CONGO, CREEPING THROUGH THE
    BLACK,
CUTTING THROUGH THE JUNGLE WITH A GOLDEN
    TRACK.

Read exactly as in first section. Lay emphasis on the delicate ideas. Keep as light-footed as possible

A negro fairyland swung into view,
A minstrel river
Where dreams come true.
The ebony palace soared on high
Through the blossoming trees to the evening sky.
The inlaid porches and casements shone

With gold and ivory and elephant-bone.
And the black crowd laughed till their sides were
    sore
At the baboon butler in the agate door,
And the well-known tunes of the parrot band
That trilled on the bushes of that magic land.
A troupe of skull-faced witch-men came
Through the agate doorway in suits of flame—   *With pom-*
Yea, long-tailed coats with a gold-leaf crust   *posity*
And hats that were covered with diamond dust.
And the crowd in the court gave a whoop and a
    call
And danced the juba from wall to wall.
But the witch-men suddenly stilled the throng   *With a great*
With a stern cold glare, and a stern old song: *deliberation*
"Mumbo-Jumbo will hoo-doo you." . . .   *and ghostli-*
    ness

Just then from the doorway, as fat as shotes   *With over-*
Came the cake-walk princes in their long red   *whelming*
    coats,   *assurance,*
Canes with a brilliant lacquer shine,   *good cheer,*
And tall silk hats that were red as wine.   *and pomp*
And they pranced with their butterfly partners   *With grow-*
    there,   *ing speed*
Coal-black maidens with pearls in their hair,   *and sharply*
Knee-skirts trimmed with the jassamine sweet,   *marked*
And bells on their ankles and little black feet.   *dance-*
And the couples railed at the chant and the frown   *rhythm*
Of the witch-men lean, and laughed them down.
(Oh, rare was the revel, and well worth while
That made those glowering witch-men smile.)

The cake-walk royalty then began   *With a touch*
To walk for a cake that was tall as a man   *of Negro dia-*
To the tune of "Boomlay, boomlay, Boom,"   *lect, and as*
While the witch-men laughed, with a sinister air,   *rapidly as*
And sang with the scalawags prancing there: *possible to-*
    ward the end

"Walk with care, walk with care,
Or Mumbo-Jumbo, god of the Congo,
And all of the other
Gods of the Congo,
Mumbo-Jumbo will hoo-doo you.
Beware, beware, walk with care,
Boomlay, boomlay, boomlay, boom,
Boomlay, boomlay, boomlay, boom,
Boomlay, boomlay, boomlay, boom,
Boomlay, boomlay, boomlay,
Boom."

Slow philo-sophic calm

Oh, rare was the revel, and well worth while
That made those glowering witch-men smile.

III—THE HOPE OF THEIR RELIGION

Heavy bass. With a literal imitation of camp-meet-ing racket and trance

A good old Negro in the slums of the town
Preached at a sister for her velvet gown.
Howled at a brother for his low-down ways,
His prowling, guzzling, sneak-thief days.
Beat on the Bible till he wore it out
Starting the jubilee revival shout.
And some had visions, as they stood on chairs,
And sang of Jacob, and the golden stairs.
And they all repented, a thousand strong,
From their stupor and savagery and sin and wrong,
And slammed with their hymn-books till they
    shook the room
With "Glory, glory, glory,"
And "Boom, boom, BOOM."
THEN I SAW THE CONGO, CREEPING THROUGH THE
    BLACK,

Exactly as in the first sec-tion. Begin with terror and power, end with joy

CUTTING THROUGH THE JUNGLE WITH A GOLDEN
    TRACK.
And the gray sky opened like a new-rent veil
And showed the apostles with their coats of mail.
In bright white steel they were seated round,

And their fire-eyes watched where the Congo
   wound.
And the twelve Apostles, from their throne on
   high,

Sung to the tune of "Hark, ten thousand harps and voices"

Thrilled all the forest with their heavenly cry:
"Mumbo-Jumbo will die in the jungle;
Never again will he hoo-doo you,
Never again will he hoo-doo you."

Then along that river, a thousand miles,
The vine-snared trees fell down in files.

With growing deliberation and joy

Pioneer angels cleared the way
For a Congo paradise, for babes at play,
For sacred capitals, for temples clean.
Gone were the skull-faced witch-men lean;
There, where the wild ghost-gods had wailed,
A million boats of the angels sailed

In a rather high key—as delicately as possible

With oars of silver, and prows of blue,
And silken pennants that the sun shone through
'Twas a land transfigured, 'twas a new creation.
Oh, a singing wind swept the Negro nation,
And on through the backwoods clearing flew:—
"Mumbo-Jumbo is dead in the jungle.
Never again will he hoo-doo you,

To the tune of "Hark, ten thousand harps and voices"

Never again will he hoo-doo you."

Redeemed were the forests, the beasts and the
   men,
And only the vulture dared again
By the far lone mountains of the moon
To cry, in the silence, the Congo tune:

Dying down into a penetrating, terrified whisper

"Mumbo-Jumbo will hoo-doo you,
Mumbo-Jumbo will hoo-doo you.
Mumbo . . . Jumbo . . . will . . . hoo-doo . . . you."

GENERAL WILLIAM BOOTH ENTERS INTO HEAVEN

(To be sung to the tune of 'The Blood of the Lamb'
with indicated instrument)

I

(Bass drum beaten loudly.)

Booth led boldly with his big bass drum—
(Are you washed in the blood of the Lamb?)
The Saints smiled gravely and they said: 'He's come.'
(Are you washed in the blood of the Lamb?)
Walking lepers followed, rank on rank,
Lurching bravos from the ditches dank,
Drabs from the alleyways and drug fiends pale—
Minds still passion-ridden, soul-powers frail:—
Vermin-eaten saints with moldy breath,
Unwashed legions with the ways of Death—
(Are you washed in the blood of the Lamb?)

(Banjos.)

Every slum had sent its half-a-score
The round world over. (Booth had groaned for more.)
Every banner that the wide world flies
Bloomed with glory and transcendent dyes.
Big-voiced lasses made their banjos bang,
Tranced, fanatical they shrieked and sang:—
'Are you washed in the blood of the Lamb?'
Hallelujah! It was queer to see
Bull-necked convicts with that land make free.
Loons with trumpets blowed a blare, blare, blare
On, on upward thro' the golden air!
(Are you washed in the blood of the Lamb?)

II

(Bass drum slower and softer.)

Booth died blind and still by faith he trod,
Eyes still dazzled by the ways of God.
Booth led boldly, and he looked the chief
Eagle countenance in sharp relief,

Beard a-flying, air of high command
Unabated in that holy land.

(Sweet flute music.)
Jesus came from out the court-house door,
Stretched his hands above the passing poor.
Booth saw not, but led his queer ones there
Round and round the mighty court-house square.
Then, in an instant all that blear review
Marched on spotless, clad in raiment new.
The lame were straightened, withered limbs uncurled
And blind eyes opened on a new, sweet world.

(Bass drum louder.)
Drabs and vixens in a flash made whole!
Gone was the weasel-head, the snout, the jowl!
Sages and sibyls now, and athletes clean,
Rulers of empires, and of forests green!

(Grand chorus of all instruments. Tambourines to the foreground.)
The hosts were sandalled, and their wings were fire!
(Are you washed in the blood of the Lamb?)
But their noise played havoc with the angel-choir.
(Are you washed in the blood of the Lamb?)
Oh, shout Salvation! It was good to see
Kings and Princes by the Lamb set free.
The banjos rattled and the tambourines
Jing-jing-jingled in the hands of Queens.

(Reverently sung, no instruments.)
And when Booth halted by the curb for prayer
He saw his Master thro' the flag-filled air.
Christ came gently with a robe and crown
For Booth the soldier, while the throng knelt down.
He saw King Jesus. They were face to face,
And he knelt a-weeping in that holy place.
Are you washed in the blood of the Lamb?

ABRAHAM LINCOLN WALKS AT MIDNIGHT

(In Springfield, Illinois)

It is portentous, and a thing of state
That here at midnight, in our little town
A mourning figure walks, and will not rest,
Near the old court-house pacing up and down,

Or by his homestead, or in shadowed yards
He lingers where his children used to play,
Or through the market, on the well-worn stones
He stalks until the dawn-stars burn away.

A bronzed, lank man! His suit of ancient black,
A famous high top-hat and plain worn shawl
Make him the quaint great figure that men love,
The prairie-lawyer, master of us all.

He cannot sleep upon his hillside now.
He is among us:—as in times before!
And we who toss and lie awake for long
Breathe deep, and start, to see him pass the door.

His head is bowed. He thinks on men and kings.
Yea, when the sick world cries, how can he sleep?
Too many peasants fight, they know not why,
Too many homesteads in black terror weep.

The sins of all the war-lords burn his heart.
He sees the dreadnaughts scouring every main.
He carries on his shawl-wrapped shoulders now
The bitterness, the folly and the pain.

He cannot rest until a spirit-dawn
Shall come;—the shining hope of Europe free:
The league of sober folk, the Workers' Earth,
Bringing long peace to Cornland, Alp and Sea.

It breaks his heart that kings must murder still,
That all his hours of travail here for men
Seem yet in vain. And who will bring white peace
That he may sleep upon his hill again?

BRYAN, BRYAN, BRYAN, BRYAN

*The Campaign of Eighteen Ninety-six, as Viewed at the Time
by a Sixteen-Year-Old, etc.*

I

In a nation of one hundred fine, mob-hearted, lynching, relent-
    ing, repenting millions,
There are plenty of sweeping, swinging, stinging, gorgeous
    things to shout about,
And knock your old blue devils out.

I brag and chant of Bryan, Bryan, Bryan,
Candidate for president who sketched a silver Zion,
The one American Poet who could sing outdoors,
He brought in tides of wonder, of unprecedented splendor,
Wild roses from the plains, that made hearts tender,
All the funny circus silks
Of politics unfurled,
Bartlett pears of romance that were honey at the cores,
And torchlights down the street, to the end of the world.

There were truths eternal in the gab and tittle-tattle.
There were real heads broken in the fustian and the rattle.
There were real lines drawn:
Not the silver and the gold,
But Nebraska's cry went eastward against the dour and old,
The mean and cold.

It was eighteen ninety-six, and I was just sixteen
And Altgeld ruled in Springfield, Illinois,
When there came from the sunset Nebraska's shout of joy:

In a coat like a deacon, in a black Stetson hat
He scourged the elephant plutocrats
With barbed wire from the Platte.
The scales dropped from their mighty eyes.
They saw that summer's noon
A tribe of wonders coming
To a marching tune.

Oh, the longhorns from Texas,
The jay hawks from Kansas,
The plop-eyed bungaroo and giant giassicus,
The varmint, chipmunk, bugaboo,
The horned-toad, prairie-dog and ballyhoo,
From all the newborn states arow,
Bidding the eagles of the west fly on,
Bidding the eagles of the west fly on.
The fawn, prodactyl and thing-a-ma-jig,
The rakaboor, the hellangone,
The whangdoodle, batfowl and pig,
The coyote, wild-cat and grizzly in a glow,
In a miracle of health and speed, the whole breed abreast,
They leaped the Mississippi, blue border of the West,
From the Gulf to Canada, two thousand miles long:—
Against the towns of Tubal Cain,
Ah,—sharp was their song.
Against the ways of Tubal Cain, too cunning for the young,
The longhorn calf, the buffalo and wampus gave tongue.

These creatures were defending things Mark Hanna never
      dreamed:
The moods of airy childhood that in desert dews gleamed,
The gossamers and whimsies,
The monkeyshines and didoes
Rank and strange
Of the canyons and the range,
The ultimate fantastics
Of the far western slope,
And of prairie schooner children

Born beneath the stars,
Beneath falling snows,
Of the babies born at midnight
In the sod huts of lost hope,
With no physician there,
Except a Kansas prayer,
With the Indian raid a howling through the air.

And all these in their helpless days
By the dour East oppressed,
Mean paternalism
Making their mistakes for them,
Crucifying half the West,
Till the whole Atlantic coast
Seemed a giant spiders' nest.

And these children and their sons
At last rode through the cactus,
A cliff of mighty cowboys
On the lope,
With gun and rope.
And all the way tó frightened Maine the old East heard them
    call,
And saw our Bryan by a mile lead the wall
Of men and whirling flowers and beasts,
The bard and the prophet of them all.
Prairie avenger, mountain lion,
Bryan, Bryan, Bryan, Bryan,
Gigantic troubadour, speaking like a siege gun,
Smashing Plymouth Rock with his boulders from the West,
And just a hundred miles behind, tornadoes piled across the
    sky,
Blotting out sun and moon,
A sign on high.

Headlong, dazed and blinking in the weird green light,
The scalawags made moan,
Afraid to fight.

II

When Bryan came to Springfield, and Altgeld gave him greet-
        ing,
Rochester was deserted, Divernon was deserted,
Mechanicsburg, Riverton, Chickenbristle, Cotton Hill,
Empty: for all Sangamon drove to the meeting—
In silver-decked racing cart,
Buggy, buckboard, carryall,
Carriage, phaeton, whatever would haul,
And silver-decked farm wagons gritted, banged and rolled,
With the new tale of Bryan by the iron tires told.

The State House loomed afar,
A speck, a hive, a football, a captive balloon!
And the town was all one spreading wing of bunting, plumes,
        and sunshine,
Every rag and flag, and Bryan picture sold,
When the rigs in many a dusty line
Jammed our streets at noon,
And joined the wild parade against the power of gold.
We roamed, we boys from High School,
With mankind, while Springfield gleamed, silk-lined.
Oh, Tom Dines, and Art Fitzgerald,
And the gangs that they could get!
I can hear them yelling yet.
Helping the incantation,
Defying aristocracy,
With every bridle gone,
Ridding the world of the low down mean,
Bidding the eagles of the West fly on,
Bidding the eagles of the West fly on,
We were bully, wild and woolly,
Never yet curried below the knees.
We saw flowers in the air,
Fair as the Pleiades, bright as Orion,
—Hopes of all mankind,
Made rare, resistless, thrice refined.
Oh, we bucks from every Springfield ward!

Colts of democracy—
Yet time-winds out of Chaos from the star-fields of the Lord.

The long parade rolled on. I stood by my best girl.
She was a cool young citizen, with wise and laughing eyes.
With my necktie by my ear, I was stepping on my dear,
But she kept like a pattern, without a shaken curl.
She wore in her hair a brave prairie rose.
Her gold chums cut her, for that was not the pose.
No Gibson Girl would wear it in that fresh way.
But we were fairy Democrats, and this was our day.

The earth rocked like the ocean, the sidewalk was a deck.
The houses for the moment were lost in the wide wreck.
And the bands played strange and stranger music as they
    trailed along.
Against the ways of Tubal Cain,
Ah, sharp was their song!
The demons in the bricks, the demons in the grass,
The demons in the bank-vaults peered out to see us pass,
And the angels in the trees, the angels in the grass,
The angels in the flags, peered out to see us pass.
And the sidewalk was our chariot, and the flowers bloomed
    higher,
And the street turned to silver and the grass turned to fire,
And then it was but grass, and the town was there again,
A place for women and men.

III

Then we stood where we could see
Every band,
And the speaker's stand.
And Bryan took the platform.
And he was introduced.
And he lifted his hand
And cast a new spell.
Progressive silence fell
In Springfield, in Illinois, around the world.

Then we heard these glacial boulders across the prairie rolled:
'The people have a right to make their own mistakes. . . .
You shall not crucify mankind
Upon a cross of gold.'
And everybody heard him—
In the streets and State House yard.
And everybody heard him in Springfield, in Illinois,
Around and around and around the world,
That danced upon its axis
And like a darling broncho whirled.

IV

July, August, suspense.
Wall Street lost to sense.
August, September, October,
More suspense,
And the whole East down like a wind-smashed fence.

Then Hanna to the rescue, Hanna of Ohio,
Rallying the roller-tops,
Rallying the bucket-shops.
Threatening drouth and death,
Promising manna,
Rallying the trusts against the bawling flannelmouth;
Invading misers' cellars, tin-cans, socks,
Melting down the rocks,
Pouring out the long green to a million workers,
Spondulix by the mountain-load, to stop each new tornado,
And beat the cheapskate, blatherskite,
Populistic, anarchistic, deacon—desperado.

V

Election night at midnight:
Boy Bryan's defeat.
Defeat of western silver.
Defeat of the wheat.
Victory of letterfiles

And plutocrats in miles
With dollar signs upon their coats,
Diamond watchchains on their vests and spats on their feet.
Victory of custodians, Plymouth Rock,
And all that inbred landlord stock.
Victory of the neat.
Defeat of the aspen groves of Colorado valleys,
The blue bells of the Rockies,
And blue bonnets of old Texas, by the Pittsburg alleys.
Defeat of alfalfa and the Mariposa lily.
Defeat of the Pacific and the long Mississippi.
Defeat of the young by the old and silly.
Defeat of tornadoes by the poison vats supreme.
Defeat of my boyhood, defeat of my dream.

VI

Where is McKinley, that respectable McKinley,
The man without an angle or a tangle,
Who soothed down the city man and soothed down the farmer,
The German, the Irish, the Southerner, the Northerner,
Who climbed every greasy pole, and slipped through every
    crack;
Who soothed down the gambling hall, the bar-room, the
    church,
The devil vote, the angel vote, the neutral vote,
The desperately wicked, and their victims on the rack,
The gold vote, the silver vote, the brass vote, the lead vote,
Every vote? . . .

Where is McKinley, Mark Hanna's McKinley,
His slave, his echo, his suit of clothes?
Gone to join the shadows, with the pomps of that time,
And the flame of that summer's prairie rose.

Where is Cleveland whom the Democratic platform
Read from the party in a glorious hour,
Gone to join the shadows with pitchfork Tillman,
And sledge-hammer Altgeld who wrecked his power.

Where is Hanna, bulldog Hanna,
Low-browed Hanna, who said: 'Stand pat'?
Gone to his place with old Pierpont Morgan.
Gone somewhere . . . with lean rat Platt.

Where is Roosevelt, the young dude cowboy,
Who hated Bryan, then aped his way?
Gone to join the shadows with mighty Cromwell
And tall King Saul, till the Judgment day.

Where is Altgeld, brave as the truth,
Whose name the few still say with tears?
Gone to join the ironies with Old John Brown,
Whose fame rings loud for a thousand years.

Where is that boy, that Heaven-born Bryan,
That Homer Bryan, who sang from the West?
Gone to join the shadows with Altgeld the Eagle,
Where the kings and the slaves and the troubadours rest.

THE APPLE-BARREL OF JOHNNY APPLESEED

On the mountain peak, called 'Going-To-The-Sun,'
I saw gray Johnny Appleseed at prayer
Just as the sunset made the old earth fair.
Then darkness came; in an instant, like great smoke,
The sun fell down as though its great hoops broke
And dark rich apples, poured from the dim flame
Where the sun set, came rolling toward the peak,
A storm of fruit, a mighty cider-reek,
The perfume of the orchards of the world,
From apple-shadows: red and russet domes
That turned to clouds of glory and strange homes
Above the mountain tops for cloud-born souls:—
Reproofs for men who build the world like moles,
Models for men, if they would build the world
As Johnny Appleseed would have it done—
Praying, and reading the books of Swedenborg
On the mountain top called 'Going-To-The-Sun.'

wallace stevens

PETER QUINCE AT THE CLAVIER

I

Just as my fingers on these keys
Make music, so the self-same sounds
On my spirit make a music too.

Music is feeling, then, not sound;
And thus it is that what I feel,
Here in this room, desiring you,

Thinking of your blue-shadowed silk,
Is music. It is like the strain
Waked in the elders by Susanna:

Of a green evening, clear and warm,
She bathed in her still garden, while
The red-eyed elders, watching, felt

The basses of their being throb
In witching chords, and their thin blood
Pulse pizzicati of Hosanna.

II

In the green water, clear and warm,
Susanna lay.
She searched
The touch of springs,
And found
Concealed imaginings.
She sighed
For so much melody.

Upon the bank she stood
In the cool
Of spent emotions.

She felt, among the leaves,
The dew
Of old devotions.

She walked upon the grass,
Still quavering.
The winds were like her maids,
On timid feet,
Fetching her woven scarves,
Yet wavering.

A breath upon her hand
Muted the night.
She turned—
A cymbal clashed,
And roaring horns.

III

Soon, with a noise like tambourines,
Came her attendant Byzantines.

They wondered why Susanna cried
Against the elders by her side:

And as they whispered, the refrain
Was like a willow swept by rain.

Anon their lamps' uplifted flame
Revealed Susanna and her shame.

And then the simpering Byzantines
Fled, with a noise like tambourines.

IV

Beauty is momentary in the mind—
The fitful tracing of a portal;
But in the flesh it is immortal.

The body dies; the body's beauty lives.
So evenings die, in their green going,
A wave, interminably flowing.

So gardens die, their meek breath scenting
The cowl of Winter, done repenting.
So maidens die, to the auroral
Celebration of a maiden's choral.

Susanna's music touched the bawdy strings
Of those white elders; but, escaping,
Left only Death's ironic scraping.
Now in its immortality, it plays
On the clear viol of her memory,
And makes a constant sacrament of praise.

CONNOISSEUR OF CHAOS

I

A. A violent order is disorder; and
B. A great disorder is an order. These
Two things are one. (Pages of illustrations.)

II

If all the green of spring was blue, and it is;
If the flowers of South Africa were bright
On the tables of Connecticut, and they are;
If Englishmen lived without tea in Ceylon, and they do;
And if all went on in an orderly way,
And it does; a law of inherent opposites,
Of essential unity, is as pleasant as port,
As pleasant as the brush-strokes of a bough,
An upper, particular bough in, say, Marchand.

III

After all the pretty contrast of life and death
Proves that these opposite things partake of one,

At least that was the theory, when bishops' books
Resolved the world. We cannot go back to that.
The squirming facts exceed the squamous mind,
If one may say so. And yet relation appears,
A small relation expanding like the shade
Of a cloud on sand, a shape on the side of a hill.

IV

A. Well, an old order is a violent one.
This proves nothing. Just one more truth, one more
Element in the immense disorder of truths.
B. It is April as I write. The wind
Is blowing after days of constant rain.
All this, of course, will come to summer soon.
But suppose the disorder of truths should ever come
To an order, most Plantagenet, most fixed. . .
A great disorder is an order. Now, A
And B are not like statuary, posed
For a vista in the Louvre. They are things chalked
On the sidewalk so that the pensive man may see.

V

The pensive man. . . He sees that eagle float
For which the intricate Alps are a single nest.

THE GLASS OF WATER

That the glass would melt in heat,
That the water would freeze in cold,
Shows that this object is merely a state,
One of many, between two poles. So,
In the metaphysical, there are these poles.

Here in the centre stands the glass. Light
Is the lion that comes down to drink. There
And in that state, the glass is a pool.
Ruddy are his eyes and ruddy are his claws
When light comes down to wet his frothy jaws

And in the water winding weeds move round.
And there and in another state—the refractions,
The *metaphysica*, the plastic parts of poems
Crash in the mind—But, fat Jocundus, worrying
About what stands here in the centre, not the glass,

But in the centre of our lives, this time, this day,
It is a state, this spring among the politicians
Playing cards. In a village of the indigenes,
One would have still to discover. Among the dogs and dung,
One would continue to contend with one's ideas.

THE IDEA OF ORDER IN KEY WEST

She sang beyond the genius of the sea.
The water never formed to mind or voice,
Like a body wholly body, fluttering
Its empty sleeves; and yet its mimic motion
Made constant cry, caused constantly a cry,
That was not ours although we understood,
Inhuman, of the veritable ocean.

The sea was not a mask. No more was she.
The song and water were not medleyed sound,
Even if what she sang was what she heard,
Since what she sang she uttered word by word.
It may be that in all her phrases stirred
The grinding water and the gasping wind;
But it was she and not the sea we heard.

For she was the maker of the song she sang.
The ever-hooded, tragic-gestured sea
Was merely a place by which she walked to sing.
Whose spirit is this? we said, because we knew
It was the spirit that we sought and knew
That we should ask this often as she sang.

If it was only the dark voice of the sea
That rose, or even colored by many waves;
If it was only the outer voice of sky
And cloud, of the sunken coral water-walled,
However clear, it would have been deep air,
The heaving speech of air, a summer sound
Repeated in a summer without end
And sound alone. But it was more than that,
More even than her voice, and ours, among
The meaningless plungings of water and the wind,
Theatrical distances, bronze shadows heaped
On high horizons, mountainous atmospheres
Of sky and sea.

              It was her voice that made
The sky acutest at its vanishing.
She measured to the hour its solitude.
She was the single artificer of the world
In which she sang. And when she sang, the sea,
Whatever self it had, became the self
That was her song, for she was maker. Then we,
As we beheld her striding there alone,
Knew that there never was a world for her
Except the one she sang and, singing, made.

Ramon Fernandez, tell me, if you know,
Why, when the singing ended and we turned
Toward the town, tell why the glassy lights,
The lights in the fishing boats at anchor there,
As the night descended, tilting in the air,
Mastered the night and portioned out the sea,
Fixing emblazoned zones and fiery poles,
Arranging, deepening, enchanting night.

Oh! Blessed rage for order, pale Ramon,
The maker's rage to order words of the sea,
Words of the fragrant portals, dimly-starred,
And of ourselves and of our origins,
In ghostlier demarcations, keener sounds.

SUNDAY MORNING

Complacencies of the peignoir, and late
Coffee and oranges in a sunny chair,
And the green freedom of a cockatoo
Upon a rug mingle to dissipate
The holy hush of ancient sacrifice.
She dreams a little, and she feels the dark
Encroachment of that old catastrophe,
As a calm darkens among water-lights.
The pungent oranges and bright, green wings
Seem things in some procession of the dead,
Winding across wide water, without sound.
The day is like wide water, without sound,
Stilled for the passing of her dreaming feet
Over the seas, to silent Palestine,
Dominion of the blood and sepulchre.

Why should she give her bounty to the dead?
What is divinity if it can come
Only in silent shadows and in dreams?
Shall she not find in comforts of the sun,
In pungent fruit and bright, green wings, or else
In any balm or beauty of the earth,
Things to be cherished like the thought of heaven?
Divinity must live within herself:
Passions of rain, or moods in falling snow;
Grievings in loneliness, or unsubdued
Elations when the forest blooms; gusty
Emotions on wet roads on autumn nights;
All pleasures and all pains, remembering
The bough of summer and the winter branch.
These are the measures destined for her soul.

Jove in the clouds had his inhuman birth.
No mother suckled him, no sweet land gave
Large-mannered motions to his mythy mind.
He moved among us, as a muttering king,
Magnificent, would move among his hinds,

Until our blood, commingling, virginal,
With heaven, brought such requital to desire
The very hinds discerned it, in a star.
Shall our blood fail? Or shall it come to be
The blood of paradise? And shall the earth
Seem all of paradise that we shall know?
The sky will be much friendlier then than now,
A part of labor and a part of pain,
And next in glory to enduring love,
Not this dividing and indifferent blue.

She says, "I am content when wakened birds,
Before they fly, test the reality
Of misty fields, by their sweet questionings;
But when the birds are gone, and their warm fields
Return no more, where, then, is paradise?"
There is not any haunt of prophecy,
Nor any old chimera of the grave,
Neither the golden underground, nor isle
Melodious, where spirits gat them home,
Nor visionary south, nor cloudy palm
Remote on heaven's hill, that has endured
As April's green endures; or will endure
Like her remembrance of awakened birds,
Or her desire for June and evening, tipped
By the consummation of the swallow's wings.

She says, "But in contentment I still feel
The need of some imperishable bliss."
Death is the mother of beauty; hence from her,
Alone, shall come fulfilment to our dreams
And our desires. Although she strews the leaves
Of sure obliteration on our paths,
The path sick sorrow took, the many paths
Where triumph rang its brassy phrase, or love
Whispered a little out of tenderness,
She makes the willow shiver in the sun
For maidens who were wont to sit and gaze

Upon the grass, relinquished to their feet.
She causes boys to pile new plums and pears
On disregarded plate. The maidens taste
And stray impassioned in the littering leaves.

Is there no change of death in paradise?
Does ripe fruit never fall? Or do the boughs
Hang always heavy in that perfect sky,
Unchanging, yet so like our perishing earth,
With rivers like our own that seek for seas
They never find, the same receding shores
That never touch with inarticulate pang?
Why set the pear upon those river-banks
Or spice the shores with odors of the plum?
Alas, that they should wear our colors there,
The silken weavings of our afternoons,
And pick the strings of our insipid lutes!
Death is the mother of beauty, mystical,
Within whose burning bosom we devise
Our earthly mothers waiting, sleeplessly.

Supple and turbulent, a ring of men
Shall chant in orgy on a summer morn
Their boisterous devotion to the sun,
Not as a god, but as a god might be,
Naked among them, like a savage source.
Their chant shall be a chant of paradise,
Out of their blood, returning to the sky;
And in their chant shall enter, voice by voice,
The windy lake wherein their lord delights,
The trees, like serafim, and echoing hills,
That choir among themselves long afterward.
They shall know well the heavenly fellowship
Of men that perish and of summer morn.
And whence they came and whither they shall go
The dew upon their feet shall manifest.

She hears, upon that water without sound,
A voice that cries, "The tomb in Palestine

Is not the porch of spirits lingering.
It is the grave of Jesus, where He lay."
We live in an old chaos of the sun,
Or old dependency of day and night,
Or island solitude, unsponsored, free,
Of that wide water, inescapable.
Deer walk upon our mountains, and the quail
Whistle about us their spontaneous cries;
Sweet berries ripen in the wilderness;
And, in the isolation of the sky,
At evening, casual flocks of pigeons make
Ambiguous undulations as they sink,
Downward to darkness, on extended wings.

THE SENSE OF THE SLEIGHT-OF-HAND MAN

One's grand flights, one's Sunday baths,
One's tootings at the weddings of the soul
Occur as they occur. So bluish clouds
Occurred above the empty house and the leaves
Of the rhododendrons rattled their gold,
As if someone lived there. Such floods of white
Came bursting from the clouds. So the wind
Threw its contorted strength around the sky.

Could you have said the bluejay suddenly
Would swoop to earth? It is a wheel, the rays
Around the sun. The wheel survives the myths.
The fire eye in the clouds survives the gods.
To think of a dove with an eye of grenadine
And pines that are cornets, so it occurs,

And a little island full of geese and stars:
It may be that the ignorant man, alone,
Has any chance to mate his life with life
That is the sensual, pearly spouse, the life
That is fluent in even the wintriest bronze.

THE POEMS OF OUR CLIMATE

I

Clear water in a brilliant bowl,
Pink and white carnations. The light
In the room more like a snowy air,
Reflecting snow. A newly-fallen snow
At the end of winter when afternoons return.
Pink and white carnations—one desires
So much more than that. The day itself
Is simplified: a bowl of white,
Cold, a cold porcelain, low and round,
With nothing more than the carnations there.

II

Say even that this complete simplicity
Stripped one of all one's torments, concealed
The evilly compounded, vital I
And made it fresh in a world of white,
A world of clear water, brilliant-edged,
Still one would want more, one would need more,
More than a world of white and snowy scents.

III

There would still remain the never-resting mind,
So that one would want to escape, come back
To what had been so long composed.
The imperfect is our paradise.
Note that, in this bitterness, delight,
Since the imperfect is so hot in us,
Lies in flawed words and stubborn sounds.

AN EXTRACT

from Addresses to the Academy of Fine Ideas

On an early Sunday in April, a feeble day,
He felt curious about the winter hills
And wondered about the water in the lake.

It had been cold since December. Snow fell, first,
At New Year and, from then until April, lay
On everything. Now it had melted, leaving
The gray grass like a pallet, closely pressed;
And dirt. The wind blew in the empty place.
The winter wind blew in an empty place—
There was that difference between the and an,
The difference between himself and no man,
No man that heard a wind in an empty place.
It was time to be himself again, to see
If the place, in spite of its witheredness, was still
Within the difference. He felt curious
Whether the water was black and lashed about
Or whether the ice still covered the lake. There was still
Snow under the trees and on the northern rocks,
The dead rocks not the green rocks, the live rocks. If,
When he looked, the water ran up the air or grew white
Against the edge of the ice, the abstraction would
Be broken and winter would be broken and done,
And being would be being himself again,
Being, becoming seeing and feeling and self,
Black water breaking into reality.

✳ A POSTCARD FROM THE VOLCANO

Children picking up our bones
Will never know that these were once
As quick as foxes on the hill;

And that in autumn, when the grapes
Made sharp air sharper by their smell
These had a being, breathing frost;

And least will guess that with our bones
We left much more, left what still is
The look of things, left what we felt

At what we saw. The spring clouds blow
Above the shuttered mansion-house,
Beyond our gate and the windy sky
Cries out a literate despair.
We knew for long the mansion's look
And what we said of it became

A part of what it is ... Children,
Still weaving budded aureoles,
Will speak our speech and never know,

Will say of the mansion that it seems
As if he that lived there left behind
A spirit storming in blank walls,

A dirty house in a gutted world,
A tatter of shadows peaked to white,
Smeared with the gold of the opulent sun.

PAROCHIAL THEME

Long-tailed ponies go nosing the pine-lands,
Ponies of Parisians shooting on the hill.

The wind blows. In the wind the voices
Have shapes that are not yet fully themselves,

Are sounds blown by a blower into shapes,
The blower squeezed to the thinnest *mi* of falsetto.

The hunters run to and fro. The heavy trees,
The grunting, shuffling branches, the robust,

The nocturnal, the antique, the blue-green pines
Deepen the feelings to inhuman depths.

These are the forest. This health is holy,
This halloo, halloo, halloo heard over the cries

Of those for whom a square room is a fire,
Of those whom the statues torture and keep down.

This health is holy, this descant of a self,
This barbarous chanting of what is strong, this blare.

But salvation here? What about the rattle of sticks
On tins and boxes? What about horses eaten by wind?

When spring comes and the skeletons of the hunters
Stretch themselves to rest in their first summer's sun,

The spring will have health of its own, with none
Of autumn's halloo in its hair. So that closely, then,

Health follows after health. Salvation there:
There's no such thing as life; or if there is,

It is faster than the weather, faster than
Any character. It is more than any scene:

Of the guillotine or of any glamorous hanging.
Piece the world together, boys, but not with your hands.

THE WOMAN THAT HAD MORE BABIES THAN THAT

I

An acrobat on the border of the sea
Observed the waves, the rising and the swell
And the first line spreading up the beach; again,
The rising and the swell, the preparation
And the first line foaming over the sand; again,
The rising and the swell, the first line's glitter,
Like a dancer's skirt, flung round and settling down.
This was repeated day by day. The waves
Were mechanical, muscular. They never changed,
They never stopped, a repetition repeated

Continually—There is a woman has had
More babies than that. The merely revolving wheel
Returns and returns, along the dry, salt shore.
There is a mother whose children need more than that.
She is not the mother of landscapes but of those
That question the repetition on the shore,
Listening to the whole sea for a sound
Of more or less, ascetically sated
By amical tones.

       The acrobat observed
The universal machine. There he perceived
The need for a thesis, a music constant to move.

II

Berceuse, transatlantic. The children are men, old men,
Who, when they think and speak of the central man,
Of the humming of the central man, the whole sound
Of the sea, the central humming of the sea,
Are old men breathed on by a maternal voice,
Children and old men and philosophers,
Bald heads with their mother's voice still in their ears.
The self is a cloister full of remembered sounds
And of sounds so far forgotten, like her voice,
That they return unrecognized. The self
Detects the sound of a voice that doubles its own,
In the images of desire, the forms that speak,
The ideas that come to it with a sense of speech.
The old men, the philosophers, are haunted by that
Maternal voice, the explanation at night.
They are more than parts of the universal machine.
Their need in solitude: that is the need,
The desire, for the fiery lullaby.

III

          If her head
Stood on a plain of marble, high and cold;
If her eyes were chinks in which the sparrows built;
If she was deaf with falling grass in her ears—

But there is more than a marble, massive head.
They find her in the crackling summer night,
In the *Duft* of towns, beside a window, beside
A lamp, in a day of the week, the time before spring,
A manner of walking, yellow fruit, a house,
A street. She has a supernatural head.
On her lips familiar words become the words
Of an elevation, an elixir of the whole.

ON AN OLD HORN

I

The bird kept saying that birds had once been men,
Or were to be, animals with men's eyes,
Men fat as feathers, misers counting breaths,
Woman of a melancholy one could sing.
Then the bird from his ruddy belly blew
A trumpet round the trees. Could one say that it was
A baby with the tail of a rat?
                                    The stones
Were violet, yellow, purple, pink. The grass
Of the iris bore white blooms. The bird then boomed.
Could one say that he sang the colors in the stones,
False as the mind, instead of the fragrance, warm
With sun?
                In the little of his voice, or the like,
Or less, he found a man, or more, against
Calamity, proclaimed himself, was proclaimed.

II

If the stars that move together as one, disband,
Flying like insects of fire in a cavern of night,
Pipperoo, pippera, pipperum . . . The rest is rot.

CUISINE BOURGEOISE

These days of disinheritance, we feast
On human heads. True, birds rebuild
Old nests and there is blue in the woods.
The church bells clap one night in the week.
But that's all done. It is what used to be,
As they used to lie in the grass, in the heat,
Men on green beds and women half of sun.
The words are written, though not yet said.

It is like the season when, after summer,
It is summer and it is not, it is autumn
And it is not, it is day and it not,
As if last night's lamps continued to burn,
As if yesterday's people continued to watch
The sky, half porcelain, preferring that
To shaking out heavy bodies in the glares
Of this present, this science, this unrecognized,

This outpost, this douce, this dumb, this dead, in which
We feast on human heads, brought in on leaves,
Crowned with the first, cold buds. On these we live,
No longer on the ancient cake of seed,
The almond and deep fruit. This bitter meat
Sustains us. . . . Who, then, are they, seated here?
Is the table a mirror in which they sit and look?
Are they men eating reflections of themselves?

THE PRESIDENT ORDAINS THE BEE TO BE

The President ordains the bee to be
Immortal. The President ordains. But does
The body lift its heavy wing, take up,

Again, an inexhaustible being, rise
Over the loftiest antagonist
To drone the green phrases of its juvenal?

Why should the bee recapture a lost blague,
Find a deep echo in a horn and buzz
The bottomless trophy, new hornsman after old?

The President has apples on the table
And barefoot servants round him, who adjust
The curtains to a metaphysical t

And the banners of the nation flutter, burst
On the flag-poles in a red-blue dazzle, whack
At the halyards. Why, then, when in golden fury

Spring vanishes the scraps of winter, why
Should there be a question of returning or
Of death in memory's dream? Is spring a sleep?

This warmth is for lovers at last accomplishing
Their love, this beginning, not resuming, this
Booming and booming of the new-come bee.

(From *Notes Toward a Supreme Fiction*)

TO AN OLD PHILOSOPHER IN ROME

On the threshold of heaven, the figures in the street
Become the figures of heaven, the majestic movement
Of men growing small in the distances of space,
Singing, with smaller and still smaller sound,
Unintelligible absolution and an end—

The threshold, Rome, and that more merciful Rome
Beyond, the two alike in the make of the mind.
It is as if in a human dignity
Two parallels become one, a perspective, of which
Men are part both in the inch and in the mile.

How easily the blown banners change to wings ..
Things dark on the horizons of perception
Become accompaniments of fortune, but
Of the fortune of the spirit, beyond the eye,
Not of its sphere, and yet not far beyond,

The human end in the spirit's greatest reach,
The extreme of the known in the presence of the extreme
Of the unknown. The newsboys' muttering
Becomes another murmuring; the smell
Of medicine, a fragrantness not to be spoiled ..

The bed, the books, the chair, the moving nuns,
The candle as it evades the sight, these are
The sources of happiness in the shape of Rome,
A shape within the ancient circles of shapes,
And these beneath the shadow of a shape

In a confusion on bed and books, a portent
On the chair, a moving transparence on the nuns,
A light on the candle tearing against the wick
To join a hovering excellence, to escape
From fire and be part only of that of which

Fire is the symbol: the celestial possible.
Speak to your pillow as if it was yourself.
Be orator but with an accurate tongue
And without eloquence, O, half-asleep,
Of the pity that is the memorial of this room,

So that we feel, in this illumined large,
The veritable small, so that each of us
Beholds himself in you, and hears his voice
In yours, master and commiserable man,
Intent on your particles of nether-do,

Your dozing in the depths of wakefulness,
In the warmth of your bed, at the edge of your chair, alive
Yet living in two worlds, impenitent
As to one, and, as to one, most penitent,
Impatient for the grandeur that you need

In so much misery; and yet finding it
Only in misery, the afflatus of ruin,

Profound poetry of the poor and of the dead,
As in the last drop of the deepest blood,
As it falls from the heart and lies there to be seen,

Even as the blood of an empire, it might be,
For a citizen of heaven though still of Rome.
It is poverty's speech that seeks us out the most.
It is older than the oldest speech of Rome.
This is the tragic accent of the scene.

And you—it is you that speak it, without speech,
The loftiest syllables among loftiest things,
The one invulnerable man among
Crude captains, the naked majesty, if you like,
Of bird-nest arches and of rain-stained vaults.

The sounds drift in. The buildings are remembered.
The life of the city never lets go. You do not
Ever want it to. It is part of the life in your room.
Its domes are the architecture of your bed.
The bells keep on repeating solemn names

In choruses and choirs of choruses,
Unwilling that mercy should be a mystery
Of silence, that any solitude of sense
Should give you more than their peculiar chords
And reverberations clinging to whisper still.

It is a kind of total grandeur at the end,
With every visible thing enlarged and yet
No more than a bed, a chair and moving nuns,
The immensest theater, the pillared porch,
The book and candle in your ambered room,

Total grandeur of a total edifice,
Chosen by an inquisitor of structures
For himself. He stops upon this threshold,
As if the design of all his words takes form
And frame from thinking and is realized.

william carlos williams

THE YACHTS

contend in a sea which the land partly encloses
shielding them from the too heavy blows
of an ungoverned ocean which when it chooses

tortures the biggest hulls, the best man knows
to pit against its beatings, and sinks them pitilessly.
Mothlike in mists, scintillant in the minute

brilliance of cloudless days, with broad bellying sails
they glide to the wind tossing green water
from their sharp prows while over them the crew crawls

ant like, solicitously grooming them, releasing,
making fast as they turn, lean far over and having
caught the wind again, side by side, head for the mark.

In a well guarded arena of open water surrounded by
lesser and greater craft which, sycophant, lumbering
and flittering follow them, they appear youthful, rare

as the light of a happy eye, live with the grace
of all that in the mind is feckless, free and
naturally to be desired. Now the sea which holds them

is moody, lapping their glossy sides, as if feeling
for some slightest flaw but fails completely.
Today no race. Then the wind comes again. The yachts

move, jockeying for a start, the signal is set and they
are off. Now the waves strike at them but they are too
well made, they slip through, though they take in canvas.

Arms with hands grasping seek to clutch at the prows.
Bodies thrown recklessly in the way are cut aside.
It is a sea of faces about them in agony, in despair

until the horror of the race dawns staggering the mind,
the whole sea become an entanglement of watery bodies
lost to the world bearing what they cannot hold. Broken,

beaten, desolate, reaching from the dead to be taken up
they cry out, failing, failing! their cries rising
in waves still as the skillful yachts pass over.

elinor wylie

WILD PEACHES

I

When the world turns completely upside down
You say we'll emigrate to the Eastern Shore
Aboard a river-boat from Baltimore;
We'll live among wild peach trees, miles from town,
You'll wear a coonskin cap, and I a gown
Homespun, dyed butternut's dark gold colour.
Lost, like your lotus-eating ancestor,
We'll swim in milk and honey till we drown.
The winter will be short, the summer long,
The autumn amber-hued, sunny and hot,
Tasting of cider and of scuppernong;
All seasons sweet, but autumn best of all.
The squirrels in their silver fur will fall
Like falling leaves, like fruit, before your shot.

II

The autumn frosts will lie upon the grass
Like bloom on grapes of purple-brown and gold.
The misted early mornings will be cold;
The little puddles will be roofed with glass.
The sun, which burns from copper into brass,
Melts these at noon, and makes the boys unfold
Their knitted mufflers; full as they can hold,
Fat pockets dribble chestnuts as they pass.

Peaches grow wild, and pigs can live in clover;
A barrel of salted herrings lasts a year;
The spring begins before the winter's over.
By February you may find the skins
Of garter snakes and water moccasins
Dwindled and harsh, dead-white and cloudy-clear.

III

When April pours the colours of a shell
Upon the hills, when every little creek
Is shot with silver from the Chesapeake
In shoals new-minted by the ocean swell,
When strawberries go begging, and the sleek
Blue plums lie open to the blackbird's beak,
We shall live well—we shall live very well.
The months between the cherries and the peaches
Are brimming cornucopias which spill
Fruits red and purple, sombre-bloomed and black;
Then, down rich fields and frosty river beaches
We'll trample bright persimmons, while you kill
Bronze partridge, speckled quail, and canvasback.

IV

Down to the Puritan marrow of my bones
There's something in this richness that I hate.
I love the look, austere, immaculate,
Of landscapes drawn in pearly monotones.
There's something in my very blood that owns
Bare hills, cold silver on a sky of slate,
A thread of water, churned to milky spate
Streaming through slanted pastures fenced with stones.
I love those skies, thin blue or snowy gray,
Those fields sparse-planted, rendering meagre sheaves;
That spring, briefer than apple-blossom's breath,
Summer, so much too beautiful to stay,
Swift autumn, like a bonfire of leaves,
And sleepy winter, like the sleep of death.

THE EAGLE AND THE MOLE

Avoid the reeking herd,
Shun the polluted flock,
Live like that stoic bird,
The eagle of the rock.

The huddled warmth of
    crowds
Begets and foster hate;
He keeps, above the clouds,
His cliff inviolate.

When flocks are folded warm,
And herds to shelter run,
He sails above the storm,
He stares into the sun.

If in the eagle's track
Your sinews cannot leap,
Avoid the lathered pack,
Turn from the steaming
    sheep.

If you would keep your soul
From spotted sight or sound,
Live like the velvet mole;
Go burrow under ground.

And there hold intercourse
With roots of trees and
    stones,
With rivers at their source,
And disembodied bones.

ADDRESS TO MY SOUL

My soul, be not disturbed
By planetary war;
Remain securely orbed
In this contracted star.

Fear not, pathetic flame;
Your sustenance is doubt:
Glassed in translucent dream
They cannot snuff you out.

Wear water, or a mask
Of unapparent cloud;
Be brave and never ask
A more defunctive shroud.

The universal points
Are shrunk into a flower;
Between its delicate joints
Chaos keeps no power.

The pure integral form,
Austere and silver-dark,
Is balanced on the storm
In its predestined arc.

Small as a sphere of rain
It slides along the groove
Whose path is furrowed plain
Among the suns that move.

The shapes of April buds
Outlive the phantom year:
Upon the void at odds
The dewdrop falls severe.

Five-petalled flame, be cold:
Be firm, dissolving star:
Accept the stricter mould
That makes you singular.

THE PURITAN'S BALLAD

My love came up from Barnegat,
    The sea was in his eyes;
He trod as softly as a cat
    And told me terrible lies.

His hair was yellow as new-cut pine
    In shavings curled and feathered;
I thought how silver it would shine
    By cruel winters weathered.

But he was in his twentieth year,
    This time I'm speaking of;
We were head over heels in love with fear
    And half a-feared of love.

His feet were used to treading a gale
    And balancing thereon;
His face was brown as a foreign sail
    Threadbare against the sun.

His arms were thick as hickory logs
    Whittled to little wrists;
Strong as the teeth of terrier dogs
    Were the fingers of his fists.

Within his arms I feared to sink
    Where lions shook their manes,
And dragons drawn in azure ink
    Leapt quickened by his veins.

Dreadful his strength and length of limb
    As the sea to foundering ships;
I dipped my hands in love for him
    No deeper than their tips.

But our palms were welded by a flame
    The moment we came to part,
And on his knuckles I read my name
    Enscrolled within a heart.

And something made our wills to bend
    As wild as trees blown over;
We were no longer friend and friend,
    But only lover and lover.

'In seven weeks or seventy years—
    God grant it may be sooner!—
I'll make a handkerchief for your tears
    From the sails of my captain's schooner.

'We'll wear our love like wedding rings
    Long polished to our touch;
We shall be busy with other things
    And they cannot bother us much.

'When you are skimming the wrinkled cream
    And your ring clinks on the pan,
You'll say to yourself in a pensive dream,
    'How wonderful a man!'

'When I am slitting a fish's head
    And my ring clanks on the knife,
I'll say with thanks, as a prayer is said,
    'How beautiful a wife!'

'And I shall fold my decorous paws
    In velvet smooth and deep,
Like a kitten that covers up its claws
    To sleep and sleep and sleep.

'Like a little blue pigeon you shall bow
    Your bright alarming crest;
In the crook of my arm you'll lay your brow
    To rest and rest and rest.'

Will he never come back from Barnegat
    With thunder in his eyes,
Treading as soft as a tiger cat,
    To tell me terrible lies?

d. h. lawrence

BAVARIAN GENTIANS

Not every man has gentians in his house
in Soft September, at slow, Sad Michaelmas.

Bavarian gentians, big and dark, only dark
darkening the day-time torch-like with the smoking blueness
of Pluto's gloom,
ribbed and torch-like, with their blaze of darkness spread blue
down flattening into points, flattened under the sweep of
white day
torch-flower of the blue-smoking darkness, Pluto's dark-blue
daze,
black lamps from the halls of Dis, burning dark blue,
giving off darkness, blue darkness, as Demeter's pale lamps
give off light,
lead me then, lead me the way.

Reach me a gentian, give me a torch
let me guide myself with the blue, forked torch of this flower
down the darker and darker stairs, where blue is darkened on
blueness.
even where Persephone goes, just now, from the
frosted September
to the sightless realm where darkness is awake upon the dark
and Persephone herself is but a voice
or a darkness invisible enfolded in the deeper dark
of the arms Plutonic, and pierced with the passion of dense
gloom,
among the splendour of torches of darkness, shedding darkness on the lost bride and her groom.

PIANO

Softly, in the dusk, a woman is singing to me;
Taking me back down the vista of years, till I see
A child sitting under the piano, in the boom of the tingling
strings

And pressing the small, poised feet of a mother who smiles as
    she sings.

In spite of myself, the insidious mastery of song
Betrays me back, till the heart of me weeps to belong
To the old Sunday evenings at home, with winter outside
And hymns in the cozy parlor, the tinkling piano our guide.

So now it is vain for the singer to burst into clamor
With the great black piano appassionato. The glamour
Of childish days is upon me, my manhood is cast
Down in the flood of remembrance, I weep like a child for the
    past.

HUMMING-BIRD

I can imagine, in some otherworld
Primeval-dumb, far back
In that most awful stillness, that only gasped and hummed,
Humming-birds raced down the avenues.

Before anything had a soul,
While life was a heave of Matter, half inanimate,
This little bit chipped off in brilliance
And went whizzing through the slow, vast, succulent stems.

I believe there were no flowers then,
In the world where the humming-bird flashed ahead of
    creation.
I believe he pierced the slow vegetable veins with his long
    beak.
Probably he was big
As mosses, and little lizards, they say, were once big.
Probably he was a jabbing, terrifying monster.

We look at him through the wrong end of the long telescope
    of Time,
Luckily for us.

THE SHIP OF DEATH

I

Now it is autumn and the falling fruit
and the long journey towards oblivion.
The apples falling like great drops of dew
to bruise themselves an exit from themselves.

And it is time to go, to bid farewell
to one's own self, and find an exit
from the fallen self.

II

Have you built your ship of death, O have you?
O build your ship of death, for you will need it.

The grim frost is at hand, when the apples will fall
thick, almost thundrous, on the hardened earth.

And death is on the air like a smell of ashes!
Ah! can't you smell it?
And in the bruised body, the frightened soul
finds itself shrinking, wincing from the cold
that blows upon it through the orifices.

III

And can a man his own quietus make
with a bare bodkin?

With daggers, bodkins, bullets, man can make
a bruise or break of exit for his life;
but is that a quietus, O tell me, is it quietus?

Surely not so! for how could murder, even self-murder,
ever a quietus make?

IV

O let us talk of quiet that we know,

that we can know, the deep and lovely quiet
of a strong heart at peace!

How can we this, our own quietus, make?

V

Build then the ship of death, for you must take
the longest journey, to oblivion.

And die the death, the long and painful death
that lies between the old self and the new.

Already our bodies are fallen, bruised, badly bruised,
already our souls are oozing through the exit
of the cruel bruise.

Already the dark and endless ocean of the end
is washing in through the breaches of our wounds,
already the flood is upon us.

O build your ship of death, your little ark
and furnish it with food, with little cakes, and wine
for the dark flight down oblivion.

VI

Piecemeal the body dies, and the timid soul
has her footing washed away, as the dark flood rises.

We are dying, we are dying, we are all of us dying
and nothing will stay the death-flood rising within us
and soon it will rise on the world, on the outside world.

We are dying, we are dying, piecemeal our bodies are dying
and our strength leaves us,
and our soul cowers naked in the dark rain over the flood,
cowering in the last branches of the tree of our life.

VII

We are dying, we are dying, so all we can do
is now to be willing to die, and to build the ship
of death to carry the soul on the longest journey.

A little ship, with oars and food
and little dishes, and all accoutrements
fitting and ready for the departing soul.

Now launch the small ship, now as the body dies
and life departs, launch out, the fragile soul
in the fragile ship of courage, the ark of faith
with its store of food and little cooking pans
and change of clothes,
upon the flood's black waste
upon the waters of the end
upon the sea of death, where still we sail
darkly, for we cannot steer, and have no port.

There is no port, there is nowhere to go
only the deepening blackness darkening still
blacker upon the soundless, ungurgling flood
darkness at one with darkness, up and down
and sideways utterly dark, so there is no direction any more
and the little ship is there; yet she is gone.
She is not seen, for there is nothing to see her by.
She is gone! gone! and yet
somewhere she is there.
Nowhere.

VIII

And everything is gone, the body is gone
completely under, gone, entirely gone.
The upper darkness is heavy as the lower,
between them the little ship
is gone

It is the end, it is oblivion

IX

And yet out of eternity a thread
separates itself on the blackness,
a horizontal thread
that fumes a little with pallor upon the dark.

Is it illusion? or does the pallor fume
A little higher?
Ah wait, wait, for there's the dawn,
the cruel dawn of coming back to life
out of oblivion
Wait, wait, the little ship
drifting, beneath the deathly ashly grey
of a flood-dawn.

Wait, wait! even so, a flush of yellow
and strangely, O chilled wan soul, a flush of rose.

A flush of rose, and the whole thing starts again.

X

The flood subsides, and the body, like a worn sea-shell
emerges strange and lovely.
And the little ship wings home, faltering and lapsing
on the pink flood,
and the frail soul steps out, into the house again
filling the heart with peace.

Swings the heart renewed with peace
even of oblivion.

Oh build your ship of death. Oh build it!
for you will need it.
For the voyage of oblivion awaits you.

ezra pound

A PACT

I make a pact with you, Walt Whitman—
I have detested you long enough.
I come to you as a grown child
Who has had a pig-headed father;
I am old enough now to make friends.
It was you that broke the new wood,
Now is a time for carving.
We have one sap and one root—
Let there be commerce between us.

ANCIENT MUSIC

Winter is icumen in,
Lhude sing Goddamm,
Raineth drop and staineth slop,
And how the wind doth ramm!
       Sing : Goddamm.
Skiddeth bus and sloppeth us,
An ague hath my ham.
Freezeth river, turneth liver,
     Damn you, sing : Goddamm.
Goddamm, Goddamm, 'tis why I am, Goddamm,
      So 'gainst the winter's balm.
Sing goddamm, damm, sing Goddamm,
Sing goddamm, sing goddamm, DAMM.

CANTO I

And then went down to the ship,
Set keel to breakers, forth on the godly sea, and
We set up mast and sail on that swart ship,
Bore sheep aboard her, and our bodies also

Heavy with weeping, and winds from sternward
Bore us out onward with bellying canvas,
Circe's this craft, the trim-coifed goddess.
Then sat we amidships, wind jamming the tiller,
Thus with stretched sail, we went over sea till day's end.
Sun to his slumber, shadows o'er all the ocean,
Came we then to the bounds of deepest water,
To the Kimmerian lands, and peopled cities
Covered with close-webbed mist, unpierced ever
With glitter of sun-ray
Nor with stars stretched, nor looking back from heaven
Swartest night stretched over wretched men there.
The ocean flowing backward, came we then to the place
Aforesaid by Circe.
Here did they rites, Perimedes and Eurylochus,
And drawing sword from my hip
I dug the ell-square pitkin;
Poured we libations unto each the dead,
First mead and then sweet wine, water mixed with white flour.
Then prayed I many a prayer to the sickly death's-heads;
As set in Ithaca, sterile bulls of the best
For sacrifice, heaping the pyre with goods,
A sheep to Tiresias only, black and a bell-sheep.
Dark blood flowed in the fosse,
Souls out of Erebus, cadaverous dead, of brides
Of youths and of the old who had borne much;
Souls stained with recent tears, girls tender,
Men many, mauled with bronze lance heads,
Battle spoil, bearing yet dreary arms,
These many crowded about me; with shouting,
Pallor upon me, cried to my men for more beasts;
Slaughtered the herds, sheep slain of bronze;
Poured ointment, cried to the gods,
To Pluto the strong, and praised Proserpine;
Unsheathed the narrow sword,
I sat to keep off the impetuous impotent dead,
Till I should hear Tiresias.
But first Elpenor came, our friend Elpenor,

Unburied, cast on the wide earth,
Limbs that we left in the house of Circe,
Unwept, unwrapped in sepulcher, since toils urged other.
Pitiful spirit. And I cried in hurried speech:
"Elpenor, how art thou come to this dark coast?
"Cam'st thou afoot, outstripping seamen?"

And he in heavy speech:
"Ill fate and abundant wine. I slept in Circe's ingle.
"Going down the long ladder unguarded,
"I fell against the buttress,
"Shattered the nape-nerve, the soul sought Avernus.
"But thou, O King, I bid remember me, unwept, unburied,
"Heap up mine arms, be tomb by sea-board, and inscribed:
" '*A man of no fortune and with a name to come.*'
"And set my oar up, that I swung mid fellows."
And Anticlea came, whom I beat off, and then Tiresias
        Theban,
Holding his golden wand, knew me, and spoke first:
"A second time? why? man of ill star,
"Facing the sunless dead and this joyless region?
"Stand from the fosse, leave me my bloody bever
"For soothsay."

And I stepped back,
And he strong with the blood, said then: "Odysseus
"Shalt return through spiteful Neptune, over dark seas,
"Lose all companions." And then Anticlea came.
Lie quiet Divus. I mean that is Andreas Divus,
In officina Wecheli, 1538, out of Homer.
And he sailed, by Sirens and thence outward and away
And unto Circe.

Venerandam,
In the Cretan's phrase, with the golden crown, Aphrodite,
Cypri munimenta sortita est, mirthful, oricalchi, with golden
Girdles and breast bands, thou with dark eyelids
Bearing the golden bough of Argicida.

SESTINA: ALTAFORTE

Loquitur: En Bertrans de Born.
> Dante Alighieri put this man in hell for that he was a stirrer up of strife.
> Eccovi! Judge ye!
> Have I dug him up again?
The scene is at his castle, Altaforte. "Papiols" is his jongleur.
"The Leopard," the device of Richard Cœur de Lion.

Damn it all! all this our South stinks peace.
You whoreson dog, Papiols, come! Let's to music!
I have no life save when the swords clash.
But ah! when I see the standards gold, vair, purple, opposing
And the broad fields beneath them turn crimson,
Then howl I my heart nigh mad with rejoicing.

In hot summer have I great rejoicing
When the tempest kills the earth's foul peace,
And the lightnings from black heav'n flash crimson,
And the fierce thunders roar me their music
And the winds shriek through the clouds mad, opposing,
And through all the riven skies God's swords clash.

Hell grant soon we hear again the swords clash!
And the shrill neighs of destriers in battle rejoicing,
Spiked breast to spiked breast opposing!
Better one hour's stour than a year's peace
With fat boards, bawds, wine and frail music!
Bah! there's no wine like the blood's crimson!

And I love to see the sun rise blood-crimson.
And I watch his spears through the dark clash
And it fills all my heart with rejoicing
And pries wide my mouth with fast music
When I see him so scorn and defy peace,
His lone might 'gainst all darkness opposing.

The man who fears war and squats opposing
My words for stour, hath no blood of crimson.
But is fit only to rot in womanish peace
For from where worth's won and the swords clash

For the death of such sluts I go rejoicing;
Yea, I fill all the air with my music.

Papiols, Papiols, to the music!
There's no sound like to swords swords opposing,
No cry like the battle's rejoicing
When our elbows and swords drip the crimson
And our charges 'gainst "The Leopard's" rush clash.
May God damn for ever all who cry "Peace!"

And let the music of the swords make them crimson!
Hell grant soon we hear again the swords clash!
Hell blot black for alway the thought "Peace"!

THE RIVER-MERCHANT'S WIFE: A LETTER

While my hair was still cut straight across my forehead
I played about the front gate, pulling flowers.
You came by on bamboo stilts, playing horse,
You walked about my seat, playing with blue plums.
And we went on living in the village of Chokan:
Two small people, without dislike or suspicion.

At fourteen I married My Lord you.
I never laughed, being bashful.
Lowering my head, I looked at the wall.
Called to, a thousand times, I never looked back.

At fifteen I stopped scowling,
I desired my dust to be mingled with yours
Forever and forever and forever.
Why should I climb the look out?

At sixteen you departed,
You went into far Ku-to-yen, by the river of swirling eddies,
And you have been gone five months.
The monkeys make sorrowful noise overhead.
You dragged your feet when you went out.

By the gate now, the moss is grown, the different mosses,
Too deep to clear them away!
The leaves fall early this autumn, in wind.
The paired butterflies are already yellow with August
Over the grass in the West garden;
They hurt me. I grow older.
If you are coming down through the narrows of the river
Please let me know beforehand,   [Kiang,
And I will come out to meet you
                    As far as Cho-fu-sa.

THE SEAFARER: *From the Anglo-Saxon*

May I for my own self song's truth reckon,
Journey's jargon, how I in harsh days
Hardship endured oft.
Bitter breast-cares have I abided,
Known on my keel many a care's hold,
And dire sea-surge, and there I oft spent
Narrow nightwatch nigh the ship's head
While she tossed close to cliffs. Coldly afflicted,
My feet were by frost benumbed.
Chill its chains are; chafing sighs
Hew my heart round and hunger begot
Mere-weary mood. Lest man know not
That he on dry land loveliest liveth,
List how I, care-wretched, on ice-cold sea,
Weathered the winter, wretched outcast
Deprived of my kinsmen;
Hung with hard ice-flakes, where hail-scur flew,
There I heard naught save the harsh sea
And ice-cold wave, at whiles the swan cries,
Did for my games the gannet's clamour,
Sea-fowls' loudness was for me laughter,
The mews' singing all my mead-drink.
Storms, on the stone-cliffs beaten, fell on the stern
In icy feathers; full oft the eagle screamed
With spray on his pinion.

Not any protector
May make merry man faring needy.
This he little believes, who aye in winsome life
Abides 'mid burghers some heavy business,
Wealthy and wine-flushed, how I weary oft
Must bide above brine.
Neareth nightshade, snoweth from north,
Frost froze the land, hail fell on earth then,
Corn of the coldest. Nathless there knocketh now
The heart's thought that I on high streams
The salt-wavy tumult traverse alone.
Moaneth alway my mind's lust
That I fare forth, that I afar hence
Seek out a foreign fastness.
For this there's no mood-lofty man over earth's midst,
Not though he be given his good, but will have in his youth
      greed;
Nor his deed to the daring, nor his kind to the faithful
But shall have his sorrow for sea-fare
Whatever his lord will.
He hath not heart for harping, nor in ring-having
Nor winsomeness to wife, nor world's delight
Nor any whit else save the wave's slash,
Yet longing comes upon him to fare forth on the water.
Bosque taketh blossom, cometh beauty of berries,
Fields to fairness, land fares brisker,
All this admonisheth man eager of mood,
The heart turns to travel so that he then thinks
On flood-ways to be far departing.
Cuckoo calleth with gloomy crying,
He singeth summerward, bodeth sorrow,
The bitter heart's blood. Burgher knows not—
He the prosperous man—what some perform
Where wandering them widest draweth.
So that but now my heart burst from my breastlock,
My mood 'mid the mere-flood,
Over the whale's acre, would wander wide.
On earth's shelter cometh oft to me,

Eager and ready, the crying lone-flyer,
Whets for the whale-path the heart irresistibly,
O'er tracks of ocean; seeing that anyhow
My lord deems to me this dead life
On loan and on land, I believe not
That any earth-weal eternal standeth
Save there be somewhat calamitous
That, ere a man's tide go, turn it to twain.
Disease or oldness or sword-hate
Beats out the breath from doom-gripped body.
And for this, every earl whatever, for those speaking after—
Laud of the living, boasteth some last word,
That he will work ere he pass onward,
Frame on the fair earth 'gainst foes his malice,
Daring ado, . . .
So that all men shall honour him after
And his laud beyond them remain 'mid the English,
Aye, for ever, a lasting life's-blast,
Delight 'mid the doughty. . . . Days little durable,
And all arrogance of earthen riches,
There come now no kings nor Cæsars
Nor gold-giving lords like those gone.
Howe'er in mirth most magnified,
Whoe'er lived in life most lordliest,
Drear all this excellence, delights undurable!
Waneth the watch, but the world holdeth.
Tomb hideth trouble. The blade is layed low.
Earthly glory ageth and seareth.
No man at all going the earth's gait,
But age fares against him, his face paleth,
Grey-haired he groaneth, knows gone companions,
Lordly men, are to earth o'ergiven,
Nor may he then the flesh-cover, whose life ceaseth,
Nor eat the sweet nor feel the sorry,
Nor stir hand nor think in mid heart,
And though he strew the grave with gold,
His born brothers, their buried bodies
Be an unlikely treasure hoard.

BALLAD OF THE GOODLY FERE

Simon Zelotes speaketh it somewhile after the Crucifixion

Ha' we lost the goodliest fere o' all
For the priests and the gallows tree?
Aye lover he was of brawny men,
O' ships and the open sea.

When they came wi' a host to take Our Man
His smile was good to see,
"First let these go!" quo' our Goodly Fere,
"Or I'll see ye damned," says he.

Aye he sent us out through the crossed high spears
And the scorn of his laugh rang free,
"Why took ye not me when I walked about
Alone in the town?" says he.

Oh we drunk his "Hale" in the good red wine
When we last made company,
No capon priest was the Goodly Fere
But a man o' men was he.

I ha' seen him drive a hundred men
Wi' a bundle o' cords swung free,
That they took the high and holy house
For their pawn and treasury.

They'll no' get him a' in a book I think
Though they write it cunningly;
No mouse of the scrolls was the Goodly Fere
But aye loved the open sea.

If they think they ha' snared our Goodly Fere
They are fools to the last degree.
"I'll go to the feast," quo' our Goodly Fere,
"Though I go to the gallows tree."

"Ye ha' seen me heal the lame and blind,
And wake the dead," says he,
"Ye shall see one thing to master all:
'Tis how a brave man dies on the tree."

A son of God was the Goodly Fere
That bade us his brothers be.
I ha' seen him cow a thousand men.
I have seen him upon the tree.

He cried no cry when they drave the nails
And the blood gushed hot and free,
The hounds of the crimson sky gave tongue
But never a cry cried he.

I ha' seen him cow a thousand men
On the hills o' Galilee,
They whined as he walked out calm between,
Wi' his eyes like the grey o' the sea,

Like the sea that brooks no voyaging
With the winds unleashed and free,
Like the sea that he cowed at Genseret
Wi' twey words spoke' suddently.

A master of men was the Goodly Fere,
A mate of the wind and sea,
If they think they ha' slain our Goodly Fere
They are fools eternally.

I ha' seen him eat o' the honey-comb
Sin' they nailed him to the tree.

CANTO XLV

With *Usura*
With usura hath no man a house of good stone
each block cut smooth and well fitting
that design might cover their face,
with usura
hath no man a painted paradise on his church wall
harpes et luthes
or where virgin receiveth message
and halo projects from incision,
with usura
seeth no man Gonzaga his heirs and his concubines
no picture is made to endure nor to live with
but it is made to sell and sell quickly
with usura, sin against nature,
is thy bread ever more of stale rags
is thy bread dry as paper,
with no mountain wheat, no strong flour
with usura the line grows thick
with usura is no clear demarcation
and no man can find site for his dwelling.
Stone cutter is kept from his stone
weaver is kept from his loom
WITH USURA
wool comes not to market
sheep bringeth no gain with usura
Usura is a murrain, usura
blunteth the needle in the maid's hand
and stoppeth the spinner's cunning. Pietro Lombardo
came not by usura
Duccio came not by usura
nor Pier della Francesca; Zuan Bellin' not by usura
nor was 'La Calunnia' painted.
Came not by usura Angelico; came not Ambrogio Praedis,
Came no church of cut stone signed: *Adamo me fecit*.
Not by usura St. Trophime
Not by usura Saint Hilaire,

Usura rusteth the chisel
It rusteth the craft and the craftsman
It gnaweth the thread in the loom
None learneth to weave gold in her pattern;
Azure hath a canker by usura; cramoisi is unbroidered
Emerald findeth no Memling
Usura slayeth the child in the womb
It stayeth the young man's courting
It hath brought palsey to bed, lyeth
between the young bride and her bridegroom
                    CONTRA NATURAM
They have brought whores for Eleusis
Corpses are set to banquet
at behest of usura.

rupert brooke

THE GREAT LOVER

I have been so great a lover: filled my days
So proudly with the splendour of Love's praise,
The pain, the calm, and the astonishment,
Desire illimitable, and still content,
And all dear names men use, to cheat despair,
For the perplexed and viewless streams that bear
Our hearts at random down the dark of life.
Now, ere the unthinking silence on that strife
Steals down, I would cheat drowsy Death so far,
My night shall be remembered for a star
That outshone all the suns of all men's days.
Shall I not crown them with immortal praise
Whom I have loved, who have given me, dared with me
High secrets, and in darkness knelt to see
The inenarrable godhead of delight?
Love is a flame;—we have beaconed the world's night.
A city:—and we have built it, these and I.

An emperor:—we have taught the world to die.
So, for their sakes I loved, ere I go hence,
And the high cause of Love's magnificence,
And to keep loyalties young, I'll write those names
Golden for ever, eagles, crying flames,
And set them as a banner, that men may know,
To dare the generations, burn, and blow
Out on the wind of Time, shining and streaming. . . .

These I have loved:
       White plates and cups, clean-gleaming,
Ringed with blue lines; and feathery, faery dust;
Wet roofs, beneath the lamp-light; the strong crust
Of friendly bread; and many-tasting food;
Rainbows; and the blue bitter smoke of wood;
And radiant raindrops couching in cool flowers;
And flowers themselves, that sway through sunny hours,
Dreaming of moths that drink them under the moon;
Then, the cool kindliness of sheets, that soon
Smooth away trouble; and the rough male kiss
Of blankets; grainy wood; live hair that is
Shining and free; blue-massing clouds; the keen
Unpassioned beauty of a great machine;
The benison of hot water; furs to touch;
The good smell of old clothes; and other such—
The comfortable smell of friendly fingers,
Hair's fragrance, and the musty reek that lingers
About dead leaves and last year's ferns. . . . Dear names,
And thousand others throng to me! Royal flames;
Sweet water's dimpling laugh from tap or spring;
Holes in the ground; and voices that do sing:
Voices in laughter, too; and body's pain,
Soon turned to peace; and the deep-panting train;
Firm sands; the little dulling edge of foam
That browns and dwindles as the wave goes home;
And washen stones, gay for an hour; the cold
Graveness of iron; moist black earthen mould;
Sleep; and high places; footprints in the dew;

And oaks; and brown horse-chestnuts, glossy-new;
And new-peeled sticks; and shining pools on grass;—
All these have been my loves. And these shall pass.
Whatever passes not, in the great hour,
Nor all my passion, all my prayers, have power
To hold them with me through the gate of Death.
They'll play deserter, turn with traitor breath,
Break the high bond we made, and sell Love's trust
And sacramented covenant to the dust.

—Oh, never a doubt but, somewhere, I shall wake,
And give what's left of love again, and make
New friends, now strangers. . . . But the best I've known,
Stays here, and changes, breaks, grows old, is blown
About the winds of the world, and fades from brains
Of living men, and dies. Nothing remains.

O dear my loves, O faithless, once again
This one last gift I give: that after men
Shall know, and later lovers, far-removed
Praise you, 'All these were lovely'; say, 'He loved.'

THE SOLDIER

If I should die, think only this of me:
That there's some corner of a foreign field
That is for ever England. There shall be
In that rich earth a richer dust concealed;
A dust whom England bore, shaped, made aware,
Gave, once, her flowers to love, her ways to roam,
A body of England's breathing English air,
Washed by the rivers, blest by suns of home.

And think, this heart, all evil shed away,
A pulse in the eternal mind, no less
Gives somewhere back the thoughts by England given;
Her sights and sounds; dreams happy as her day;
And laughter, learnt of friends; and gentleness,
In hearts at peace, under an English heaven.

STILL FALLS THE RAIN

(The Raids, 1940. Night and Dawn)

Still falls the Rain—
Dark as the world of man, black as our loss—
Blind as the nineteen hundred and forty nails
Upon the Cross.

Still falls the Rain
With a sound like the pulse of the heart that is changed to the
    hammer-beat
In the Potter's Field, and the sound of the impious feet
On the Tomb:

          Still falls the Rain
In the Field of Blood where the small hopes breed and the hu-
    man brain
Nurtures its greed, that worm with the brow of Cain.

Still falls the Rain
At the feet of the Starved Man hung upon the Cross.
Christ that each day, each night, nails there, have mercy on
    us—
On Dives and on Lazarus:
Under the Rain the sore and the gold are as one.

Still falls the Rain—
Still falls the Blood from the Starved Man's wounded Side:
He bears in His Heart all wounds,—those of the light that died,
The last faint spark
In the self-murdered heart, the wounds of the sad uncompre-
    hending dark,
The wounds of the baited bear,—
The blind and weeping bear whom the keepers beat
On his helpless flesh . . . the tears of the hunted hare.

Still falls the Rain—
Then—O Ile leape up to my God: who pulles me doune—
See, see where Christ's blood streames in the firmament:

It flows from the Brow we nailed upon the tree
Deep to the dying, to the thirsting heart
That holds the fires of the world,—dark-smirched with pain
As Caesar's laurel crown.

Then sounds the voice of One who like the heart of man
Was once a child who among beasts has lain—
"Still do I love, still shed my innocent light, my Blood, for
    thee."

HEART AND MIND

Said the Lion to the Lioness—'When you are amber dust,—
No more a raging fire like the heat of the Sun
(No liking but all lust)—
Remember still the flowering of the amber blood and bone
The rippling of bright muscles like a sea,
Remember the rose-prickles of bright paws
Though we shall mate no more
Till the fire of that sun the heart and the moon-cold bone are
                                                    [one.'

Said the Skeleton lying upon the sands of Time—
'The great gold planet that is the mourning heat of the Sun
Is greater than all gold, more powerful
Than the tawny body of a Lion that fire consumes
Like all that grows or leaps . . . so is the heart
More powerful than all dust. Once I was Hercules
Or Samson, strong as the pillars of the seas:
But the flames of the heart consumed me, and the mind
Is but a foolish wind.'

Said the Sun to the Moon—'When you are but a lonely white
    crone,
And I, a dead King in my golden armour somewhere in a dark
    wood,
Remember only this of our hopeless love
That never till Time is done
Will the fire of the heart and the fire of the mind be one.'

AN OLD WOMAN

I, an old woman in the light of the sun,
Wait for my Wanderer, and my upturned face
Has all the glory of the remembering Day
The hallowed grandeur of the primeval clay
That knew the Flood, and suffered all the dryness
Of the uncaring heaven, the sun its lover.

For the sun is the first lover of the world,
Blessing all humble creatures, all life-giving,
Blessing the end of life and the work done,
The clean and the unclean, ores in earth, and splendours
Within the heart of man, that second sun.

For when the first founts and deep waterways
Of the young light flow down and lie like peace
Upon the upturned faces of the blind
From life, it comes to bless
Eternity in its poor mortal dress,—
Shining upon young lovers and old lechers
Rising from their beds, and laying gold
Alike in the unhopeful path of beggars
And in the darkness of the miser's heart.
The crookèd has a shadow light made straight,
The shallow places gain their strength again,—
And desert hearts, waste heavens, the barren height
Forget that they are cold.
The man-made chasm between man and man
Of creeds and tongues are fill'd, the guiltless light
Remakes all men and things in holiness.

And he who blessed the fox with a golden fleece
And covered earth with ears of corn like the planets
Bearded with thick ripe gold,
For the holy bread of mankind, blessed my clay:
For the sun cares not that I am a simple woman,
To him, laughing, the veins in my arms and the wrinkles
From work on my nursing hands are sacred as branches

And furrows of harvest . . . to him, the heat of the earth
And beat of the heart are one,—
Born from the energy of the world, the love
That keeps the Golden Ones in their place above,
And hearts and blood of beasts even in motion,—
Without which comets, sun, plants, and all living beings
And warmth in the inward parts of the earth would freeze.
And the sun does not care if I live in holiness,
To him, my mortal dress
Is sacred, part of the earth, a lump of the world
With my splendours, ores, impurities, and harvest,
Over which shines my heart, that ripening sun.

Though the dust, the shining racer, overtake me,
I too was a golden woman like those that walk
In the fields of the heavens:—but am now grown old
And must sit by the fire and watch the fire grow cold,
—A country Fate whose spool is the household task.
Yet still I am loved by the sun, and still am part
Of earth. In the evenings bringing home the workers,
Bringing the wanderer home and the dead child,
The child unborn and never to be conceived,
Home to the mother's breast, I sit by the fire
Where the seed of gold drops dead and the kettle simmers
With a sweet sound like that of a hive of bees,
And I wait for my Wanderer to come home to rest—
Covered with earth as if he had been working
Among the happy gardens, the holy fields
Where the bread of mankind ripens in the stillness.
Unchanged to me by death, I shall hold to my breast
My little child in his sleep, I shall seem the consoling
Earth, the mother of corn, nurse of the unreturning.

Wise is the earth, consoling grief and glory,
The golden heroes proud as pomp of waves,—
Great is the earth embracing them, their graves,
And great is the earth's story.
For though the soundless wrinkles fall like snow
On many a golden cheek, and creeds grow old

And change,—man's heart, that sun,
Outlives all terrors shaking the old night:
The world's huge fevers burn and shine, turn cold,
Yet the heavenly bodies and young lovers burn and shine,
The golden lovers walk in the holy fields,
Where the Abraham-bearded sun, the father of all things
Is shouting of ripeness, and the whole world of dews and
    splendours are singing
To the cradles of earth, of men, beasts, harvests, swinging
In the peace of God's heart. And I, the primeval clay
That has known earth's grief and harvest's happiness,
Seeing mankind's dark seed-time, come to bless,—
Forgive and bless all men like the holy light.

TEARS

To Pavel Tchelitchew

My tears were Orion's splendour with sextuple suns and the
    million
Flowers in the fields of the heaven, where solar systems are
    setting,—
The rocks of great diamonds in the midst of the clear wave
By May dews and early light ripened, more diamonds beget-
I wept for the glories of air, for the millions of dawns   [ting.
And the splendours within Man's heart with the darkness war-
    ring,
I wept for the beautiful queens of the world, like a flower-bed
    shining,—
Now gathered, some at six, some at seven, but all in Eternity's
    morning.
But now my tears have shrunk and like hours are falling:
I weep for Venus whose body has changed to a metaphysical
    city
Whose heart-beat is now the sound of the revolutions,—for love
    changed
To the hospital mercy, the scientists' hope for the future,
And for darkened Man, that complex multiplicity
Of air and water, plant and animal,
Hard diamond, infinite sun.

STREET SONG

"Love my heart for an hour, but my bone for a day—
At least the skeleton smiles, for it has a morrow:
But the hearts of the young are now the dark treasure of
And summer is lonely.   [Death,

Comfort the lonely light and the sun in its sorrow,
Come like the night, for terrible is the sun
As truth, and the dying light shows only the skeleton's hunger
For peace, under the flesh like the summer rose.

Come through the darkness of death, as once through the
     branches
Of youth you came, through the shade like the flowering door
That leads into Paradise, far from the street,—you, the unborn
City seen by the homeless, the night of the poor.

You walk in the city ways, where Man's threatening shadow
Red-edged by the sun like Cain, has a changing shape—
Elegant like the Skeleton, crouched like the Tiger,
With the age-old wisdom and aptness of the Ape.

The pulse that beats in the heart is changed to the hammer
That sounds in the Potter's Field where they build a new
     world
From our Bone, and the carrion-bird days' foul droppings and
     clamour—
But you are my night, and my peace,—

The holy night of conception, of rest, the consoling
Darkness when all men are equal,—the wrong and the right,
And the rich and the poor are no longer separate nations,—
They are brothers in night."

This was the song I heard; but the Bone is silent!
Who knows if the sound was that of the dead light calling,—
Of Caesar rolling onward his heart, that stone,
Or the burden of Atlas falling.

arthur waley

CENSORSHIP

A poem in the Chinese style

TO HSIAO CH'IEN

I have been a censor for fifteen months;
The building where I work has four times
    been bombed.
Glass, boards and paper, each in turn,
Have been blasted from the windows—where
    windows are left at all.
It is not easy to wash, keep warm and eat;
At times we lack gas, water or light.
The rules for censors are difficult to keep;
In six months there were over a thousand
    'stops'.
The Air Raid Bible alters from day to day;
Official orders are not clearly expressed.
One may mention Harrods, but not Derry and
    Toms;
One may write of mist, but may not write of rain.
Japanese, scribbled on thin paper
In faint scrawl tires the eyes to read.
In a small room with ten telephones
And a tape-machine concentration is hard.
Yet the Blue Pencil is a mere toy to wield,
There are worse knots than the tangles of Red
    Tape.
It is not difficult to censor foreign news,
What is hard to-day is to censor one's own
    thoughts,—
To sit by and see the blind man
On the sightless horse, riding into the
    bottomless abyss.

robinson jeffers

THE EYE

The Atlantic is a stormy moat, and the Mediterranean,
The blue pool in the old garden,
More than five thousand years has drunk sacrifice
Of ships and blood and shines in the sun; but here the Pacific:
The ships, planes, wars are perfectly irrelevant.
Neither our present blood-feud with the brave dwarfs
Nor any future world-quarrel of westering
And eastering man, the bloody migrations, greed of power,
      battle-falcons,
Are a mote of dust in the great scale-pan.
Here from this mountain shore, headland beyond stormy head-
      land plunging like dolphins through the gray sea-smoke
Into pale sea, look west at the hill of water: it is half the
      planet: this dome, this half-globe, this bulging
Eyeball of water, arched over to Asia,
Australia and white Antarctica: those are the eyelids that never
      close; this is the staring unsleeping
Eye of the earth, and what it watches is not our wars.

TO THE STONE-CUTTERS

Stone-cutters fighting time with marble, you fore-defeated
Challengers of oblivion
Eat cynical earnings, knowing rock splits, records fall down,
The square-limbed Roman letters
Scale in the thaws, wear in the rain. The poet as well
Builds his monument mockingly;
For man will be blotted out, the blithe earth die, the brave sun
Die blind and blacken to the heart:
Yet stones have stood for a thousand years, and pained
      thoughts found
The honey of peace in old poems.

NIGHT

The ebb slips from the rock, the sunken
Tide-rocks lift streaming shoulders
Out of the slack, the slow west
Sombering its torch; a ship's light
Shows faintly, far out,
Over the weight of the prone ocean
On the low cloud.

Over the dark mountain, over the dark pinewood,
Down the long dark valley along the shrunken river,
Returns the splendor without rays, the shining of shadow,
Peace-bringer, the matrix of all shining and quieter of shining.
Where the shore widens on the bay she opens dark wings
And the ocean accepts her glory. O soul worshipful of her
You like the ocean have grave depths where she dwells always,
And the film of waves above that takes the sun takes also
Her, with more love. The sun-lovers have a blond favorite,
A father of lights and noises, wars, weeping and laughter,
Hot labor, lust and delight and the other blemishes. Quietness
Flows from her deeper fountain; and he will die; and she is
     immortal.

Far off from here the slender
Flocks of the mountain forest
Move among stems like towers
Of the old redwoods to the stream,
No twig crackling; dip shy
Wild muzzles into the mountain water
Among the dark ferns.

O passionately at peace you being secure will pardon
The blasphemies of glowworms, the lamp in my tower, the
    fretfulness
Of cities, the cressets of the planets, the pride of the stars.
This August night in a rift of cloud Antares reddens,
The great one, the ancient torch, a lord among lost children,

The earth's orbit doubled would not girdle his greatness, one
    fire
Globed, out of grasp of the mind enormous; but to you O
    Night
What? Not a spark? What flicker of a spark in the faint far
    glimmer
Of a lost fire dying in the desert, dim coals of a sand-pit the
    Bedouins
Wandered from at dawn . . . Ah singing prayer to what gulfs
    tempted
Suddenly are you more lost? To us the near-hand mountain
Be a measure of height, the tide-worn cliff at the sea-gate a
    measure of continuance.

The tide, moving the night's
Vastness with lonely voices,
Turns, the deep dark-shining
Pacific leans on the land,
Feeling his cold strength
To the outmost margins: you Night will resume
The stars in your time.

O passionately at peace when will that tide draw shoreward?
Truly the spouting fountains of light, Antares, Arcturus,
Tire of their flow, they sing one song but they think silence.
The striding winter giant Orion shines, and dreams darkness.
And life, the flicker of men and moths and the wolf on the hill,
Though furious for continuance, passionately feeding, passion-
    ately
Remaking itself upon its mates, remembers deep inward
The calm mother, the quietness of the womb and the egg,
The primal and the latter silences: dear Night it is memory
Prophesies, prophecy that remembers, the charm of the dark.

And I and my people, we are willing to love the four-score
    years
Heartily; but as a sailor loves the sea, when the helm is for
    harbor.

Have men's minds changed,
Or the rock hidden in the deep of the waters of the soul
Broken the surface? A few centuries
Gone by, was none dared not to people
The darkness beyond the stars with harps and habitations.
But now, dear is the truth. Life is grown sweeter and lonelier,
And death is no evil.

BOATS IN A FOG

Sports and gallantries, the stage, the arts, the antics of dancers,
The exuberant voices of music,
Have charm for children but lack nobility; it is bitter earnest-
ness
That makes beauty; the mind
Knows, grown adult.
                    A sudden fog-drift muffled the ocean,
A throbbing of engines moved in it,
At length, a stone's throw out, between the rocks and the
vapor,
One by one moved shadows
Out of the mystery, shadows, fishing-boats, trailing each other
Following the cliff for guidance,
Holding a difficult path between the peril of the sea-fog
And the foam on the shore granite.
One by one, trailing their leader, six crept by me,
Out of the vapor and into it,
The throb of their engines subdued by the fog, patient and
cautious,
Coasting all round the peninsula
Back to the buoys in Monterey harbor. A flight of pelicans
Is nothing lovelier to look at;
The flight of the planets is nothing nobler; all the arts lose
virtue
Against the essential reality
Of creatures going about their business among the equally
Earnest elements of nature.

PHENOMENA

Great-enough both accepts and subdues; the great frame takes
    all creatures;
From the greatness of their element they all take beauty.
Gulls; and the dingy freightship lurching south in the eye of a
    rain-wind;
The airplane dipping over the hill; hawks hovering
The white grass of the headland; cormorants roosting upon the
    guano-
Whitened skerries; pelicans awind; sea-slime
Shining at night in the wave-stir like drowned men's lanterns;
    smugglers signaling
A cargo to land; or the old Point Pinos lighthouse
Lawfully winking over dark water; the flight of the twilight
    herons,
Lonely wings and a cry; or with motor-vibrations
That hum in the rock like a new storm-tone of the ocean's to
    turn eyes westward
The navy's new-bought Zeppelin going by in the twilight,
Far out seaward; relative only to the evening star and the
    ocean
It slides into a cloud over Point Lobos.

HAUNTED COUNTRY

Here the human past is dim and feeble and alien to us
Our ghosts draw from the crowded future.
Fixed as the past how could it fail to drop weird shadows
And make strange murmurs about twilight?
In the dawn twilight metal falcons flew over the mountain,
Multitudes, and faded in the air; at moonrise
The farmer's girl by the still river is afraid of phantoms,
Hearing the pulse of a great city
Move on the water-meadow and stream off south; the country's
Children for all their innocent minds
Hide dry and bitter lights in the eye, they dream without
    knowing it

The inhuman years to be accomplished,
The inhuman powers, the servile cunning under pressure,
In a land grown old, heavy and crowded.
There are happy places that fate skips; here is not one of them;
The tides of the brute womb, the excess
And weight of life spilled out like water, the last migration
Gathering against this holier valley-mouth
That knows its fate beforehand, the flow of the womb, banked
    back
By the older flood of the ocean, to swallow it.

SCIENCE

Man, introverted man, having crossed
In passage and but a little with the nature of things this latter
    century
Has begot giants; but being taken up
Like a maniac with self-love and inward conflicts cannot man-
    age his hybrids.
Being used to deal with edgeless dreams,
Now he's bred knives on nature turns them also inward:
    they have thirsty points though.
His mind forebodes his own destruction;
Actæon who saw the goddess naked among leaves and his
    hounds tore him.
A little knowledge, a pebble from the shingle,
A drop from the oceans: who would have dreamed this infi-
    nitely little too much?

APOLOGY FOR BAD DREAMS

I

In the purple light, heavy with redwood, the slopes drop sea-
    ward,
Headlong convexities of forest, drawn in together to the steep
    ravine. Below, on the sea-cliff,
A lonely clearing; a little field of corn by the streamside; a roof
    under spared trees. Then the ocean

Like a great stone someone has cut to a sharp edge and pol-
ished to shining. Beyond it, the fountain
And furnace of incredible light flowing up from the sunk sun.
In the little clearing a woman
Is punishing a horse; she had tied the halter to a sapling at the
edge of the wood, but when the great whip
Clung to the flanks the creature kicked so hard she feared he
would snap the halter; she called from the house
The young man her son; who fetched a chain tie-rope, they
working together
Noosed the small rusty links round the horse's tongue
And tied him by the swollen tongue to the tree.
Seen from this height they are shrunk to insect size.
Out of all human relation. You cannot distinguish
The blood dripping from where the chain is fastened,
The beast shuddering; but the thrust neck and the legs
Far apart. You can see the whip fall on the flanks . . .
The gesture of the arm. You cannot see the face of the woman.
The enormous light beats up out of the west across the cloud-
bars of the trade-wind. The ocean
Darkens, the high clouds brighten, the hills darken together.
Unbridled and unbelievable beauty
Covers the evening world . . . not covers, grows apparent out
of it, as Venus down there grows out
From the lit sky. What said the prophet? 'I create good: and I
create evil: I am the Lord.'

II

This coast crying out for tragedy like all beautiful places,
(The quiet ones ask for quieter suffering: but here the granite
cliff the gaunt cypresses crown
Demands what victim? The dykes of red lava and black what
Titan? The hills like pointed flames
Beyond Soberanes, the terrible peaks of the bare hills under
the sun, what immolation?)
This coast crying out for tragedy like all beautiful places: and
like the passionate spirit of humanity

Pain for its bread: God's, many victims', the painful deaths,
    the horrible transfigurations: I said in my heart,
'Better invent than suffer: imagine victims
Lest your own flesh be chosen the agonist, or you
Martyr some creature to the beauty of the place.' And I said,
'Burn sacrifices once a year to magic
Horror away from the house, this little house here
You have built over the ocean with your own hands
Beside the standing boulders: for what are we,
The beast that walks upright, with speaking lips
And little hair, to think we should always be fed,
Sheltered, intact, and self-controlled? We sooner more liable
Than the other animals. Pain and terror, the insanities of de-
    sire; not accidents but essential,
And crowd up from the core:' I imagined victims for those
    wolves, I made them phantoms to follow,
They have hunted the phantoms and missed the house. It is
    not good to forget over what gulfs the spirit
Of the beauty of humanity, the petal of a lost flower blown
    seaward by the night-wind, floats to its quietness.

III

Boulders blunted like an old bear's teeth break up from the
    headland; below them
All the soil is thick with shells, the tide-rock feasts of a dead
    people.
Here the granite flanks are scarred with ancient fire, the ghosts
    of the tribe
Crouch in the nights beside the ghost of a fire, they try to re-
    member the sunlight,
Light has died out of their skies. These have paid something
    for the future
Luck of the country, while we living keep old griefs in mem-
    ory: though God's
Envy is not a likely fountain of ruin, to forget evils calls down
Sudden reminders from the cloud: remembered deaths be our
    redeemers;

Imagined victims our salvation: white as the half moon at
    midnight
Someone flamelike passed me, saying, 'I am Tamar Cauldwell,
    I have my desire,'
Then the voice of the sea returned, when she had gone by, the
    stars to their towers.
. . . Beautiful country burn again, Point Pinos down to the
    Sur Rivers
Burn as before with bitter wonders, land and ocean and the
    Carmel water.

IV

He brays humanity in a mortar to bring the savor
From the bruised root: a man having bad dreams, who invents
    victims, is only the ape of that God.
He washes it out with tears and many waters, calcines it with
    fire in the red crucible,
Deforms it, makes it horrible to itself: the spirit flies out and
    stands naked, he sees the spirit,
He takes it in the naked ecstasy; it breaks in his hand, the
    atom is broken, the power that massed it
Cries to the power that moves the stars, 'I have come home
    to myself, behold me.
I bruised myself in the flint mortar and burnt me
In the red shell, I tortured myself, I flew forth,
Stood naked of myself and broke me in fragments,
And here am I moving the stars that are me.'
I have seen these ways of God: I know of no reason
For fire and change and torture and the old returnings.
He being sufficient might be still. I think they admit no reason;
    they are the ways of my love.
Unmeasured power, incredible passion, enormous craft: no
    thought apparent but burns darkly
Smothered with its own smoke in the human brain-vault: no
    thought outside: a certain measure in phenomena:
The fountains of the boiling stars, the flowers on the foreland,
    the ever-returning roses of dawn.

SUMMER HOLIDAY

When the sun shouts and people abound
One thinks there were the ages of stone and the age of bronze
And the iron age; iron the unstable metal;
Steel made of iron, unstable as his mother; the towered-up
    cities
Will be stains of rust on mounds of plaster.
Roots will not pierce the heaps for a time, kind rains will cure
    them,
Then nothing will remain of the iron age
And all these people but a thigh-bone or so, a poem
Stuck in the world's thought, splinters of glass
In the rubbish dumps, a concrete dam far off in the moun-
    tain . . .

I SHALL LAUGH PURELY

[I]

Turn from that girl
Your fixed blue eyes.
Boy-slender she is,
And a face as beautiful as a
    hawk's face.
History passes like falling
    rocks.

I am old as a stone,
But she is beautiful.
War is coming.
All the fine boys will go off
    to war.
History passes like falling
    rocks.

Oh, that one's to marry

Another old man;
You won't be helped
When your tall sons go
    away to war.
History falls on your head
    like rocks.

Keep a straight mind
In the evil time.
In the mad-dog time
Why may not an old man
    run mad?
History falls like rocks in
    the dark,
All will be worse confounded
    soon.

ii]   Count the glories of this time,
        Count that girl's beauty, then count England,
        Bleeding, at bay, magnificent,
        At last a lion,
        For all will be worse confounded soon.

        Count that girl's beauty, count the coast-range,
        The steep rock that stops the Pacific,
        Count the surf on its precipice,
        The hawks in its air,
        For all will be worse confounded soon.

        Count its eagles and wild boars,
        Count the great blue-black winter storms,
        Heavy rain and the hurricane,
        Get them by heart,
        For all will be worse confounded soon.

        Count no human thing but only
        England's great fight and that girl's beauty,
        History passes like falling
        Rocks in the dark,
        And all will be worse confounded soon.

iii] But this, I steadily assure you, is not the world's end,
Nor even the end of a civilization. It is not so late as you think:
        give nature time.
These wars will end, and I shall lead a troupe of shaky old
        men through Europe and America,
Old drunkards, worn-out lechers; fallen dictators, cast kings,
        a disgraced president; some cashiered generals
And collapsed millionaires: we shall enact a play, I shall
        announce to the audience:
"All will be worse confounded soon."

We shall beware of wild dogs in Europe, and of the police in
        armed imperial America:—
For all that pain was mainly a shift of power:—we shall enact
        our play: "Oh Christian era,

Make a good end," but first I announce to our audiences:
"This play is prophetic, it will be centuries.
This play does not represent the world's end,
But only the fall of a civilization. It is not so late as you think:
    give nature time."

In Europe we shall beware of starving dogs and political
    commissars, and of the police in America.
We shall rant on our makeshift stages in our cracked voices:
    "Oh Christian era,
Era of chivalry and the barbarians and the machines, era of
    science and the saints,
When you go down make a good sunset.
Never linger superfluous, old and holy and paralytic like India,
Go down in conclusive war and a great red sunset, great age
    go down,
For all will be worse confounded soon."

We shall tour to the last verge and the open Pacific, we shall
    sit on the yellow cliffs at Hurricane Point
And watch the centaurs come from the sea; their splayed
    hooves plunge and stutter on the tide-rocks, watch them
    swarm up,
The hairy and foamy flanks, the naked destructive shoulders,
    the brutal faces and the bent bows,
Horde after horde under the screaming gulls: my old men
    will cough in the fog and baa like sheep,
"Here comes the end of a civilization. Give nature time,"
And spit, and make lewd jokes. But I shall laugh purely,
Remembering what old enthusiast named a girl's beauty and
    England's battle
Among the lights of his time: she being by then a dyed hag,
    or more likely
One of those embalmer-fingered smiles in the subsoil; and
    England will be
Not admirable. I shall laugh purely, knowing the next age
Lives on not-human beauty, waiting on circumstance and its
    April, weaving its winter chrysalis;
Thin snow falls on historical rocks.

edwin muir

THE CASTLE

All through that summer at ease we lay,
And daily from the turret wall
We watched the mowers in the hay
And the enemy half a mile away.
They seemed no threat to us at all.

For what, we thought, had we to fear
With our arms and provender, load on load,
Our towering battlements, tier on tier,
And friendly allies drawing near
On every leafy summer road.

Our gates were strong, our walls were thick,
So smooth and high, no man could win
A foothold there, no clever trick
Could take us, have us dead or quick.
Only a bird could have got in.

What could they offer us for bait?
Our captain was brave and we were true. . . .
There was a little private gate,
A little wicked wicket gate.
The wizened warder let them through.

Oh then our maze of tunnelled stone
Grew thin and treacherous as air.
The cause was lost without a groan,
The famous citadel overthrown,
And all its secret galleries bare.

How can this shameful tale be told?
I will maintain until my death
We could do nothing, being sold;
Our only enemy was gold,
And we had no arms to fight it with.

THE ROAD

There is a road that turning always
    Cuts off the country of Again.
Archers stand there on every side
    And as it runs Time's deer is slain,
    And lies where it has lain.

That busy clock shows never an hour.
    All flies and all in flight must tarry.
The hunter shoots the empty air
    Far on before the quarry,
    Which falls though nothing's there to parry.

The lion couching in the centre
    With mountain head and sunset brow
Rolls down the everlasting slope
    Bones picked an age ago,
    And the bones rise up and go.

There the beginning finds the end
    Before beginning ever can be,
And the great runner never leaves
    The starting and the finishing tree,
    The budding and the fading tree.

There the ship sailing safe in harbour
    Long since in many a sea was drowned.
The treasure burning in her hold
    So near will never be found,
    Sunk past all sound.

There a man on a summer evening
    Reclines at ease upon his tomb
And in his mortal effigy.
    And there within the womb,
    The cell of doom,

The ancestral deed is thought and done,
    And in a million Edens fall

A million Adams drowned in darkness,
    For small is great and great is small,
    And a blind seed all.

THE INTERROGATION

We could have crossed the road but hesitated.
And then came the patrol;
The leader conscientious and intent,
The men surly, indifferent.
While we stood by and waited
The interrogation began. He says the whole
Must come out now, who, what we are,
Where we have come from, with what purpose, whose
Country or camp we plot for or betray.
Question on question.
We have stood and answered through the standing day
And watched across the road beyond the hedge
The careless lovers in pairs go by,
Hand linked in hand, wandering another star,
So near we could shout to them. We cannot choose
Answer or action here,
Though still the careless lovers saunter by
And the thoughtless field is near.
We are on the very edge,
Endurance almost done,
And still the interrogation is going on.

THE ANIMALS

    They do not live in the world,
    Are not in time and space,
    From birth to death hurled
    No word do they have, not one
    To plant a foot upon,
    Were never in any place.

For by words the world was called
Out of the empty air,
With words was shaped and walled —
Line and circle and square,
Mud and emerald, —
Snatched from deceiving death
By the articulate breath.

But these have never trod
Twice the familiar track,
Never never turned back
Into the memoried day;
All is new and near
In the unchanging Here
Of the fifth great day of God,
That shall remain the same,
Never shall pass away.

On the sixth day we came.

THE DEBTOR

I am debtor to all, to all am I bounden,
Fellowman and beast, season and solstice, darkness and light,
And life and death. On the backs of the dead,
See, I am borne, on lost errands led,
By spent harvests nourished. Forgotten prayers
To gods forgotten bring blessings upon me.
Rusted arrow and broken bow, look, they preserve me
Here in this place. The never-won stronghold
That sank in the ground as the years into time,
Slowly with all its men stedfast and watching,
Keeps me safe now. The ancient waters
Cleanse me, revive me. Victor and vanquished
Give me their passion, their peace and the field.
The meadows of Lethe shed twilight around me.
The dead in their silences keep me in memory,
Have me in hold. To all I am bounden.

marianne moore

POETRY

I, too, dislike it: there are things that are important
        beyond all this fiddle.
    Reading it, however, with a perfect contempt for it, one
        discovers in
    it after all, a place for the genuine.
        Hands that can grasp, eyes
        that can dilate, hair that can rise
            if it must, these things are important not because a

high-sounding interpretation can be put upon them but be-
        cause they are
    useful. When they become so derivative as to become
        unintelligible,
    the same thing may be said for all of us, that we
        do not admire what
        we cannot understand: the bat
            holding on upside down or in quest of something to

eat, elephants pushing, a wild horse taking a roll, a tireless
        wolf under
    a tree, the immovable critic twitching his skin like a
        horse that feels a flea, the base-
    ball fan, the statistician—
        nor is it valid
        to discriminate against 'business documents and

school-books'; all these phenomena are important. One
        must make a distinction
    however: when dragged into prominence by half poets,
        the result is not poetry,
    nor till the poets among us can be
        'literalists of
        the imagination'—above
            insolence and triviality and can present

for inspection, imaginary gardens with real toads in them,
   shall we have
it. In the meantime, if you demand on the one hand,
   the raw material of poetry in
 all its rawness and
 that which is on the other hand
  genuine, then you are interested in poetry.

WHAT ARE YEARS?

   What is our innocence,
  what is our guilt? All are
   naked, none is safe. And whence
 is courage: the unanswered question,
 the resolute doubt,—
  dumbly calling, deafly listening—that
 in misfortune, even death,
    encourages others
    and in its defeat, stirs

   the soul to be strong? He
  sees deep and is glad, who
   accedes to mortality
 and in his imprisonment, rises
 upon himself as
  the sea in a chasm, struggling to be
 free and unable to be,
    in its surrendering
    finds its continuing.

   So he who strongly feels,
  behaves. The very bird,
   grown taller as he sings, steels
 his form straight up. Though he is captive,
 his mighty singing
  says, satisfaction is a lowly
 thing, how pure a thing is joy.
    This is mortality,
    this is eternity.

SPENSER'S IRELAND

has not altered;—
   the kindest place I've never been,
   the greenest place I've never seen.
Every name is a tune.
Denunciations do not affect
     the culprit;   nor blows, but it
is torture to him to not be spoken to.
They're natural,—
      the coat, like Venus'
mantle lined with stars,
buttoned close at the neck,—the
      sleeves new from disuse.

If in Ireland
   they play the harp backward at need,
   and gather at midday the seed
of the fern, eluding
their 'giants all covered with iron,' might
     there be fern   seed for unlearn-
ing obduracy and for reinstating
the enchantment?
      Hindered characters
seldom have mothers—
in Irish stories—
     but they all have grandmothers.

It was Irish;
   a match not a marriage was made
   when my great great grandmother'd said
with native genius for
disunion, 'although your suitor be
     perfection,   one objection
is enough; he is not
Irish.' Outwitting
     the fairies, befriending the furies,
whoever again

and again says, 'I'll never
     give in,' never sees

that you're not free
  until you've been made captive by
  supreme belief,—credulity
you say? When large dainty
fingers tremblingly divide the wings
    of the fly   for mid-July
with a needle and wrap it with peacock-tail,
or tie wool and
     buzzard's wing, their pride,
like the enchanter's
is in care, not madness. Con-
    curring hands divide

flax for damask
  that when bleached by Irish weather
  has the silvered chamois-leather
water-tightness of a
skin. Twisted torcs and gold new-moon-shaped
    lunulae   aren't jewelry
like the purple-coral fuchsia-tree's. If Eire—
the guillemot
     so neat and the hen
of the heath and the
linnet spinet-sweet—bespeak
    relentlessness, then

they are to me
  like enchanted Earl Gerald who
  changed himself into a stag, to
a great green-eyed cat of
the mountain. Discommodity makes
    them invis   ible; they've dis-
appeared. The Irish say your trouble is their
trouble and your
     joy their joy? I wish

I could believe it;
I am troubled; I'm dissat-
    isfied, I'm Irish.

THE MIND IS AN ENCHANTING THING

is an enchanted thing
    like the glaze on a
katydid-wing
            subdivided by sun
            till the nettings are legion.
Like Gieseking playing Scarlatti;

like the apteryx-awl
    as a beak, or the
kiwi's rain-shawl
            of haired feathers, the mind
            feeling its way as though blind,
walks along with its eyes on the ground.

It has memory's ear
    that can hear without
having to hear.
            Like the gyroscope's fall,
            truly unequivocal
because trued by regnant certainty,

it is a power of
    strong enchantment. It
is like the dove-
            neck animated by
            sun; it is memory's eye;
it's conscientious inconsistency.

It tears off the veil; tears
    the temptation, the
mist the heart wears,
            from its eyes,—if the heart
            has a face; it takes apart
dejection. It's fire in the dove-neck's

iridescence, in the
    inconsistencies
of Scarlatti.
        Unconfusion submits
          its confusion to proof; it's
not a Herod's oath that cannot change.

IN DISTRUST OF MERITS

Strengthened to live, strengthened to die for
    medals and position victories?
They're fighting, fighting, fighting the blind
    man who thinks he sees,—
who cannot see that the enslaver is
enslaved; the hater, harmed. O shining O
      firm star, O tumultuous
        ocean lashed till small things go
      as they will, the mountainous
        wave makes us who look, know

depth. Lost at sea before they fought! O
    star of David, star of Bethlehem,
O black imperial lion
    of the Lord—emblem
of a risen world—be joined at last, be
joined. There is hate's crown beneath which all is
      death; there's love's without which none
        is king; the blessed deeds bless
      the halo. As contagion
        of sickness makes sickness,

contagion of trust can make trust. They're
    fighting in deserts and caves, one by
one, in battalions and squadrons;
    they're fighting that I
may yet recover from the disease, My
Self; some have it lightly, some will die. "Man's
      wolf to man" and we devour

ourselves. The enemy could not
have made a greater breach in our
defenses. One pilot-

ing a blind man can escape him, but
        Job disheartened by false comfort knew
that nothing can be so defeating
        as a blind man who
can see. O alive who are dead, who are
proud not to see, O small dust of the earth
        that walks so arrogantly,
                trust begets power and faith is
        an affectionate thing. We
        vow, we make this promise

to the fighting—it's a promise—"We'll
        never hate black, white, red, yellow, Jew,
Gentile, Untouchable." We are
        not competent to
make our vows. With set jaw they are fighting,
fighting, fighting,—some we love whom we know,
        some we love but know not—that
                hearts may feel and not be numb.
        It cures me; or am I what
                I can't believe in? Some

in snow, some on crags, some in quicksands,
        little by little, much by much, they
are fighting fighting fighting that where
        there was death there may
be life. "When a man is prey to anger,
he is moved by outside things; when he holds
        his ground in patience
                patience, that is action or
        beauty," the soldier's defense
        and hardest armor for

the fight. The world's an orphans' home. Shall
        we never have peace without sorrow?

without pleas of the dying for
    help that won't come? O
quiet form upon the dust, I cannot
look and yet I must. If these great patient
      dyings—all these agonies
         and woundbearings and blood shed—
    can teach us how to live, these
      dyings were not wasted.

Hate-hardened heart, O heart of iron,
    iron is iron till it is rust.
There never was a war that was
    not inward; I must
fight till I have conquered in myself what
causes war, but I would not believe it.
    I inwardly did nothing.
      O Iscariotlike crime!
    Beauty is everlasting
      and dust is for a time.

SILENCE

My father used to say,
"Superior people never make long visits,
have to be shown Longfellow's grave
or the glass flowers at Harvard.
Self-reliant like the cat—
that takes its prey to privacy,
the mouse's limp tail hanging like a shoelace from its mouth—
they sometimes enjoy solitude,
and can be robbed of speech
by speech which has delighted them.
The deepest feeling always shows itself in silence;
not in silence, but restraint."
Nor was he insincere in saying, "Make my house your inn."
Inns are not residences.

john crowe ransom

BLUE GIRLS

Twirling your blue skirts, traveling the sward
Under the towers of your seminary,
Go listen to your teachers old and contrary
Without believing a word.

Tie the white fillets then about your lustrous hair
And think no more of what will come to pass
Than bluebirds that go walking on the grass
And chattering on the air.

Practice your beauty, blue girls, before it fail;
And I will cry with my loud lips and publish
Beauty which all our power shall never establish,
It is so frail.

For I could tell you a story which is true:
I know a lady with a terrible tongue,
Blear eyes fallen from blue,
All her perfections tarnished—yet it is not long
Since she was lovelier than any of you.

HERE LIES A LADY

Here lies a lady of beauty and high degree.
Of chills and fever she died, of fever and chills,
The delight of her husband, her aunts, an infant of three,
And of medicos marveling sweetly on her ills.

For either she burned, and her confident eyes would blaze,
And her fingers fly in a manner to puzzle their heads—
What was she making? Why, nothing; she sat in a maze
Of old scraps of laces, snipped into curious shreds—

Or this would pass, and the light of her fire decline
Till she lay discouraged and cold as a thin stalk white and
    blown,
And would not open her eyes, to kisses, to wine.
The sixth of these states was her last; the cold settled down.

Sweet ladies, long may ye bloom, and toughly I hope ye may
    thole,
But was she not lucky? In flowers and lace and mourning,
In love and great honor we bade God rest her soul
After six little spaces of chill, and six of burning.

MAN WITHOUT SENSE OF DIRECTION

Tell this to ladies: how a hero man
Assail a thick and scandalous giant
Who casts true shadow in the sun,
And die, but play no truant.

This is more horrible: that the darling egg
Of the chosen people hatch a creature
Of noblest mind and powerful leg
Who cannot fathom nor perform his nature.

The larks' tongues are never stilled
Where the pale spread straw of sunlight lies.
Then what invidious gods have willed
Him to be seized so otherwise?

Birds of the field and beasts of the stable
Are swollen with rapture and make uncouth
Demonstration of joy, which is a babble
Offending the ear of the fervorless youth.

Love—is it the cause? the proud shamed spirit?
Love has slain some whom it possessed,
But his was requited beyond his merit
And won him in bridal the loveliest.

Yet scarcely he issues from the warm chamber,
Flushed with her passion, when cold as dead
Once more he walks where waves past number
Of sorrow buffet his curse-hung head.

Whether by street, or in field full of honey,
Attended by clouds of the creatures of air
Or shouldering the city's companioning many,
His doom is on him; and how can he care

For the shapes that would fiddle upon his senses,
Wings and faces and mists that move,
Words, sunlight, the blue air which rinses
The pure pale head which he must love?

And he writhes like an antique man of bronze
That is beaten by furies visible,
Yet he is punished not knowing his sins
And for his innocence walks in hell.

He flails his arms, he moves his lips:
"Rage have I none, cause, time, nor country—
Yet I have traveled land and ships
And knelt my seasons in the chantry."

So he stands muttering; and rushes
Back to the tender thing in his charge
With clamoring tongue and taste of ashes
And a small passion to feign large.

But let his cold lips be her omen,
She shall not kiss that harried one
To peace, as men are served by women
Who comfort them in darkness and in sun.

CAPTAIN CARPENTER

Captain Carpenter rose up in his prime
Put on his pistols and went riding out
But he got well nigh nowhere at that time
Till he fell in with ladies in a rout.

It was a pretty lady and all her train
That played with him so sweetly but before
An hour she'd taken a sword with all her main
And twined him of his nose for evermore.

Captain Carpenter mounted up one day
And rode straightway into a stranger rogue
That looked unchristian but be that as it may
The Captain did not wait upon prologue.

But drew upon him out of his great heart
The other swung against him with a club
And cracked his two legs at the shinny part
And let him roll and stick like any tub.

Captain Carpenter rode many a time
From male and female took he sundry harms
He met the wife of Satan crying "I'm
The she-wolf bids you shall bear no more arms."

Their strokes and counters whistled in the wind
I wish he had delivered half his blows
But where she should have made off like a hind
The bitch bit off his arms at the elbows.

And Captain Carpenter parted with his ears
To a black devil that used him in this wise
O Jesus ere his threescore and ten years
Another had plucked out his sweet blue eyes.

Captain Carpenter got up on his roan
And sallied from the gate in hell's despite

I heard him asking in the grimmest tone
If any enemy yet there was to fight?

"To any adversary it is fame
If he risk to be wounded by my tongue
Or burnt in two beneath my red heart's flame
Such are the perils he is cast among.

"But if he can he has a pretty choice
From an anatomy with little to lose
Whether he cut my tongue and take my voice
Or whether it be my round red heart he choose."

It was the neatest knave that ever was seen
Stepping in perfume from his lady's bower
Who at this word put in his merry mien
And fell on Captain Carpenter like a tower.

I would not knock old fellows in the dust
But there lay Captain Carpenter on his back
His weapons were the old heart in his bust
And a blade shook between rotten teeth alack.

The rogue in scarlet and gray soon knew his mind
He wished to get his trophy and depart;
With gentle apology and touch refined
He pierced him and produced the Captain's heart.

God's mercy rest on Captain Carpenter now
I thought him Sirs an honest gentleman
Citizen husband soldier and scholar enow
Let jangling kites eat of him if they can.

But God's deep curses follow after those
That shore him of his goodly nose and ears
His legs and strong arms at the two elbows
And eyes that had not watered seventy years.

The curse of hell upon the sleek upstart
Who got the Captain finally on his back
And took the red red vitals of his heart
And made the kites to whet their beaks clack clack.

PAINTED HEAD

By dark severance the apparition head
Smiles from the air a capital on no
Column or a Platonic perhaps head
On a canvas sky depending from nothing;

Stirs up an old illusion of grandeur
By tickling the instinct of heads to be
Absolute and to try decapitation
And to play truant from the body bush;

But too happy and beautiful for those sorts
Of head (homekeeping heads are happiest)
Discovers maybe thirty unwidowed years
Of not dishonoring the faithful stem;

Is nameless and has authored for the evil
Historian headhunters neither book
Nor state and is therefore distinct from tart
Heads with crowns and guilty gallery heads;

So that the extravagant device of art
Unhousing by abstraction this once head
Was capital irony by a loving hand
That knew the no treason of a head like this;

Makes repentance in an unlovely head
For having vinegarly traduced the flesh
Till, the hurt flesh recusing, the hard egg
Is shrunken to its own deathlike surface;

And an image thus. The body bears the head
(So hardly one they terribly are two)
Feeds and obeys and unto please what end?
Not to the glory of tyrant head but to

The increase of body. Beauty is of body.
The flesh contouring shallowly on a head
Is a rock-garden needing body's love
And best bodiness to colorify

The big blue birds sitting and sea-shell flats
And caves, and on the iron acropolis
To spread the hyacinthine hair and rear
The olive garden for the nightingales.

PHILOMELA

Procne, Philomela, and Itylus,
Your names are liquid, your improbable tale
Is recited in the classic numbers of the nightingale.
Ah, but our numbers are not felicitous,
It goes not liquidly for us.

Perched on a Roman ilex, and duly apostrophized,
The nightingale descanted unto Ovid;
She has even appeared to the Teutons, the swilled and gravid;
At Fontainebleau it may be the bird was gallicized;
Never was she baptized.

To England came Philomela with her pain,
Fleeing the hawk her husband; querulous ghost,
She wanders when he sits heavy on his roost,
Utters herself in the original again,
The untranslatable refrain.

Not to these shores she came! this other Thrace,
Environ barbarous to the royal Attic;

How could her delicate dirge run democratic,
Delivered in a cloudless boundless public place
To an inordinate race?

I pernoctated with the Oxford students once,
And in the quadrangles, in the cloisters, on the Cher,
Precociously knocked at antique doors ajar,
Fatuously touched the hems of the hierophants,
Sick of my dissonance.

I went out to Bagley Wood, I climbed the hill;
Even the moon had slanted off in a twinkling,
I heard the sepulchral owl and a few bells tinkling,
There was no more villainous day to unfulfil,
The diuturnity was still.

Up from the darkest wood where Philomela sat,
Her fairy numbers issued. What then ailed me?
My ears are called capacious but they failed me,
Her classics registered a little flat!
I rose, and venomously spat.

Philomela, Philomela, lover of song,
I am in despair if we may make us worthy,
A bantering breed sophistical and swarthy;
Unto more beautiful, persistently more young,
Thy fabulous provinces belong.

conrad aiken

MORNING SONG OF SENLIN

It is morning, Senlin says, and in the morning
When the light drips through the shutters like the dew,
I arise, I face the sunrise,
And do the things my fathers learned to do.
Stars in the purple dusk above the rooftops
Pale in a saffron mist and seem to die,
And I myself on a swiftly tilting planet
Stand before a glass and tie my tie.

Vine leaves tap my window,
Dew-drops sing to the garden stones,
The robin chirps in the chinaberry tree
Repeating three clear tones.

It is morning. I stand by the mirror
And tie my tie once more.
While waves far off in a pale rose twilight
Crash on a white sand shore.
I stand by a mirror and comb my hair:
How small and white my face!—
The green earth tilts through a sphere of air
And bathes in a flame of space.
There are houses hanging above the stars
And stars hung under a sea . . .
And a sun far off in a shell of silence
Dapples my walls for me . . .

It is morning, Senlin says, and in the morning
Should I not pause in the light to remember god?
Upright and firm I stand on a star unstable,
He is immense and lonely as a cloud.
I will dedicate this moment before my mirror
To him alone, for him I will comb my hair.
Accept these humble offerings, cloud of silence!
I will think of you as I descend the stair.

Vine leaves tap my window,
The snail-track shines on the stones,
Dew-drops flash from the chinaberry tree
Repeating two clear tones.

It is morning, I awake from a bed of silence,
Shining I rise from the starless waters of sleep.
The walls are about me still as in the evening,
I am the same, and the same name still I keep.

The earth revolves with me, yet makes no motion,
The stars pale silently in a coral sky.
In a whistling void I stand before my mirror,
Unconcerned, and tie my tie.

There are horses neighing on far-off hills
Tossing their long white manes,
And mountains flash in the rose-white dusk,
Their shoulders black with rains . . .
It is morning. I stand by the mirror
And surprise my soul once more;
The blue air rushes above my ceiling,
There are suns beneath my floor . . .

. . . It is morning, Senlin says, I ascend from darkness
And depart on the winds of space for I know not where,
My watch is wound, a key is in my pocket,
And the sky is darkened as I descend the stair.
There are shadows across the windows, clouds in heaven,
And a god among the stars; and I will go
Thinking of him as I might think of daybreak
And humming a tune I know . . .

Vine-leaves tap at the window,
Dew-drops sing to the garden stones,
The robin chirps in the chinaberry tree
Repeating three clear tones.

THE ROOM

Through that window—all else being extinct
Except itself and me—I saw the struggle
Of darkness against darkness. Within the room
It turned and turned, dived downward. Then I saw
How order might—if chaos wished—become:
And saw the darkness crush upon itself,
Contracting powerfully; it was as if
It killed itself, slowly: and with much pain.
Pain. The scene was pain, and nothing but pain.
What else, when chaos draws all forces inward
To shape a single leaf? . . .
                            For the leaf came
Alone and shining in the empty room;
After a while the twig shot downward from it;
And from the twig a bough; and then the trunk,
Massive and coarse; and last the one black root.
The black root cracked the walls. Boughs burst the window:
The great tree took possession.
                            Tree of trees!
Remember (when time comes) how chaos died
To shape the shining leaf. Then turn, have courage,
Wrap arms and roots together, be convulsed
With grief, and bring back chaos out of shape.
I will be watching then as I watch now.
I will praise darkness now, but then the leaf.

WINTER FOR A MOMENT TAKES THE MIND

Winter for a moment takes the mind; the snow
Falls past the arclight; icicles guard a wall;
The wind moans through a crack in the window;
A keen sparkle of frost is on the sill.
Only for a moment; as spring too might engage it,
With a single crocus in the loam, or a pair of birds;
Or summer with hot grass; or autumn with a yellow leaf.

Winter is there, outside, is here in me:
Drapes the planets with snow, deepens the ice on the moon,
Darkens the darkness that was already darkness.
The mind too has its snows, its slippery paths,
Walls bayonetted with ice, leaves ice-encased.
Here is the in-drawn room, to which you return
When the wind blows from Arcturus: here is the fire
At which you warm your hands and glaze your eyes;
The piano, on which you touch the cold treble;
Five notes like breaking icicles; and then silence.

The alarm-clock ticks, the pulse keeps time with it,
Night and the mind are full of sounds. I walk
From the fire-place, with its imaginary fire,
To the window, with its imaginary view.
Darkness, and snow ticking the window: silence,
And the knocking of chains on a motor-car, the tolling
Of a bronze bell, dedicated to Christ.
And then the uprush of angelic wings, the beating
Of wings demonic, from the abyss of the mind:
The darkness filled with a feathery whistling, wings
Numberless as the flakes of angelic snow,
The deep void swarming with wings and sound of wings,
The winnowing of chaos, the aliveness
Of depth and depth and depth dedicated to death.

Here are the bickerings of the inconsequential,
The chatterings of the ridiculous, the iterations
Of the meaningless. Memory, like a juggler,
Tosses its colored balls into the light, and again
Receives them into darkness. Here is the absurd,
Grinning like an idiot, and the omnivorous quotidian,
Which will have its day. A handful of coins,
Tickets, items from the news, a soiled handkerchief,
A letter to be answered, notice of a telephone call,
The petal of a flower in a volume of Shakespeare,
The program of a concert. The photograph, too,

Propped on the mantel, and beneath it a dry rosebud;
The laundry bill, matches, an ash-tray, Utamaro's
Pearl-fishers. And the rug, on which are still the crumbs
Of yesterday's feast. These are the void, the night,
And the angelic wings that make it sound.

What is the flower? It is not a sigh of color,
Suspiration of purple, sibilation of saffron,
Nor aureate exhalation from the tomb.
Yet it is these because you think of these,
An emanation of emanations, fragile
As light, or glisten, or gleam, or coruscation,
Creature of brightness, and as brightness brief.
What is the frost? It is not the sparkle of death,
The flash of time's wing, seeds of eternity;
Yet it is these because you think of these.
And you, because you think of these, are both
Frost and flower, the bright ambiguous syllable
Of which the meaning is both no and yes.

Here is the tragic, the distorting mirror
In which your gesture becomes grandiose;
Tears form and fall from your magnificent eyes,
The brow is noble, and the mouth is God's.
Here is the God who seeks his mother, Chaos,—
Confusion seeking solution, and life seeking death.
Here is the rose that woos the icicle; the icicle
That woos the rose. Here is the silence of silences
Which dreams of becoming a sound, and the sound
Which will perfect itself in silence. And all
These things are only the uprush from the void,
The wings angelic and demonic, the sound of the abyss
Dedicated to death. And this is you.

edna st. vincent millay

ON HEARING A SYMPHONY OF BEETHOVEN

Sweet sounds, oh, beautiful music, do not cease!
Reject me not into the world again.
With you alone is excellence and peace,
Mankind made plausible, his purpose plain.
Enchanted in your air benign and shrewd,
With limbs a-sprawl and empty faces pale,
The spiteful and the stingy and the rude
Sleep like the scullions in the fairy-tale.
This moment is the best the world can give:
The tranquil blossom on the tortured stem.
Reject me not, sweet sounds; oh, let me live,
Till Doom espy my towers and scatter them,
A city spell-bound under the aging sun.
Music my rampart, and my only one.

LOVE IS NOT ALL: IT IS NOT MEAT NOR DRINK

Love is not all: it is not meat nor drink
Nor slumber nor a roof against the rain;
Nor yet a floating spar to men that sink
And rise and sink and rise and sink again;
Love can not fill the thickened lung with breath,
Nor clean the blood, nor set the fractured bone;
Yet many a man is making friends with death
Even as I speak, for lack of love alone.
It well may be that in a difficult hour,
Pinned down by pain and moaning for release,
Or nagged by want past resolution's power,
I might be driven to sell your love for peace,
Or trade the memory of this night for food.
It well may be. I do not think I would.

AND YOU AS WELL MUST DIE, BELOVÈD DUST

And you as well must die, belovèd dust,
And all your beauty stand you in no stead;
This flawless, vital hand, this perfect head,
This body of flame and steel, before the gust
Of Death, or under his autumnal frost,
Shall be as any leaf, be no less dead
Than the first leaf that fell,—this wonder fled.
Altered, estranged, disintegrated, lost.

Nor shall my love avail you in your hour.
In spite of all my love, you will arise
Upon that day and wander down the air
Obscurely as the unattended flower,
It mattering not how beautiful you were,
Or how belovèd above all else that dies.

WHAT LIPS MY LIPS HAVE KISSED

What lips my lips have kissed, and where, and why,
I have forgotten, and what arms have lain
Under my head till morning; but the rain
Is full of ghosts tonight, that tap and sigh
Upon the glass and listen for reply;
And in my heart there stirs a quiet pain
For unremembered lads that not again
Will turn to me at midnight with a cry.

Thus in the winter stands the lonely tree,
Nor knows what birds have vanished one by one,
Yet knows its boughs more silent than before:
I cannot say what loves have come and gone;
I only know that summer sang in me
A little while, that in me sings no more.

MORITURUS

If I could have
Two things in one:
The peace of the grave,
And the light of the sun;

My hands across
My thin breast-bone,
But aware of the moss
Invading the stone,

Aware of the flight
Of the golden flicker
With his wing to the light;
To hear him nicker

And drum with his bill
On the rotted window;
Snug and still
On a gray pillow

Deep in the clay
Where digging is hard,
One of the way,—
The blue shard

Of a broken platter—
If I might be
Insensate matter
With sensate me

Sitting within,
Harking and prying,
I might begin
To dicker with dying.

For the body at best
Is a bundle of aches,
Longing for rest;
It cries when it wakes

"Alas, 'tis light!"
At set of sun
"Alas, 'tis night,
And nothing done!"

Death, however,
Is a spongy wall,
Is a sticky river,
Is nothing at all.

Summon the weeper,
Wail and sing;
Call him Reaper,
Angel, King;

Call him Evil
Drunk to the lees,
Monster, Devil—
He is less than these.

Call him Thief,
The Maggot in the Cheese,
The Canker in the Leaf—
He is less than these.

Dusk without sound,
Where the spirit by pain
Uncoiled, is wound
To spring again;

The mind enmeshed
Laid straight in repose,
And the body refreshed
By feeding the rose—

These are but visions;
These would be
The grave's derisions,
Could the grave see.

Here is the wish
Of one that died
Like a beached fish
On the ebb of the tide:

That he might wait
Till the tide came back,
To see if a crate,
Or a bottle, or a black

Boot, or an oar,
Or an orange peel
Be washed ashore. . . .
About his heel

The sand slips;
The last he hears
From the world's lips
Is the sand in his ears.

What thing is little?—
The aphis hid
In a house of spittle?
The hinge of the lid

Of the spider's eye
At the spider's birth?

"Greater am I
By the earth's girth

"Than Mighty Death!"
All creatures cry
That can summon breath—
And speak no lie.

For he is nothing;
He is less
Than Echo answering
"Nothingness!"—

Less than the heat
Of the furthest star
To the ripening wheat;
Less by far,

When all the lipping
Is said and sung,
Than the sweat dripping
From a dog's tongue.

This being so,
And I being such,
I would liever go
On a cripple's crutch,

Lopped and felled;
Liever be dependent
On a chair propelled
By a surly attendant

With a foul breath,
And be spooned my food,
Than go with Death
Where nothing good,

Not even the thrust
Of the summer gnat,
Consoles the dust
For being that.

Needy, lonely,
Stitched by pain,
Left with only
The drip of the rain

Out of all I had;
The books of the wise,
Badly read
By other eyes,

Lewdly bawled
At my closing ear;
Hated, called
A lingerer here—

Withstanding Death
Till Life be gone,
I shall treasure my breath,
I shall linger on.

I shall bolt my door
With a bolt and a cable;
I shall block my door
With a bureau and a table;

With all my might
My door shall be barred.
I shall put up a fight,
I shall take it hard.

With his hand on my mouth
He shall drag me forth,
Shrieking to the south
And clutching at the north.

RECUERDO

We were very tired, we were very merry—
We had gone back and forth all night on the ferry.
It was bare and bright, and smelled like a stable—
But we looked into a fire, we leaned across a table,
We lay on a hill-top underneath the moon;
And the whistles kept blowing, and the dawn came soon.

We were very tired, we were very merry—
We had gone back and forth all night on the ferry;
And you ate an apple, and I ate a pear,
From a dozen of each we had bought somewhere;
And the sky went wan, and the wind came cold,
And the sun rose dripping, a bucketful of gold.

We were very tired, we were very merry,
We had gone back and forth all night on the ferry.
We hailed, "Good-morrow, mother!" to a shawl-covered head,
And bought a morning paper, which neither of us read;
And she wept ,"God bless you!" for the apples and pears,
And we gave her all our money but our subway fares.

DIRGE WITHOUT MUSIC

I am not resigned to the shutting away of loving hearts in the
  hard ground.
So it is, and so it will be, for so it has been, time out of mind:
Into the darkness they go, the wise and the lovely. Crowned
With lilies and with laurel they go; but I am not resigned.

Lovers and thinkers, into the earth with you.
Be one with the dull, the indiscriminate dust.
A fragment of what you felt, of what you knew,
A formula, a phrase remains,—but the best is lost.

The answers quick & keen, the honest look, the laughter, the
  love,
They are gone. They have gone to feed the roses. Elegant and
  curled
Is the blossom. Fragrant is the blossom. I know. But I do not
  approve.
More precious was the light in your eyes than all the roses in
  the world.

Down, down, down into the darkness of the grave
Gently they go, the beautiful, the tender, the kind;
Quietly they go, the intelligent, the witty, the brave.
I know. But I do not approve. And I am not resigned.

THE RETURN

Earth does not understand her child,
   Who from the loud gregarious town
Returns, depleted and defiled,
   To the still woods, to fling him down.

Earth can not count the sons she bore:
   The wounded lynx, the wounded man
Come trailing blood unto her door;
   She shelters both as best she can.

But she is early up and out,
   To trim the year or strip its bones;
She has no time to stand about
   Talking of him in undertones

Who has no aim but to forget,
   Be left in peace, be lying thus
For days, for years, for centuries yet,
   Unshaven and anonymous;

Who, marked for failure, dulled by grief,
   Has traded in his wife and friend
For this warm ledge, this alder leaf:
   Comfort that does not comprehend.

john peale bishop

SPEAKING OF POETRY

The ceremony must be found
that will wed Desdemona to the huge Moor.

      It is not enough—
to win the approval of the Senator
or to outwit his disapproval; honest Iago

can manage that: it is not enough. For then,
though she may pant again in his black arms
(his weight resilient as a Barbary stallion's)
she will be found
when the ambassadors of the Venetian state arrive
again smothered. These things have not been changed,
not in three hundred years.

       (Tupping is still tupping
though that particular word is obsolete.
Naturally, the ritual would not be in Latin.)

For though Othello had his blood from kings
his ancestry was barbarous, his ways African,
his speech uncouth. It must be remembered
that though he valued an embroidery—
three mulberries proper on a silk like silver—
it was not for the subtlety of the stitches,
but for the magic in it. Whereas, Desdemona
once contrived to imitate in needlework
her father's shield, and plucked it out
three times, to begin again, each time
with diminished colors. This is a small point
but indicative.

       Desdemona was small and fair,
delicate as a grasshopper
at the tag-end of summer: a Venetian
to her noble finger tips.

       O, it is not enough
that they should meet, naked, at dead of night
in a small inn on a dark canal. Procurers
less expert than Iago can arrange as much.

The ceremony must be found

Traditional, with all its symbols

ancient as the metaphors in dreams;
strange, with never before heard music; continuous
until the torches deaden at the bedroom door.

THE RETURN

(After a phrase by Giorgio de Chirico)

Night and we heard heavy and cadenced hoofbeats
Of troops departing: the last cohorts left
By the North Gate. That night some listened late
Leaning their eyelids toward Septentrion.

Morning flared and the young tore down the trophies
And warring ornaments: arches were strong
And in the sun but stone; no longer conquests
Circled our columns; all our state was down

In fragments. In the dust, old men with tufted
Eyebrows whiter than sunbaked faces gulped
As it fell. But they no more than we remembered
The old sea-fights, the soldiers' names and sculptors'.

We did not know the end was coming: nor why
It came; only that long before the end
Were many wanted to die. Then vultures starved
And sailed more slowly in the sky.

We still had taxes. Salt was high. The soldiers
Gone. Now there was much drinking and lewd
Houses all night loud with riot. But only
For a time. Soon the taverns had no roofs.

Strangely it was the young the almost boys
Who first abandoned hope; the old still lived
A little, at last a little lived in eyes.
It was the young whose child did not survive.

Some slept beneath the simulacra, until
The gods' faces froze. Then was fear.
Some had response in dreams, but morning restored
Interrogation. Then O then, O ruins!

Temples of Neptune invaded by the sea
And dolphins streaked like streams sportive
As sunlight rode and over the rushing floors
The sea unfurled and what was blue raced silver.

archibald macleish

YOU, ANDREW MARVELL

And here face down beneath the sun
And here upon earth's noonward height
To feel the always coming on
The always rising of the night

To feel creep up the curving east
The earthy chill of dusk and slow
Upon those under lands the vast
And ever climbing shadow grow

And strange at Ecbatan the trees
Take leaf by leaf the evening strange
The flooding dark about their knees
The mountains over Persia change

And now at Kermanshah the gate
Dark empty and the withered grass
And through the twilight now the late
Few travelers in the westward pass

And Baghdad darken and the bridge
Across the silent river gone

And through Arabia the edge
Of evening widen and steal on

And deepen on Palmyra's street
The wheel rut in the ruined stone
And Lebanon fade out and Crete
High through the clouds and overblown

And over Sicily the air
Still flashing with the landward gulls
And loom and slowly disappear
The sails above the shadowy hulls

And Spain go under and the shore
Of Africa the gilded sand
And evening vanish and no more
The low pale light across that land

Nor now the long light on the sea

And here face downward in the sun
To feel how swift how secretly
The shadow of the night comes on...

ARS POETICA

A poem should be palpable and mute
As a globed fruit

Dumb
As old medallions to the thumb

Silent as the sleeve-worn stone
Of casement ledges where the moss has grown—

A poem should be wordless
As the flight of birds

A poem should be motionless in time
As the moon climbs

Leaving, as the moon releases
Twig by twig the night-entangled trees,

Leaving, as the moon behind the winter leaves,
Memory by memory the mind—

A poem should be motionless in time
As the moon climbs

A poem should be equal to:
Not true

For all the history of grief
An empty doorway and a maple leaf

For love
The leaning grasses and two lights above the sea—

A poem should not mean
But be.

WHAT ANY LOVER LEARNS

Water is heavy silver over stone.
Water is heavy silver over stone's
Refusal. It does not fall. It fills. It flows
Every crevice, every fault of the stone,
Every hollow. River does not run.
River presses its heavy silver self
Down into stone and stone refuses.

What runs,
Swirling and leaping into sun, is stone's
Refusal of the river, not the river.

wilfred owen

GREATER LOVE

Red lips are not so red
  As the stained stones kissed by the English dead.
Kindness of wooed and wooer
Seems shame to their love pure.
O Love, your eyes lose lure
  When I behold eyes blinded in my stead!

Your slender attitude
  Trembles not exquisite like limbs knife-skewed,
Rolling and rolling there
Where God seems not to care;
Till the fierce Love they bear
  Cramps them in death's extreme decrepitude.

Your voice sings not so soft,—
  Though even as wind murmuring through raftered loft,—
Your dear voice is not dear,
Gentle, and evening clear,
As theirs whom none now hear,
  Now earth has stopped their piteous mouths that coughed.

Heart, you were never hot,
  Nor large, nor full like hearts made great with shot;
And though your hand be pale,
Paler are all which trail
Your cross through flame and hail:
  Weep, you may weep, for you may touch them not.

THE SEND-OFF

Down the close, darkening lanes they sang their way
To the siding-shed,
And lined the train with faces grimly gay.
Their breasts were stuck all white with wreath and spray
As men's are, dead.

Dull porters watched them, and a casual tramp
Stood staring hard,
Sorry to miss them from the upland camp.
Then, unmoved, signals nodded, and a lamp
Winked to the guard.

So secretly, like wrongs hushed-up, they went.
They were not ours:
We never heard to which front these were sent.
Nor there if they yet mock what women meant
Who gave them flowers.
Shall they return to beatings of great bells
In wild train-loads?
A few, a few, too few for drums and yells,
May creep back, silent, to village wells
Up half-known roads.

THE SHOW

We have fallen in the dreams the ever-living
Breathe on the tarnished mirror of the world,
And then smooth out with ivory hands and sigh.

W. B. YEATS.

My soul looked down from a vague height with Death,
As unremembering how I rose or why,
And saw a sad land, weak with sweats of dearth,
Gray, cratered like the moon with hollow woe,
And pitted with great pocks and scabs of plagues.
Across its beard, that horror of harsh wire,
There moved thin caterpillars, slowly uncoiled.
It seemed they pushed themselves to be as plugs
Of ditches, where they writhed and shrivelled, killed.
By them had slimy paths been trailed and scraped
Round myriad warts that might be little hills.
From gloom's last dregs these long-strung creatures crept,
And vanished out of dawn down hidden holes.
(And smell came up from those foul openings
As out of mouths, or deep wounds deepening.)

On dithering feet upgathered, more and more,
Brown strings, towards strings of gray, with bristling spines,
All migrants from green fields, intent on mire.
Those that were gray, of more abundant spawns,
Ramped on the rest and ate them and were eaten.
I saw their bitten backs curve, loop, and straighten,
I watched those agonies curl, lift, and flatten.
Whereat, in terror what that sight might mean,
I reeled and shivered earthward like a feather.
And Death fell with me, like a deepening moan.
And He, picking a manner of worm, which half had hid
Its bruises in the earth, but crawled no further,
Showed me its feet, the feet of many men,
And the fresh-severed head of it, my head.

APOLOGIA PRO POEMATE MEO

I, too, saw God through mud,—
    The mud that cracked on cheeks when wretches smiled.
    War brought more glory to their eyes than blood,
    And gave their laughs more glee than shakes a child.

Merry it was to laugh there—
    Where death becomes absurd and life absurder.
    For power was on us as we slashed bones bare
    Not to feel sickness or remorse of murder.

I, too, have dropped off fear—
    Behind the barrage, dead as my platoon,
    And sailed my spirit surging, light and clear
    Past the entanglement where hopes lay strewn;

And witnessed exultation—
    Faces that used to curse me, scowl for scowl,
    Shine and lift up with passion of oblation,
    Seraphic for an hour; though they were foul.

I have made fellowships—
    Untold of happy lovers in old song.

For love is not the binding of fair lips
With the soft silk of eyes that look and long, ⟩ romance

By Joy, whose ribbon slips,— package of romance
But wound with war's hard wire whose stakes are strong;
Bound with the bandage of the arm that drips;
Knit in the webbing of the rifle-thong.

I have perceived much beauty
In the hoarse oaths that kept our courage straight;
Heard music in the silentness of duty;
Found peace where shell-storms spouted reddest spate.

Nevertheless, except you share
With them in hell the sorrowful dark of hell,
Whose world is but the trembling of a flare,
And heaven but as the highway for a shell,

You shall not hear their mirth:
You shall not come to think them well content
By any jest of mine. These men are worth
Your tears. You are not worth their merriment.

DULCE ET DECORUM EST

Bent double, like old beggars under sacks,
Knock-kneed, coughing like hags, we cursed through sludge,
Till on the haunting flares we turned our backs,
And towards our distant rest began to trudge.
Men marched asleep. Many had lost their boots,
But limped on, blood-shod. All went lame, all blind;
Drunk with fatigue; deaf even to the hoots
Of gas-shells dropping softly behind.

Gas! GAS! Quick, boys!—An ecstasy of fumbling,
Fitting the clumsy helmets just in time,
But someone still was yelling out and stumbling
And floundering like a man in fire or lime.—

Dim through the misty panes and thick green light,
As under a green sea, I saw him drowning.
In all my dreams before my helpless sight   *keeps coming*
He plunges at me, guttering, choking, drowning.   *back to*

If in some smothering dreams, you too could pace
Behind the wagon that we flung him in,
And watch the white eyes writhing in his face,
His hanging face, like a devil's sick of sin;
If you could hear, at every jolt, the blood
Come gargling from the froth-corrupted lungs,
Bitter as the cud
Of vile, incurable sores on innocent tongues,
My friend, you would not tell with such high zest
To children ardent for some desperate glory,
The old Lie: Dulce et decorum est
Pro patria mori.

ANTHEM FOR DOOMED YOUTH

What passing-bells for these who die as cattle?
Only the monstrous anger of the guns.
Only the stuttering rifles' rapid rattle
Can patter out their hasty orisons.
No mockeries for them from prayers or bells,
Nor any voice of mourning save the choirs,—
The shrill, demented choirs of wailing shells;
And bugles calling for them from sad shires.
What candles may be held to speed them all?
Not in the hands of boys, but in their eyes
Shall shine the holy glimmers of good-byes.
The pallor of girls' brows shall be their pall;
Their flowers the tenderness of silent minds,
And each slow dusk a drawing-down of blinds.

ARMS AND THE BOY

Let the boy try along this bayonet-blade
How cold steel is, and keen with hunger of blood;
Blue with all malice, like a madman's flash;
And thinly drawn with famishing for flesh.

Lend him to stroke these blind, blunt bullet-heads
Which long to nuzzle in the hearts of lads,
Or give him cartridges of fine zinc teeth,
Sharp with the sharpness of grief and death.

For his teeth seem for laughing round an apple.
There lurk no claws behind his fingers supple;
And God will grow no talons at his heels,
Nor antlers through the thickness of his curls.

STRANGE MEETING

It seemed that out of battle I escaped
Down some profound dull tunnel, long since scooped
Through granites which titanic wars had groined.
Yet also there encumbered sleepers groaned,
Too fast in thought or death to be bestirred.
Then, as I probed them, one sprang up, and stared
With piteous recognition in fixed eyes,
Lifting distressful hands as if to bless.
And by his smile, I knew that sullen hall,
By his dead smile I knew we stood in Hell.
With a thousand pains that vision's face was grained;
Yet no blood reached there from the upper ground,
And no guns thumped, or down the flues made moan.
"Strange friend," I said, "here is no cause to mourn."
"None," said the other, "save the undone years,
The hopelessness. Whatever hope is yours,
Was my life also; I went hunting wild
After the wildest beauty in the world,
Which lies not calm in eyes, or braided hair,

But mocks the steady running of the hour,
And if it grieves, grieves richlier than here.
For by my glee might many men have laughed,
And of my weeping something had been left,
Which must die now. I mean the truth untold,
The pity of war, the pity war distilled.
Now men will go content with what we spoiled.
Or, discontent, boil bloody, and be spilled.
They will be swift with swiftness of the tigress,
None will break ranks, though nations trek from progress.
Courage was mine, and I had mystery,
Wisdom was mine, and I had mastery;
To miss the march of this retreating world
Into vain citadels that are not walled.
Then, when much blood had clogged their chariot-wheels
I would go up and wash them from sweet wells,
Even with truths that lie too deep for taint.
I would have poured my spirit without stint
But not through wounds; not on the cess of war.
Foreheads of men have bled where no wounds were.
I am the enemy you killed, my friend.
I knew you in this dark; for so you frowned
Yesterday through me as you jabbed and killed.
I parried; but my hands were loath and cold.
Let us sleep now. . . ."

ON SEEING A PIECE OF OUR ARTILLERY BROUGHT INTO ACTION

Being slowly lifted up, thou long black arm,
Great gun towering toward Heaven, about to curse;
Sway steep against them, and for years rehearse
Huge imprecations like a blasting charm!
Reach at that arrogance which needs thy harm,
And beat it down before its sins grow worse;
Spend our resentment, cannon, yea, disburse
Our gold in shapes of flame, our breaths in storm.
Yet, for men's sakes whom thy vast malison

Must wither innocent of enmity,
Be not withdrawn, dark arm, thy spoilure done,
Safe to the bosom of our prosperity.
But when thy spell be cast complete and whole,
May God curse thee, and cut thee from our soul!

INSENSIBILITY

Happy are men who yet before they are killed
Can let their veins run cold.
Whom no compassion fleers
Or makes their feet
Sore on the alleys cobbled with their brothers.
The front line withers,
But they are troops who fade, not flowers
For poets' tearful fooling:
Men, gaps for filling:
Losses who might have fought
Longer; but no one bothers.

And some cease feeling
Even themselves or for themselves.
Dullness best solves
The tease and doubt of shelling,
And Chance's strange arithmetic
Comes simpler than the reckoning of their shilling.
They keep no check on armies' decimation.

Happy are these who lose imagination:
They have enough to carry with ammunition.
Their spirit drags no pack,
Their old wounds save with cold can not more ache.
Having seen all things red,
Their eyes are rid
Of the hurt of the colour of blood for ever.
And terror's first constriction over,
Their hearts remain small-drawn.

Their senses in some scorching cautery of battle
Now long since ironed,
Can laugh among the dying, unconcerned.

Happy the soldier home, with not a notion
How somewhere, every dawn, some men attack,
And many sighs are drained.
Happy the lad whose mind was never trained:
His days are worth forgetting more than not.
He sings along the march
Which we march taciturn, because of dusk,
The long, forlorn, relentless trend
From larger day to huger night.

We wise, who with a thought besmirch
Blood over all our soul,
How should we see our task
But through his blunt and lashless eyes?
Alive, he is not vital overmuch;
Dying, not mortal overmuch;
Nor sad, nor proud,
Nor curious at all.
He cannot tell
Old men's placidity from his.

But cursed are dullards whom no cannon stuns,
That they should be as stones;
Wretched are they, and mean
With paucity that never was simplicity.
By choice they made themselves immune
To pity and whatever moans in man
Before the last sea and the hapless stars;
Whatever mourns when many leave these shores;
Whatever shares
The eternal reciprocity of tears.

e. e. cummings

PITY THIS BUSY MONSTER, MANUNKIND

pity this busy monster,manunkind,

not.   Progress is a comfortable disease:
your victim(death and life safely beyond)

plays with the bigness of his littleness
—electrons deify one razorblade
into a mountainrange;lenses extend

unwish through curving wherewhen till unwish
returns on its unself.
                                    A world of made
is not a world of born—pity poor flesh

and trees,poor stars and stones,but never this
fine specimen of hypermagical

ultraomnipotence.   We doctors know

a hopeless case if—listen:there's a hell
of a good universe next door;let's go

WHAT IF A MUCH OF A WHICH OF A WIND

what if a much of a which of a wind
gives the truth to summer's lie;
bloodies with dizzying leaves the sun
and yanks immortal stars awry?
Blow king to beggar and queen to seem
(blow friend to fiend: blow space to time)
—when skies are hanged and oceans drowned,
the single secret will still be man

what if a keen of a lean wind flays
screaming hills with sleet and snow:
strangles valleys by ropes of thing
and stifles forests in white ago?
Blow hope to terror; blow seeing to blind
(blow pity to envy and soul to mind)
—whose hearts are mountains, roots are trees,
it's they shall cry hello to the spring

what if a dawn of a doom of a dream
bites this universe in two,
peels forever out of his grave
and sprinkles nowhere with me and you?
Blow soon to never and never to twice
(blow life to isn't: blow death to was)
—all nothing's only our hugest home;
the most who die, the more we live

ALL IGNORANCE TOBOGGANS INTO KNOW

all ignorance toboggans into know
and trudges up to ignorance again:
but winter's not forever,even snow
melts;and if spring should spoil the game,what then?

all history's a winter sport or three:
but were it five,i'd still insist that all
history is too small for even me;
for me and you,exceedingly too small.

Swoop(shrill collective myth)into thy grave
merely to toil the scale to shrillerness
per every madge and mabel dick and dave
—tomorrow is our permanent address

and there they'll scarcely find us(if they do,
we'll move away still further:into now

DARLING! BECAUSE MY BLOOD CAN SING

darling! because my blood can sing
and dance (and does with each your least
your any most very amazing now
or here) let pitiless fear play host
to every isn't that's under the spring
—but if a look should april me,
down isn't's own isn't go ghostly they

doubting can turn men's see to stare
their faith to how their joy to why
their stride and breathing to limp and prove
—but if a look should april me,
some thousand million hundred more
bright worlds than merely by doubting have
darkly themselves unmade makes love

armies (than hate itself and no
meanness unsmaller) armies can
immensely meet for centuries
and (except nothing) nothing's won
—but if a look should april me
for half a when, whatever is less
alive than never begins to yes

but if a look should april me
(though such as perfect hope can feel
only despair completely strikes
forests of mind, mountains of soul)
quite at the hugest which of his who
death is killed dead.   Hills jump with brooks:
trees tumble out of twigs and sticks;

AS FREEDOM IS A BREAKFASTFOOD

as freedom is a breakfastfood
or truth can live with right and wrong

or molehills are from mountains made
—long enough and just so long
will being pay the rent of seem
and genius please the talentgang
and water most encourage flame

as hatracks into peachtrees grow
or hopes dance best on bald men's hair
and every finger is a toe
and any courage is a fear
—long enough and just so long
will the impure think all things pure
and hornets wail by children stung

or as the seeing are the blind
and robins never welcome spring
nor flatfolk prove their world is round
nor dingsters die at break of dong
and common's rare and millstones float
—long enough and just so long
tomorrow will not be too late

worms are the words but joy's the voice
down shall go which and up come who
breasts will be breasts thighs will be thighs
deeds cannot dream what dreams can do
—time is a tree (this life one leaf)
but love is the sky and i am for you
just so long and long enough

MY FATHER MOVED THROUGH DOOMS OF LOVE

my father moved through dooms of love
through sames of am through haves of give,
singing each morning out of each night
my father moved through depths of height

this motionless forgetful where
turned at his glance to shining here;
that if (so timid air is firm)
under his eyes would stir and squirm

newly as from unburied which
floats the first who, his april touch
drove sleeping selves to swarm their fates
woke dreamers to their ghostly roots

and should some why completely weep
my father's fingers brought her sleep:
vainly no smallest voice might cry
for he could feel the mountains grow.

Lifting the valleys of the sea
my father moved through griefs of joy;
praising a forehead called the moon
singing desire into begin

joy was his song and joy so pure
a heart of star by him could steer
and pure so now and now so yes
the wrists of twilight would rejoice

keen as midsummer's keen beyond
conceiving mind of sun will stand,
so strictly (over utmost him
so hugely) stood my father's dream

his flesh was flesh his blood was blood:
no hungry man but wished him food;
no cripple wouldn't creep one mile
uphill to only see him smile.

Scorning the pomp of must and shall
my father moved through dooms of feel;
his anger was as right as rain
his pity was as green as grain

septembering arms of year extend
less humbly wealth to foe and friend
than he to foolish and to wise
offered immeasurable is

proudly and (by octobering flame
beckoned) as earth will downward climb,
so naked for immortal work
his shoulders marched against the dark

his sorrow was as true as bread:
no liar looked him in the head;
if every friend became his foe
he'd laugh and build a world with snow.

My father moved through theys of we,
singing each new leaf out of each tree
(and every child was sure that spring
danced when she heard my father sing)

then let men kill which cannot share,
let blood and flesh be mud and mire,
scheming imagine, passion willed,
freedom a drug that's bought and sold

giving to steal and cruel kind,
a heart to fear, to doubt a mind,
to differ a disease of same,
conform the pinnacle of am

though dull were all we taste as bright,
bitter all utterly things sweet,
maggoty minus and dumb death
all we inherit, all bequeath

and nothing quite so least as truth
—i say though hate were why men breathe—
because my father lived his soul
love is the whole and more than all

I SING OF OLAF

i sing of Olaf glad and big
whose warmest heart recoiled at war:
a conscientious object-or

his well-belovéd colonel (trig
westpointer most succinctly bred)
took erring Olaf soon in hand;
but—though an host of overjoyed
noncoms (first knocking on the head
him) do through icy waters roll
that helplessness which others stroke
with brushes recently employed
anent this muddy toiletbowl,
while kindred intellects evoke
allegiance per blunt instruments—
Olaf (being to all intents
a corpse and wanting any rag
upon what God unto him gave)
responds, without getting annoyed
"I will not kiss your f.ing flag"

straightway the silver bird looked grave
(departing hurriedly to shave)

but—though all kinds of officers
(a yearning nation's blueeyed pride)
their passive prey did kick and curse
until for wear their clarion
voices and boots were much the worse,
and egged the firstclassprivates on
his rectum wickedly to tease
by means of skilfully applied
bayonets roasted hot with heat—
Olaf (upon what were once knees)
does almost ceaselessly repeat
"there is some s. I will not eat"

our president, being of which
assertions duly notified
threw the yellowsonofabitch
into a dungeon, where he died

Christ (of His mercy infinite)
i pray to see; and Olaf, too

preponderatingly because
unless statistics lie he was
more brave than me: more blond than you.

ANYONE LIVED IN A PRETTY HOW TOWN

anyone lived in a pretty how town
(with up so floating many bells down)
spring summer autumn winter
he sang his didn't he danced his did.

Women and men (both little and small)
cared for anyone not at all
they sowed their isn't they reaped their same
sun moon stars rain

children guessed (but only a few
and down they forgot as up they grew
autumn winter spring summer)
that noone loved him more by more

when by now and tree by leaf
she laughed his joy she cried his grief
bird by snow and stir by still
anyone's any was all to her

someones married their everyones
laughed their cryings and did their dance
(sleep wake hope and then) they
said their nevers they slept their dream

stars rain sun moon
(and only the snow can begin to explain
how children are apt to forget to remember
with up so floating many bells down)

one day anyone died i guess
(and noone stooped to kiss his face)
busy folk buried them side by side
little by little and was by was

all by all and deep by deep
and more by more they dream their sleep
noone and anyone earth by april
wish by spirit and if by yes.

Women and men (both dong and ding)
summer autumn winter spring
reaped their sowing and went their came
sun moon stars rain

SOMEWHERE I HAVE NEVER TRAVELLED

somewhere i have never travelled, gladly beyond
any experience, your eyes have their silence:
in your most frail gesture are things which enclose me,
or which i cannot touch because they are too near

your slightest look easily will unclose me
though i have closed myself as fingers,
you open always petal by petal myself as Spring opens
(touching skilfully, mysteriously) her first rose

or if your wish be to close me, i and
my life will shut very beautifully, suddenly,
as when the heart of this flower imagines
the snow carefully everywhere descending;

nothing which we are to perceive in this world equals
the power of your intense fragility: whose texture

compels me with the colour of its countries,
rendering death and forever with each breathing

(i do not know what it is about you that closes
and opens; only something in me understands
the voice of your eyes is deeper than all roses)
nobody, not even the rain, has such small hands

robert graves

INTERRUPTION

If ever against this easy blue and silver
Hazed-over countryside of thoughtfulness
Far behind in the mind and above,
Boots from before and below approach tramping,
Watch how their premonition will display
A forward countryside, low in the distance,
A picture-postcard square of June grass,
Will warm a summer season, trim the hedges,
Cast the river about on either flank,
Start the late cuckoo emptily calling,
Invent a rambling tale of moles and voles,
Furnish a path with stiles.
Watch how the field will broaden, the feet nearing
Sprout with great dandelions and buttercups,
Widen and heighten. The blue and silver
Fogs at the border of this all-grass.
Interruption looms gigantified,
Lurches against, treads thundering through,
Blots the landscape, scatters all,
Roars and rumbles like a dark tunnel,
Is gone.

        The picture-postcard grass and trees
Swim back to central: it is a large patch,
It is a modest, failing patch of green,

The postage-stamp of its departure,
Clouded with blue and silver, closing in now
To a plain countryside of less and less,
Unpeopled and unfeathered blue and silver,
Before, behind, above.

OGRES AND PYGMIES

    Those famous men of old, the Ogres—
They had long beards and stinking arm-pits.
They were wide-mouthed, long-yarded and great-bellied
Yet of not taller stature, Sirs, than you.
They lived on Ogre-Strand, which was no place
But the churl's terror of their proud extent,
Where every foot was three-and-thirty inches,
And every penny bought a whole sheep.
Now of their company none survive, not one,
The times being, thank God, unfavourable
To all but nightmare memory of them.
Their images stand howling in the waste,
(The winds enforced against their wide mouths)
Whose granite haunches king and priest must yearly
Buss, and their cold knobbed knees.

So many feats they did to admiration:
With their enormous lips they sang louder
Than ten cathedral choirs, and with their grand yards
Stormed the most rare and obstinate maidenheads,
With their strong-gutted and capacious bellies
Digested stones and glass like ostriches.
They dug great pits and heaped great cairns,
Deflected rivers, slew whole armies,
And hammered judgments for posterity—
For the sweet-cupid-lipped and tassel-yarded
Delicate-stomached dwellers
In Pygmy Alley, where with brooding on them
A foot is shrunk to seven inches
And twelve-pence will not buy a spare rib.

And who would choose between Ogres and Pygmies—
The thundering text, the snivelling commentary—
Reading between such covers he will likely
Prove his own disproportion and not laugh.

ROCKY ACRES

This is a wild land, country of my choice,
    With harsh craggy mountain, moor ample and bare.
Seldom in these acres is heard any voice
    But voice of cold water that runs here and there
    Through rocks and lank heather growing without care.
No mice in the heath run nor no birds cry
For fear of the dark speck that floats in the sky.

He soars and he hovers, rocking on his wings,
    He scans his wide parish with a sharp eye,
He catches the trembling of small hidden things,
    He tears them in pieces, dropping from the sky:
    Tenderness and pity the land will deny
Where life is but nourished from water and rock,
A hardy adventure, full of fear and shock.

Time has never journeyed to this lost land,
    Crakeberries and heather bloom out of date,
The rocks jut, the streams flow singing on either hand,
    Careless if the season be early or late.
    The skies wander overhead, now blue, now slate:
Winter would be known by his cold cutting snow
If June did not borrow his armor also.

Yet this is my country beloved by me best,
    The first land that rose from Chaos and the Flood,
Nursing no fat valleys for comfort and rest,
    Trampled by no hard hooves, stained with no blood.
    Bold immortal country whose hill-tops have stood
Strongholds for the proud gods when on earth they go,
Terror for fat burghers in far plains below.

A LOVE STORY

The full moon easterly rising, furious,
Against a winter sky ragged with red;
The hedges high in snow, and owls raving—
Solemnities not easy to withstand:
A shiver wakes the spine.

In boyhood, having encountered the scene,
I suffered horror: I fetched the moon home,
With owls and snow, to nurse in my head
Throughout the trials of a new spring,
Famine unassuaged.

But fell in love, and made a lodgement
Of love on those frozen ramparts.
Her image was my ensign: snows melted,
Hedges sprouted, the moon tenderly shone,
The owls trilled with tongues of nightingale.

These were all lies, though they matched the time,
And brought me less than luck: her image
Warped in the weather, turned beldamish.
Then back came winter on me at a bound,
The pallid sky heaved with a moon-quake.

Dangerous it had been with love-notes
To serenade Queen Famine.
In tears I recomposed the former scene,
Let the snow lie, watched the moon rise, suffered
    the owls,
Paid homage to them of unevent.

THE EREMITES

We may well wonder at those froward hermits
Who like the scorpion and the basilisk
Crouched in the desert sands, to undo
Their scurfy flesh with tortures.

They drank from pools fouled by the ass and camel,
Chewed uncooked millet pounded between stones,
Wore but a shame-rag, dusk or dawn,
And rolled in thorny places.

In the wilderness there are no women;
Yet hermits harbour in their shrunken loins
A penitential paradise,
A leaping-house of glory.

Solomons of a thousand lusty love-chants,
These goatish men, burned Aethiopian black,
Kept vigil till the angelic whores
Should lift the latch of pleasure.

And what Atellan orgies of the soul
Were celebrated then among the rocks
They testify themselves in books
That rouse Atellan laughter.

Haled back at last to wear the ring and mitre,
They clipped their beards and, for their stomachs' sake,
Drank now and then a little wine,
And tasted cakes and honey.

Observe then how they disciplined the daughters
Of noble widows, who must fast and thirst,
Abjure down-pillows, rouge and curls,
Deform their delicate bodies:

Whose dreams were curiously beset with visions
Of stinking hermits in a wilderness
Pressing unnatural lusts on them
Until they wakened screaming.

Such was the virtue of our pious fathers:
To refine pleasure in the hungry dream.
Pity for them, but pity too for us—
Our beds by their leave lain in.

WARNING TO CHILDREN

Children, if you dare to think
Of the greatness, rareness, muchness,
Fewness of this precious only
Endless world in which you say
You live, you think of things like this:
Blocks of slate enclosing dappled
Red and green, enclosing tawny
Yellow nets, enclosing white
And black acres of dominoes,
Where a neat brown paper parcel
Tempts you to untie the string.
In the parcel a small island,
On the island a large tree,
On the tree a husky fruit.
Strip the husk and cut the rind off:
In the centre you will see
Blocks of slate enclosed by dappled
Red and green, enclosed by tawny
Yellow nets, enclosed by white
And black acres of dominoes,
Where the same brown paper parcel—
Children, leave the string untied!
For who dares undo the parcel
Finds himself at once inside it,
On the island, in the fruit,
Blocks of slate about his head,
Finds himself enclosed by dappled
Green and red, enclosed by yellow
Tawny nets, enclosed by black
And white acres of dominoes,
But the same brown paper parcel
Still untied upon his knee.
And, if he then should dare to think
Of the fewness, muchness, rareness,
Greatness of this endless only
Precious world in which he says
He lives—he then unties the string.

SEA SIDE

Into a gentle wildness and confusion,
Of here and there, of one and everyone,
Of windy sandhills by an unkempt sea,
Came two and two in search of symmetry,
Found symmetry of two in sea and sand,
In left foot, right foot, left hand and right hand.

The beast with two backs is a single beast,
Yet by his love of singleness increased
To two and two and two and two again,
Until, instead of sandhills, is a plain
Patterned in two and two, by two and two—
And the sea parts in horror at a view
Of rows of houses coupling, back to back,
While love smokes from the common chimney-stack
With two-four-eight-sixteenish single same
Re-registration of the duple name.

TO JUAN AT THE WINTER SOLSTICE

There is one story and one story only
That will prove worth your telling,
Whether as learned bard or gifted child;
To it all lines or lesser gauds belong
That startle with their shining
Such common stories as they stray into.

Is it of trees you tell, their months and virtues,
Of strange beasts that beset you,
Of birds that croak at you the Triple will?
Or of the Zodiac and how slow it turns
Below the Boreal Crown,
Prison of all true kings that ever reigned?

Water to water, ark again to ark,
From woman back to woman:

So each new victim treads unfalteringly
The never altered circuit of his fate,
Bringing twelve peers as witness
Both to his starry rise and starry fall.

Or is it of the Virgin's silver beauty,
All fish below the thighs?
She in her left hand bears a leafy quince;
When with her right she crooks a finger, smiling,
How may the King hold back?
Royally then he barters life for love.

Or of the undying snake from chaos hatched,
Whose coils contain the ocean,
Into whose chops with naked sword he springs,
Then in black water, tangled by the reeds,
Battles three days and nights,
To be spewed up beside her scalloped shore?

Much snow is falling, winds roar hollowly,
The owl hoots from the elder,
Fear in your heart cries to the loving-cup:
Sorrow to sorrow as the sparks fly upward.
The log groans and confesses
There is one story and one story only.

Dwell on her graciousness, dwell on her smiling,
Do not forget what flowers
The great boar trampled down in ivy time.
Her brow was creamy as the long ninth wave,
Her sea-blue eyes were wild.
But nothing promised that is not performed.

frederick mortimer clapp

TO DIE INTO YOURSELF

To die into yourself would not now be a martyrdom,
or stratagem embedded in an ingrown blur in seeing,
but just a sneak collision of aberrant stars
that flung themselves from being into a light
encased in dust so thick the paternity of its flight
from nowhere to some anywhere is far too far
away to be conceived in our self-centered time's
clicking, and yet too near to match the rod and perch of
        space,
the license of these eyes. So you keep counting autumn flies
that die as hazy spots on your window-pane
as some the fleeing of universes trapped in their rainbows'
fingerprints on silvered gelatine. There is no formula
clean of falsehood
for such conjunctions and absorptions at the telltale
end of reason, nor any record of a knowable direction
receding into the absconded body of what once seemed a
        whence.

ONCE WHEN MARS

Once when Mars was sliding backward slowly
across midsummer stars
in a great loop, birth came unasked to me
in a mean street much meaner now than then.
A life has passed. Mars many times has traced its July loop
between the Archer and the fish-tailed Goat,
slipping a sailor's overhanded knot
falsely yet visibly.
Wars not a few have flashed white-hot then smouldered red;
tyrants have risen and misery.

Yet, but for a brief turn, I have been held apart
from danger and death. By what? For what? By whom?
Others in their millions stuck on the tines of an iron rake
have burned in autumns not yet theirs, the answer
to being born not clearly made by death for any life.
All answers are fuzzed now and choke with smoke
from vents the industrious heavens try to hide
as Mars, tying its preconforming knot,
backtracks again across remoter stars
whose eyes on the tilt of earth's planisphere
glitter with distance and, as if, disdain.

PUSHED NUDE INTO THIS ASSIGNMENT

Pushed nude into this assignment
where with delinquent brain the imminent lunatic cultivates
the backyard of his illusions and passions,
we might as well disown the clouds that streak the moon-
    mirror
of our sleep and reprobate their foliated logic.

For being but ourselves, should we not weep now in our mirth
and laugh on the ice-cloaked pinnacles of grief and make
under the farcical scowl of death
perverse gestures as obscene and ludicrous as birth?

Dull to the betrayal of their own decay
our nerves, choked by the strangler fig-tree
of our love-seeking lives,
cry out for a despised ransom lost
on a yesterday of ages ago
when inanimate we came hurtling through
regions beyond space to reach the earth.
It waits, it only waits the advent of your eyes.

a. j. m. smith

THE SORCERER

There is a sorcerer in Lachine
Who for a small fee will put a spell
On my beloved, who has sea-green
Eyes, and on my doting self as well.

He will transform us, if we like, to goldfish:
We shall swim in a crystal bowl,
And the bright water will go swish
Over our naked bodies; we shall have no soul.

In the morning the syrupy sunshine
Will dance on our tails and fins.
I shall have her then all for mine,
And Father Lebeau will hear no more of her sins.

Come along, good sir, change us into goldfish.
I would put away intellect and lust,
Be but a red gleam in a crystal dish,
But kin of the trembling ocean, not of the dust.

THE ARCHER

Bend back thy bow, O Archer, till the string
Is level with thine ear, thy body taut,
Its nature art, thyself thy statue wrought
Of marble blood, thy weapon the poised wing
Of coiled and aquiline Fate. Then, loosening, fling
The hissing arrow like a burning thought
Into the empty sky that smokes as the hot
Shaft plunges to the bullseye's quenching ring.

So for a moment, motionless, serene,
Fixed between time and time, I aim and wait;
Nothing remains for breath now but to waive
His prior claim and let the barb fly clean
Into the heart of what I know and hate—
That central black, the ringed and targeted grave.

louise bogan

SONG FOR THE LAST ACT

Now that I have your face by heart, I look
Less at its features than its darkening frame
Where quince and melon, yellow as young flame,
Lie with quilled dahlias and the shepherd's crook.
Beyond, a garden. There, in insolent ease
The lead and marble figures watch the show
Of yet another summer loath to go
Although the scythes hang in the apple trees.

Now that I have your face by heart, I look.

Now that I have your voice by heart, I read
In the black chords upon a dulling page
Music that is not meant for music's cage,
Whose emblems mix with words that shake and bleed.
The staves are shuttled over with a stark
Unprinted silence. In a double dream
I must spell out the storm, the running stream.
The beat's too swift. The notes shift in the dark.

Now that I have your voice by heart, I read.

Now that I have your heart by heart, I see
The wharves with their great ships and architraves;
The rigging and the cargo and the slaves
On a strange beach under a broken sky.
O not departure, but a voyage done!
The bales stand on the stone; the anchor weeps
Its red rust downward, and the long vine creeps
Beside the salt herb, in the lengthening sun.

Now that I have your heart by heart, I see.

f. r. higgins

SONG FOR THE CLATTER-BONES

God rest that Jewy woman,
Queen Jezebel, the bitch
Who peeled the clothes from her shoulder-bones
Down to her spent teats
As she stretched out of the window
Among the geraniums, where
She chaffed and laughed like one half daft
Titivating her painted hair—

King Jehu he drove to her,
She tipped him a fancy beck;
But he from his knacky side-car spoke,
'Who'll break that dewlapped neck?'
And so she was thrown from the window;
Like Lucifer she fell
Beneath the feet of the horses and they beat
The light out of Jezebel.

That corpse wasn't planted in clover;
Ah, nothing of her was found
Save those grey bones that Hare-foot Mike
Gave me for their lovely sound;
And as once her dancing body
Made star-lit princes sweat,
So I'll just clack: though her ghost lacks a back
There's music in the old bones yet.

allen tate

ODE TO THE CONFEDERATE DEAD

Row after row with strict impunity
The headstones yield their names to the element,
The wind whirrs without recollection;
In the riven troughs the splayed leaves
Pile up, of nature the casual sacrament
To the seasonal eternity of death;
Then driven by the fierce scrutiny
Of heaven to their election in the vast breath,
They sough the rumour of mortality.

Autumn is desolation in the plot
Of a thousand acres where these memories grow
From the inexhaustible bodies that are not
Dead, but feed the grass row after rich row.
Think of the autumns that have come and gone!—
Ambitious November with the humors of the year,
With a particular zeal for every slab,
Staining the uncomfortable angels that rot
On the slabs, a wing chipped here, an arm there:
The brute curiosity of an angel's stare
Turns you, like them, to stone,
Transforms the heaving air
Till plunged to a heavier world below
You shift your sea-space blindly
Heaving, turning like the blind crab.

Dazed by the wind, only the wind
The leaves flying, plunge

You know who have waited by the wall
The twilight certainty of an animal,
Those midnight restitutions of the blood

You know—the immitigable pines, the smoky frieze
Of the sky, the sudden call: you know the rage,
The cold pool left by the mounting flood,
Of muted Zeno and Parmenides.
You who have waited for the angry resolution
Of those desires that should be yours tomorrow,
You know the unimportant shrift of death
And praise the vision
And praise the arrogant circumstance
Of those who fall
Rank upon rank, hurried beyond decision—
Here by the sagging gate, stopped by the wall.

    Seeing, seeing only the leaves
    Flying, plunge and expire

Turn your eyes to the immoderate past,
Turn to the inscrutable infantry rising
Demons out of the earth—they will not last.
Stonewall, Stonewall, and the sunken fields of hemp,
Shiloh, Antietam, Malvern Hill, Bull Run.
Lost in that orient of the thick-and-fast
You will curse the setting sun.

    Cursing only the leaves crying
    Like an old man in a storm

You hear the shout, the crazy hemlocks point
With troubled fingers to the silence which
Smothers you, a mummy, in time.

                    The hound bitch
Toothless and dying, in a musty cellar
Hears the wind only.

              Now that the salt of their blood
Stiffens the saltier oblivion of the sea,
Seals the malignant purity of the flood,

What shall we who count our days and bow
Our heads with a commemorial woe
In the ribboned coats of grim felicity,
What shall we say of the bones, unclean,
Whose verdurous anonymity will grow?
The ragged arms, the ragged heads and eyes
Lost in these acres of the insane green?
The gray lean spiders come, they come and go;
In a tangle of willows without light
The singular screech-owl's tight
Invisible lyric seeds the mind
With the furious murmur of their chivalry.

    We shall say only the leaves
    Flying, plunge and expire

We shall say only the leaves whispering
In the improbable mist of nightfall
That flies on multiple wing;
Night is the beginning and the end
And in between the ends of distraction
Waits mute speculation, the patient curse
That stones the eyes, or like the jaguar leaps
For his own image in a jungle pool, his victim.

What shall we say who have knowledge
Carried to the heart? Shall we take the act
To the grave? Shall we, more hopeful, set up the grave
In the house? The ravenous grave?

                        Leave now
The shut gate and the decomposing wall:
The gentle serpent, green in the mulberry bush,
Riots with his tongue through the hush—
Sentinel of the grave who counts us all!

LAST DAYS OF ALICE

Alice grown lazy, mammoth but not fat,
Declines upon her lost and twilight age;
Above in the dozing leaves the grinning cat
Quivers forever with his abstract rage:

Whatever light swayed on the perilous gate
Forever sways, nor will the arching grass,
Caught when the world clattered, undulate
In the deep suspension of the looking-glass.

Bright Alice! always pondering to gloze
The spoiled cruelty she had meant to say
Gazes learnedly down her airy nose
At nothing, nothing thinking all the day.

Turned absent-minded by infinity
She cannot move unless her double move,
The All-Alice of the world's entity
Smashed in the anger of her hopeless love,

Love for herself who, as an earthly twain,
Pouted to join her two in a sweet one;
No more the second lips to kiss in vain
The first she broke, plunged through the glass alone—

Alone to the weight of impassivity,
Incest of spirit, theorem of desire,
Without will as chalky cliffs by the sea,
Empty as the bodiless flesh of fire:

All space, that heaven is a dayless night,
A nightless day driven by perfect lust
For vacancy, in which her bored eyesight
Stares at the drowsy cubes of human dust.

—We too back to the world shall never pass
Through the shattered door, a dumb shade-harried crowd

Being all infinite, function depth and mass
Without figure, a mathematical shroud

Hurled at the air—bléssed without sin!
O God of our flesh, return us to Your wrath,
Let us be evil could we enter in
Your grace, and falter on the stony path!

THE WOLVES

There are wolves in the next room waiting
With heads bent low, thrust out, breathing
At nothing in the dark; between them and me
A white door patched with light from the hall
Where it seems never (so still is the house)
A man has walked from the front door to the stair.
It has all been forever. Beasts claw the floor.
I have brooded on angels and archfiends
But no man has ever sat where the next room's
Crowded with wolves, and for the honor of man
I affirm that never have I before. Now while
I have looked for the evening star at a cold window
And whistled when Arcturus spilt his light,
I've heard the wolves scuffle, and said: So this
Is man; so—what better conclusion is there—
The day will not follow night, and the heart
Of man has a little dignity, but less patience
Than a wolf's, and a duller sense that cannot
Smell its own mortality. (This and other
Meditations will be suited to other times
After dog silence howls his epitaph.)
Now remember courage, go to the door,
Open it and see whether coiled on the bed
Or cringing by the wall, a savage beast
Maybe with golden hair, with deep eyes
Like a bearded spider on a sunlit floor
Will snarl—and man can never be alone.

THE CROSS

There is a place that some men know,
I cannot see the whole of it
Nor how I came there. Long ago
Flame burst out of a secret pit
Crushing the world with such a light
The day-sky fell to moonless black,
The kingly sun to hateful night
For those, once seeing, turning back:
For love so hates mortality
Which is the providence of life
She will not let it blesséd be
But curses it with mortal strife,
Until beside the blinding rood
Within that world-destroying pit
—Like young wolves that have tasted blood,
Of death, men taste no more of it.
So blind, in so severe a place
(All life before in the black grave)
The last alternatives they face
Of life, without the life to save,
Being from all salvation weaned—
A stag charged both at heel and head:
Who would come back is turned a fiend
Instructed by the fiery dead.

THE MEDITERRANEAN

Quem das finem, rex magne, dolorum?

Where we went in the boat was a long bay
A slingshot wide, walled in by towering stone—
Peaked margin of antiquity's delay,
And we went there out of time's monotone:

Where we went in the black hull no light moved
But a gull white-winged along the feckless wave,

The breeze, unseen but fierce as a body loved,
That boat drove onward like a willing slave:

Where we went in the small ship the seaweed
Parted and gave to us the murmuring shore
And we made feast and in our secret need
Devoured the very plates Aeneas bore:

Where derelict you see through the low twilight
The green coast that you, thunder-tossed, would win,
Drop sail, and hastening to drink all night
Eat dish and bowl—to take that sweet land in!

Where we feasted and caroused on the sandless
Pebbles, affecting our day of piracy,
What prophecy of eaten plates could landless
Wanderers fulfil by the ancient sea?

We for that time might taste the famous age
Eternal here yet hidden from our eyes
When lust of power undid its stuffless rage;
They, in a wineskin, bore earth's paradise.

Let us lie down once more by the breathing side
Of Ocean, where our live forefathers sleep
As if the Known Sea still were a month wide—
Atlantis howls but is no longer steep!

What country shall we conquer, what fair land
Unman our conquest and locate our blood?
We've cracked the hemispheres with careless hand!
Now, from the Gates of Hercules we flood

Westward, westward till the barbarous brine
Whelms us to the tired land where tasseling corn,
Fat beans, grapes sweeter than muscadine
Rot on the vine: in that land were we born.

SONNETS AT CHRISTMAS

I

This is the day His hour of life draws near,
Let me get ready from head to foot for it
Most handily with eyes to pick the year
For small feed to reward a feathered wit.
Some men would see it an epiphany
At ease, at food and drink, others at chase
Yet I, stung lassitude, with ecstasy
Unspent argue the season's difficult case

So: Man, dull critter of enormous head,
What would he look at in the coiling sky?
But I must kneel again unto the Dead
While Christmas bells of paper white and red,
Figured with boys and girls spilt from a sled,
Ring out the silence I am nourished by.

II

Ah, Christ, I love you rings to the wild sky
And I must think a little of the past:
When I was ten I told a stinking lie
That got a black boy whipped; but now at last
The going years, caught in an accurate glow,
Reverse like balls englished upon green baize—
Let them return, let the round trumpets blow
The ancient crackle of the Christ's deep gaze.

Deafened and blind, with senses yet unfound,
Am I, untutored to the after-wit
Of knowledge, knowing a nightmare has no sound;
Therefore with idle hands and head I sit
In late December before the fire's daze
Punished by crimes of which I would be quit.

hart crane

BLACK TAMBOURINE

The interests of a black man in a cellar
Mark tardy judgment on the world's closed door.
Gnats toss in the shadow of a bottle,
And a roach spans a crevice in the floor.

Æsop, driven to pondering, found
Heaven with the tortoise and the hare;
Fox brush and sow ear top his grave
And mingling incantations on the air.

The black man, forlorn in the cellar,
Wanders in some mid-kingdom, dark, that lies,
Between his tambourine, stuck on the wall,
And, in Africa, a carcass quick with flies.

PRAISE FOR AN URN

In Memoriam: Ernest Nelson

It was a kind and northern face
That mingled in such exile guise
The everlasting eyes of Pierrot
And, of Gargantua, the laughter.

His thoughts, delivered to me
From the white coverlet and pillow,
I see now, were inheritances—
Delicate riders of the storm.

The slant moon on the slanting hill
Once moved us toward presentiments
Of what the dead keep, living still,
And such assessments of the soul

As, perched in the crematory lobby,
The insistent clock commented on,
Touching as well upon our praise
Of glories proper to the time.

Still, having in mind gold hair,
I cannot see that broken brow
And miss the dry sound of bees
Stretching across a lucid space.

Scatter these well-meant idioms
Into the smoky spring that fills
The suburbs, where they will be lost.
They are no trophies of the sun.

CHAPLINESQUE

We make our meek adjustments,
Contented with such random consolations
As the wind deposits
In slithered and too ample pockets.

For we can still love the world, who find
A famished kitten on the step, and know
Recesses for it from the fury of the street,
Or warm torn elbow coverts.

We will sidestep, and to the final smirk
Dally the doom of that inevitable thumb
That slowly chafes its puckered index toward us,
Facing the dull squint with what innocence
And what surprise!

And yet these fine collapses are not lies
More than the pirouettes of any pliant cane;
Our obsequies are, in a way, no enterprise.
We can evade you, and all else but the heart:
What blame to us if the heart live on.

The game enforces smirks; but we have seen
The moon in lonely alleys make
A grail of laughter of an empty ash can,
And through all sound of gaiety and quest
Have heard a kitten in the wilderness.

REPOSE OF RIVERS

The willows carried a slow sound,
A sarabande the wind mowed on the mead.
I could never remember
That seething, steady leveling of the marshes
Till age had brought me to the sea.

Flags, weeds. And remembrance of steep alcoves
Where cypresses shared the noon's
Tyranny; they drew me into hades almost.
And mammoth turtles climbing sulphur dreams
Yielded, while sun-silt rippled them
Asunder ...

How much I would have bartered! the black gorge
And all the singular nestings in the hills
Where beavers learn stitch and tooth.
The pond I entered once and quickly fled—
I remember now its singing willow rim.

And finally, in that memory all things nurse;
After the city that I finally passed
With scalding unguents spread and smoking darts
The monsoon cut across the delta
At gulf gates ... There, beyond the dykes

I heard wind flaking sapphire, like this summer,
And willows could not hold more steady sound.

THE WINE MENAGERIE

Invariably when wine redeems the sight,
Narrowing the mustard scansions of the eyes,
A leopard ranging always in the brow
Asserts a vision in the slumbering gaze.

Then glozening decanters that reflect the street
Wear me in crescents on their bellies. Slow
Applause flows into liquid cynosures:
—I am conscripted to their shadows' glow.

Against the imitation onyx wainscoting
(Painted emulsion of snow, eggs, yarn, coal, manure)
Regard the forceps of the smile that takes her.
Percussive sweat is spreading to his hair. Mallets,
Her eyes, unmake an instant of the world . . .

What is it in this heap the serpent pries—
Whose skin, facsimile of time, unskeins
Octagon, sapphire transepts round the eyes;
—From whom some whispered carillon assures
Speed to the arrow into feathered skies?

Sharp to the window-pane guile drags a face,
And as the alcove of her jealousy recedes
An urchin who has left the snow
Nudges a cannister across the bar
While August meadows somewhere clasp his brow.

Each chamber, transept, coins some squint,
Remorseless line, minting their separate wills—
Poor streaked bodies wreathing up and out,
Unwitting the stigma that each turn repeals:
Between black tusks the roses shine!

New thresholds, new anatomies! Wine talons
Build freedom up about me and distill

This competence—to travel in a tear
Sparkling alone, within another's will.

Until my blood dreams a receptive smile
Wherein new purities are snared; where chimes
Before some flame of gaunt repose a shell
Tolled once, perhaps, by every tongue in hell.
—Anguished, the wit that cries out of me:

'Alas,—these frozen billows of your skill!
Invent new dominoes of love and bile . . .
Ruddy, the tooth implicit of the world
Has followed you. Though in the end you know
And count some dim inheritance of sand,
How much yet meets the treason of the snow.

'Rise from the dates and crumbs. And walk away,
Stepping over Holofernes' shins—
Beyond the wall, whose severed head floats by
With Baptist John's. Their whispering begins.

'—And fold your exile on your back again;
Petrushka's valentine pivots on its pin.'

VOYAGES

I

Above the fresh ruffles of the surf
Bright striped urchins flay each other with sand.
They have contrived a conquest for shell shucks,
And their fingers crumble fragments of baked weed
Gaily digging and scattering.

And in answer to their treble interjections
The sun beats lightning on the waves,
The waves fold thunder on the sand;
And could they hear me I would tell them:

O brilliant kids, frisk with your dog,
Fondle your shells and sticks, bleached
By time and the elements; but there is a line
You must not cross nor ever trust beyond it
Spry cordage of your bodies to caresses
Too lichen-faithful from too wide a breast.
The bottom of the sea is cruel.

II

And yet this great wink of eternity,
Of rimless floods, unfettered leewardings,
Samite sheeted and processioned where
Her undinal vast belly moonward bends,
Laughing the wrapt inflections of our love;

Take this Sea, whose diapason knells
On scrolls of silver snowy sentences,
The sceptred terror of whose sessions rends
As her demeanors motion well or ill,
All but the pieties of lovers' hands.

And onward, as bells off San Salvador
Salute the crocus lustres of the stars,
In these poinsettia meadows of her tides,—
Adagios of islands, O my Prodigal,
Complete the dark confessions her veins spell.

Mark how her turning shoulders wind the hours,
And hasten while her penniless rich palms
Pass superscription of bent foam and wave,—
Hasten, while they are true,—sleep, death, desire,
Close round one instant in one floating flower.

Bind us in time, O Seasons clear, and awe.
O minstrel galleons of Carib fire,
Bequeath us to no earthly shore until
Is answered in the vortex of our grave
The seal's wide spindrift gaze toward paradise.

III

Infinite consanguinity it bears—
This tendered theme of you that light
Retrieves from sea plains where the sky
Resigns a breast that every wave enthrones;
While ribboned water lanes I wind
Are laved and scattered with no stroke
Wide from your side, whereto this hour
The sea lifts, also, reliquary hands.

And so, admitted through black swollen gates
That must arrest all distance otherwise,—
Past whirling pillars and lithe pediments,
Light wrestling there incessantly with light,
Star kissing star through wave on wave unto
Your body rocking!
                and where death, if shed,
Presumes no carnage, but this single change,—
Upon the steep floor flung from dawn to dawn
The silken skilled transmemberment of song;

Permit me voyage, love, into your hands . . .

TO BROOKLYN BRIDGE

How many dawns, chill from his rippling rest
The seagull's wings shall dip and pivot him,
Shedding white rings of tumult, building high
Over the chained bay waters Liberty—

Then, with inviolate curve, forsake our eyes
As apparitional as sails that cross
Some page of figures to be filed away;
—Till elevators drop us from our day . . .

I think of cinemas, panoramic sleights
With multitudes bent toward some flashing scene

Never disclosed, but hastened to again,
Foretold to other eyes on the same screen;

And Thee, across the harbor, silver-paced
As though the sun took step of thee, yet left
Some motion ever unspent in thy stride,—
Implicitly thy freedom staying thee!

Out of some subway scuttle, cell or loft
A bedlamite speeds to thy parapets,
Tilting there momently, shrill shirt ballooning,
A jest falls from the speechless caravan.

Down Wall, from girder into street noon leaks,
A rip-tooth of the sky's acetylene;
All afternoon the cloud-flown derricks turn . . .
Thy cables breathe the North Atlantic still.

And obscure as that heaven of the Jews,
Thy guerdon . . . Accolade thou dost bestow
Of anonymity time cannot raise:
Vibrant reprieve and pardon thou dost show.

O harp and altar, of the fury fused,
(How could mere toil align thy choiring strings!)
Terrific threshold of the prophet's pledge,
Prayer of pariah, and the lover's cry,—

Again the traffic lights that skim thy swift
Unfractioned idiom, immaculate sigh of stars,
Beading thy path—condense eternity:
And we have seen night lifted in thine arms.

Under thy shadow by the piers I waited;
Only in darkness is thy shadow clear.
The City's fiery parcels all undone,
Already snow submerges an iron year . . .

O Sleepless as the river under thee,
Vaulting the sea, the prairies' dreaming sod,
Unto us lowliest sometime sweep, descend
And of the curveship lend a myth to God.

THE BROKEN TOWER

The bell-rope that gathers God at dawn
Dispatches me as though I dropped down the knell
Of a spent day—to wander the cathedral lawn
From pit to crucifix, feet chill on steps from hell.

Have you not heard, have you not seen that corps
Of shadows in the tower, whose shoulders sway
Antiphonal carillons launched before
The stars are caught and hived in the sun's ray?

The bells, I say, the bells break down their tower;
And swing I know not where. Their tongues engrave
Membrane through marrow, my long-scattered score
Of broken intervals . . . And I, their sexton slave!

Oval encyclicals in canyons heaping
The impasse high with choir. Banked voices slain!
Pagodas, campaniles with reveilles outleaping—
O terraced echoes prostrate on the plain! . . .

And so it was I entered the broken world
To trace the visionary company of love, its voice
An instant in the wind (I know not whither hurled)
But not for long to hold each desperate choice.

My word I poured. But was it cognate, scored
Of that tribunal monarch of the air
Whose thigh embronzes earth, strikes crystal Word
In wounds pledged once to hope—cleft to despair?

The steep encroachments of my blood left me
No answer (could blood hold such a lofty tower
As flings the question true?)—or is it she
Whose sweet mortality stirs latent power?—

And through whose pulse I hear, counting the strokes
My veins recall and add, revived and sure
The angelus of wars my chest evokes:
What I hold healed, original now, and pure . . .

And builds, within, a tower that is not stone
(Not stone can jacket heaven)—but slip
Of pebbles—visible wings of silence sown
In azure circles, widening as they dip

The matrix of the heart, lift down the eye
That shrines the quiet lake and swells a tower . . .
The commodious, tall decorum of that sky
Unseals her earth, and lifts love in its shower.

léonie adams

LIGHT AT EQUINOX

The realm is here and masque of light,
When struck rent wood and cornland by
The belled heaven claps the ground.
Husk, seed, pale straw, pale ear, the year reposes,
And a thinned frieze of earth rims round
The whey-gleamed, wet-ash-dimming sky,
And whole trodden floor of light,
Where that slant limb winds with its shadowing closes.

Distant, as lustrally, the sun
Within their pearl of nimble play,
Where traverse with rehearsing tread
Orients of prime to their all-reaping west,

Strangered from every grave glissade
Of blue enduskings or of milky day,
And wan, with silvery nimbus on,
Keeps now his burning sojourn unprofessed.

Past barks mouse-sleek, wattled as serpent skin
Rare acorn-fall, rare squirrel-flash;
Without and in a silenced scene
The gamin wanderer of immense day
Can with luxuriant bendings preen,
And in his pebble-scoopings plash,
To alarmless Eden flown,
And suddenly for nothing flies away.

And all are sole in the estranging day.
Forms of all things the candour wear
Of the undefending dead,
And forth from out a mortal stricture gaze
Of unperspective radiance shed
Through everywhere horizoned air,
Tasking precising love to say,
For its dense words the azuring periphrase.

To her own brink light glides, intent
An unsphering sense to bind
By narrowing measures in;
Sidelong as then up branching March she bade
Stiff buds into the glancing skein,
And the green reel unwind.
Now towards another pole she's leant,
And netherward for partner draws her shade.

THIN AIR

Thin air I breathe and birds use for flying
Over and through trees standing breathing in air
Air insects drop through in insect dying
And deer that use it to listen in, share—
Thickens with mist on the lake, or rain
Cuts it with tasteless water and a grey
Day colors it and it is the thin and plain
Air in my mouth the air for miles away.

So close it feeds me each second, everyone's friend
Hugging outside and inside, I can't get rid
Of air, I know it, till the hateful end
When with it I give up the insanely hid
The airless secret I strangle not to share
With all the others as others share the air.

SMELLING OR FEELING

Smelling or feeling of the several holes
Above the jawbone and below the belly
Suggests to searching lovers that the soul's
A slippery gumdrop filled with a sweet jelly.
A mouth tastes spicy like geraniums
Eyes like sweet trout, ears like snails to eat,
And when it's lower down the lover comes
He's washed all through by something awfully sweet.

And though in the full course of his research
Each lover must deceive himself at will,
Must falsify, forget, betray, besmirch,
Debase and doublecross and nearly kill,
Yet licking their lips all lovers are agreed
The soul's a something very sweet indeed.

yvor winters

THE REALIZATION

Death. Nothing is simpler. One is dead.
The set face now will fade out; the bare fact,
Related movement, regular, intact,
Is reabsorbed, the clay is on the bed.
The soul is mortal, nothing: the dim head
On the dim pillow, less. But thought clings flat
To this, since it can never follow that
Where no precision of the mind is bred.
Nothing to think of between you and All!
Screaming processionals of infinite
Logic are grinding down receding cold!
O fool! Madness again! Turn not, for it
Lurks in each paintless cranny, and you sprawl
Blurring a definition. Quick! you are old.

THE INVADERS

They have won out at last and laid us bare,
The demons of the meaning of the dead,
Stripped us with wheel and flame. Oh, where they tread,
Dissolves our heritage of earth and air!
Till as a locomotive plunges through
Distance that has no meaning and no bound
Thundering some interminable sound
To inward metal where its motion grew—
Grew and contracted down through infinite
And sub-atomic roar of Time on Time
Toward meaning that its changing cannot find;
So, stripped of color of an earth, and lit
With motion only of some inner rime,
The naked passion of the human mind.

JEREMIAD

When the bird flew from the Columbus hull
And swung our canyons from its fabled beak,
Or gravitation donned long gloves of bough
To drop its apple in perception's lap,
How was the embattled Spirit to conceive
Monstrosities lay breathing in the good,
That limbs of lambs could grow the heads of wolves?

The multitudes who built a wall of graves
Around the golden calf of nothingness
And faced the deathrays of the deathless smile
Through the vast stretches of injustice brought
The flower brimming in the crack of light—
They open valves to brimstone on our sleep
And freight our air with tons of memory.

Now out of reservoirs of misery
Our language glistens with a flow of tears
And history sweats its worms out of the books;
While prodded by war planes of an angry day
Out of abstraction's bed we turn to meet
The gigantic sense of failure darkening
The many windowed framework of the skull.

And once again, and maybe more than once
Again, must we put down the clockwheel tools
And apron of our carelessness, and rise
And throw our bodies, our bags of blood, against
The rocks of Mammonhood and so blot out
The evil writing on the tidal wall,
The Red Sea running down the heart of God.

THE SEESAW

I

I sit on the surge called ten stories tall
My eye flattens to a floor, a wall,
Like any bird on the nest anywhere
I live in a constant nothing of air
Some forty years up and ten glories high
A hundred inventions ahead of the sky,
With a ladder of ancestors holding me up
Whose rungs into history mystery drop,
But here I am where faith's feathers fly
Like the child in the rhyme in the sky so high.

Over the plumes of your thoughts I see
Your tired heart resting beside a tree;
From the tenth platform of my tithe of time
I perceive you exhausted in your prime,
With heaven collaterally circling around
Your presence that holds the landscape down,
With birds disappearing in the sponge of leaves
And sundown painting your hopes in sheaves—
I speak into a tube for your distant ear,
You look up at me across the miles so clear.

Is it your look makes my room to descend
As though I were inside the shaft of the end?
The floorspace edges from under my feet
The breadth of a sword's edge of monstrous speed;
I grasp for the desperate point of a tear,
For the bend in space or the turn of the year,
But out of the thousands not the least star
Can keep me from falling too fast too far;
And suddenly there beneath your tree I lie
With you at the window all stories too high.

II

My face hung out its search in front of me,
A mask to try the outer storm of space,
Or net of form cast in the sea to be,
To catch at things not safely in their place
Out building coral pinnacles; on the fly
When heaven was stretched on rocks of cloud I caught
A tall star in the corner of my eye—
Lassoed was I, prone on the floor of thought—

Thrown, like the fisherman's wife who asked too much
In wanting to be God; the lightning's hiss
Foamed at the peak of earth, full height to touch
And hope, but death-rayed down to an abyss,
This now-deep nothingness on which we're curled.
It is the stars that make a valley of the world.

III

Divine seesaw! Ply thy twin ways of higher!
The valley of the grave upholds the stars.
The hand on the big Dipper trembles, pours
The fields of gold that roll out on the mire;
And in those fields there boils another sun
Stamping his weight until the night's stars drive
My unlived ages to the land of none
From which the sunflower shakes his flames alive—

And fire breaks out in my friend's house of rules,
The light in my neighbor's window burns my soul,
My enemy falls heir to all of Christ's jewels,
The loved one in the moving grave swings clear.
As grave and window seesaw before the whole
The hill swirls orbits of the dust and wind.
O pivot's pressure at the heart, through you I hear
The universe hallooing for an end.

MILK AT THE BOTTOM OF THE SEA

In the bowl of buildings *alias* the back yard
The milk of snow endlessly pours, but the bowl never
Fills. The century's live inhabitant caught behind
The window pane watches the single rakish tree
Blaze forth in ponderously immaculate italics.
The snowflakes pour everywhere in a panic, dizzyingly,
Or whirl to re-organize in the mid-air and float
Undecided; the sky tilts its ominous mountain, insuring
Another waterfall of snowflakes with all feathery speed.
Such activity should be noisy, a school's-out! of sounds,
But the silence is reverberating on the window glass
Exploring the deep-sea life of waywardness.

I am the traveller in the middle of the winter
In a wood-and-glass ship on the deeps of the age.
From peril's hold I watch the white germs from heaven
And blithe nothingness, the delicate roe of purity
Splurging to fill the air with their multipleness.
Making not even the sound of rain against rock.
I am an eye, I know, frozen in an undersea facade,
And have lost my hearing in such fantastic depths
Where the pressures cave in the senses, but still
My eye kindles to all this whiteness bearing down
In a dance of spiritual blindspots on our town.

In the end the wandering snowflakes are driven
Together, foam fat in the bottom of time, and I
Assuage through the mouth of the mind my entity;
The army of my veins, blood-drops, pores, thoughts,
Crowds to my bones in one supreme act of gravity,
Closer than earth to a hill, than leaves to a tree,
Till I am the very body of oneness and cannot go
Pure, cold, diffuse and wayward like the snow.

THE MIRAGE

I lived a life without love, and saw the being
I loved on every branch; then that bare tree
Stood up with all its branches up, a great harp
Growing straight out of the ground, and there I saw
A squadron of bright birds clothing the bare limbs;
The music notes sat on the harp; it was all love.

This was the heart inside the starved body;
Love grew images like cactus, and planted roses
On the walls of the mirage, and the garden grew
Shining with perfume and the senses dwindled to dew,
The century was rolled into one formation aloft,
A cloud, like St. Veronica's handkerchief of love.

There I saw the face of the one without whom
I lived, two soft jewels implanted in her face,
Her hair pouring around her face without sound,
And her love for me sprang on her skin like dew,
Pearl-grey as the flower of the brain she lay
Quivering on the soft cushion of the great day.

I heard a roar of buildings at my conscience,
I looked up and saw a wall of windows glowing,
And there my love leaned out of each window,
There she leaned out multiplied like heaven
In that vast wall of lights, every light her face,
Suns of a thousand mornings ranging on one day.

And all the machines were running, and yes, great
Was the sound of their running downward and down
Into the blind chutes of their rooted feet,
And all of the windows quivered with my many loves,
Like apples they fell off, at one windfall, all,
And I awoke on the starved pavements of no love.

SHOPPING FOR MEAT IN WINTER

What lewd, naked and revolting shape is this?
A frozen oxtail in the butcher's shop
Long and lifeless upon the huge block of wood
On which the ogre's axe begins *chop chop.*

The sun like incense fumes on the smoky glass,
The street frets with people, the winter wind
Throws knives, prices dangle from shoppers' mouths
While the grim vegetables, on parade, bring to mind

The great countryside bathed in golden sleep,
The trees, the bees, the soft peace everywhere—
I think of the cow's tail, how all summer long
It beat the shapes of harps into the air.

THE LAST SUPPER

i Apostles of the hidden sun
Are come unto the room of breath
Hung with the banging blinds of death,
The body twelve, the spirit one,
Far as the eye, in earth arrayed,
The night shining, the supper laid.

ii The wine shone on the table that evening of history
Like an enormous ruby in the bauble and mystery.

In the glowing walls of the flickering decanter
There moved His face as at the world's center.

The hands of Judas showed up red and hurried
And the light hit them so, like a cross carried.

The faces of the others were there and moving
In the crystal of the dome, swiftly hovering.

The saints, under a lens, shrunken to pigmies,
Gesticulated in birds or in colored enigmas.

Outside there was a storm, the sound of temblors,
The blood bubbled and sprang into the tumblers.

When the morning came like a white wall of stone,
The day lay in the glass and the blood was gone.

VARIATIONS ON A THEME

I

ON THE DEATH OF AN ACQUAINTANCE

Friend, when I think of your delicate feminine face
And of your little hopes common as hearing or seeing,
How singlehanded you moved the massive stone of space
To find a cranny for the flower from the soil of your being,

And how now you manage to keep open in the universe
Under all-time strain that lighted crack in the reckoning
I am haunted by your grimace O steadily getting worse
Awaiting the vast glad look that reduces everything.

For long I thought you another human being in doubt,
One of the millions ordinary as daylight is everywhere,
One of those usual people that one meets with all about—
Now I see you were capable of decision and despair.

Forgive me if my heart cringes with those who die,
Forgive me, friend, when even in thought I cannot be brave
Who think of your clear face agonized under tons of sky
Hourly growing more haggard from the weight of the grave.

II

THE SPRITELY DEAD

There was a man within our tenement
who died upon a worn down step of day:
the wreath they hung upon the doorway meant
that there was nothing else for him to do.

But he was obstinate, he would not rest:
he dragged the flesh of silence everywhere
on crippled wings, and we would hear him whir
while on our memory's sill his eyes would roost.
We saw him wring his thoughts in deep despair
and stamp the color from our backyard scene:
careless, without his body, he would peer
to find out if we noticed his new sin.
He was afraid, afraid: he climbed our vines
and hid, on hands and knees, along our veins.

III

THE BORROWER OF SALT

The man who saw the light hanging on the tall end
Of the road thought it was a lantern on the distant wall
Of the mysterious neighbor, so he said, friend, friend,
I am coming out to borrow some of the savor of your salt.

Wherewith he started running toward the light that hung
In the neighbor's window, and as he kept going the light
Danced, saying with a mocking step, isn't it wrong
That I dance in my glory while you walk in the night?

Yes, said the man, it is wrong, and what is worse
The wind is getting bad, the mud thicker, the road
Harder to follow and I move as slowly as a hearse,
In fact I feel my body itself turning into the load.

The gleam tittered like a light on the end of a spar
But the man was up to his knees in road as if roots
Sprouted from his feet; alas, said the man, it is too hard,
Those who would walk in great men's tracks wear boots.

He turned around and the wind opened spigots of swift air
On his head, up his thighs he felt the earth's lips creep,
And lo, the light gleamed spiritedly from his own fair
Housetop, but he couldn't move, the track was so deep.

THE ECLIPSE

This real expanse collapsed beneath our feet
Upholds us. In the hollow of a hand,
God's rocking hand, along the stars we sweep.
We glimpse the melting skies, round-shouldered stones,
Each other, and the décor of our lives.
The world curls down its edges as we move
Not to debate the view, man's mortal view.
Yet the horizon our lush vision scythes
And curbs the barbarous appetite of reach.
All riches rationed at the source of each,
Which one, of us who dare the edge of good,
Will steal a look between God's fingers glued?

God's fearful hand is out, blocking His face.
We ride a deck that all but covers us
Nor see the deep, love's living deep, we race.
The journey kindles in a reign of dusk.
We hang on to the rock of an eclipse
Of larger heavens where the great rock stops,
A shade before God's eye. It is our birth.
Our hearts upleaping in corona flame,
The blood dimmed to its color by the one
Vast shadow bolting in its final frame,
All life that darkened moment is, the earth
Looms, rocking, black, against our sun, the sun.

THE NEW SPHINX

The new sphinx with the lips of economics
Propounds the question, the gears grinding in the throat:
—What is reality?—and the man with the demon skin
Lets his amorphous eyes upward toward Paradise float.

And with wet seas of astonishment he now beholds
The insect glitterings of the amorphous sphere,

Huge foreign body trafficking in the blood stream,
Shrieking and disgorging the synthetic year.

From the back way, from the backyards of justification
Comes the question, its feet weighted with factories,
Sashweighted by the turbines, dynamos, dividends,
While the holy ghost of freedom cries among the trees.

The vandals are rebuilding the theatres again,
The crumpled curtains are smeared with imaginations:
The sequins are the glistering eyeballs of the men
Whose colossal virtue was their incredible patience.

The capacious demeanors of the gods are still unwilted,
The fields of molten corn come gliding from their hands:
The untiring sunsets have not yet—not yet succeeded
In designing an iron moment to cover the lands.

But the question hangs, a cloud frozen into chromium,
Frightening the pink-toed senses in their heated nest:
The sackcloth of martyrdom shines like a coat of mail,
And there are guns up the sleeve that sleep on the breast.

The radio, that angel's upper lip, repeats the question,
In the private air, in the closet mouldy with conscience:
The slough of the Sunday papers slaps at the windows:
Termites are living in the rotted music of the ancients.

The personal aggrandizement of earning a living
Prejudices the sincerity and the desire for an answer:
The sky fills the eye until it brims with the past,
And the search for reality grows keener and tenser:

And the opponent who disagrees remains the forerunner
Of that perilous matter, that element, the real:
And only when the drums stop to let the future pass
Does the man hear the small feet of the frightened ideal.

j. v. cunningham

TWO EPIGRAMS

I

The Elders at their services begin
With paper offerings. They release from sin
The catechumens on the couches lying
In visions, testimonies, prophesying:
Not, "Are you saved?" they ask, but in informal
Insistent query, "Brother, are you normal?"

II

You ask me how Contempt who claims to sleep
With every woman that has ever been
Can still maintain that women are skin deep?
They never let him any deeper in.

roy fuller

MEDITATION

Now the ambassadors have gone, refusing
Our gifts, treaties, anger, compliance;
And in their place the winter has arrived,
Icing the culture-bearing water.
We brood in our respective empires on
The words we might have said which would have breached
The Chinese wall round our superfluous love
And manufactures. We do not brood too deeply.
There are our friends' perpetual, subtle demands
For understanding: visits to those who claim
To show us what is meant by death,
And therefore life, our short and puzzling lives,
And to explain our feelings when we look
Through the dark sky to other lighted worlds—

The well-shaved owners of sanatoria,
And raving, grubby oracles: the books
On diet, posture, prayer and aspirin art:
The claims of frightful weapons to be investigated:
Mad generals to be promoted: and
Our private gulfs to slither down in bed.

Perhaps in spring the ambassadors will return.
Before then we shall find perhaps that bombs,
Books, people, planets, worry, even our wives,
Are not at all important. Perhaps
The preposterous fishing-line tangle of undesired
Human existence will suddenly unravel
Before some staggering equation
Or mystic experience, and God be released
From the moral particle or blue-lit room.
Or, better still, perhaps we shall, before
Anything really happens, be safely dead.

julian symons

PUB

The glasses are raised, the voices drift into laughter,
The clock hands have stopped, the beer in the hands of the
    soldiers
Is blond, the faces are calm and the fingers can feel
The wet touch of glasses, the glasses print rings on the table,
The smoke rings curl and go up and dissolve near the ceiling,
        This moment exists and is real.

What is reality? Do not ask that. At this moment
Look at the butterfly eyes of the girls, watch the barmaid's
Precision in pouring a Scotch, and remember this day,
This day at this moment you were no longer an island,
People were friendly, the clock in the hands of the soldiers
        For this moment had nothing to say.

And nothing to say and the glasses are raised, we are happy
Drinking through time, and a world that is gentle and helpless
Survives in the pub and goes up in the smoke of our breath,
The regulars doze in the corner, the talkers are fluent;
Look now in the faces of those you love and remember
      That you are not thinking of death.

But thinking of death as the lights go out and the glasses
Are lowered, the people go out and the evening
Goes out, ah, goes out like a light and leaves you alone,
As the heart goes out, the door opens out into darkness,
The foot takes a step, and the moment, the moment of falling
      Is here, you go down like a stone,

Are you able to meet the disaster, able to meet the
Cold air of the street and the touch of corruption, the rotting
Fingers that murder your own in the grip of love?
Can you bear to find hateful the faces you once thought were
    lovely,
Can you bear to find comfort alone in the evil and stunted,
      Can you bear to abandon the dove?

The houses are shut and the people go home, we are left in
Our island of pain, the clocks start to move and the powerful
To act, there is nothing now, nothing at all
To be done: for the trouble is real: and the verdict is final
Against us. The clocks go round faster and faster. And fast as
    confetti
      The days are beginning to fall.

henry treece

IN THE BEGINNING WAS THE BIRD

In the beginning was the bird,
A spume of feathers on the face of time,
Man's model for destruction, God's defence.

Before man, a bird, a feather before time,
And music growing outward into space,
The feathered shears cutting dreams in air.

Before birds, a God, a Nothing with a shape
More horrible than mountains or the Plague,
A Voice as large as fate, a tongue of bronze.

Before this, O no before was there.
Where? Among the placeless atoms, mad
As tale the maggot makes locked in the skull.

And so I state a bird. For sanity
My brain's lips blow the tumbled plume.
I see it prophesy the path winds take.

THE DYKE-BUILDER

On the seventh day the storm lay dead,
The god who built the dyke strolled out to see
Blind men, blind windows, widows and the daft,
And the cracked shore carpeted with gulls.

On the ninth day no sunset red
Daubed the damp stubble: peacock blue, bright harmony
Of gold and purple laced the sky, and soft
Ripe as a plum with joy danced the quick girls.

But on the eleventh day the dead
Looked from their priest-holes, seeing only sea,
And the green shark-cradles with their swift
Cruel fingers setting the ocean's curls.

michael roberts

THE WORLD'S END

Those who have visited the North Pole
Or other pubs beyond a two-mile limit
Will know, at least by hearsay, this one, too.
Here is no glory of the Star and Garter,
Nor the obscure theology of the Goat and Compasses,
But a somewhat plain home truth,
That the world lives by labour and barter,
And all things, in the long run, end up shabby.

Here is the ash of history. But we recall
When fire came down from heaven and the house rocked
(A sensation mildly exhilarating to those in love with life)
And we remember tracer-bullets and the white flares,
And a general atmosphere of form and colour,
With possible extinction giving flavour to the stewed pears.

Well, here is the World's End, or so it seems;
But Oh, my love, tenacity is all:
'Her years of pain and glory' are not ended.
Silent, invisible, the bombs explode,
The dead and wounded walk the cancelled streets,
Colour and form run through the brittle pages,
And Time can crumble all, but cannot touch
The book that burns, faster than we can read.

kenneth fearing

END OF THE SEERS' CONVENTION

We were walking and talking on the roof of the world,
In an age that seemed, at that time, an extremely modern age
Considering a merger, last on the agenda, of the Seven Great
    Leagues that held the Seven True Keys to the Seven
    Ultimate Spheres of all moral, financial, and occult life.

"I foresee a day," said one of the delegates, an astroanalyst
    from Idaho, "when men will fly through the air, and talk
    across space;
They will sail in ships that float beneath the water;
They will emanate shadows of themselves upon a screen, and
    the shadows will move, and talk, and seem as though
    real."

"Very interesting, indeed," declared a Gypsy delegate. "But I
    should like to ask, as a simple reader of tea leaves and
    palms:
How does this combat the widespread and growing evil of the
    police?"

The astrologer shrugged, and an accidental meteor fell from
    his robes and smoldered on the floor.
"In addition," he said, "I foresee a war,
And a victory after that one, and after the victory, a war
    again."

"Trite," was the comment of a crystal-gazer from Miami Beach.
"Any damn fool, at any damn time, can visualize wars, and
    more wars, and famines and plagues.
The real question is: How to seize power from entrenched
    and organized men of Common Sense?"

"I foresee a day," said the Idaho astrologer, "when human
    beings will live on top of flag-poles,

And dance, at some profit, for weeks and months without any rest,
And some will die very happily of eating watermelons, and nails, and cherry pies."

"Why," said a bored numerologist, reaching for his hat, "can't these star-gazers keep their feet on the ground?"
"Even if it's true," said a Bombay illusionist, "it is not, like the rope-trick, altogether practical."

"And furthermore, and finally," shouted the astrologer, with comets and halfmoons dropping from his pockets, and his agitated sleeves,
"I prophesy an age of triumph for laziness and sleep, and dreams and utter peace.
I can see couples walking through the public parks in love, and those who do not are wanted by the sheriff.
I see men fishing beside quiet streams, and those who do not are pursued by collectors, and plastered with liens."
"This does not tell us how to fight against skepticism," muttered a puzzled mesmerist, groping for the door.
"I think," agreed a lady who interpreted the cards, "we are all inclined to accept too much on faith."

A sprinkling of rain, or dragon's blood,
Or a handful of cinders fell on the small, black umbrellas they raised against the sky.

ogden nash

PORTRAIT OF THE ARTIST AS A PREMATURELY OLD MAN

It is common knowledge to every schoolboy and even every
    Bachelor of Arts,
That all sin is divided into two parts.
One kind of sin is called a sin of commission, and that is very
    important,
And it is what you are doing when you are doing something
    you ortant,
And the other kind of sin is just the opposite and is called a
    sin of omission and is equally bad in the eyes of all right-
    thinking people, from Billy Sunday to Buddha,
And it consists of not having done something you shudda.
I might as well give you my opinion of these two kinds of sin
    as long as, in a way, against each other we are pitting them,
And that is, don't bother your head about sins of commission
    because however sinful, they must at least be fun or else
    you wouldn't be committing them.
It is the sin of omission, the second kind of sin,
That lays eggs under your skin.
The way you get really painfully bitten
Is by the insurance you haven't taken out and the checks you
    haven't added up the stubs of and the appointments you
    haven't kept and the bills you haven't paid and the letters
    you haven't written.
Also, about sins of omission there is one particularly painful
    lack of beauty,
Namely, it isn't as though it had been a riotous red letter day
    or night every time you neglected to do your duty;
You didn't get a wicked forbidden thrill
Every time you let a policy lapse or forgot to pay a bill;
You didn't slap the lads in the tavern on the back and loudly
    cry Whee,
Let's all fail to write just one more letter before we go home,
    and this round of unwritten letters is on me.

No, you never get any fun
Out of the things you haven't done,
But they are the things that I do not like to be amid,
Because the suitable things you didn't do give you a lot more trouble than the unsuitable things you did.
The moral is that it is probably better not to sin at all, but if some kind of sin you must be pursuing,
Well, remember to do it by doing rather than by not doing.

BANKERS ARE JUST LIKE ANYBODY ELSE, EXCEPT RICHER

This is a song to celebrate banks,
Because they are full of money and you go into them and all you hear is clinks and clanks,
Or maybe a sound like the wind in the trees on the hills,
Which is the rustling of the thousand dollar bills.
Most bankers dwell in marble halls,
Which they get to dwell in because they encourage deposits and discourage withdrawals,
And particularly because they all observe one rule which woe betides the banker who fails to heed it,
Which is you must never lend any money to anybody unless they don't need it.
I know you, you cautious conservative banks!
If people are worried about their rent it is your duty to deny them the loan of one nickel, yes, even one copper engraving of the martyred son of the late Nancy Hanks;
Yes, if they request fifty dollars to pay for a baby you must look at them like Tarzan looking at an uppity ape in the jungle,
And tell them what do they think a bank is, anyhow, they had better go get the money from their wife's aunt or ungle.
But suppose people come in and they have a million and they want another million to pile on top of it,
Why, you brim with the milk of human kindness and you urge them to accept every drop of it,
And you lend them the million so then they have two million

and this gives them the idea that they would be better off with four,

So they already have two million as security so you have no hesitation in lending them two more,

And all the vice-presidents nod their heads in rhythm,

And the only question asked is do the borrowers want the money sent or do they want to take it withm.

But please do not think that I am not fond of banks,

Because I think they deserve our appreciation and thanks,

Because they perform a valuable public service in eliminating the jackasses who go around saying that health and happiness are everything and money isn't essential,

Because as soon as they have to borrow some unimportant money to maintain their health and happiness they starve to death so they can't go around any more sneering at good old money, which is nothing short of providential.

THE ANATOMY OF HAPPINESS

Lots of truisms don't have to be repeated but there is one that has got to be,

Which is that it is much nicer to be happy than it is not to be,

And I shall even add to it by stating unequivocally and without restraint

That you are much happier when you are happy than when you ain't.

Some people are just naturally Pollyanna,

While others call for sugar and cream and strawberries on their manna.

Now, I think we all ought to say a fig for the happiness that comes of thinking helpful thoughts and searching your soul,

The most exciting happiness is the happiness generated by forces beyond your control,

Because if you just depend on your helpful thoughts for your happiness and would just as soon drink buttermilk as champagne, and if mink is no better than lapin to you,

Why you don't even deserve to have anything nice and exciting happen to you.

If you are really Master of your Fate,

It shouldn't make any difference to you whether Cleopatra or the Bearded Lady is your mate,

So I hold no brief for the kind of happiness or the kind of unhappiness that some people constantly carry around in their breast,

Because that kind of happiness simply consists of being resigned to the worst just as that kind of unhappiness consists of being resentful of the best.

No, there is only one kind of happiness that I take the stump for,

Which is the kind that comes when something so wonderful falls in your lap that joy is what you jump for,

Something not of your own doing,

When the blue sky opens and out pops a refund from the Government or an invitation to a terrapin dinner or an unhoped-for Yes from the lovely creature you have been disconsolately wooing.

And obviously such miracles don't happen every day,

But here's hoping they may,

Because then everybody would be happy except the people who pride themselves on creating their own happiness who as soon as they saw everybody who didn't create their own happiness happy they would probably grieve over sharing their own heretofore private sublimity,

A condition which I could face with equanimity.

I NEVER EVEN SUGGESTED IT

I know lots of men who are in love and lots of men who are married and lots of men who are both,

And to fall out with their loved ones is what all of them are most loth.

They are conciliatory at every opportunity,
Because all they want is serenity and a certain amount of impunity.
Yes, many the swain who has finally admitted that the earth is flat
Simply to sidestep a spat,
Many the masculine Positively or Absolutely which has been diluted to an If
Simply to avert a tiff,
Many the two-fisted executive whose domestic conversation is limited to a tactfully interpolated Yes,
And then he is amazed to find that he is being raked backwards over a bed of coals nevertheless.
These misguided fellows are under the impression that it takes two to make a quarrel, that you can sidestep a crisis by nonaggression and nonresistance,
Instead of removing yourself to a discreet distance.
Passivity can be a provoking *modus operandi;*
Consider the Empire and Gandhi.
Silence is golden, but sometimes invisibility is golder. .
Because loved ones may not be able to make bricks without straw but often they don't need any straw to manufacture a bone to pick or blood in their eye or a chip for their soft white shoulder.
It is my duty, gentlemen, to inform you that women are dictators all, and I recommend to you this moral:
In real life it takes only one to make a quarrel.

KINDLY UNHITCH THAT STAR, BUDDY

I hardly suppose I know anybody who wouldn't rather be a success than a failure,
Just as I suppose every piece of crabgrass in the garden would much rather be an azalea,
And in celestial circles all the run-of-the-mill angels would rather be archangels or at least cherubim and seraphim,

And in the legal world all the little process-servers hope to
 grow up into great big bailiffim and sheriffim.
Indeed, everybody wants to be a wow,
But not everybody knows exactly how.
Some people think they will eventually wear diamonds instead
 of rhinestones
Only by everlastingly keeping their noses to their grhinestones,
And other people think they will be able to put in more time
 at Palm Beach and the Ritz
By not paying too much attention to attendance at the office
 but rather in being brilliant by starts and fits.
Some people after a full day's work sit up all night getting a
 college education by correspondence,
While others seem to think they'll get just as far by devoting
 their evenings to the study of the difference in temperament
 between brunettance and blondance.
Some stake their all on luck,
And others put their faith in their ability to pass the buck.
In short, the world is filled with people trying to achieve
 success,
And half of them think they'll get it by saying No and half of
 them by saying Yes,
And if all the ones who say No said Yes, and vice versa, such
 is the fate of humanity that ninety-nine per cent of them
 still wouldn't be any better off than they were before,
Which perhaps is just as well because if everybody was a
 success nobody could be contemptuous of anybody else and
 everybody would start in all over again trying to be a bigger
 success than everybody else so they would have somebody
 to be contemptuous of and so on forevermore,
Because when people start hitching their wagons to a star,
That's the way they are.

c. day lewis

CONSIDER THESE, FOR WE HAVE CONDEMNED THEM

Consider these, for we have condemned them;
Leaders to no sure land, guides their bearings lost
Or in league with robbers have reversed the signposts,
Disrespectful to ancestors, irresponsible to heirs.
Born barren, a freak growth, root in rubble,
Fruitlessly blossoming, whose foliage suffocates,
Their sap is sluggish, they reject the sun.

The man with his tongue in his cheek, the woman
With her heart in the wrong place, unhandsome, unwhole-
    some;
Have exposed the new-born to worse than weather,
Exiled the honest and sacked the seer.
These drowned the farms to form a pleasure-lake,
In time of drought they drain the reservoir
Through private pipes for baths and sprinklers.

Getters not begetters; gainers not beginners;
Whiners, no winners; no triers, betrayers;
Who steer by no star, whose moon means nothing.
Daily denying, unable to dig:
At bay in villas from blood relations,
Counters of spoons and content with cushions
They pray for peace, they hand down disaster.

They that take the bribe shall perish by the bribe,
Dying of dry rot, ending in asylums,
A curse to children, a charge on the state.
But still their fears and frenzies infect us;
Drug nor isolation will cure this cancer:
It is now or never, the hour of the knife,
The break with the past, the major operation.

DO NOT EXPECT AGAIN A PHOENIX HOUR

Do not expect again a phoenix hour,
The triple-towered sky, the dove complaining,
Sudden the rain of gold and heart's first ease
Tranced under trees by the eldritch light of sundown.

By a blazed trail our joy will be returning:
One burning hour throws light a thousand ways,
And hot blood stays into familiar gestures.
The best years wait, the body's plenitude.

Consider then, my lover, this is the end
Of the lark's ascending, the hawk's unearthly hover:
Spring season is over soon and first heatwave;
Grave-browed with cloud ponders the huge horizon.

Draw up the dew. Swell with pacific violence.
Take shape in silence. Grow as the clouds grew.
Beautiful brood the cornlands, and you are heavy;
Leafy the boughs—they also hide big fruit.

NEARING AGAIN THE LEGENDARY ISLE

Nearing again the legendary isle
Where sirens sang and mariners were skinned,
We wonder now what was there to beguile
That such stout fellows left their bones behind.
Those chorus-girls are surely past their prime,
Voices grow shrill and paint is wearing thin,
Lips that sealed up the sense from gnawing time
Now beg the favour with a graveyard grin.
We have no flesh to spare and they can't bite,
Hunger and sweat have stripped us to the bone;
A skeleton crew we toil upon the tide
And mock the theme-song meant to lure us on:
No need to stop the ears, avert the eyes
From purple rhetoric of evening skies.

THE CONFLICT

I sang as one
Who on a tilting deck sings
To keep their courage up, though the wave hangs
That shall cut off their sun.

As storm-cocks sing,
Flinging their natural answer in the wind's teeth,
And care not if it is waste of breath
Or birth-carol of spring.

As ocean-flyer clings
To height, to the last drop of spirit driving on
While yet ahead is land to be won
And work for wings.

Singing I was at peace,
Above the clouds, outside the ring:
For sorrow finds a swift release in song
And pride its poise.

Yet living here,
As one between two massing powers I live
Whom neutrality cannot save
Nor occupation cheer.

None such shall be left alive:
The innocent wing is soon shot down,
And private stars fade in the blood-red dawn
Where two worlds strive.

The red advance of life
Contracts pride, calls out the common blood,
Beats song into a single blade,
Makes a depth-charge of grief.

Move then with new desires,
For where we used to build and love
Is no man's land, and only ghosts can live
Between two fires.

THE UNWANTED

On a day when the breath of roses
    Plumpened a swooning breeze
And all the silken combes of summer
    Opened wide their knees,
Between two sighs they planted one—
A willed one, a wanted one—
And he will be the sign, they said, of our felicities.

Eager the loins he sprang from,
    Happy the sheltering heart:
Seldom had the seed of man
    So charmed, so clear a start.
And he was born as frail a one,
As ailing, freakish, pale a one
As ever the wry planets knotted their beams to thwart.

Sun locked up for winter;
    Earth an empty rind:
Two strangers harshly flung together
    As by a flail of wind.
Oh was it not a furtive thing,
A loveless, damned, abortive thing—
This flurry of the groaning dust, and what is left behind!

Sure, from such warped beginnings
    Nothing debonair
Can come? But neither shame nor panic,
    Drugs nor sharp despair
Could uproot that untoward thing,
That all too fierce and froward thing:
Willy-nilly born it was, divinely formed and fair.

IN THE HEART OF CONTEMPLATION

In the heart of contemplation—
Admiring, say, the frost-flowers of the white lilac,
Or lark's song busily sifting like sand-crystals
Through the pleased hourglass an afternoon of summer,
Or your beauty, dearer to me than these—
Discreetly a whisper in the ear,
The glance of one passing my window recall me
From lark, lilac, you, grown suddenly strangers.

In the plump and pastoral valley
Of a leisure time, among the trees like seabirds
Asleep on a glass calm, one shadow moves—
The sly reminder of the forgotten appointment.
All the shining pleasures, born to be innocent,
Grow dark with a truant's guilt:
The day's high heart falls flat, the oaks tremble,
And the shadow sliding over your face divides us.

In the act of decision only,
In the hearts cleared for action like lovers naked
For love, this shadow vanishes: there alone
There is nothing between our lives for it to thrive on.
You and I with lilac, lark and oak-leafed
Valley are bound together
As in the astounded clarity before death.
Nothing is innocent now but to act for life's sake.

roy campbell

THE ZEBRAS

From the dark woods that breathe of fallen showers,
Harnessed with level rays in golden reins,
The zebras draw the dawn across the plains
Wading knee-deep among the scarlet flowers.
The sunlight, zithering their flanks with fire,

Flashes between the shadows as they pass
Barred with electric tremors through the grass
Like wind along the gold strings of a lyre.
Into the flushed air snorting rosy plumes
That smoulder round their feet in drifting fumes,
With dove-like voices call the distant fillies,
While round the herds the stallion wheels his flight,
Engine of beauty volted with delight,
To roll his mare among the trampled lilies.

CHOOSING A MAST

This mast, new-shaved, through whom I rive the ropes,
Says she was once an oread of the slopes,
Graceful and tall upon the rocky highlands,
A slender tree as vertical as noon,
And her low voice was lovely as the silence
Through which a fountain whistles to the moon,
Who now of the white spray must take the veil
And, for her songs, the thunder of the sail.

I chose her for her fragrance, when the spring
With sweetest resins swelled her fourteenth ring
And with live amber welded her young thews:
I chose her for the glory of the Muse,
Smoother of forms that her hard-knotted grain,
Grazed by the chisel, shaven by the plane,
Might from the steel as cool a burnish take
As from the bladed moon a windless lake.

I chose her for her eagerness of flight
Where she stood tiptoe on the rocky height
Lifted by her own perfume to the sun,
While through her rustling plumes with eager sound
Her eagle spirit, with the gale at one,
Spreading wide pinions, would have spurned the ground
And her own sleeping shadow, had they not
With thymy fragrance charmed her to the spot.

Lover of song, I chose this mountain pine
Not only for the straightness of her spine
But for her songs: for there she loved to sing
Through a long noon's repose of wave and wing,
The fluvial swirling of her scented hair
Sole rill of song in all that windless air,
And her slim form the naiad of the stream
Afloat upon the languor of its theme;

And for the soldier's fare on which she fed:
Her wine the azure, and the snow her bread;
And for her stormy watches on the height,
For only out of solitude or strife
Are born the sons of valour and delight;
And lastly for her rich exulting life,
That with the wind stopped not its singing breath
But carolled on, the louder for its death.

Under a pine, when summer days were deep,
We loved the most to lie in love or sleep;
And when in long hexameters the west
Rolled his grey surge, the forest for his lyre,
It was the pines that sang us to our rest,
Loud in the wind and fragrant in the fire,
With legioned voices swelling all night long,
From Pelion to Provence, their storm of song.

It was the pines that fanned us in the heat,
The pines, that cheered us in the time of sleet,
For which sweet gifts I set one dryad free;
No longer to the wind a rooted foe,
This nymph shall wander where she longs to be
And with the blue north wind arise and go,
A silver huntress with the moon to run
And fly through rainbows with the rising sun;

And when to pasture in the glittering shoals
The guardian mistral drives his thundering foals,

And when like Tartar horsemen racing free
We ride the snorting fillies of the sea,
My pine shall be the archer of the gale
While on the bending willow curves the sail
From whose great bow the long keel shooting home
Shall fly, the feathered arrow of the foam.

richard eberhart

THE GROUNDHOG

In June, amid the golden fields,
I saw a groundhog lying dead.
Dead lay he; my senses shook,
And mind outshot our naked frailty.
There lowly in the vigorous summer
His form began its senseless change,
And made my senses waver dim
Seeing nature ferocious in him.
Inspecting close his maggots' might
And seething cauldron of his being,
Half with loathing, half with a strange love,
I poked him with an angry stick.
The fever arose, became a flame
And Vigour circumscribed the skies,
Immense energy in the sun,
And through my frame a sunless trembling.
My stick had done nor good nor harm.
Then stood I silent in the day
Watching the object, as before;
And kept my reverence for knowledge
Trying for control, to be still,
To quell the passion of the blood;
Until I had bent down on my knees
Praying for joy in the sight of decay.
And so I left; and I returned
In Autumn strict of eye, to see

The sap gone out of the groundhog,
But the bony sodden hulk remained.
But the year had lost its meaning,
And in intellectual chains
I lost both love and loathing,
Mured up in the wall of wisdom.
Another summer took the fields again
Massive and burning, full of life,
But when I chanced upon the spot
There was only a little hair left,
And bones bleaching in the sunlight
Beautiful as architecture;
I watched them like a geometer,
And cut a walking stick from a birch.
It has been three years, now.
There is no sign of the groundhog.
I stood there in the whirling summer,
My hand capped a withered heart,
And thought of China and of Greece,
Of Alexander in his tent;
Of Montaigne in his tower,
Of Saint Theresa in her wild lament.

THE FURY OF AERIAL BOMBARDMENT

You would think the fury of aerial bombardment
Would rouse God to relent; the infinite spaces
Are still silent. He looks on shock-pried faces.
History, even, does not know what is meant.

You would feel that after so many centuries
God would give man to repent; yet he can kill
As Cain could, but with multitudinous will,
No farther advanced than in his ancient furies.

Was man made stupid to see his own stupidity?
Is God by definition indifferent, beyond us all?

Is the eternal truth man's fighting soul
Wherein the Beast ravens in its own avidity?

Of Van Wettering I speak, and Averill,
Names on a list, whose faces I do not recall
But they are gone to early death, who late in school
Distinguished the belt feed lever from the belt holding pawl.

DAM NECK, VIRGINIA

Anti-aircraft seen from a certain distance
On a steely blue night say a mile away
Flowers on the air absolutely dream-like,
The vision has no relation to the reality.

The floating balls of light are tossed easily
And float out into space without a care,
They the sailors of the gentlest parabolas
In a companionship and with a kind of stare.

They are a controlled kind of falling stars,
But not falling, rising and floating and going out,
Teaming together in efflorescent spectacle
Seemingly better than nature's: man is on the lookout.

The men are firing tracers, practising at night.
Each specialist himself precision's instrument,
These expert prestidigitators press the luminance
In knowledge of and ignorance of their doing.

They do not know the dream-like vision ascending
In me, one mile away: they had not thought of that.
Huddled in darkness behind their bright projectors
They are the scientists of the skill to kill.

As this sight and show is gentle and false,
The truth of guns is fierce that aims at death.
Of war in the animal sinews let us speak not,
But of the beautiful disrelation of the spiritual.

THE NOBLE MAN

An Olympian before the Olympics, that inhuman backdrop.
The possible man, it is him I posit, him preempt,
The not incalculable master of the braced mountains.
He does not have to lose himself in them. His spirit
Creates their newest hazard as idyllic only.
He has confronted man, Olympian of the dark mark.

Rage is the substratum of pure animal poise;
A strenuosity, exquisite, roves in the controlled eye;
Multiple actions, muted, gaze upon the world;
Leaping tensions exhale the formidable and graceful;
Masterworking modulations enter every day;
Oval kingdoms quell the old volcanoes.

The Olympian looks at the Olympics olympianly,
Openly. To him they are fractures of the Alpine.
Their height is modified in his height. Hurls
Fireballs out of himself when he wills it. Towers
Over his own music, lofty, sensitive, possessed.
The Olympian is master of his own mystery,

Mystified in his own mastery, recognizing
His relation to the real, the impersonal mountains.
He knows his own reality and that of the world,
The most human one, testator of furor and quiet,
He fears not, having feared all, love's altitude,
Gives off love's avalanche, mountainous man-make.

Fear that undoes many straightens him;
Contemplation is his burly action;
Round is the eye of his understanding;
Fear of death has not shaken him;
He looks upon all things with fervor of tenderness;
His laughter is ready. He has overcome pride.

An Olympian will not drown in the rain forests
Of self-pity. Life gives him its own mountains.

Active love is the mark of a noble man,
By cynicism, by asceticism not betrayed. Nature
Works in him her balance. A bright perfection
Plays around the brows of the Olympian.

THE HORSE CHESTNUT TREE

Boys in sporadic but tenacious droves
Come with sticks, as certainly as Autumn,
To assault the great horse chestnut tree.

There is a law governs their lawlessness.
Desire is in them for a shining amulet
And the best are those that are highest up.

They will not pick them easily from the ground.
With shrill arms they fling to the higher branches,
To hurry the work of nature for their pleasure.

I have seen them trooping down the street
Their pockets stuffed with chestnuts shucked, unshucked.
It is only evening keeps them from their wish.

Sometimes I run out in a kind of rage
To chase the boys away; I catch an arm,
Maybe, and laugh to think of being the lawgiver.

I was once such a young sprout myself
And fingered in my pocket the prize and trophy.
But still I moralize upon the day

And see that we, outlaws on God's property,
Fling out imagination beyond the skies
Wishing a tangible good from the unknown.

And likewise death will drive us from the scene
With the great flowering world unbroken yet,
Which we held in idea, a little handful.

THE SOUL LONGS TO RETURN WHENCE IT CAME

I drove up to the graveyard, which
Used to frighten me as a boy,
When I walked down the river past it,
And evening was coming on. I'd make sure
I came home from the woods early enough.
I drove in, I found to the place, I
Left the motor running. My eyes hurried,
To recognize the great oak tree
On the little slope, among the stones.
It was a high day, a crisp day,
The cleanest kind of Autumn day,
With brisk intoxicating air, a
Little wind that frisked, yet there was
Old age in the atmosphere, nostalgia,
The subtle heaviness of the Fall.
I stilled the motor. I walked a few paces;
It was good, the tree; the friendliness of it.
I touched it, I thought of the roots;
They would have pierced her seven years.
O all peoples! O mighty shadows!
My eyes opened along the avenue
Of tombstones, the common land of death.
Humiliation of all loves lost,
That might have had full meaning in any
Plot of ground, come, hear the silence,
See the quivering light. My mind worked
Almost imperceptibly, I
In the command, I the wilful ponderer.
I must have stood silent and thoughtful there.
A host of dry leaves
Danced on the ground in the wind.
They startled, they curved up from the ground,
There was a dry rustling, rattling.
The sun was motionless and brittle.
I felt the blood darken in my cheeks
And burn. Like running. My eyes

Telescoped on decay, I out of command.
Fear, tenderness, they seized me.
My eyes were hot, I dared not look
At the leaves. A pagan urge swept me.
Multitudes, O multitudes in one.
The urge of the earth, the titan
Wild and primitive lust, fused
On the ground of her grave.
I was a being of feeling alone.
I flung myself down on the earth
Full length on the great earth, full length,
I wept out the dark load of human love.
In pagan adoration I adored her.
I felt the actual earth of her.
Victor and victim of humility,
I closed in the wordless ecstasy
Of mystery: where there is no thought
But feeling lost in itself forever,
Profound, remote, immediate, and calm.
Frightened, I stood up, I looked about
Suspiciously, hurriedly (A rustling),
As if the sun, the air, the trees
Were human, might not understand.
I drew breath, it made a sound,
I stepped gingerly away. Then
The mind came like a fire, it
Tortured man, I thought of madness.
The mind will not accept the blood.
The sun and sky, the trees and grasses,
And the whispering leaves, took on
Their usual characters. I went away,
Slowly, tingling, elated, saying, saying
Mother, Great Being, O Source of Life
To whom in wisdom we return,
Accept this humble servant evermore.

peter quennell

THE FLIGHT INTO EGYPT

Within Heaven's circle I had not guessed at this,
I had not guessed at pleasure such as this,
So sharp a pleasure,
That, like a lamp burning in foggy night,
Makes its own orb and sphere of flowing gold
And tents itself in light.

Going before you, now how many days,
Thoughts, all turned back like birds against the wind,
Wheeled sullenly towards my Father's house,
Considered his blind presence and the gathered, bustling
    pæan,
The affluence of his sweetness, his grace and unageing might.

My flesh glowed then in the shadow of a loose cloak
And my brightness troubled the ground with every pulse of
    the blood,
My wings lax on the air, my eyes open and grave,
With the vacant pride of hardly less than a god.

We passed thickets that quaked with hidden deer,
And wide shallows dividing before my feet,
Empty plains threaded, and between stiff aloes
I took the ass's bridle to climb into mountain pathways.

When cold bit you, through your peasant's mantle,
And my Father filled the air with meaningless stars,
I brought dung and dead white grass for fuel,
Blowing a fire with the breath of the holy word.

Your drudge, Joseph, slept; you would sit unmoving,
In marble quiet, or by the unbroken voice of a river,
Would sometimes bare your maiden breast to his mouth,
The suckling, to the conscious God balanced upon your knees.

Apart I considered the melodious names of my brothers,
As again in my Father's house, and the even spheres
Slowly, nightlong recalled the splendour of numbers;
I heard again the voluptuous measure of praise.

Sometimes pacing beneath clarity immeasurable
I saw my mind lie open and desert,
The wavering streams frozen up and each coppice quieted,
A whole valley in starlight with leaves and waters.

Coming at last to these farthest Syrian hills,
Attis or Adon, some ambushed lust looked out;
My skin grows pale and smooth, shrunken as silk,
Without the rough effulgence of a God.

And here no voice has spoken;
There is no shrine of any godhead here;
No grove or hallowed fires,
And godhead seems asleep.

Only the vine has woven
Strange houses and blind rooms and palaces,
Into each hollow and crevice continually
Dropped yearlong irrecoverable flowers.

The sprawling vine has built us a close room
Obedient Hymen fills the air with mist;
And to make dumb our theft
The white and moving sand that will not bear a print.

robert penn warren

ORIGINAL SIN: A SHORT STORY

Nodding, its great head rattling like a gourd,
And locks like seaweed strung on the stinking stone,
The nightmare stumbles past, and you have heard
It fumble your door before it whimpers and is gone:
It acts like the old hound that used to snuffle your door and
  moan.

You thought you had lost it when you left Omaha,
For it seemed connected then with your grandpa, who
Had a wen on his forehead and sat on the veranda
To finger the precious protuberance, as was his habit to do,
Which glinted in sun like rough garnet or the rich old brain
  bulging through.

But you met it in Harvard Yard as the historic steeple
Was confirming the midnight with its hideous racket,
And you wondered how it had come, for it stood so imbecile,
With empty hands, humble, and surely nothing in pocket:
Riding the rods, perhaps—or grandpa's will paid the ticket.

You were almost kindly then, in your first homesickness,
As it tortured its stiff face to speak, but scarcely mewed;
Since then you have outlived all your homesickness,
But have met it in many another distempered latitude:
Oh, nothing is lost, ever lost! at last you understood.

But it never came in the quantum glare of sun
To shame you before your friends, and had nothing to do
With your public experience or private reformation:
But it thought no bed too narrow—it stood with lips askew
And shook its great head sadly like the abstract Jew.

Never met you in the lyric arsenical meadow
When children call and your heart goes stone in the bosom;

At the orchard anguish never, nor ovoid horror,
Which is furred like a peach or avid like the delicious plum.
It takes no part in your classic prudence or fondled axiom.

Not there when you exclaimed: "Hope is betrayed by
Disastrous glory of sea-capes, sun-torment of whitecaps
—There must be a new innocence for us to be stayed by."
But there it stood, after all the timetables, all the lamps,
In the crepuscular clutter of *always, always,* or *perhaps.*

You have moved often and rarely left an address,
And hear of the deaths of friends with a sly pleasure,
A sense of cleansing and hope, which blooms from distress;
But it has not died, it comes, its hand childish, unsure,
Clutching the bribe of chocolate or a toy you used to treasure.

It tries the lock; you hear, but simply drowse:
There is nothing remarkable in that sound at the door.
Later you hear it wander the dark house
Like a mother who rises at night to seek a childhood picture;
Or it goes to the backyard and stands like an old horse cold in
    the pasture.

william empson

LEGAL FICTION

Law makes long spokes of the short stakes of men.
Your well fenced out real estate of mind
No high flat of the nomad citizen
Looks over, or train leaves behind.

Your rights extend under and above your claim
Without bound; you own land in Heaven and Hell;
Your part of earth's surface and mass the same,
Of all cosmos' volume, and all stars as well.

Your rights reach down where all owners meet, in Hell's
Pointed exclusive conclave, at earth's centre
(Your spun farm's root still on that axis dwells);
And up, through galaxies, a growing sector.

You are nomad yet; the lighthouse beam you own
Flashes, like Lucifer, through the firmament.
Earth's axis varies; your dark central cone
Wavers a candle's shadow, at the end.

MISSING DATES

Slowly the poison the whole blood stream fills.
It is not the effort nor the failure tires.
The waste remains, the waste remains and kills.

It is not your system or clear sight that mills
Down small to the consequence a life requires;
Slowly the poison the whole blood stream fills.

They bled an old dog dry yet the exchange rills
Of young dog blood gave but a month's desires;
The waste remains, the waste remains and kills.

It is the Chinese tombs and the slag hills
Usurp the soil, and not the soil retires.
Slowly the poison the whole blood stream fills.

Not to have fire is to be a skin that shrills.
The complete fire is death. From partial fires
The waste remains, the waste remains and kills.

It is the poems you have lost, the ills
From missing dates, at which the heart expires.
Slowly the poison the whole blood stream fills.
The waste remains, the waste remains and kills.

vernon watkins

DISCOVERIES

The poles are flying where the two eyes set:
America has not found Columbus yet.

Ptolemy's planets, playing fast and loose,
Foretell the wisdom of Copernicus.

Dante calls Primum Mobile, the First Cause:
Love that moves the world and the other stars.

Great Galileo, twisted by the rack,
Groans the bright sun from heaven, then breathes it back.

Blake, on the world alighting, holds the skies,
And all the stars shine down through human eyes.

Donne sees those stars, yet will not let them lie:
'We're tapers, too, and at our own cost die.'

The shroud-lamp catches. Lips are smiling there.
'Les flammes—déjà?'—The world dies, or Voltaire.

Swift, a cold mourner at his burial-rite,
Burns to the world's heart like a meteorite.

Beethoven deaf, in deafness hearing all,
Unwinds all music from sound's funeral.

Three prophets fall, the litter of one night,
Blind Milton gazes in fixed deeps of light.

Beggar of those Minute Particulars,
Yeats lights again the turmoil of the stars.

Motionless motion! Come, Tiresias,
The eternal flies, what's passing cannot pass.

'Solace in flight,' old Heraclitus cries;
Light changing to Von Hügel's butterflies.

Rilke bears all, thinks like a tree, believes,
Sinks in the hand that bears the falling leaves.

The stars! The signs! Great Angelo hurls them back.
His whirling ceiling draws the zodiac.

The pulse of Keats testing the axiom;
The second music when the sound is dumb.

The Christian Paradox, bringing its great reward
By loss; the moment known to Kierkegaard.

MUSIC OF COLOURS—WHITE BLOSSOM

White blossom, white, white shell; the Nazarene
Walking in the ear; white touched by souls
Who know the music by which white is seen,
Blinding white, from strings and aureoles,
Until that is not white, seen at the two poles,
Nor white the Scythian hills, nor Marlowe's queen.

The spray looked white until this snowfall.
Now the foam is grey, the wave is dull.
Call nothing white again, we were deceived.
The flood of Noah dies, the rainbow is lived.
Yet from the deluge of illusions an unknown colour is saved.

White must die black, to be born white again
From the womb of sounds, the inscrutable grain,
From the crushed, dark fibre, breaking in pain.

The bud of the apple is already forming there.
The cherry-bud, too, is firm, and behind it the pear
Conspires with the racing cloud. I shall not look.
The rainbow is diving through the wide-open book
Past the rustling paper of birch, the sorceries of bark.

Buds in April, on the waiting branch,
Starrily opening, light raindrops drench,
Swinging from world to world when starlings sweep,
Where they alight in air, are white asleep.
They will not break, not break, until you say
White is not white again, nor may may.

White flowers die soonest, die into that chaste
Bride-bed of the moon, their lives laid waste.
Lilies of Solomon, taken by the gust,
Sigh, make way. And the dark forest
Haunts the lowly crib near Solomon's dust,
Rocked to the end of majesty, warmed by the low beast,
Locked in the liberty of his tremendous rest.

If there is white, or has been white, it must have been
When His eyes looked down and made the leper clean.
White will not be, apart, though the trees try
Spirals of blossom, their green conspiracy.
She who touched His garment saw no white tree.

Lovers speak of Venus, and the white doves,
Jubilant, the white girl, myth's whiteness, Jove's,
Of Leda, the swan, whitest of his loves.
Lust imagines him, web-footed Jupiter, great down
Of thundering light; love's yearning pulls him down
On the white swan-breast, the magical lawn,
Involved in plumage, mastered by the veins of dawn.

In the churchyard the yew is neither green nor black.
I know nothing of Earth or colour until I know I lack
Original white, by which the ravishing bird looks wan.
The mound of dust is nearer, white of mute dust that dies
In the soundfall's great light, the music in the eyes,
Transfiguring whiteness into shadows gone,
Utterly secret. I know you, black swan.

w. h. auden

PETITION

Sir, no man's enemy, forgiving all
But will his negative inversion, be prodigal:
Send to us power and light, a sovereign touch
Curing the intolerable neural itch,
The exhaustion of weaning, the liar's quinsy,
And the distortions of ingrown virginity.
Prohibit sharply the rehearsed response
And gradually correct the coward's stance;
Cover in time with beams those in retreat
That, spotted, they turn though the reverse were great;
Publish each healer that in city lives
Or country house at the end of drives;
Harrow the house of the dead; look shining at
New styles of architecture, a change of heart.

MUSÉE DES BEAUX ARTS

About suffering they were never wrong,
The Old Masters: how well they understood
Its human position; how it takes place
While someone else is eating or opening a window or just
    walking dully along;
How, when the aged are reverently, passionately waiting
For the miraculous birth, there always must be
Children who did not specially want it to happen, skating
On a pond at the edge of the wood:
They never forgot
That even the dreadful martyrdom must run its course
Anyhow in a corner, some untidy spot
Where the dogs go on with their doggy life and the torturer's
    horse
Scratches its innocent behind on a tree.

In Brueghel's *Icarus*, for instance: how everything turns away
Quite leisurely from the disaster; the ploughman may
Have heard the splash, the forsaken cry,
But for him it was not an important failure; the sun shone
As it had to on the white legs disappearing into the green
Water; and the expensive delicate ship that must have seen
Something amazing, a boy falling out of the sky,
Had somewhere to get to and sailed calmly on.

PAYSAGE MORALISÉ

Hearing of harvests rotting in the valleys,
Seeing at end of street the barren mountains,
Round corners coming suddenly on water,
Knowing them shipwrecked who were launched for islands,
We honour founders of these starving cities
Whose honour is the image of our sorrow,

Which cannot see its likeness in their sorrow
That brought them desperate to the brink of valleys;
Dreaming of evening walks through learned cities
They reined their violent horses on the mountains,
Those fields like ships to castaways on islands,
Visions of green to them who craved for water.

They built by rivers and at night the water
Running past windows comforted their sorrow;
Each in his little bed conceived of islands
Where every day was dancing in the valleys
And all the green trees blossomed on the mountains
Where love was innocent, being far from cities.

But dawn came back and they were still in cities;
No marvellous creature rose up from the water;
There was still gold and silver in the mountains
But hunger was a more immediate sorrow,
Although to moping villagers in valleys
Some waving pilgrims were describing islands . . .

'The gods,' they promise, 'visit us from islands,
Are stalking, head-up, lovely, through our cities;
Now is the time to leave your wretched valleys
And sail with them across the lime-green water,
Sitting at their white sides, forget your sorrow,
The shadow cast across your lives by mountains.'

So many, doubtful, perished in the mountains,
Climbing up crags to get a view of islands,
So many, fearful, took with them their sorrow
Which stayed them when they reached unhappy cities,
So many, careless, dived and drowned in water,
So many, wretched, would not leave their valleys.

It is our sorrow. Shall it melt? Ah, water
Would gush, flush, green these mountains and these valleys,
And we rebuild our cities, not dream of islands.

IN MEMORY OF W. B. YEATS

(d. Jan. 1939)

I

He disappeared in the dead of winter:
The brooks were frozen, the airports almost deserted,
And snow disfigured the public statues;
The mercury sank in the mouth of the dying day.
O all the instruments agree
The day of his death was a dark cold day.

Far from his illness
The wolves ran on through the evergreen forests,
The peasant river was untempted by the fashionable quays;
By mourning tongues
The death of the poet was kept from his poems.

But for him it was his last afternoon as himself,
An afternoon of nurses and rumours;

The provinces of his body revolted,
The squares of his mind were empty,
Silence invaded the suburbs,
The current of his feeling failed: he became his admirers.

Now he is scattered among a hundred cities
And wholly given over to unfamiliar affections;
To find his happiness in another kind of wood
And be punished under a foreign code of conscience.
The words of a dead man
Are modified in the guts of the living.

But in the importance and noise of tomorrow
When the brokers are roaring like beasts on the floor of the
    Bourse,
And the poor have the sufferings to which they are fairly ac-
    customed,
And each in the cell of himself is almost convinced of his free-
    dom;
A few thousand will think of this day
As one thinks of a day when one did something slightly un-
    usual.
O all the instruments agree
The day of his death was a dark cold day.

II

You were silly like us: your gift survived it all;
The parish of rich women, physical decay,
Yourself; mad Ireland hurt you into poetry.
Now Ireland has her madness and her weather still,
For poetry makes nothing happen: it survives
In the valley of its saying where executives
Would never want to tamper; it flows south
From ranches of isolation and the busy griefs,
Raw towns that we believe and die in; it survives,
A way of happening, a mouth.

III

Earth, receive an honoured
    guest;
William Yeats is laid to rest:
Let the Irish vessel lie
Emptied of its poetry.

Time that is intolerant
Of the brave and innocent,
And indifferent in a week
To a beautiful physique,

Worships language and
    forgives
Everyone by whom it lives;
Pardons cowardice, conceit,
Lays its honours at their feet.

Time that with this strange
    excuse
Pardoned Kipling and his
    views,
And will pardon Paul Claudel,
Pardons him for writing well.

In the nightmare of the dark
All the dogs of Europe bark,
And the living nations wait,
Each sequestered in its hate;

Intellectual disgrace
Stares from every human face,
And the seas of pity lie
Locked and frozen in each
    eye.

Follow, poet, follow right
To the bottom of the night,
With your unconstraining
    voice
Still persuade us to rejoice;

With the farming of a verse
Make a vineyard of the curse,
Sing of human unsuccess
In a rapture of distress;

In the deserts of the heart
Let the healing fountain start,
In the prison of his days
Teach the free man how to
    praise.

LAY YOUR SLEEPING HEAD, MY LOVE

Lay your sleeping head, my love,
Human on my faithless arm;
Time and fevers burn away
Individual beauty from
Thoughtful children, and the grave
Proves the child ephemeral:

But in my arms till break of day
Let the living creature lie,
Mortal, guilty, but to me
The entirely beautiful.

Soul and body have no bounds:
To lovers as they lie upon
Her tolerant enchanted slope
In their ordinary swoon,
Grave the vision Venus sends
Of supernatural sympathy,
Universal love and hope;
While an abstract insight wakes
Among the glaciers and the rocks
The hermit's sensual ecstasy.

Certainty, fidelity
On the stroke of midnight pass
Like vibrations of a bell,
And fashionable madmen raise
Their pedantic boring cry:
Every farthing of the cost,
All the dreaded cards foretell,
Shall be paid, but from this night
Not a whisper, not a thought,
Not a kiss nor look be lost.

Beauty, midnight, vision dies:
Let the winds of dawn that blow
Softly round your dreaming head
Such a day of sweetness show
Eye and knocking heart may bless,
Find the mortal world enough;
Noons of dryness see you fed
By the involuntary powers,
Nights of insult let you pass
Watched by every human love.

THE UNKNOWN CITIZEN

(To JS/07/M/378 This Marble Monument Is Erected by the State)

He was found by the Bureau of Statistics to be
One against whom there was no official complaint,
And all the reports on his conduct agree
That, in the modern sense of an old-fashioned word, he was a
    saint,
For in everything he did he served the Greater Community.
Except for the War till the day he retired
He worked in a factory and never got fired,
But satisfied his employers, Fudge Motors Inc.
Yet he wasn't a scab or odd in his views,
For his Union reports that he paid his dues,
(Our report on his Union shows it was sound)
And our Social Psychology workers found
That he was popular with his mates and liked a drink.
The Press are convinced that he bought a paper every day
And that his reactions to advertisements were normal in every
    way.
Policies taken out in his name prove that he was fully insured,
And his Health-card shows he was once in hospital but left it
    cured.
Both Producers Research and High-Grade Living declare
He was fully sensible to the advantages of the Installment Plan
And had everything necessary to the Modern Man,
A phonograph, a radio, a car and a frigidaire.
Our researchers into Public Opinion are content
That he held the proper opinions for the time of year;
When there was peace, he was for peace; when there was war,
    he went.
He was married and added five children to the population,
Which our Eugenist says was the right number for a parent
    of his generation,
And our teachers report that he never interfered with their
    education.
Was he free? Was he happy? The question is absurd:
Had anything been wrong, we should certainly have heard.

O WHAT IS THAT SOUND

O what is that sound which so thrills the ear
   Down in the valley drumming, drumming?
Only the scarlet soldiers, dear,
   The soldiers coming.

O what is that light I see flashing so clear
   Over the distance brightly, brightly?
Only the sun on their weapons, dear,
   As they step lightly.

O what are they doing with all that gear,
   What are they doing this morning, this morning?
Only their usual manoeuvres, dear,
   Or perhaps a warning.

O why have they left the road down there,
   Why are they suddenly wheeling, wheeling?
Perhaps a change in their orders, dear.
   Why are you kneeling?

O haven't they stopped for the doctor's care,
   Haven't they reined their horses, their horses?
Why, they are none of them wounded, dear,
   None of these forces.

O is it the parson they want, with white hair,
   Is it the parson, is it, is it?
No, they are passing his gateway, dear,
   Without a visit.

O it must be the farmer who lives so near.
   It must be the farmer so cunning, so cunning?
They have passed the farmyard already, dear,
   And now they are running.

O where are you going? Stay with me here!
   Were the vows you swore deceiving, deceiving?

No, I promised to love you, dear,
  But I must be leaving.

O it's broken the lock and splintered the door,
  O it's the gate where they're turning, turning;
Their boots are heavy on the floor
  And their eyes are burning.

O WHERE ARE YOU GOING

'O where are you going?' said reader to rider,
'That valley is fatal when furnaces burn,
Yonder's the midden whose odours will madden,
That gap is the grave where the tall return.'

'O do you imagine,' said fearer to farer,
'That dusk will delay on your path to the pass,
Your diligent looking discover the lacking
Your footsteps feel from granite to grass?'

'O what was that bird,' said horror to hearer,
'Did you see that shape in the twisted trees?
Behind you swiftly the figure comes softly,
The spot on your skin is a shocking disease?'

'Out of this house'—said rider to reader,
'Yours never will'—said farer to fearer,
'They're looking for you'—said hearer to horror,
As he left them there, as he left them there.

CONSIDER

Consider this and in our time
As the hawk sees it or the helmeted airman:
The clouds rift suddenly—look there
At cigarette-end smouldering on a border
At the first garden party of the year.

Pass on, admire the view of the massif
Through plate-glass windows of the Sport Hotel;
Join there the insufficient units
Dangerous, easy, in furs, in uniform
And constellated at reserved tables
Supplied with feelings by an efficient band
Relayed elsewhere to farmers and their dogs
Sitting in kitchens in the stormy fens.

Long ago, supreme Antagonist,
More powerful than the great northern whale
Ancient and sorry at life's limiting defect,
In Cornwall, Mendip, or the Pennine moor
Your comments on the highborn mining-captains,
Found they no answer, made them wish to die
—Lie since in barrows out of harm.
You talk to your admirers every day
By silted harbours, derelict works,
In strangled orchards, and the silent comb
Where dogs have worried or a bird was shot.
Order the ill that they attack at once:
Visit the ports and, interrupting
The leisurely conversation in the bar
Within a stone's throw of the sunlit water,
Beckon your chosen out. Summon
Those handsome and diseased youngsters, those women
Your solitary agents in the country parishes;
And mobilize the powerful forces latent
In soils that make the farmer brutal
In the infected sinus, and the eyes of stoats.
Then, ready, start your rumour, soft
But horrifying in its capacity to disgust
Which, spreading magnified, shall come to be
A polar peril, a prodigious alarm,
Scattering the people, as torn-up paper
Rags and utensils in a sudden gust,
Seized with immeasurable neurotic dread.

Seekers after happiness, all who follow
The convolutions of your simple wish,
It is later than you think; nearer that day
Far other than that distant afternoon
Amid rustle of frocks and stamping feet
They gave the prizes to the ruined boys.
You cannot be away, then, no
Not though you pack to leave within an hour,
Escaping humming down arterial roads:
The date was yours; the prey to fugues,
Irregular breathing and alternate ascendancies
After some haunted migratory years
To disintegrate on an instant in the explosion of mania
Or lapse for ever into a classic fatigue.

MUNDUS ET INFANS

Kicking his mother until she let go of his soul
Has given him a healthy appetite: clearly, her rôle
    In the New Order must be
To supply and deliver his raw materials free;
    Should there be any shortage,
She will be held responsible; she also promises
To show him all such attentions as befit his age.
    Having dictated peace,

With one fist clenched behind his head, heel drawn up to
        thigh,
The cocky little ogre dozes off, ready,
    Though, to take on the rest
Of the world at the drop of a hat or the mildest
    Nudge of the impossible,
Resolved, cost what it may, to seize supreme power and
Sworn to resist tyranny to the death with all
    Forces at his command.

A pantheist not a solipsist, he co-operates
With a universe of large and noisy feeling-states
    Without troubling to place
Them anywhere special, for, to his eyes, Funnyface
    Or Elephant as yet
Mean nothing. His distinction between Me and Us
Is a matter of taste; his seasons are Dry and Wet;
    He thinks as his mouth does.

Still his loud iniquity is still what only the
Greatest of saints become—someone who does not lie:
    He because he cannot
Stop the vivid present to think, they by having got
    Past reflection into
A passionate obedience in time. We have our Boy-
Meets-Girl era of mirrors and muddle to work through,
    Without rest, without joy.

Therefore we love him because his judgments are so
Frankly subjective that his abuse carries no
    Personal sting. We should
Never dare offer our helplessness as a good
    Bargain; without at least
Promising to overcome a misfortune we blame
History or Banks or the Weather for: but this beast
    Dares to exist without shame.

Let him praise our Creator with the top of his voice,
Then, and the motions of his bowels; let us rejoice
    That he lets us hope, for
He may never become a fashionable or
    important personage:
However bad he may be, he has not yet gone mad;
Whoever we are now, we were no worse at his age;
    So of course we ought to be glad

When he bawls the house down. Has he not a perfect right
To remind us at every moment how we quite
   Rightly expect each other
To go upstairs or for a walk if we must cry over
   Spilt milk, such as our wish
That, since, apparently, we shall never be above
Either or both, we had never learned to distinguish
   Between hunger and love?

THE SHIELD OF ACHILLES

     She looked over his shoulder
       For vines and olive trees,
     Marble, well-governed cities
       And ships upon wine-dark seas;
     But there on the shining metal
       His hands had put instead
     An artificial wilderness
       And a sky like lead.

A plain without a feature, bare and brown,
   No blade of grass, no sign of neighborhood,
Nothing to eat and nowhere to sit down;
   Yet, congregated on that blankness, stood
   An unintelligible multitude,
A million eyes, a million boots, in line,
Without expression, waiting for a sign.

Out of the air a voice without a face
   Proved by statistics that some cause was just
In tones as dry and level as the place;
   No one was cheered and nothing was discussed,
   Column by column, in a cloud of dust,
They marched away, enduring a belief
Whose logic brought them, somewhere else, to grief.

She looked over his shoulder
    For ritual pieties,
White flower-garlanded heifers,
    Libation and sacrifice:
But there on the shining metal
    Where the altar should have been
She saw by his flickering forge-light
    Quite another scene.

Barbed wire enclosed an arbitrary spot
    Where bored officials lounged (one cracked a joke)
And sentries sweated for the day was hot;
    A crowd of ordinary decent folk
    Watched from outside and neither moved nor spoke
As three pale figures were led forth and bound
To three posts driven upright in the ground.

The mass and majesty of this world, all
    That carries weight and always weighs the same,
Lay in the hands of others; they were small
    And could not hope for help, and no help came;
    What their foes liked to do was done; their shame
Was all the worst could wish: they lost their pride
And died as men before their bodies died.

She looked over his shoulder
    For athletes at their games,
Men and women in a dance
    Moving their sweet limbs,
Quick, quick, to music;
    But there on the shining shield
His hands had set no dancing-floor
    But a weed-choked field.

A ragged urchin, aimless and alone,
    Loitered about that vacancy; a bird
Flew up to safety from his well-aimed stone:

That girls are raped, that two boys knife a third,
  Were axioms to him, who'd never heard
Of any world where promises were kept
Or one could weep because another wept.

The thin-lipped armorer
  Hephaestos hobbled away;
Thetis of the shining breasts
  Cried out in dismay
At what the God had wrought
  To please her son, the strong
Iron-hearted man-slaying Achilles
  Who would not live long.

PRECIOUS FIVE

Be patient, solemn nose,
Serve in a world of prose
The present moment well
Nor surlily contrast
Its brash ill-mannered smell
With grand scents of the past;
That calm enchanted wood,
That grave world where you
    stood
So gravely at its middle,
Its oracle and riddle,
Has all been altered, now
In anxious times you serve
As bridge from mouth to
    brow,
As asymmetric curve
Thrust outward from a face
Time-conscious into space,
Whose oddness may provoke
To a mind-saving joke

A mind that would it were
An apathetic sphere:
Point, then, for honor's sake
Up the storm-beaten slope
From memory to hope
The way you cannot take.

Be modest, lively ears,
Spoiled darlings of a stage
Where any caper cheers
The paranoiac mind
Of this undisciplined
And concert-going age,
So lacking in conviction
It cannot take pure fiction
And what it wants from you
Are rumors partly true;
Before you catch its sickness
Submit your lucky quickness
And levity to rule,

o back again to school,
rudge patiently until
o whisper is too much
nd your precision such
t any sound that all
em natural, not one
antastic or banal,
nd then do what you will:
ance with angelic grace,
 ecstasy and fun,
he luck you cannot place.

 civil, hands; on you
though you cannot read
 written what you do
ad blows you struck so
 blindly
 temper or in greed
ur tricks of long ago,
es, kindly or unkindly,
known to you will know;
vere those hairy wrists
nd leg-of-mutton fists
hich pulverised the trolls
nd carved deep Donts in
 stone,
eat hands which under
 knolls
e now disjointed bone,
t what has been has been;
tight arthritic claw
 aldermanic paw
aving about in praise
 those homeric days
impious and obscene:
ow, hands, into those living
nds which true hands
should be

By making and by giving
To hands you cannot see.

Look, naked eyes, look
    straight
At all eyes but your own
Lest in a tête-à-tête
Of glances double-crossed,
Both knowing and both
    known,
Your nakedness be lost;
Rove curiously about
But look from inside out,
Compare two eyes you meet
By dozens on the street,
One shameless, one ashamed,
Too lifeless to be blamed,
With eyes met now and then
Looking from living men,
Which in petrarchan fashion
Play opposite the heart,
Their humor to her passion,
Her nature to their art,
For mutual undeceiving;
True seeing is believing
(What sight can never prove)
There is a world to see:
Look outward, eyes, and love
Those eyes you cannot be.

Praise, tongue, the Earthly
    Muse
By number and by name
In any style you choose,
For nimble tongues and lame
Have both found favor;
    praise
Her port and sudden ways,

Now fish-wife and now
    queen,
Her reason and unreason:
Though freed from that
    machine,
Praise Her revolving wheel
Of appetite and season
In honor of Another,
The old self you become
At any drink or meal,
That animal of taste
And of his twin, your
    brother,
Unlettered, savage, dumb,
Down there below the waist:
Although your style be
    fumbling,
Half stutter and half song,
Give thanks however
    bumbling,
Telling for Her dear sake
To whom all styles belong
The truth She cannot make.

Be happy, precious five,
So long as I'm alive
Nor try to ask me what
You should be happy for;
Think, if it helps, of love
Or alcohol or gold,
But do as you are told.
I could (which you cannot)
Find reasons fast enough
To face the sky and roar
In anger and despair
At what is going on,
Demanding that it name
Whoever is to blame:
The sky would only wait
Till all my breath was gone
And then reiterate
As if I wasn't there
That singular command
I do not understand,
Bless what there is for being,
Which has to be obeyed, for
What else am I made for,
Agreeing or disagreeing.

CANZONE

When shall we learn, what should be clear as day,
We cannot choose what we are free to love?
Although the mouse we banished yesterday
Is an enraged rhinoceros today,
Our value is more threatened than we know:
Shabby objections to our present day
Go snooping round its outskirts; night and day
Faces, orations, battles, bait our will
As questionable forms and noises will;
Whole phyla of resentments every day

Give status to the wild men of the world
Who rule the absent-minded and this world.

We are created from and with the world
To suffer with and from it day by day:
Whether we meet in a majestic world
Of solid measurements or a dream world
Of swans and gold, we are required to love
All homeless objects that require a world.
Our claim to own our bodies and our world
Is our catastrophe. What can we know
But panic and caprice until we know
Our dreadful appetite demands a world
Whose order, origin, and purpose will
Be fluent satisfaction of our will?

Drift, Autumn, drift; fall, colours, where you will:
Bald melancholia minces through the world.
Regret, cold oceans, the lymphatic will
Caught in reflection on the right to will:
While violent dogs excite their dying day
To bacchic fury; snarl, though, as they will,
Their teeth are not a triumph for the will
But utter hesitation. What we love
Ourselves for is our power not to love,
To shrink to nothing or explode at will,
To ruin and remember that we know
What ruins and hyaenas cannot know.

If in this dark now I less often know
That spiral staircase where the haunted will
Hunts for its stolen luggage, who should know
Better than you, beloved, how I know
What gives security to any world,
Or in whose mirror I begin to know
The chaos of the heart as merchants know
Their coins and cities, genius its own day?
For through our lively traffic all the day,

In my own person I am forced to know
How much must be forgotten out of love,
How much must be forgiven, even love.

Dear flesh, dear mind, dear spirit, O dear love,
In the depths of myself blind monsters know
Your presence and are angry, dreading Love
That asks its images for more than love;
The hot rampageous horses of my will,
Catching the scent of Heaven, whinny: Love
Gives no excuse to evil done for love,
Neither in you, nor me, nor armies, nor the world
Of words and wheels, nor any other world.
Dear fellow-creature, praise our God of Love
That we are so admonished, that no day
Of conscious trial be a wasted day.

Or else we make a scarecrow of the day,
Loose ends and jumble of our common world,
And stuff and nonsense of our own free will;
Or else our changing flesh may never know
There must be sorrow if there can be love.

THE DIASPORA

How he survived them they could never understand:
Had they not beggared him themselves to prove
They could not live without their dogmas or their land?
No worlds they drove him from were ever big enough:
How *could* it be the earth the Unconfined
Meant when It bade them set no limits to their love?
And he fulfilled the rôle for which he was designed:
On heat with fear, he drew their terrors to him,
And was a godsend to the lowest of mankind.
Till there was no place left where they could still pursue him
Except that exile which he called his Race.
But, envying him even that, they plunged right through him
Into a land of mirrors without time or space,
And all they had to strike now was the human face.

SEPTEMBER 1, 1939

I sit in one of the dives
On Fifty-second Street
Uncertain and afraid
As the clever hopes expire
Of a low dishonest decade:
Waves of anger and fear
Circulate over the bright
And darkened lands of the earth,
Obsessing our private lives;
The unmentionable odour of death
Offends the September night.

Accurate scholarship can
Unearth the whole offence
From Luther until now
That has driven a culture mad,
Find what occurred at Linz,
What huge imago made
A psychopathic god:
I and the public know
What all schoolchildren learn,
Those to whom evil is done
Do evil in return.

Exiled Thucydides knew
All that a speech can say
About Democracy,
And what dictators do,
The elderly rubbish they talk
To an apathetic grave;
Analysed all in his book,
The enlightenment driven away,
The habit-forming pain,
Mismanagement and grief:
We must suffer them all again.

Into this neutral air
Where blind skyscrapers use
Their full height to proclaim
The strength of Collective Man,
Each language pours its vain
Competitive excuse:
But who can live for long
In an euphoric dream;
Out of the mirror they stare,
Imperialism's face
And the international wrong.

Faces along the bar
Cling to their average day:
The lights must never go out,
The music must always play,
All the conventions conspire
To make this fort assume
The furniture of home;
Lest we should see where we are,
Lost in a haunted wood,
Children afraid of the night
Who have never been happy or good.

The windiest militant trash
Important Persons shout
Is not so crude as our wish:
What mad Nijinsky wrote
About Diaghilev
Is true of the normal heart;
For the error bred in the bone
Of each woman and each man
Craves what it cannot have,
Not universal love
But to be loved alone.

From the conservative dark
Into the ethical life
The dense commuters come,

Repeating their morning vow;
'I *will* be true to the wife,
I'll concentrate more on my work,'
And helpless governors wake
To resume their compulsory game:
Who can release them now,
Who can reach the deaf,
Who can speak for the dumb?

All I have is a voice
To undo the folded lie,
The romantic lie in the brain
Of the sensual man-in-the-street
And the lie of Authority
Whose buildings grope the sky:
There is no such thing as the State
And no one exists alone;
Hunger allows no choice
To the citizen or the police;
We must love one another or die.

Defenceless under the night
Our world in stupor lies;
Yet, dotted everywhere,
Ironic points of light
Flash out wherever the Just
Exchange their messages:
May I, composed like them
Of Eros and of dust,
Beleaguered by the same
Negation and despair,
Show an affirming flame.

NONES

What we know to be not possible
    Though time after time foretold
By wild hermits, by shaman and sybil
    Gibbering in their trances,

Or revealed to a child in some chance rhyme
    Like *will* and *kill*, comes to pass
Before we realise it: we are surprised
    At the ease and speed of our deed
And uneasy: it is barely three,
    Mid afternoon, yet the blood
Of our sacrifice is already
    Dry on the grass; we are not prepared
For silence so sudden and so soon;
    The day is too hot, too bright, too still,
Too ever, the dead remains too nothing.
    What shall we do till nightfall?

The wind has dropped and we have lost our public.
    The faceless many who always
Collect when any world is to be wrecked,
    Blown up, burnt down, cracked open,
Felled, sawn in two, hacked through, torn apart,
    Have all melted away: not one
Of these who in the shade of walls and trees
    Lie sprawled now, calmly sleeping,
Harmless as sheep, can remember why
    He shouted or what about
So loudly in the sunlight this morning;
    All, if challenged, would reply
—'It was a monster with one red eye,
    A crowd that saw him die, not I—.'
The hangman has gone to wash, the soldiers to eat:
    We are left alone with our feat.

The Madonna with the green woodpecker,
    The Madonna of the fig tree,
The Madonna beside the yellow dam,
    Turn their kind faces from us
And our projects under construction,
    Look only in one direction,
Fix their gaze on our completed work.
    Pile-driver, concrete-mixer,

Crane and pickaxe wait to be used again,
  But how can we repeat this?
Outliving our act we stand where we are
  As disregarded as some
Discarded artifact of our own,
  Like torn gloves, rusted kettles,
Abandoned branchlines, worn lop-sided
  Grindstones buried in nettles.

This mutilated flesh, our victim,
  Explains too nakedly, too well,
The spell of the asparagus garden,
  The aim of our chalk-pit game: stamps,
Bird's eggs are not the same: behind the wonder
  Of tow-paths and sunken lanes,
Behind the rapture on the spiral stair,
  We shall always now be aware
Of the deed into which they lead, under
  The mock chase and mock capture,
The racing and tussling and splashing,
  The panting and the laughter,
Be listening for the cry and stillness
  To follow after. Wherever
The sun shines, brooks run, books are written,
  There will also be this death.

Soon cool tramontana will stir the leaves,
  The shops will re-open at four,
The empty blue bus in the empty pink square
  Fill up and drive off: we have time
To misrepresent, excuse, deny,
  Mythify, use this event
While, under a hotel bed, in prison,
  Down wrong turnings, its meaning
Waits for our lives. Sooner than we would choose
  Bread will melt, water will burn,
And the great quell begin; Abaddon
  Set up his triple gallows

At our seven gates, fat Belial make
   Our wives waltz naked: meanwhile
It would be best to go home, if we have a home,
   In any case good to rest.

That our dreaming wills may seem to escape
   This dead calm, wander instead
On knife edges, on black and white squares,
   Across moss, baize, velvet, boards,
Over cracks and hillocks, in mazes
   Of string and penitent cones,
Down granite ramps and damp passages,
   Through gates that will not relatch
And doors marked Private, pursued by Moors
   And watched by latent robbers,
To hostile villages at the heads of fjords,
   To dark châteaux where wind sobs
In the pine-trees and telephones ring
   Inviting trouble, to a room
Lit by one weak bulb where our double sits
   Writing and does not look up.

That while we are thus away our own wronged flesh
   May work undisturbed, restoring
The order we try to destroy, the rhythm
   We spoil out of spite: valves close
And open exactly, glands secrete,
   Vessels contract and expand
At the right moment, essential fluids
   Flow to renew exhausted cells,
Not knowing quite what has happened but awed
   By death like all the creatures
Now watching this spot, like the hawk looking down
   Without blinking, the smug hens
Passing close by in their pecking order,
   The bug whose view is baulked by grass,
Or the deer who shyly from afar
   Peer through chinks in the forest.

louis macneice

SUNDAY MORNING

Down the road someone is practicing scales,
The notes like little fishes vanish with a wink of tails,
Man's heart expands to tinker with his car
For this is Sunday morning, Fate's great bazaar,
Regard these means as ends, concentrate on this Now,
And you may grow to music or drive beyond Hindhead any-
    how,
Take corners on two wheels until you go so fast
That you can clutch a fringe or two of the windy past,
That you can abstract this day and make it to the week of time
A small eternity, a sonnet self-contained in rhyme.

But listen, up the road, something gulps, the church spire
Opens its eight bells out, skulls' mouths which will not tire
To tell how there is no music or movement which secures
Escape from the weekday time. Which deadens and endures.

AMONG THESE TURF-STACKS

Among these turf-stacks graze no iron horses
Such as stalk such as champ in towns and the soul of crowds,
Here is no mass-production of neat thoughts
No canvas shrouds for the mind nor any black hearses:
The peasant shambles on his boots like hooves
Without thinking at all or wanting to run in grooves.

But those who lack the peasant's conspirators
The tawny mountain, the unregarded buttress,
Will feel the need of a fortress against ideas and against the
Shuddering insidious shock of the theory-vendors
The little sardine men crammed in a monster toy
Who tilt their aggregate beast against our crumbling Troy.

For we are obsolete who like the lesser things,
Who play in corners with looking-glasses and beads;
It is better we should go quickly, go into Asia
Or any other tunnel where the world recedes,
Or turn blind wantons like the gulls who scream
And rip the edge off any ideal or dream.

BAGPIPE MUSIC

It's no go the merry-go-round, it's no go the rickshaw,
All we want is a limousine and a ticket for the peepshow.
Their knickers are made of crêpe-de-chine, their shoes are
    made of python.
Their halls are lined with tiger rugs and their walls with heads
    of bison.

John MacDonald found a corpse, put it under the sofa,
Waited till it came to life and hit it with a poker,
Sold its eyes for souvenirs, sold its blood for whiskey,
Kept its bones for dumb-bells to use when he was fifty.

It's no go the Yogi-Man, it's no go Blavatsky,
All we want is a bank balance and a bit of skirt in a taxi.

Annie MacDougall went to milk, caught her foot in the
    heather,
Woke to hear a dance record playing of Old Vienna.
It's no go your maidenheads, it's no go your culture,
All we want is a Dunlop tire and the devil mend the puncture.

The laird o'Phelps spent Hogmannay declaring he was sober;
Counted his feet to prove the fact and found he had one foot
    over.
Mrs. Carmichael had her fifth, looked at the job with repulsion,
Said to the midwife 'Take it away; I'm through with over-
    production.'

It's no go the gossip column, it's no go the Ceilidh,
All we want is a mother's help and a sugar-stick for the baby.
Willie Murray cut his thumb, couldn't count the damage,
Took the hide of an Ayrshire cow and used it for a bandage.
His brother caught three hundred cran when the seas were
    lavish,
Threw the bleeders back in the sea and went upon the parish.

It's no go the Herring Board, it's no go the Bible,
All we want is a packet of fags when our hands are idle.

It's no go the picture palace, it's no go the stadium,
It's no go the country cot with a pot of pink geraniums.
It's no go the Government grants, it's no go the elections,
Sit on your arse for fifty years and hang your hat on a pension.

It's no go my honey love, it's no go my poppet;
Work your hands from day to day, the winds will blow the
    profit.
The glass is falling hour by hour, the glass will fall forever,
But if you break the bloody glass you won't hold up the
    weather.

REFUGEES

With prune-dark eyes, thick lips, jostling each other
These, disinterred from Europe, throng the deck
To watch their hope heave up in steel and concrete
Powerful but delicate as a swan's neck,

Thinking, each of them, the worst is over
And we do not want any more to be prominent or rich,
Only to be ourselves, to be unmolested
And make ends meet—an ideal surely which

Here if anywhere is feasible. Their glances
Like wavering antennae feel
Around the sliding limber towers of Wall Street
And count the numbered docks and gingerly steal

Into the hinterland of their own future
Behind this excessive annunciation of towers,
Tracking their future selves through a continent of strangeness.
The liner moves to the magnet; the quay flowers

With faces of people's friends. But these are mostly
Friendless and all they look to meet
Is a secretary who holds his levée among ledgers,
Tells them to take a chair and wait . . .

And meanwhile the city will go on, regardless
Of any new arrival, trains like prayers
Radiating from stations haughty as cathedrals,
Tableaux of spring in milliners' windows, great affairs

Being endorsed on a vulcanite table, lines of washing
Feebly garnish among grimy brick and dour
Iron fire-escapes; barrows of cement are rumbling
Up airy planks; a florist adds a flower

To a bouquet that is bound for somebody's beloved
Or for someone ill; in a sombre board-room great
Problems wait to be solved or shelved. The city
Goes on but you, you will probably find, must wait

Till something or other turns up. Something-or-Other
Becomes an expected angel from the sky
But do not trust the sky, the blue that looks so candid
Is non-committal, frigid as a harlot's eye.

Gangways—the handclasp of the land. The resurrected,
The brisk or resigned Lazaruses, who want
Another chance, go trooping ashore. But chances
Are dubious. Fate is stingy, recalcitrant.

And officialdom greets them blankly as they fumble
Their foreign-looking baggage; they still feel
The movement of the ship while through their imagination
Seen and unheard-of constellations wheel.

theodore roethke

ELEGY FOR JANE

(My student, thrown by a horse)

I remember the neckcurls, limp and damp as tendrils;
And her quick look, a sidelong pickerel smile;
And how, once startled into talk, the light syllables leaped for
her,
And she balanced in the delight of her thought,
A wren, happy, tail into the wind,
Her song trembling the twigs and small branches.
The shade sang with her;
The leaves, their whispers turned to kissing,
And the mould sang in the bleached valleys under the rose.

Oh, when she was sad, she cast herself down into such a pure
depth,
Even a father could not find her:
Scraping her cheek against straw,
Stirring the clearest water.

My sparrow, you are not here,
Waiting like a fern, making a spiney shadow.
The sides of wet stones cannot console me,
Nor the moss, wound with the last light.

If only I could nudge you from this sleep,
My maimed darling, my skittery pigeon.
Over this damp grave I speak the words of my love:
I, with no rights in this matter,
Neither father nor lover.

EPIDERMAL MACABRE

Indelicate is he who loathes
The aspect of his fleshy clothes,—
The flying fabric stitched on bone,
The vesture of the skeleton,
The garment neither fur nor hair,
The cloak of evil and despair,
The veil long violated by
Caresses of the hand and eye.
Yet such is my unseemliness:
I hate my epidermal dress,
The savage blood's obscenity,
The rags of my anatomy,
And willingly would I dispense
With false accoutrements of sense,
To sleep immodestly, a most
Incarnadine and carnal ghost.

PIPLING

Behold a critic, pitched like the *castrati,*
Imperious youngling, though approaching forty:
He heaps few honours on a living head,
He loves himself, and the illustrious dead;
He pipes, he squeaks, he quivers through his nose,—
Some cannot praise him: *I* am one of those.

stephen spender

ULTIMA RATIO REGUM

The guns spell money's ultimate reason
In letters of lead on the spring hillside.
But the boy lying dead under the olive trees
Was too young and too silly
To have been notable to their important eye.
He was a better target for a kiss.

When he lived, tall factory hooters never summoned him.
Nor did restaurant plate-glass doors revolve to wave him in.
His name never appeared in the papers.
The world maintained its traditional wall
Round the dead with their gold sunk deep as a well,
Whilst his life, intangible as a Stock Exchange rumour, drifted
    outside.

O too lightly he threw down his cap
One day when the breeze threw petals from the trees.
The unflowering wall sprouted with guns,
Machine-gun anger quickly scythed the grasses;
Flags and leaves fell from hands and branches;
The tweed cap rotted in the nettles.

Consider his life which was valueless
In terms of employment, hotel ledgers, news files.
Consider. One bullet in ten thousand kills a man.
Ask. Was so much expenditure justified
On the death of one so young and so silly
Lying under the olive trees, O world, O death?

NOT PALACES, AN ERA'S CROWN

Not palaces, an era's crown
Where the mind dreams, intrigues, rests;
The architectural gold-leaved flower
From people ordered like a single mind,
I build. This only will I tell:
It is too late for rare accumulation,
For family pride, for beauty's filtered dusts;
I say, stamping the words with emphasis,
Drink from here energy and only energy,
As from the electric charge of a battery,
To will this time's change.

Eye, gazelle, delicate wanderer,
Drinker of horizon's fluid line;
Ear that suspends on a chord
The spirit drinking timelessness;
Touch, love—all senses—
Leave your gardens, your singing feasts,
Your dreams of suns circling before our sun,
Of heaven after our world.
Instead, watch images of flashing brass
That strike the outward sense, the polished will,
Flag of our purpose which the wind engraves.
No spirit seek here rest. But this: No man
Shall hunger; Man shall spend equally.
Our goal which we compel: Man shall be man.

The program of the antique Satan
Bristling with guns on the indented page,
With battleship towering from hilly waves:
For what? Drive of a ruining purpose,
Destroying all but its age-long exploiters.
Our program like this, yet opposite:
Death to the killers, bringing light to life.

I THINK CONTINUALLY OF THOSE WHO WERE TRULY GREAT

I think continually of those who were truly great
Who, from the womb, remembered the soul's history
Through corridors of light where the hours are suns,
Endless and singing. Whose lovely ambition
Was that their lips, still touched with fire,
Should tell of the spirit clothed from head to foot in song.
And who hoarded from the spring branches
The desires falling across their bodies like blossoms.

What is precious is never to forget
The delight of the blood drawn from ageless springs
Breaking through rocks in worlds before our earth;
Never to deny its pleasure in the simple morning light,
Nor its grave evening demand for love;
Never to allow gradually the traffic to smother
With noise and fog the flowering of the spirit.

Near the snow, near the sun, in the highest fields
See how these names are fêted by the waving grass,
And by the streamers of white cloud,
And whispers of wind in the listening sky;
The names of those who in their lives fought for life,
Who wore at their hearts the fire's center.
Born of the sun they traveled a short while towards the sun,
And left the vivid air signed with their honour.

bernard spencer

PART OF PLENTY

When she carries food to the table and stoops down
—Doing this out of love—and lays soup with its good
Tickling smell, or fry winking from the fire
And I look up, perhaps from a book I am reading
Or other work: there is an importance of beauty
Which can't be accounted for by there and then,

And attacks me, but not separately from the welcome
Of the food, or the grace of her arms.

When she puts a sheaf of tulips in a jug
And pours in water and presses to one side
The upright stems and leaves that you hear creak,
Or loosens them, or holds them up to show me,
So that I see the tangle of their necks and cups
With the curls of her hair, and the body they are held
Against, and the stalk of the small waist rising
And flowering in the shape of breasts;

Whether in the bringing of the flowers or the food
She offers plenty, and is part of plenty,
And whether I see her stooping, or leaning with the flowers,
What she does is ages old, and she is not simply,
No, but lovely in that way.

w. r. rodgers

NEITHER HERE NOR THERE

In that land all Is and nothing's Ought;
No owners or notices, only birds;
No walls anywhere, only lean wire of words
Worming brokenly out from eaten thought;
No oats growing, only ankle-lace grass
Easing and not resenting the feet that pass;
No enormous beasts, only names of them;
No bones made, bans laid, or boons expected,
No contracts, entails, hereditaments,
Anything at all that might tie or hem.

In that land all's lackadaisical;
No lakes of coddled spawn, and no locked ponds
Of settled purpose, no netted fishes;

But only inkling streams and running fronds,
Fritillaried with dreams, weedy with wishes;
Nor arrogant talk is heard, haggling phrase,
But undertones, and hesitance, and haze;
On clear days mountains of meaning are seen
Humped high on the horizon; no one goes
To con their meaning, no one cares or knows.

In that land all's flat, indifferent; there
Is neither springing house nor hanging tent,
No aims are entertained, and nothing is meant,
For there are no ends and no trends, no roads,
Only follow your nose to anywhere.
No one is born there, no one stays or dies,
For it is a timeless land, it lies
Between the act and the attrition, it
Marks off bound from rebound, make from break, tit
From tat, also to-day from to-morrow.
No Cause there comes to term, but each departs
Elsewhere to whelp its deeds, expel its darts;
There are no homecomings, of course, no good-byes
In that land, neither yearning nor scorning,
Though at night there is the smell of morning.

WHITE CHRISTMAS

Punctually at Christmas the soft plush
Of sentiment snows down, embosoms all
The sharp and pointed shapes of venom, shawls
The hills and hides the shocking holes of this
Uneven world of want and wealth, cushions
With cosy wish like cotton-wool the cool
Arm's-length interstices of caste and class,
And into obese folds subtracts from sight
All truculent acts, bleeding the world white.

Punctually that glib pair, Peace and Goodwill,
Emerges royally to take the air,

Collect the bows, assimilate the smiles,
Of waiting men. It is a genial time;
Angels, like stalactites, descend from heaven;
Bishops distribute their own weight in words,
Congratulate the poor on Christlike lack;
And the member for the constituency
Feeds the five thousand, and has plenty back.

Punctually, to-night, in old stone circles
Of set reunion, families stiffly sit
And listen: this is the night and this the happy time
When the tinned milk of human kindness is
Upheld and holed by radio-appeal:
Hushed are hurrying heels on hard roads,
And every parlour's a pink pond of light
To the cold and travelling man going by
In the dark, without a bark or a bite.

But punctually to-morrow you will see
All this silent and dissembling world
Of stilted sentiment suddenly melt
Into mush and watery welter of words
Beneath the warm and moving traffic of
Feet and actual fact. Over the stark plain
The silted mill-chimneys once again spread
Their sackcloth and ashes, a flowing mane
Of repentance for the false day that's fled.

THE TOWER

Pile upon pile of thought he drove
Into the sobbing bog below,
While others on the shaking raft
Of laughter travelled to and fro;
Light after light of love sailed by
His single and unseeing eye.

Coldly he willed and boldly strove
To build the lean and winding stair,
While, wide and high, the idle drove
Swung on hyperboles of air;
In hoops of happiness they curled
Bat-like about his darkening world.

Whose was the hand that laid the pyre?
What was the foot that fled the stair?
Look how the jarring tongues of fire
Roll out and glory-hole the air.
From the charred arches of his brain
The golden girders fall like rain
Upon the unforgiving plain.

AUTUMN DAY

Going out, those bold days,
O what a gallery-roar of trees and gale-wash
Of leaves abashed me, what a shudder and shore
Of bladdery shadows dashed on windows ablaze,
What hedge-shingle seething, what vast lime-splashes
Of light clouting the land. Never had I seen
Such a running-over of clover, such tissue sheets
Of cloud poled asunder by sun, such plunges
And thunder-load of fun. Trees, grasses, wings—all
On a hone of wind sluiced and sleeked one way,
Smooth and close as the pile of a pony's coat,
But, in a moment, smoke-slewed, glared, squinted back
And up like sticking bones shockingly unkinned.
How my heart, like all these, was silk and thistle
By turns, how it fitted and followed the stiff lifts
And easy falls of them, or, like that bird above me,
No longer crushing against cushions of air,
Hung in happy apathy, waiting for wind-rifts:
Who could not dance on, and be dandled by, such a day
Of loud expansion? when every flash and shout

Took the hook of the mind and reeled out the eye's line
Into whips and whirl-spools of light, when every ash-shoot
    shone
Like a weal and was gone in the gloom of the wind's lash.
Who could not feel it? the uplift and total subtraction
Of breath as, now bellying, now in abeyance,
The gust poured up from the camp's throat below, bringing
Garbled reports of guns and bugle-notes,
But, gullible, then drank them back again.
And I, dryly shuffling through the scurf of leaves
Fleeing like scuffled toast, was host to all these things;
In me were the spoon-swoops of wind, in me too
The rooks dying and settling like tea-leaves over the trees;
And, rumbling on rims of rhyme, mine were the haycarts
    home-creeping
Leaving the rough hedge-cheeks long-strawed and streaked
    with their weeping.

elizabeth bishop

THE IMAGINARY ICEBERG

We'd rather have the iceberg than the ship,
Although it meant the end of travel.
Although it stood stock still like cloudy rock
And all the sea were moving marble.
We'd rather have the iceberg than the ship;
We'd rather own this breathing plain of snow
Though the ship's sails were laid upon the sea
As the snow lies undissolved upon the water.
O solemn, floating field,
Are you aware an iceberg takes repose
With you, and when it wakes may pasture on your snows?

This is a scene a sailor'd give his eyes for.
The ship's ignored. The iceberg rises

And sinks again; its glassy pinnacles
Correct elliptics in the sky.
This is a scene where he who treads the boards
Is artlessly rhetorical. The curtain
Is light enough to rise on finest ropes
That airy twists of snow provide.
The wits of these white peaks
Spar with the sun. Its weight the iceberg dares
Upon a shifting stage and stands and stares.

This iceberg cuts its facets from within.
Like jewelry from a grave
It saves itself perpetually and adorns
Only itself, perhaps the snows
Which so surprise us lying on the sea.
Goodbye, we say, goodbye, the ship steers off
Where waves give in to one another's waves
And clouds run in a warmer sky.
Icebergs behoove the soul
(Both being self-made from elements least visible)
To see them so: fleshed, fair, erected indivisible.

A MIRACLE FOR BREAKFAST

At six o'clock we were waiting for coffee,
waiting for coffee and the charitable crumb
that was going to be served from a certain balcony,
—like kings of old, or like a miracle.
It was still dark. One foot of the sun
steadied itself on a ripple in the river.

The first ferry of the day had just crossed the river.
It was so cold we hoped that the coffee
would be very hot, seeing that the sun
was not going to warm us; and that the crumb
would be a loaf each, buttered, by a miracle.
At seven a man stepped out on the balcony.

He stood for a minute alone on the balcony
looking over our heads toward the river.
A servant handed him the makings of a miracle,
consisting of one lone cup of coffee
and one roll, which he proceeded to crumb,
his head, so to speak, in the clouds—along with the sun.

Was the man crazy? What under the sun
was he trying to do, up there on his balcony!
Each man received one rather hard crumb,
which some flicked scornfully into the river,
and, in a cup, one drop of the coffee.
Some of us stood around, waiting for the miracle.

I can tell what I saw next; it was not a miracle.
A beautiful villa stood in the sun
and from its doors came the smell of hot coffee.
In front, a baroque white plaster balcony
added by birds, who nest along the river,
—I saw it with one eye close to the crumb—

and galleries and marble chambers. My crumb
my mansion, made for me a miracle,
through ages, by insects, birds, and the river
working the stone. Every day, in the sun,
at breakfast time I sit on my balcony
with my feet up, and drink gallons of coffee.

We licked up the crumb and swallowed the coffee.
A window across the river caught the sun
as if the miracle were working, on the wrong balcony.

f. t. prince

SOLDIERS BATHING

The sea at evening moves across the sand,
And under a sunset sky I watch the freedom of a band
Of soldiers who belong to me: stripped bare
For bathing in the sea, they shout and run in the warm air.
Their flesh, worn by the trade of war, revives
And watching them, my mind towards the meaning of it
[strives.

All's pathos now. The body that was gross,
Rank, ravening, disgusting in the act and in repose,
All fever, filth and sweat, all bestial strength
And bestial decay, by pain and labour grows at length
Fragile and luminous. 'Poor bare forked animal,'
Conscious of his desires and needs and flesh that rise and fall,
Stands in the soft air, tasting after toil
The sweetness of his nakedness: letting the sea-waves coil
Their frothy tongues about his feet, forgets
His hatred of the war, its terrible pressure that begets
A machinery of death and slavery,
Each being a slave and making slaves of others: finds that he
Remembers his old freedom in a game
Mocking himself, and comically mimics fear and shame.

He plays with death and animality,
And reading in the shadows of his pallid flesh, I see
The idea of Michelangelo's cartoon
Of soldiers bathing, breaking off before they were half done
At some sortie of the enemy, an episode
Of the Pisan wars with Florence. I remember how he showed
Their muscular limbs that clamber from the water
And heads that turn across the shoulder, eager for the slaugh-
ter,
Forgetful of their bodies that are bare,
And hot to buckle on and use the weapons lying there.
And I think too of the theme another found
When, shadowing lean bodies on a sinister red ground—

Was it Antonio Pollaiuolo?—
Painted a naked battle: warriors straddled, hacked the foe,
Dug their bare toes into the soil and slew
The brother-naked man who lay between their feet and drew
His lips back from his teeth in a grimace.

They were Italians who knew war's sorrow and disgrace
And showed the thing suspended, stripped, a theme
Born out of the experience of war's horrible extreme
Beneath a sky where even the air flows
With *Lachrimae Christi;* and that rage, that bitterness, those
That hatred of the slain, what could it be   [blows,
But indirectly or brutally a commentary
On the Crucifixion? for the picture burns
With indignation and pity and despair and love by turns
Because it is the obverse of the scene
Where Christ hangs murdered, stripped, upon the Cross: I
    mean,
That is the explanation of its rage.

And we too have our bitterness and pity that engage
Thought, horror in this war. But night begins,
Night of the mind: who nowadays is conscious of our sins?
Though every human deed concerns our blood,
And even we must know what no one yet has understood,
That some great love is over what we do,
And that is what has driven us to this fury, for so few
Can suffer all the terror of that love:
The terror of that love has set us spinning in this groove
Greased with our blood.
                              These dry themselves and dress,
Resume their shirts, forget the fear and shame of nakedness.
Because to love is frightening we prefer
The freedom of our crimes. Yet as I drink the dusky air,
I feel a strange delight that fills me full,
A gratitude, as if evil itself were beautiful;
And kiss the wound in thought, while in the west
I watch a streak of red that might have issued from Christ's
    breast.

delmore schwartz

THE HEAVY BEAR

"the withness of the body"—WHITEHEAD

The heavy bear who goes with me,
A manifold honey to smear his face,
Clumsy and lumbering here and there,
The central ton of every place,
The hungry beating brutish one
In love with candy, anger, and sleep,
Crazy factotum, dishevelling all,
Climbs the building, kicks the football,
Boxes his brother in the hate-ridden city.

Breathing at my side, that heavy animal,
That heavy bear who sleeps with me,
Howls in his sleep for a world of sugar,
A sweetness intimate as the water's clasp,
Howls in his sleep because the tight-rope
Trembles and shows the darkness beneath.
—The strutting show-off is terrified,
Dressed in his dress-suit, bulging his pants,
Trembles to think that his quivering meat
Must finally wince to nothing at all.

That inescapable animal walks with me,
Has followed me since the black womb held,
Moves where I move, distorting my gesture,
A caricature, a swollen shadow,
A stupid clown of the spirit's motive,
Perplexes and affronts with his own darkness,
The secret life of belly and bone,
Opaque, too near, my private, yet unknown,
Stretches to embrace the very dear
With whom I would walk without him near,
Touches her grossly, although a word

Would bare my heart and make me clear,
Stumbles, flounders, and strives to be fed
Dragging me with him in his mouthing care,
Amid the hundred million of his kind,
The scrimmage of appetite everywhere.

FOR RHODA

Calmly we walk through this April's day,
Metropolitan poetry here and there,
In the park sit pauper and *rentier*,
The screaming children, the motor car
Fugitive about us, running away,
Between the worker and the millionaire
Number provides all distances,
It is Nineteen Thirty-Seven now,
Many great dears are taken away,
What will become of you and me
(This is the school in which we learn . . .)
Besides the photo and the memory?
(. . . that time is the fire in which we burn.)

(This is the school in which we learn . . .)
What is the self amid this blaze?
What am I now that I was then
Which I shall suffer and act again,
The theodicy I wrote in my high school days
Restored all life from infancy,
The children shouting are bright as they run
(This is the school in which they learn . . .)
Ravished entirely in their passing play!
(. . . that time is the fire in which they burn.)

Avid its rush, that reeling blaze!
Where is my father and Eleanor?
Not where are they now, dead seven years,
But what they were then?

No more? No more?
From Nineteen-Fourteen to the present day,
Bert Spira and Rhoda consume, consume
Not where they are now (where are they now?)
But what they were then, both beautiful;
Each minute bursts in the burning room,
The great globe reels in the solar fire,
Spinning the trivial and unique away.
(How all things flash! How all things flare!)
What am I now that I was then?
May memory restore again and again
The smallest color of the smallest day:
Time is the school in which we learn,
Time is the fire in which we burn.

A DOG NAMED EGO

A dog named Ego, the snowflakes as kisses
Fluttered, ran, came with me in December,
Snuffing the chill air, changing, and halting,
There where I walked toward seven o'clock,
Sniffed at some interests hidden and open,
Whirled, descending, and stood still, attentive,
Seeking their peace, the stranger, unknown,
With me, near me, kissed me, touched my wound,
My simple face, obsessed and pleasure bound.

"Not free, no liberty, rock that you carry,"
So spoke Ego in his cracked and harsh voice,
While snowflakes kissed me and satisfied minutes,
Falling from some place half believed and unknown,
"You will not be free, nor ever alone,"
So spoke Ego, "Mine is the kingdom,
Dynasty's bone: you will not be free,
Go, choose, run, you will not be alone."

"Come, come, come," sang the whirling snowflakes,
Evading the dog who barked at their smallness,

"Come!" sang the snowflakes, "Come here! and here!"
How soon at the sidewalk, melted, and done,
One kissed me, two kissed me! So many died!
While Ego barked at them, swallowed their touch,
Ran this way! And that way! While they slipped to the ground,
Leading him further and farther away,
While night collapsed amid the falling,
And left me no recourse, far from my home,
And left me no recourse, far from my home.

karl shapiro

THE MINUTE

The office building treads the marble dark,
The mother-clock with wide and golden dial
Suffers and glows. Now is the hour of birth
Of the tremulous egg. Now is the time of correction.
O midnight, zero of eternity,
Soon on a million bureaus of the city
Will lie the new-born minute.

The new-born minute on the bureau lies,
Scratching the glass with infant kick, cutting
With diamond cry the crystal and expanse
Of timelessness. This pretty tick of death
Etches its name upon the air. I turn
Titanically in distant sleep, expelling
From my lungs the bitter gas of life.

The loathsome minute grows in length and strength,
Bending its spring to forge an iron hour
That rusts from link to link, the last one bright,
The late one dead. Between the shining works
Range the clean angels, studying that tick
Like a strange dirt, but will not pick it up.
Nor move it gingerly out of harm's way.

An angel is stabbed and is carried aloft howling,
For devils have gathered on a ruby jewel
Like red mites on a berry; others arrive
To tend the points with oil and smooth the heat.
See how their vicious faces, lit with sweat,
Worship the train of wheels; see how they pull
The tape-worm Time from nothing into thing.

I with my distant heart lie wide awake
Smiling at that Swiss-perfect engine room
Driven by tiny evils. Knowing no harm
Even of gongs that loom and move in towers,
And hands as high as iron masts, I sleep,
At which sad sign the angels in a flock
Rise and sweep past me, spinning threads of fear.

muriel rukeyser

AJANTA

NOTE: *In India, between the second century B. C. and the sixth century A. D., a school of Buddhist painter-monks worked on the walls of the Ajanta caves, keeping a tradition in painting that was lost in the East after them and never known in the West. Based on the religious analogy between the space of the body and the space of the universe, the treatment of bodies in these scenes of the life of the gods is such that the deepest background is the wall on which the paintings are done—the figures in the round but shadowless, start forward, seeming to fill the cave. Reality is fully accepted, then, the function of such an art is to fill with creation an accepted real world.*

Came in my full youth to the midnight cave
nerves ringing; and this thing I did alone.
Wanting my fulness and not a field of war,
for the world considered annihilation, a star
called Wormwood rose and flickered, shattering
bent light over the dead boiling up in the ground,
the biting yellow of their corrupted lives
streaming to war, denying all our words.
Nothing was left among the tainted weather

but world-walking and shadowless Ajanta.
Hallucination and the metal laugh
in clouds, and the mountain-spectre riding storm.
Nothing was certain but a moment of peace,
a hollow behind the unbreakable waterfall.
All the way to the cave, the teeming forms of death,
and death, the price of the body, cheap as air.
I blessed my heart on the expiation journey
for it had never been unable to suffer:
when I met the man whose face looked like the future,
when I met the whore with the dying red hair,
the child myself who is my murderer.
So came I between heaven and my grave
past the serene smile of the *voyeur*, to
this cave where the myth enters the heart again.

II. THE CAVE

Space to the mind, the painted cave of dream.
This is not a womb, nothing but good emerges:
this is a stage, neither unreal nor real
where the walls are the world, the rocks and palaces
stand on a borderland of blossoming ground.
If you stretch your hand, you touch the slope of the world
reaching in interlaced gods, animals, and men.
There is no background. The figures hold their peace
in a web of movement. There is no frustration,
every gesture is taken, everything yields connections.
The heavy sensual shoulders, the thighs, the blood-born flesh
and earth turning into color, rocks into their crystals,
water to sound, fire to form; life flickers
uncounted into the supple arms of love.
The space of these walls is the body's living space;
tear open your ribs and breathe the color of time
where nothing leads away, the world comes forward
in flaming sequences. Pillars and prisms. Riders
and horses and the figures of consciousness,
red cow grows long, goes running through the world.
Flung into movement in carnal purity,

these bodies are sealed—warm lip and crystal hand
in a jungle of light. Color-sheeted, seductive
foreboding eyelid lowered on the long eye,
fluid and vulnerable. The spaces of the body
are suddenly limitless, and riding flesh
shapes constellations over the golden breast,
confusion of scents and illuminated touch—
monster touch, the throat printed with brightness,
wide outlined gesture where the bodies ride.
Bells, and the spirit flashing. The religious bells,
bronze under the sunlight like breasts ringing,
bronze in the closed air, the memory of walls,
great sensual shoulders in the web of time.

III. LES TENDRESSES BESTIALES

A procession of caresses alters the ancient sky
until new constellations are the body shining:
There's the Hand to steer by, there the horizon Breast,
and the Great Stars kindling the fluid hill.
All the rooms open into magical boxes,
nothing is tilted, everything flickers
sexual and exquisite.
The panther with its throat along my arm
turns black and flows away.
Deep in all streets passes a faceless whore
and the checkered men are whispering one word.
The face I know becomes the night-black rose.
The sharp face is now an electric fan
and says one word to me.
The dice and the alcohol and the destruction
have drunk themselves and cast.
Broken bottle of loss, and the glass
turned bloody into the face.
Now the scene comes forward, very clear.
Dream-singing, airborne, surrenders the recalled,
the gesture arrives riding over the breast,
singing, singing, tender atrocity,
the silver derelict wearing fur and claws.

Oh love, I stood under the apple branch,
I saw the whipped bay and the small dark islands,
and night sailing the river and the foghorn's word.
My life said to you: I want to love you well.
The wheel goes back and I shall live again,
but the wave turns, my birth arrives and spills
over my breast the world bearing my grave,
and your eyes open in earth. You touched my life.
My life reaches the skin, moves under your smile,
and your shoulders & your throat & your face & your thighs
flash.
    I am haunted by interrupted acts,
introspective as a leper, enchanted
by a repulsive clew,
a gross and fugitive movement of the limbs.
Is this the love that shook the lights to flame?
Sheeted avenues thrash in the wind,
torn streets, the savage parks.
I am plunged deep. Must find the midnight cave.

IV. BLACK BLOOD

A habit leading to murder, smoky laughter
hated at first, but necessary later.
Alteration of motives. To stamp in terror
around the deserted harbor, down the hill
until the woman laced into a harp
screams and screams and the great clock strikes,
swinging its giant figures past the face.
The Floating Man rides on the ragged sunset
asking and asking. Do not say, Which loved?
Which was beloved? Only, Who most enjoyed?
Armored ghost of rage, screaming and powerless.
Only find me and touch my blood again.
Find me. A girl runs down the street
singing Take me, yelling Take me Take
Hang me from the clapper of a bell
and you as hangman ring it sweet tonight,
for nothing clean in me is more than cloud

unless you call it.—As I ran I heard
a black voice beating among all that blood:
"Try to live as if there were a God."

V. THE BROKEN WORLD

Came to Ajanta cave, the painted space of the breast,
the real world where everything is complete,
there are no shadows, the forms of incompleteness.
The great clack blows in the light, rider and horse arrive,
the shoulders turn and every gift is made.
No shadows fall. There is no source of distortion.
In our world, a tree casts the shadow of a woman,
a man the shadow of a phallus, a hand raised
the shadow of the whip.
Here everything is itself,
here all may stand
on summer earth.
Brightness has overtaken every light,
and every myth netted itself in flesh.
New origins, and peace given entire
and the spirit alive.
In the shadowless cave
the naked arm is raised.
Animals arrive,
interlaced, and gods
interlaced, and men
flame-woven.
I stand and am complete.

Crawls from the door,
black at my two feet
the shadow of the world.
World, not yet one,
enters the heart again.
The naked world, and the old noise of tears,
the fear, the expiation and the love,
a world of the shadowed and alone.
The journey, and the struggles of the moon.

reuel denney

McSORLEY'S BAR

Mac had a place to drink and talk downtown
Where only men were welcome, or grown boys.
When the grey snow flew, there was the forum stove
Where arguments were slow, and out of noise.
The dust was old as Sumter, and the talking
Had never stopped since Dixie went to war;
And all the men from Grant to Hayes to now
Had lived beside, been buried from that bar.
There, in the evening, the city carpenter
Bumped up a drink with one of Croker's men
And politics and poetry were one
From supper-time until it closed at ten.
The grey-haired men considered from their chairs
How time is emptied like a single ale;
Their china eyes saw tabby woo the fire
As men their recollections, at the rail.
Here, among blackened walls, men's time
Flowed past like peaceful dreams of Chinamen
Who sat in temples thinking of those flowers
That die, and live, and close their blooms again.
Here the day's passions, after dusk,
Would, while the children called beneath the L,
Draw in like coals in pipes to gleam a silence
Between the words that cursed or wished them well.
Privilege, and extortion, and corruption,
Or the wreck of the city, or some newer way to power
Described the moving lives of living men
In voices where each hero had his hour.
And sorrow that rendezvoused in here
Flowed like a stellar scheme whose dying ions
Cascade toward night, when orders somewhere else
Gather the suns like a summer's dandelions.

SUPPOSE IN PERFECT REASON

Suppose in perfect reason
you want to die, you want earnestly
knowing for years the meaning,
you want above all to die—
recall the eager, the blonde
beavers who died in shelterhalves
of steel or ground like coral
to reefs where there was no choice.
Life defines the power to choose
and when you cut the thread
you are chosen, you become
a total, a togetherness.
More difficult to go on
bowlining silk-end
to end with awkward hand.
If for any cause you want to die
recall the dead who wanted simply
to live and who had every reason
to go on yet who died
for no accurate reason that you
could name. The pure line
is never poetry
but in walking down the street
to the store. —Wrong or right
they could not be colder dead
whatever side of the fence
the beast is. They eat
out of our mouths, they gaze
through our eyes that look
at a plant. If for any cause
you want profoundly to die,
remember the dead. Re-
collect the dead.
Recall the finished dead.

george barker

RESOLUTION OF DEPENDENCE

We poets in our youth begin in gladness
But thereof come in the end despondency and madness.
> Wordsworth: 'Resolution and Independence'

I encountered the crowd returning from amusements,
The Bournemouth Pavilion, or the marvellous gardens,
The Palace of Solace, the Empyrean Cinema: and saw
William Wordsworth was one, tawdrily conspicuous,
Obviously emulating the old man of the mountain-moor,
Traipsing along on the outskirts of the noisy crowd.

Remarkable I reflected that after all it is him
The layers of time falling continually on Grasmere Church
    yard,
The accumulation of year and year like calendar,
The acute superstition that Wordsworth is after all dead,
Should have succeeded in keeping him quiet and cold.
I resent the resurrection when I feel the updraft of fear.

But approaching me with a watch in his hand, he said:
'I fear you are early; I expected a man; I see
That already your private rebellion has been quelled.
Where are the violent gestures of the individualist?
I observe the absence of the erratic, the strange;
Where is the tulip, the rose, or the bird in hand?'

I had the heart to relate the loss of my charms,
The paradise pets I kept in my pocket, the bird,
The tulip trumpet, the phallic water pistol;
I had the heart to have mourned them, but no word.
'I have done little reading,' I murmured, 'I have
Most of the time been trying to find an equation.'

He glanced over my shoulder at the evening promenade.
The passing people, like Saint Vitus, averted their eyes:
I saw his eyes like a bent pin searching for eyes
To grip and catch. 'It is a species,' he said,
I feel I can hardly cope with—it is ghosts,
Trailing, like snails, an excrement of blood.

I have passed my hand like a postman's into them;
The information I dropped in at once dropped out.'
No,' I answered, 'they received your bouquet of daffodils,
They speak of your feeling for Nature even now.'
He glanced at his watch. I admired a face.
The town clock chimed like a cat in a well.

Since the private rebellion, the personal turn,
Leads down to the river with the dead cat and dead dog,
Since the single act of protest like a foggy film
Looks like women bathing, the Irish Lakes, or Saint Vitus,
Susceptible of innumerable interpretations,
I can only advise a suicide or a resolution.'

I can resolve,' I answered, 'if you can absolve.
Relieve me of my absurd and abysmal past.'
I cannot relieve or absolve—the only absolution
Is final resolution to fix on the facts.
I mean more and less than Birth and Death; I also mean
The mechanical paraphernalia in between.

Not you and not him, not me, but all of them.
It is the conspiracy of five hundred million
To keep alive and kick. This is the resolution,
To keep us alive and kicking with strength or joy.
The past's absolution is the present's resolution.
The equation is the interdependence of parts.'

ALLEGORY OF THE ADOLESCENT AND THE ADULT

It was when weather was Arabian I went
Over the downs to Alton where winds were wounded
With flowers and swathed me with aroma, I walked
Like Saint Christopher Columbus through a sea's welter
Of gaudy ways looking for a wonder.

Who was I, who knows, no one when I started,
No more than the youth who takes longish strides,
Gay with a girl and obstreperous with strangers,
Fond of some songs, not unusually stupid,
I ascend hills anticipating the strange.

Looking for a wonder I went on a Monday,
Meandering over the Alton down and moor;
When was it I went, an hour a year or more,
That Monday back, I cannot remember.
I only remember I went in a gay mood.

Hollyhock here and rock and rose there were,
I wound among them knowing they were no wonder;
And the bird with a worm and the fox in a wood
Went flying and flurrying in front, but I was
Wanting a worse wonder, a rarer one.

So I went on expecting miraculous catastrophe.
What is it, I whispered, shall I capture a creature
A woman for a wife, or find myself a king,
Sleep and awake to find Sleep is my kingdom?
How shall I know my marvel when it comes?

Then after long striding and striving I was where
I had so long longed to be, in the world's wind,
At the hill's top, with no more ground to wander
Excepting downward, and I had found no wonder.
Found only the sorrow that I had missed my marvel.

Then I remembered, was it the bird or worm,
The hollyhock, the flower or the strong rock,
Was it the mere dream of the man and woman
Made me a marvel? It was not. It was
When on the hilltop I stood in the world's wind.

The world is my wonder, where the wind
Wanders like wind, and where the rock is
Rock. And man and woman flesh on a dream.
I look from my hill with the woods behind,
And Time, a sea's chaos, below.

SONNET TO MY MOTHER

Most near, most dear, most loved and most far,
Under the window where I often found her
Sitting as huge as Asia, seismic with laughter,
Gin and chicken helpless in her Irish hand,
Irresistible as Rabelais but most tender for
The lame dogs and hurt birds that surround her,—
She is a procession no one can follow after
But be like a little dog following a brass band.
She will not glance up at the bomber or condescend
To drop her gin and scuttle to a cellar,
But lean on the mahogany table like a mountain
Whom only faith can move, and so I send
O all my faith and all my love to tell her
That she will move from mourning into morning.

DOG, DOG IN MY MANGER

Dog, dog in my manger, drag at my heathen
Heart where the swearing smoke of Love
Goes up as I give everything to the blaze.
Drag at my fires, dog, drag at my altars
Where Aztec I over my tabernacle raise
The Absalom assassination I my murder.

Dog, drag off the gifts too much I load
My life as wishing tree too heavy with:
And, dog, guide you my stray down quiet roads
Where peace is—be my engine of myth
That, dog, so drags me down my time
Sooner I shall rest from my overload.

Dog, is my shake when I come from water,
The cataract of my days, as red as danger?
O my joy has jaws that seize in fangs
The gift and hand of love always I sought for.
They come to me with kingdoms for my paucity—
Dog, why is my tooth red with their charity?

Mourn, dog, mourn over me where I lie
Not dead but spinning on the pinpoint hazard,
The fiftieth angel. Bay, bay in the blizzard
That brings a tear to my snowman's eye
And buries us all in what we most treasured.
Dog, why do we die so often before we die?

Dog, good dog, trick do and make me take
Calmly the consciousness of the crime
Born in the blood simply because we are here.
Your father burns for his father's sake,
So will a son burn in the further time
Under the bush of joy you planted here.

Dog, dog, your bone I am, who tear my life
Tatterdemalion from me. From you I have no peace,
No life at all unless you break my bone,
No bed unless I sleep upon my grief
That without you we are too much alone,
No peace until no peace is a happy home:
O dog my god, how can I cease to praise!

SACRED ELEGY: SEPARATION OF MAN FROM GOD

I These errors loved no less than the saint loves arrows
  Repeat, Love has left the world. He is not here.
  O God, like Love revealing yourself in absence
  So that, though farther than stars, like Love that sorrows
  In separation, the desire in the heart of hearts
  To come home to you makes you most manifest.
  The booming zero spins as his halo where
  Ashes of pride on all the tongues of sense
  Crown us with negatives. O deal us in our deserts
  The crumb of falling vanity. It is eucharist.

II Everyone walking everywhere goes in a glow
  Of geometrical progression, all meteors in praise:
  Hosannas on the tongues of the dumb shall raise
  Roads for the gangs in chains to return to
  God. They go hugging the traumas like halleluias
  To the bodies that earn this beatitude. The Seven
  Seas they crowd like the great sailing Clippers,
  Those homing migrants that, with their swallow-like sails
    set,
  Swayed forward along the loneliness that opposed,
  For nothing more than a meeting in heaven.

III Therefore all things, in all three tenses,
  Alone like the statue in an alcove of love,
  Moving in obedient machinery, sleeping
  Happy in impossible achievements, keeping
  Close to each other because the night is dark;
  The great man dreaming on the stones of circumstances,
  The small wringing hands because rocks will not move:
  The beast in its red kingdom, the star in its arc:
  O all things, therefore, in shapes or in senses,
  Know that they exist in the kiss of his Love.

IV Incubus. Anæsthetist with glory in a bag,
  Foreman with a sweatbox and a whip. Asphyxiator

Of the ecstatic. Sergeant with a grudge
Against the lost lovers in the park of creation,
Fiend behind the fiend behind the fiend behind the
Friend. Mastodon with mastery, monster with an ache
At the tooth of the ego, the dead drunk judge:
Wheresoever Thou art our agony will find Thee
Enthroned on the darkest altar of our heartbreak
Perfect. Beast, brute, bastard. O dog my God!

THE DEATH OF YEATS

That dolphin-torn, that gong-tormented face
With the trumpets of Andromeda rose and spoke,
Blaring the pitiful blast and airing hope
So hope and pity flourished. Now the place
Cold is where he was, and the gold face
Shimmers only through the echoes of a poem.

The swan mourns on the long abandoned lake,
And on the verge gather the great Irish ghosts
Whom only he could from their myth awaken
And make a kingdom. The luckless and the lost
Got glory from the shake of his hand as he passed,
The lunar emperor whom Time could not break.

The boulder where he rested his shoulder is
Luckier than most, who know nothing of
The tremendous gentleness of the poet's kiss,
Thwarted by passion and impelled by love.
But the lost leaf lashed in a March above
Shares sense of action that is also his.

Saints on mountains or animals in the ground
Often found the feather of his wing on their lips
Proving and loving them; stars in their eclipse
Saw his face watching through intervening ground:

And the small fry like fish came up at the sound
Of his voice and listened to his whistling lips.

But now the cloud only shall hear: the ant,
The winter bulb under the ground, and the hidden
Stream be made dumb by his murmur in death,
Lying between the rock and the jealous plant.
No matter how close to the ground I bend, his breath
Is not for me, and all divisions widen.

Remember the lion's head and the blonde angel
Whispering in the chimney; remember the river
Singing sweeter and sweeter as it grows older and older;
Remember the moon sees things from a better angle.
O forget the echoes that go on for ever,
And remember that the great harp-breasted eagle
    Is now a grave.

SECULAR ELEGY III

Satan is on your tongue, sweet singer, with
Your eye on the income and the encomium:
Angels rhapsodise for and from their faith.
And in the studios of chromium
Lucifer seduces Orpheus with a myth.

But the principle of evil is not autonomous.
Like the Liberty Horse with a plume at a circus
Under the whipmaster it steps proud in its circles.
When I let slip one instant the whip of the will
All hell's scot free with fire at the nostril.

Thus if the crux and judgement never is
Left to our own to do with as we will,
But the decision, like a master key, lies
Wholly in the higher hands that hold all—
How can we be as innocent as this?

Everything that is profound loves the mask,
Said the Dionysian who never wore one.
Thus our damnation and our condemnation,
Wiser than Nietzsche, never taking a risk,
Wears the mask of a necessary satisfaction.

Not, Love, when we kiss do the archangels weep
For we are naked then wherever we are,
Like tigers in the night: but in our sleep
The masks go down, and the beast is bare:
It is not Love but double damnation there.

Marooned on the islands of pride, lonely
And mad on the pyramids of achievement,
Disillusioned in the cathedrals of doxology,
The sad man senses his continual bereavement:
God has just died, and now there is only

Us. The gold bull with its horns of finances
Over the sensual mountains goes gallivanting
In glory: all night and all day it dances,
Absurd and happy because nothing is wanting.
The sad man hides his grief in his five senses.

SECULAR ELEGY V

O Golden Fleece she is where she lies tonight
Trammelled in her sheets like midsummer on a bed,
Kisses like moths flitter over her bright
Mouth, and, as she turns her head,
I feel all space move close to give her right.

Where her hand, like a bird on the branch of her arm,
Droops its wings over the bedside as she sleeps,
There the air perpetually remains warm
Since, nested, her hand rested there. And she keeps
Under her green thumb life like a growing poem.

My nine-tiered tigress in the cage of sex
I feed with meat that you tear from my side
To crown your nine months with the paradox:
The love that kisses with a homicide
In robes of generation resurrects.

The bride who rides the hymeneal waterfall
Spawning all possibles in her pools of surplus,
Whom the train rapes going into a tunnel,
The imperial multiplicator nothing can nonplus:
My mother Nature is the origin of it all.

At Pharaoh's Feast and in the family cupboard,
Gay corpse, bright skeleton, and the fly in amber,
She sits with her laws like antlers from her forehead
Enmeshing everyone, with flowers and thunder
Adorning the head that destiny never worried.

EPISTLE I

To Dylan Thomas

Meeting a monster of mourning wherever I go
Who crosses me at morning and evening also,
For whom are you miserable I ask and he murmurs
I am miserable for innumerable man: for him
Who wanders through Woolworth's gazing at tin stars;
I mourn the maternal future tense, Time's mother,
Who has him in her lap, and I mourn also her,
Time whose dial face flashes with scars.

I gave the ghost my money and he smiled and said,
Keep it for the eyeballs of the dead instead.
Why here, I asked, why is it here you come
Breaking into the evening line going to another,
Edging your axe between my pencil fingers,
Twisting my word from a comedy to a crime?

I am the face once seen never forgotten,
Whose human look your dirty page will smother.

I know what it was, he said, that you were beginning;
The rigmarole of private life's belongings.
Birth, boyhood, and the adolescent baloney. So I say
Good go ahead, and see what happens then.
I promise you horror shall stand in your shoes,
And when your register of youth is through
What will it be but about the horror of man?
Try telling about birth and observe the issue.

Epping Forest where the deer and girls
Mope like lost ones looking for Love's gaols—
Among the dilapidated glades my mother wandered
With me as a kid, and sadly we saw
The deer in the rain near the trees, the leaf-hidden dung,
The Sunday papers, and the foliage's falling world;
I not knowing nothing was our possession,
Not knowing Poverty my position.

Epping Forest glutted with the green tree
Grew up again like a sea wood inside me.
I had the deer browsing on my heart,
This was my mother; and I had the dirt.
Inside was well with the green well of love,
Outside privation, poverty, all dearth.
Thus like the pearl I came from hurt,
Like the prize pig I came from love.

Now I know what was wanting in my youth,
It was not water or a loving mouth.
It was what makes the apple-tree grow big,
The mountain fall, and the minnow die.
It was hard cash I needed at my root.
I now know that how I grew was due
To echoing guts and the empty bag—
My song was out of tune for a few notes.

Oh, my ghost cried, the charming chimes of coincidence!
I was born also there, where distress collects the rents.
Guttersnipe gutless, I was planted in your guts there,
The tear of time my sperm. I rose from
The woe-womb of the want-raped mind,
Empty hunger cracked with stomach's thunder.
Remember the rags that flattered your frame
Froze hard and formed this flesh my rind.

So close over the chapter of my birth,
Blessed by distress, baptized by dearth.
How I swung myself from the tree's bough
Demonstrating death in my gay play:
How the germ of the sperm of this ghost like a worm
I caught from the cold comfort of never enough.
How by being miserable for myself I began,
And now am miserable for the mass of man.

norman nicholson

ROCKFERNS

On quarry walls the spleenwort spreads
Its green zipfasteners and black threads,
And pinches tight its unfurled purses
In every crevice with the cresses,
As if a blast of dynamite
Had spattered it upon the slate
That where the bluestone spine was broken
Spores might penetrate and quicken.
For in the fractures of the rock
Roots dig further than a pick,
As, though the sinews may not feel it,
The worm probes deeper than the bullet.
When this pen is dropped, my hand

May thrust up in a buckler frond,
And then my crushed and calcined bones
Prove better soil than arid stones.
Why need I fear the bursting bomb
Or whatsoever death shall come,
If brains and bowels be cast forth
Splintered to spleenwort on the earth?
And if a subtler part may cruise
Twice round the sun and Betelgeuse,
My soul shall detonate on high
And plant itself in cracks of sky.

henry reed

LESSONS OF WAR: JUDGING DISTANCES

Not only how far away, but the way that you say it
Is very important. Perhaps you may never get
The knack of judging a distance, but at least you know
How to report on a landscape: the central sector,
The right of arc and that, which we had last Tuesday,
    And at least you know

That maps are of time, not place, so far as the army
Happens to be concerned—the reason being,
Is one which need not delay us. Again, you know
There are three kinds of tree, three only, the fir and the poplar,
And those which have bushy tops too; and lastly
    That things only seem to be things.

A barn is not called a barn, to put it more plainly,
Or a field in the distance, where sheep may be safely grazing.
You must never be over-sure. You must say, when reporting:
At five o'clock in the central sector is a dozen
Of what appear to be animals; whatever you do,
    Don't call the bleeders *sheep*.

British
jerks

I am sure that's quite clear; and suppose, for the sake of
  example,
The one at the end, asleep, endeavours to tell us
What he sees over there to the west, and how far away,
After first having come to attention. There to the west,
On the fields of summer the sun and the shadows bestow
    Vestments of purple and gold.

The still white dwellings are like a mirage in the heat,
And under the swaying elms a man and a woman
Lie gently together. Which is, perhaps, only to say
That there is a row of houses to the left of arc,
And that under some poplars a pair of what appears to be
  humans
    Appear to be loving.

Well that, for an answer, is what we might rightly call
Moderately satisfactory only, the reason being,
Is that two things have been omitted, and those are important.
The human beings, now: in what direction are they,
And how far away, would you say? And do not forget
    There may be dead ground in between.

There may be dead ground in between; and I may not have
  got
The knack of judging a distance; I will only venture
A guess that perhaps between me and the apparent lovers,
(Who, incidentally, appear by now to have finished,)
At seven o'clock from the houses, is roughly a distance
    Of about one year and a half.

john manifold

THE SIRENS

Odysseus heard the sirens; they were singing
Music by Wolf and Weinberger and Morley
About a region where the swans go winging,
Vines are in colour, girls are growing surely
Into nubility, and pylons bringing
Leisure and power to farms that live securely
Without a landlord. Still, his eyes were stinging
With salt and seablink, and the ropes hurt sorely.
Odysseus saw the sirens; they were charming,
Blonde, with snub breasts and little neat posteriors,
But could not take his mind off the alarming
Weather report, his mutineers in irons,
The radio failing; it was bloody serious.
In twenty minutes he forgot the sirens.

FIFE TUNE

(6/8) for Sixth Platoon, 308th I.T.C.

One morning in spring
We marched from Devizes
All shapes and all sizes
Like beads on a string,
But yet with a swing
We trod the bluemetal
And full of high fettle
We started to sing.

She ran down the stair
A twelve-year-old darling
And laughing and calling
She tossed her bright hair;
Then silent to stare

At the men flowing past
  her—
There were all she could
  master
Adoring her there.

It's seldom I'll see
A sweeter or prettier;
I doubt we'll forget her
In two years or three.
And lucky he'll be
She takes for a lover
While we are far over
The treacherous sea.

WITH GOD CONVERSING

Red paths that wander through the gray, and cells
Of strangeness, rutted mouldings in the brain,
Untempered fevers heated by old kills,
By the pampered word, by the pat printed rune,
Unbalanced coil under glaucous blooms of thought,
A turning mind, unmitigated thinking that
Feeds human hunger and eats us alive
While cringing to the death, expecting love,—
Such make the self we are. And do you make it?
And practice on us? For we cannot take it.

Listen. Grow mild before the flicking lash
Seems welded to your hand, self-wounder.
What are we, cry we, while our pain leaps lush,
Too jungle thick: the jungle where we wander,
No seeded faith before, nor after, miracle,
Of bidden faith in things unseen, no particle.
For we think only through our troubled selves;
We note the worm that in the apple delves,
See gibbous moons and spots upon the sun,
Speak gibberish, and keep the poor in sin.

Plus birth and death must war-lash winnow
While every pod-burst leaf of May sucks life?
Because we think shall we be less than minnow,
Cat, carrot, rat, bat and such from sense aloof?
What doorless maze is this we wander through
With fuming souls parched of our morning dew?
Reason confounds as it presents to NAUGHT:
Earth worn, man moving into self-made night.
Reason-begotten science sets war's pace
And, civil-mouthed, makes civilization pass.

Created in your image, made up of words,
Till words reduce you to a zero-O,
We, then, reflecting you, are less than birds,
Bugs, or empty dugs, still less than minus no.
There must be something wrong with being wise—
Talking we go, wondering and wandering with woes,
Big thoughts have got us, hence we organize,
Govern our heroes with unmeant yeas and nays,
And breathe in dungeons of our nervous mesh
An air too blank to snare meandering flesh.

Night melting dawn shall turn the renewed sky,
Aurora Borealis and Australis
Fanfaring leap the poles, the moon fall by;
But if our science does not quickly fail us
How long for us will space blue light the dun
Of populaces, while wonderers eye the sun?
The gloomy silhouettes of wings we forged
With reason reasonless, are now enlarged,
The falsified subconscious, beast a-woken?
We-you? Post-suicides, shall we awaken?

ELEGY

On Gordon Barber, Lamentably Drowned in his Eighteenth Ye

When in the mirror of a permanent tear
Over the iris of your mother's eye
I beheld the dark tremor of your face, austere
With space of death, spun too benign for youth,
Icicle of the past to pierce her living sigh—
I saw you wish the last kiss of mother's mouth,
Who took the salted waters rather in the suck
Of seas, sighing yourself to fill and drench
With water the plum-rich glory of your breast
Where beat the heart escaping from war's luck.

Gordon, I mourn your wrist, your running foot,
Your curious brows, your thigh, your unborn daughters,
Yet mourn more deep the drought-caught war dry boy
Who goes, a killer, to join you in your sleep
And envy you what made you blench
Taking your purple back to drought-less waters.
What choke of terror filled you in the wet
What fierce surprise caught you when play turned fate
And all the rains you loved became your net,
Formlessly yielding, yet stronger than your breath?
Then did you dream of mother or hopes hatched
When the cold cramp held you from nape to foot
And time dissolved, promise dissolved, in Death?
Did you cry 'cruel' to all the hands that stretched
Not near, but played afar, when you sank down
Your sponge of lungs hurt to the quick
Till you had left the quick to join the dead,
Whom, now, your mother mourns grief-sick.
You were too young to drown.

Never will you take bride to happy bed,
Who lay awash in water, yet no laving
Needed, so pure so young for sudden leaving.

Gone, gone is Gordon, tall and brilliant lad
Whose mind was science. Now hollow his skull,
A noble sculpture, is but sunken bone,
His cells from water come, by water laid
Grave-deep, to water *gone*.
Lost, lost the hope he had,
Washed to a cipher his splendour and his skill.

But Gordon's gone, it's other boys who live afraid.

Two years, and lads have grown to hold a gun.
In dust must splendid lads go down and choke,
Red dry their hands and dry their one day's sun

From which they earthward fall to fiery tomb
Bomb-weighted, from bloodying children's hair.

Never a boy but takes as cross Cain's crime
And goes to death by making death, to pass
Death's gate distorted with the dried brown grime—
Better the watery death than death by air,
Or death by sand
Where fall hard fish of fear
Loud in unwetted dust.

Spun on a lucky wave, O early boy!
Now ocean's fish you are
As heretofore.
Perhaps you had sweet mercy's tenderness
To win so soon largesse of choice
That you, by grace, went gayly to the wave
And all our mourning should be to rejoice.

AFTER READING ST. JOHN THE DIVINE

Moon's glow by seven fold multiplied, turned red,
Burned fierce by the coronal limbs at last
Out-leaping insulating space, a-blast
The searing heat sheeting round earth ahead
Of the scorched geoid's course; and I a-bed
Watching that increased flame and holding fast
To pulse and pillow. Worse! No shadow cast
By chair or cat. All people waking dead . . .
Earth lurches spacial waste; my room is hot;
That moon waxes her monstrous, brimstone disk;
Thick fear stretches before the febrile light;
Green fires pierce at my clenching eye's blind spot . . .
My buried soul, rising to face the risk,
With one pure deed restores the natural night.

N. B., SYMMETRIANS

We, the symmetrians, seek justice here,
And asymmetric nature makes a drought.
We wrap up handouts for the martyred poor,
Making sure to put in books and tin-can beer.
Each man relieved goes home and gives a clout
To mrs man, or pal-man, and slams the door.

The speechful day in knowing languors goes,
We seek again for salt and summer sky.
The pure-blue meteor flares and falls unburnt;
We take to our heels standing on staunch tiptoes.
We read half-works of science for the why
And scheme to balance marxly with what's learnt.

Fastened and fasting in the bed-rock man
The assainted, snuffed-down halo strives to rise;
The unstabilized land still slips up out of ocean,—
Bears odd, imperilled flora built to plan.
A natural start is now no one's surmise,
To take things as presented, no one's notion.

They used to start a-fresh, but we try burdened,
Trimming the present's future with the past.
It's all the fault of inter-communication,
Mountains of dove-tailed pebbles and words wordened.
The newest prism is moulded from the last.
The simplest thing is: to laud the massive nation.

The moon still shines beside the daytime star,
The waters weave, rain cools, dunes move, grain grows,
Soft words bring soft replies, muscles expand.
Whether we say the stars are near or far,
The polar lights still paint the glacier floes,
The temperate zones are yet more fully manned.

SPRING AIR

In blows the loitering air of spring,
Scarcely a-blow, a-blow, a lively gas.
It makes the secret life-cells ring
And quicken, while the blood-waves pass.
Floss nothingness, we feel it cling,
Resile,—silent as space, unseen as glass
Unlustred, softer than the weakest thing.
Such air can enter nostrils, sudden as light
The eye, fair words the ear, or flight
The nerve-knot, or your unexpected love
My startled heart. Down from above,
Or from the south, or flowered west,
Or from the oceaned east, or here
Blown first by spring, this air possessed
By spring is Ah! so lithe this year.
The curtain flies before this wonder.
Talk fast. Speak swift before the heart's asunder.

And for this guile . . . no cold-ice gates?
Nothing to hold it quietly down, a-down,
The while the senses sleep? Full spates
Of air enter this room in town.
Such air draws creatures to their mates
And, wild, peels off the winter's brown
From tree; ruffles the bird and motivates
The northern winging to the utmost nest;
Breaks out the bud's first scent and, lest
Two living things escape and keep hearts steady,
Beguiles us at this window; heady
And rich, murmurs; touches like flesh
Of loving fingers, timorous but sure.
Intoxicant is this mild, fresh
Warm breath of spring, all mad and pure.
Is this my hand in yours? Am I
So close? Wait till the insinuant wind's gone by . . .

BIRD, BIRD

Age after age our bird through incense flies,
Angel or daw, dove, phoenix, falcon or roc,
Till this last net of wings dark charged to wreck
The hoops of heaven, dove's arc, and all that cries.
The clotted frets of Daedalus unlock
An egg of paradox the gods disguise;
Men as the organs of the bird demise
Heaven's breath under the bombers' moon, flac-flac.
Plunge, boy, to paradise that in heart's choir
Is home, rocked on the cords of birth, low
Again home, bringing to earth your found fire.
Be hound or vine, not entrail to the crow
Of metal death,—explode the skies of fear—
Come down, O Icarus, come down, down, O.

RIDES

So we ride, and ride through milked heaven
               Above earth.
No more for us the housed and fatted standing still.
The train is carrier of us on the two-striped road-bed;
We sit in thunder over miles, calm as chairs,
               At will?
Look again; we zoom in planes over the hill's head;
Motion, motion, our motion, up, down, and on,
               World's girth.

And laughing under the town-world's crust,
               Thus riding
At the open and rushed dark subway doors;
Swung singing and talking with the unnoticed horses;
Or unfoamed by the spray, on liners,
               Changing lores
Of bored speed; or rivalling winds in their (our?) courses
In the air we flight, to air-pressure-up
               Confiding.

Sometimes on the tumbled skin of laced seas,
> Thus cresting
With staunch legs and opened hallooing, of surf
Making a race-shot thrill, on board with pair of reins,
Lengthened freedom of running covering the inland
> Fraught turf. . . .
Ah, from riding, and the riding, who abstains?
In the cars, to the stars, waves, wars, riding
> And questing.

IN THE PROSCENIUM

The night, too long illumined, comes a stranger
Driving to roof this audience hard-weathered
Through the play of rage and bitter luck of danger.
Born to these uniform seats, they claim
No hunter's pleasure, the historic name.

Long foundered is our prow that feathered
The warm archaic wave.

The limelight warns, the need to worship waits
A serious humour, the laud-lifted clown.
The lights are fluorescent,
Pale, pale and cold, ice flickering incessant
As at Asgärd's fall, were north gods' twilight
Ceaselessly from no star.
The nerveless curtain, like dead water, parts.
Increasing thousands raise their long slow stare
To the pacified shroud, our silver screen of fêtes.

No choral song arises, no drama starts.
This pantomime, like beauty, only lies
In the entrancèd eyes.
Our mask of shadow comes, there pantaloon
How massive stands, anabasis of stone
Toward the prickling cells: the final form of Gilles.

Quick with electric chill
All profiles right and left unending freeze
Not as at death's pole or Gorgon's locks,
But tight to one grounded wire, in paralysis.

Nothing will happen but fear's thrill on the nerve
Which makes the heart a nave.

If this were but enchantment or a dream
Even of solstice sacrifice, a rite
Of Druids moving with dark seasonal pace
Barefoot beneath Stonehenge's antique weight,
Endurance might ennoble the tranced face
Or quell emotion with a natural light.

But here projection worse than mirror's spell
Our clown's oiled paradox
Drips from his skull and sockets' peacock pride.
The last cry for justice dies.
The sterile form of megalomaniac woe
Is malice; violence at recurrent speed
Is death's boredom motionless, thus is hell
Gone vacant, and so mocks.
The fawn has horned the doe.

The old, below their naked eyeballs' trance,
Recall Pierrot, the dance,
The silken lips, the fluttering love whose lease
Was years, fountains of smiles, the tears' duet
Before the risk was hate, the vines' empurpled lace.
The young lack memory. They fiercely throw
From the blank iris gun-glances for Gilles,
At Gilles, whose mask has the strength they make grow.

Innocent are their eyes, as pure as cruel,
Innocent of compassion, innocent as rue.
For the tuberose scent of love
Takes time and time to breathe;

This is amusement, to see the skull heave
Hard on the plastic ruff of hardened milk.

Even the young remember Punch. They're tough.
Punch had these heavy hands, but not this bat-winged hulk.
They have two hands for sticks, and hands enough.
Tyros of flowers and veterans of flight,
Born without firmament
In the planetary prison with a ceiling for skies,
One hour for love, short days,
They may not wing like bees through hearts of flowers
But wing like ants in regiments
Capturing aphides.

The undecipherable fate of Cain,
His mark, may saturate us with clown's pain.

Gilles sates our hunger and bloats hypnotized
In the proscenium. But he'll burst
In the easy rain of bombs, our uranium sin.
The ascending dust will sift the son of Cain,
This generation dust, or lost, or dazed.

O animals were equal at the first.
We studied hunch of bison claw of cat
For duels. In the deep caves of the bat
Our risk was beautiful.
Now, at the slaughter pen, moans the young bull.

Christ's love! Who dreed our weird? Nobility
Troubles the heart in unexpected moments,
Heart's ease.
          New Human creatures tranquilly
New seasons will inhabit, safe as the wren,
Like the lion the chicken the hyena,
Natural as the veronica and the verbena,
In agricultural health.

SHELTER

While people hunt for what can satisfy their wants,
There is a watching and a sharp recording.
Both seekers and the watchers are the palpitants,
And much is said with no deep, ferny wording.

Under the various shelters sits the soul
Not necessarily in misty, devious hiding;
The body housed, the body's firm, pale bole
Clothed, the body's self a blank abiding.

There sometimes goes a woman, fur on neck,
A man with hands immersed in pockets,
An insect crouched behind a built-up speck,
Or memories enclosed in fastened lockets.

But cease! The peering sleight-of-sight
Probing behind such partial enclosures
Is more befooled, because the definite might
Is open, like water seen through osiers.

Walking or languid, through the night or day,
Something familiar for a hiding wall
We carry, as a glove, or stare, or play
Of lips and brows. That's just a stall

That balks no frankness of the essence,
The too lightning truth of what we are—
No man can hide the presence or the absence,
We've come too quickly and too far.

THIRD MADRIGAL

My wand strikes me no joy till loosened weeping
Prints my blue air with clouded beauty lying
In milky pools of silk, the cipolin
Smooth floor his momentary couch, and sighing,

My throaty ocarina blows to win
His hearing, though his madder ear lies sleeping
Among the browny spirals of his curls.

My clouds are grey on black, grey unworn pearls,
No broody moonstone quiet for his sight.
His sun-tipped clouds fly with soft angel golds;
Weathers all raw roam through my cyclone night.
I have long hot skies and cold snows in folds,
No mild green light of spring to weave him laurels.
My future floods be such as angels ford!

Noble sport of the vain cells that overlord
This massive heart with double gorgeous spate,
Now dare I hurl the jewel that drives him far,
Earth moving under beauty's feet, for where I wait
Even that mouth, my music's gate, and war,
My clouds in rains hold mirrored, a wound a word
Struck on my gong my heart, while his live bell

Chimes as he sleeps in my clouds' citadel.
My sea rolled tremor pierce his heaven's ear,
Plunge to his dream my restless echo's flash,
And wandering draw this source of song more near,
Made of so known a substance as the flesh,
Quick with his dream, live from my vision's shell . .
His throat and eyes struck open in my room.

Curse my night mourning witch's power and doom!
His pinions stir with throbbing flowers for feathers,
My rains in haloes fall round beauty's head,
May noose my wrist, so a smile hovers and quivers,
Such blossoms blow, his white, his dark, his red,
What artist's steady hand could hold their bloom?
Unloose eyes stare! I breathe his dream's excess,

My clouds rain curtains, my vision's jewel is his.

dylan thomas

AUTHOR'S PROLOGUE

This day winding down now
At God speeded summer's end
In the torrent salmon sun,
In my seashaken house
On a breakneck of rocks
Tangled with chirrup and fruit,
Froth, flute, fin and quill
At a wood's dancing hoof,
By scummed, starfish sands
With their fishwife cross
Gulls, pipers, cockles, and sails,
Out there, crow black, men
Tackled with clouds, who kneel
To the sunset nets,
Geese nearly in heaven, boys
Stabbing, and herons, and shells
That speak seven seas,
Eternal waters away
From the cities of nine
Days' night whose towers will catch
In the religious wind
Like stalks of tall, dry straw,
At poor peace I sing
To you strangers (though song
Is a burning and crested act,
The fire of birds in
The world's turning wood,
For my sawn, splay sounds),
Out of these seathumbed leaves
That will fly and fall
Like leaves of trees and as soon
Crumble and undie
Into the dogdayed night.

Seaward the salmon, sucked sun slips,
And the dumb swans drub blue
My dabbed bay's dusk, as I hack
This rumpus of shapes
For you to know
How I, a spinning man,
Glory also this star, bird
Roared, sea born, man torn, blood blest.
Hark: I trumpet the place,
From fish to jumping hill! Look:
I build my bellowing ark
To the best of my love
As the flood begins,
Out of the fountainhead
Of fear, rage red, manalive,
Molten and mountainous to stream
Over the wound asleep
Sheep white hollow farms

To Wales in my arms,
Hoo, there, in castle keep,
You king singsong owls, who moonbeam
The flickering runs and dive
The dingle furred deer dead!
Huloo, on plumbed bryns,
O my ruffled ring dove
In the hooting, nearly dark
With Welsh and reverent rook,
Coo rooing the woods' praise,
Who moons her blue notes from her nest
Down to the curlew herd!
Ho, hullaballoing clan
Agape, with woe
In your beaks, on the gabbing capes!
Heigh, on horseback hill, jack
Whisking hare! who
Hears, there, this fox light, my flood ship's
Clangour as I hew and smite

(A clash of anvils for my
Hubbub and fiddle, this tune
On a tongued puffball)
But animals thick as thieves
On God's rough tumbling grounds
(Hail to His beasthood!).
Beasts who sleep good and thin,
Hist, in hogsback woods! The haystacked
Hollow farms in a throng
Of waters cluck and cling,
And barnroofs cockcrow war!
O kingdom of neighbours, finned
Felled and quilled, flash to my patch
Work ark and the moonshine
Drinking Noah of the bay,
With pelt, and scale, and fleece:
Only the drowned deep bells
Of sheep and churches noise
Poor peace as the sun sets
And dark shoals every holy field.
We will ride out alone, and then,
Under the stars of Wales,
Cry, Multitudes of arks! Across
The water lidded lands,
Manned with their loves they'll move,
Like wooden islands, hill to hill.
Huloo, my prowed dove with a flute!
Ahoy, old, sea-legged fox,
Tom tit and Dai mouse!
My ark sings in the sun
At God speeded summer's end
And the flood flowers now.

ESPECIALLY WHEN THE OCTOBER WIND

Especially when the October wind
With frosty fingers punishes my hair,
Caught by the crabbing sun I walk on fire
And cast a shadow crab upon the land,
By the sea's side, hearing the noise of birds,
Hearing the raven cough in winter sticks,
My busy heart who shudders as she talks
Sheds the syllabic blood and drains her words.

Shut, too, in a tower of words, I mark
On the horizon walking like the trees
The wordy shapes of women, and the rows
Of the star-gestured children in the park.
Some let me make you of the vowelled beeches,
Some of the oaken voices, from the roots
Of many a thorny shire tell you notes,
Some let me make you of the water's speeches.

Behind a pot of ferns the wagging clock
Tells me the hour's word, the neural meaning
Flies on the shafted disk, declaims the morning
And tells the windy weather in the cock.
Some let me make you of the meadow's signs;
The signal grass that tells me all I know
Breaks with the wormy winter through the eye.
Some let me tell you of the raven's sins.

Especially when the October wind
(Some let me make you of autumnal spells,
The spider-tongued, and the loud hill of Wales)
With fists of turnips punishes the land,
Some let me make you of the heartless words.
The heart is drained that, spelling in the scurry
Of chemic blood, warned of the coming fury.
By the sea's side hear the dark-vowelled birds.

LIGHT BREAKS WHERE NO SUN SHINES

Light breaks where no sun shines;
Where no sea runs, the waters of the heart
Push in their tides;
And, broken ghosts with glow-worms in their heads,
The things of light
File through the flesh where no flesh decks the bones.

A candle in the thighs
Warms youth and seed and burns the seeds of age;
Where no seed stirs,
The fruit of man unwrinkles in the stars,
Bright as a fig;
Where no wax is, the candle shows its hairs.

Dawn breaks behind the eyes;
From poles of skull and toe the windy blood
Slides like a sea;
Nor fenced, nor staked, the gushers of the sky
Spout to the rod
Divining in a smile the oil of tears.

Night in the sockets rounds,
Like some pitch moon, the limit of the globes;
Day lights the bone;
Where no cold is, the skinning gales unpin
The winter's robes;
The film of spring is hanging from the lids.

Light breaks on secret lots,
On tips of thought where thoughts smell in the rain;
When logics die,
The secret of the soil grows through the eye,
And blood jumps in the sun;
Above the waste allotments the dawn halts.

IF I WERE TICKLED BY THE RUB OF LOVE

If I were tickled by the rub of love,
A rooking girl who stole me for her side,
Broke through her straws, breaking my bandaged string,
If the red tickle as the cattle calve
Still set to scratch a laughter from my lung,
I would not fear the apple nor the flood
Nor the bad blood of spring.

Shall it be male or female? say the cells,
And drop the plum like fire from the flesh.
If I were tickled by the hatching hair,
The winging bone that sprouted in the heels,
The itch of man upon the baby's thigh,
I would not fear the gallows nor the axe
Nor the crossed sticks of war.

Shall it be male or female? say the fingers
That chalk the walls with green girls and their men.
I would not fear the muscling-in of love
If I were tickled by the urchin hungers
Rehearsing heat upon a raw-edged nerve.
I would not fear the devil in the loin
Nor the outspoken grave.

If I were tickled by the lovers' rub
That wipes away not crow's-foot nor the lock
Of sick old manhood on the fallen jaws,
Time and the crabs and the sweethearting crib
Would leave me cold as butter for the flies,
The sea of scums could drown me as it broke
Dead on the sweethearts' toes.

This world is half the devil's and my own,
Daft with the drug that's smoking in a girl
And curling round the bud that forks her eye.
An old man's shank one-marrowed with my bone,

And all the herrings smelling in the sea,
I sit and watch the worm beneath my nail
Wearing the quick away.

And that's the rub, the only rub that tickles.
The knobbly ape that swings along his sex
From damp love-darkness and the nurse's twist
Can never raise the midnight of a chuckle,
Nor when he finds a beauty in the breast
Of lover, mother, lovers, or his six
Feet in the rubbing dust.

And what's the rub? Death's feather on the nerve?
Your mouth, my love, the thistle in the kiss?
My Jack of Christ born thorny on the tree?
The words of death are dryer than his stiff,
My wordy wounds are printed with your hair.
I would be tickled by the rub that is:
Man be my metaphor.

HOLD HARD, THESE ANCIENT MINUTES IN THE CUCKOO'S MONTH

Hold hard, these ancient minutes in the cuckoo's month,
Under the lank, fourth folly on Glamorgan's hill,
As the green blooms ride upward, to the drive of time;
Time, in a folly's rider, like a county man
Over the vault of ridings with his hound at heel,
Drives forth my men, my children, from the hanging south.

Country, your sport is summer, and December's pools
By crane and water-tower by the seedy trees
Lie this fifth month unskated, and the birds have flown;
Hold hard, my country children in the world of tales,
The greenwood dying as the deer fall in their tracks,
This first and steepled season, to the summer's game.

And now the horns of England, in the sound of shape,
Summon your snowy horsemen, and the four-stringed hill,
Over the sea-gut loudening, sets a rock alive;
Hurdles and guns and railings, as the boulders heave,
Crack like a spring in a vice, bone breaking April,
Spill the lank folly's hunter and the hard-held hope.

Down fall four padding weathers on the scarlet lands,
Stalking my children's faces with a tail of blood,
Time, in a rider rising, from the harnessed valley;
Hold hard, my county darlings, for a hawk descends,
Golden Glamorgan straightens, to the falling birds.
Your sport is summer as the spring runs angrily.

ALTARWISE BY OWL-LIGHT

I

Altarwise by owl-light in the half-way house
The gentleman lay graveward with his furies;
Abaddon in the hangnail cracked from Adam,
And, from his fork, a dog among the fairies,
The atlas-eater with a jaw for news,
Bit out the mandrake with to-morrow's scream.
Then, penny-eyed, that gentleman of wounds,
Old cock from nowheres and the heaven's egg,
With bones unbuttoned to the half-way winds,
Hatched from the windy salvage on one leg,
Scraped at my cradle in a walking word
That night of time under the Christward shelter:
I am the long world's gentleman, he said,
And share my bed with Capricorn and Cancer.

II

Death is all metaphors, shape in one history;
The child that sucketh long is shooting up,
The planet-ducted pelican of circles
Weans on an artery the gender's strip;

Child of the short spark in a shapeless country
Soon sets alight a long stick from the cradle;
The horizontal cross-bones of Abaddon,
You by the cavern over the black stairs,
Rung bone and blade, the verticals of Adam,
And, manned by midnight, Jacob to the stars.
Hairs of your head, then said the hollow agent,
Are but the roots of nettles and of feathers
Over these groundworks thrusting through a pavement
And hemlock-headed in the wood of weathers.

III

First there was the lamb on knocking knees
And three dead seasons on a climbing grave
That Adam's wether in the flock of horns,
Butt of the tree-tailed worm that mounted Eve,
Horned down with skullfoot and the skull of toes
On thunderous pavements in the garden time;
Rip of the vaults, I took my marrow-ladle
Out of the wrinkled undertaker's van,
And, Rip Van Winkle from a timeless cradle,
Dipped me breast-deep in the descended bone;
The black ram, shuffling of the year, old winter,
Alone alive among his mutton fold,
We rung our weathering changes on the ladder,
Said the antipodes, and twice spring chimed.

IV

What is the metre of the dictionary?
The size of genesis? the short spark's gender?
Shade without shape? the shape of Pharaoh's echo?
(My shape of age nagging the wounded whisper.)
Which sixth of wind blew out the burning gentry?
(Questions are hunchbacks to the poker marrow.)
What of a bamboo man among your acres?
Corset the boneyards for a crooked boy?
Button your bodice on a hump of splinters,
My camel's eyes will needle through the shroud.

Love's reflection of the mushroom features,
Stills snapped by night in the bread-sided field,
Once close-up smiling in the wall of pictures,
Arc-lamped thrown back upon the cutting flood.

v

And from the windy West came two-gunned Gabriel,
From Jesu's sleeve trumped up the king of spots,
The sheath-decked jacks, queen with a shuffled heart;
Said the fake gentleman in suit of spades,
Black-tongued and tipsy from salvation's bottle.
Rose my Byzantine Adam in the night.
For loss of blood I fell on Ishmael's plain,
Under the milky mushrooms slew my hunger,
A climbing sea from Asia had me down
And Jonah's Moby snatched me by the hair,
Cross-stroked salt Adam to the frozen angel
Pin-legged on pole-hills with a black medusa
By waste seas where the white bear quoted Virgil
And sirens singing from our lady's sea-straw.

vi

Cartoon of slashes on the tide-traced crater,
He in a book of water tallow-eyed
By lava's light split through the oyster vowels
And burned sea silence on a wick of words.
Pluck, cock, my sea eye, said medusa's scripture,
Lop, love, my fork tongue, said the pin-hilled nettle;
And love plucked out the stinging siren's eye,
Old cock from nowheres lopped the minstrel tongue
Till tallow I blew from the wax's tower
The fats of midnight when the salt was singing;
Adam, time's joker, on a witch of cardboard
Spelt out the seven seas, an evil index,
The bagpipe-breasted ladies in the deadweed
Blew out the blood gauze through the wound of manwax.

VII

Now stamp the Lord's Prayer on a grain of rice,
A Bible-leaved of all the written woods
Strip to this tree: a rocking alphabet,
Genesis in the root, the scarecrow word,
And one light's language in the book of trees.
Doom on deniers at the wind-turned statement.
Time's tune my ladies with the teats of music,
The scaled sea-sawers, fix in a naked sponge
Who sucks the bell-voiced Adam out of magic,
Time, milk, and magic, from the world beginning.
Time is the tune my ladies lend their heartbreak,
From bald pavilions and the house of bread
Time tracks the sound of shape on man and cloud,
On rose and icicle the ringing handprint.

VIII

This was the crucifixion on the mountain,
Time's nerve in vinegar, the gallow grave
As tarred with blood as the bright thorns I wept;
The world's my wound, God's Mary in her grief,
Bent like three trees and bird-papped through her shift,
With pins for teardrops is the long wound's woman.
This was the sky, Jack Christ, each minstrel angle
Drove in the heaven-driven of the nails
Till the three-coloured rainbow from my nipples
From pole to pole leapt round the snail-waked world.
I by the tree of thieves, all glory's sawbones,
Unsex the skeleton this mountain minute,
And by this blowclock witness of the sun
Suffer the heaven's children through my heartbeat.

IX

From the oracular archives and the parchment,
Prophets and fibre kings in oil and letter,
The lamped calligrapher, the queen in splints,
Buckle to lint and cloth their natron footsteps.

Draw on the glove of prints, dead Cairo's henna
Pour like a halo on the caps and serpents.
This was the resurrection in the desert,
Death from a bandage, rants the mask of scholars
Gold on such features, and the linen spirit
Weds my long gentleman to dusts and furies;
With priest and pharaoh bed my gentle wound,
World in the sand, on the triangle landscape,
With stones of odyssey for ash and garland
And rivers of the dead around my neck.

x

Let the tale's sailor from a Christian voyage
Atlaswise hold half-way off the dummy bay
Time's ship-racked gospel on the globe I balance:
So shall winged harbours through the rockbirds' eyes
Spot the blown word, and on the seas I image
December's thorn screwed in a brow of holly.
Let the first Peter from a rainbow's quayrail
Ask the tall fish swept from the bible east,
What rhubarb man peeled in her foam-blue channel
Has sown a flying garden round that sea-ghost?
Green as beginning, let the garden diving
Soar, with its two bark towers, to that Day
When the worm builds with the gold straws of venom
My nest of mercies in the rude, red tree.

AFTER THE FUNERAL

(In memory of Ann Jones)

After the funeral, mule praises, brays,
Windshake of sailshaped ears, muffle-toed tap
Tap happily of one peg in the thick
Grave's foot, blinds down the lids, the teeth in black,
The spittled eyes, the salt ponds in the sleeves,
Morning smack of the spade that wakes up sleep,
Shakes a desolate boy who slits his throat

In the dark of the coffin and sheds dry leaves,
That breaks one bone to light with a judgment clout,
After the feast of tear-stuffed time and thistles
In a room with a stuffed fox and a stale fern,
I stand, for this memorial's sake, alone
In the snivelling hours with dead, humped Ann
Whose hooded, fountain heart once fell in puddles
Round the parched worlds of Wales and drowned each sun
(Though this for her is a monstrous image blindly
Magnified out of praise; her death was a still drop;
She would not have me sinking in the holy
Flood of her heart's fame; she would lie dumb and deep
And need no druid of her broken body).
But I, Ann's bard on a raised hearth, call all
The seas to service that her wood-tongued virtue
Babble like a bellbuoy over the hymning heads,
Bow down the walls of the ferned and foxy woods
That her love sing and swing through a brown chapel,
Bless her bent spirit with four, crossing birds.
Her flesh was meek as milk, but this skyward statue
With the wild breast and blessed and giant skull
Is carved from her in a room with a wet window
In a fiercely mourning house in a crooked year.
I know her scrubbed and sour humble hands
Lie with religion in their cramp, her threadbare
Whisper in a damp word, her wits drilled hollow,
Her fist of a face died clenched on a round pain;
And sculptured Ann is seventy years of stone.
These cloud-sopped, marble hands, this monumental
Argument of the hewn voice, gesture and psalm,
Storm me forever over her grave until
The stuffed lung of the fox twitch and cry Love
And the strutting fern lay seeds on the black sill.

A REFUSAL TO MOURN THE DEATH, BY FIRE, OF A CHILD IN LONDON

Never until the mankind making
Bird beast and flower
Fathering and all humbling darkness
Tells with silence the last light breaking
And the still hour
Is come of the sea tumbling in harness

And I must enter again the round
Zion of the water bead
And the synagogue of the ear of corn
Shall I let pray the shadow of a sound
Or sow my salt seed
In the least valley of sackcloth to mourn

The majesty and burning of the child's death.
I shall not murder
The mankind of her going with a grave truth
Nor blaspheme down the stations of the breath
With any further
Elegy of innocence and youth.

Deep with the first dead lies London's daughter,
Robed in the long friends,
The grains beyond age, the dark veins of her mother,
Secret by the unmourning water
Of the riding Thames.
After the first death, there is no other.

POEM IN OCTOBER

It was my thirtieth year to heaven
Woke to my hearing from harbour and neighbour wood
And the mussel pooled and the heron
Priested shore

The morning beckon
With water praying and call of seagull and rook
And the knock of sailing boats on the net webbed wall
    Myself to set foot
      That second
In the still sleeping town and set forth.

My birthday began with the water-
Birds and the birds of the winged trees flying my name
    Above the farms and the white horses
      And I rose
      In rainy autumn
And walked abroad in a shower of all my days.
High tide and the heron dived when I took the road
    Over the border
      And the gates
Of the town closed as the town awoke.

A springful of larks in a rolling
Cloud and the roadside bushes brimming with whistling
    Blackbirds and the sun of October
      Summery
    On the hill's shoulder,
Here were fond climates and sweet singers suddenly
Come in the morning where I wandered and listened
    To the rain wringing
      Wind blow cold
In the wood faraway under me.

Pale rain over the dwindling harbour
And over the sea wet church the size of a snail
    With its horns through mist and the castle
      Brown as owls
      But all the gardens
Of spring and summer were blooming in the tall tales
Beyond the border and under the lark full cloud.
    There could I marvel

My birthday
Away but the weather turned around.

It turned away from the blithe country
And down the other air and the blue altered sky
Streamed again a wonder of summer
With apples
Pears and red currants
And I saw in the turning so clearly a child's
Forgotten mornings when he walked with his mother
Through the parables
Of sun light
And the legends of the green chapels

And the twice told fields of infancy
That his tears burned my cheeks and his heart moved in mine
These were the woods the river and sea
Where a boy
In the listening
Summertime of the dead whispered the truth of his joy
To the trees and the stones and the fish in the tide.
And the mystery
Sang alive
Still in the water and singingbirds.

And there could I marvel my birthday
Away but the weather turned around. And the true
Joy of the long dead child sang burning
In the sun.
It was my thirtieth
Year to heaven stood there then in the summer noon
Though the town below lay leaved with October blood.
O may my heart's truth
Still be sung
On this high hill in a year's turning.

FERN HILL

Now as I was young and easy under the apple boughs
About the lilting house and happy as the grass was green,
      The night above the dingle starry,
        Time let me hail and climb
      Golden in the heydays of his eyes,
And honoured among wagons I was prince of the apple towns
And once below a time I lordly had the trees and leaves
        Trail with daisies and barley
      Down the rivers of the windfall light.

And as I was green and carefree, famous among the barns
About the happy yard and singing as the farm was home,
      In the sun that is young once only,
        Time let me play and be
      Golden in the mercy of his means,
And green and golden I was huntsman and herdsman, the
    calves
Sang to my horn, the foxes on the hills barked clear and cold,
        And the sabbath rang slowly
      In the pebbles of the holy streams.

All the sun long it was running, it was lovely, the hay-
Fields high as the house, the tunes from the chimneys, it was
    air
        And playing, lovely and watery
        And fire green as grass.
        And nightly under the simple stars
As I rode to sleep the owls were bearing the farm away,
All the moon long I heard, blessed among stables, the nightjars
        Flying with the ricks, and the horses
      Flashing into the dark.

And then to awake, and the farm, like a wanderer white
With the dew, come back, the cock on his shoulder: it was all
      Shining, it was Adam and maiden,

The sky gathered again
And the sun grew round that very day.
So it must have been after the birth of the simple light
In the first, spinning place, the spellbound horses walking
    warm
        Out of the whinnying green stable
        On to the fields of praise.

And honoured among foxes and pheasants by the gay house
Under the new made clouds and happy as the heart was long,
        In the sun born over and over,
           I ran my heedless ways,
      My wishes raced through the house-high hay
And nothing I cared, at my sky blue trades, that time allows
In all his tuneful turning so few and such morning songs
        Before the children green and golden
          Follow him out of grace,

Nothing I cared, in the lamb white days, that time would take
    me
Up to the swallow thronged loft by the shadow of my hand,
        In the moon that is always rising,
          Nor that riding to sleep
      I should hear him fly with the high fields
And wake to the farm forever fled from the childless land.
Oh as I was young and easy in the mercy of his means,
        Time held me green and dying
    Though I sang in my chains like the sea.

POEM ON HIS BIRTHDAY

    In the mustardseed sun,
By full tilt river and switchback sea
    Where the cormorants scud,
In his house on stilts high among beaks
    And palavers of birds
This sandgrain day in the bent bay's grave

He celebrates and spurns
His driftwood thirty-fifth wind turned age;
  Herons spire and spear.

Under and round him go
Flounders, gulls, on their cold, dying trails,
  Doing what they are told,
Curlews aloud in the congered waves
  Work at their ways to death,
And the rhymer in the long tongued room,
  Who tolls his birthday bell,
Toils towards the ambush of his wounds;
  Herons, steeple stemmed, bless.

In the thistledown fall,
He sings towards anguish; finches fly
  In the claw tracks of hawks
On a seizing sky; small fishes glide
  Through wynds and shells of drowned
Ship towns to pastures of otters. He
* In his slant, racking house
And the hewn coils of his trade perceives
  Herons walk in their shroud,

The livelong river's robe
Of minnows wreathing around their prayer;
  And far at sea he knows,
Who slaves to his crouched, eternal end
  Under a serpent cloud,
Dolphins dive in their turnturtle dust,
  The rippled seals streak down
To kill and their own tide daubing blood
  Slides good in the sleek mouth.

In a cavernous, swung
Wave's silence, wept white angelus knells.
  Thirty-five bells sing struck
On skull and scar where his loves lie wrecked,

Steered by the falling stars.
And to-morrow weeps in a blind cage
  Terror will rage apart
Before chains break to a hammer flame
  And love unbolts the dark

And freely he goes lost
In the unknown, famous light of great
  And fabulous, dear God.
Dark is a way and light is a place,
  Heaven that never was
Nor will be ever is always true,
  And, in that brambled void,
Plenty as blackberries in the woods
  The dead grow for His joy.

There he might wander bare
With the spirits of the horseshoe bay
  Or the stars' seashore dead,
Marrow of eagles, the roots of whales
  And wishbones of wild geese,
With blessed, unborn God and His Ghost,
  And every soul His priest,
Gulled and chanter in young Heaven's fold
  Be at cloud quaking peace,

But dark is a long way.
He, on the earth of the night, alone
  With all the living, prays,
Who knows the rocketing wind will blow
  The bones out of the hills,
And the scythed boulders bleed, and the last
  Rage shattered waters kick
Masts and fishes to the still quick stars,
  Faithlessly unto Him

Who is the light of old
And air shaped Heaven where souls grow wild

As horses in the foam:
Oh, let me midlife mourn by the shrined
And druid herons' vows
The voyage to ruin I must run,
Dawn ships clouted aground,
Yet, though I cry with tumbledown tongue,
Count my blessings aloud:

Four elements and five
Senses, and man a spirit in love
Tangling through this spun slime
To his nimbus bell cool kingdom come
And the lost, moonshine domes,
And the sea that hides his secret selves
Deep in its black, base bones,
Lulling of spheres in the seashell flesh,
And this last blessing most,

That the closer I move
To death, one man through his sundered hulks,
The louder the sun blooms
And the tusked, ramshackling sea exults;
And every wave of the way
And gale I tackle, the whole world then,
With more triumphant faith
Than ever was since the world was said,
Spins its morning of praise,

I hear the bouncing hills
Grow larked and greener at berry brown
Fall and the dew larks sing
Taller this thunderclap spring, and how
More spanned with angels ride
The mansouled fiery islands! Oh,
Holier then their eyes,
And my shining men no more alone
As I sail out to die.

DO NOT GO GENTLE INTO THAT GOOD NIGHT

Do not go gentle into that good night,
Old age should burn and rave at close of day;
Rage, rage against the dying of the light.

Though wise men at their end know dark is right,
Because their words had forked no lightning they
Do not go gentle into that good night.

Good men, the last wave by, crying how bright
Their frail deeds might have danced in a green bay,
Rage, rage against the dying of the light.

Wild men who caught and sang the sun in flight,
And learn, too late, they grieved it on its way,
Do not go gentle into that good night.

Grave men, near death, who see with blinding sight
Blind eyes could blaze like meteors and be gay,
Rage, rage against the dying of the light.

And you, my father, there on the sad height,
Curse, bless, me now with your fierce tears, I pray.
Do not go gentle into that good night.
Rage, rage against the dying of the light.

LAMENT

When I was a windy boy and a bit
And the black spit of the chapel fold,
(Sighed the old ram rod, dying of women),
I tiptoed shy in the gooseberry wood,
The rude owl cried like a telltale tit,
I skipped in a blush as the big girls rolled
Ninepin down on the donkey's common,
And on seesaw sunday nights I wooed

Whoever I would with my wicked eyes,
The whole of the moon I could love and leave
All the green leaved little weddings' wives
In the coal black bush and let them grieve.

When I was a gusty man and a half
And the black beast of the beetles' pews,
(Sighed the old ram rod, dying of bitches),
Not a boy and a bit in the wick-
Dipping moon and drunk as a new dropped calf,
I whistled all night in the twisted flues,
Midwives grew in the midnight ditches,
And the sizzling beds of the town cried, Quick!—
Whenever I dove in a breast high shoal,
Wherever I ramped in the clover quilts,
Whatsoever I did in the coal-
Black night, I left my quivering prints.

When I was a man you could call a man
And the black cross of the holy house,
(Sighed the old ram rod, dying of welcome),
Brandy and ripe in my bright, bass prime,
No springtailed tom in the red hot town
With every simmering woman his mouse
But a hillocky bull in the swelter
Of summer come in his great good time
To the sultry, biding herds, I said,
Oh, time enough when the blood creeps cold,
And I lie down but to sleep in bed,
For my sulking, skulking, coal black soul!

When I was a half of the man I was
And serve me right as the preachers warn,
(Sighed the old ram rod, dying of downfall),
No flailing calf or cat in a flame
Or hickory bull in milky grass
But a black sheep with a crumpled horn,
At last the soul from its foul mousehole

Slunk pouting out when the limp time came;
And I gave my soul a blind, slashed eye,
Gristle and rind, and a roarers' life,
And I shoved it into the coal black sky
To find a woman's soul for a wife.

Now I am a man no more no more
And a black reward for a roaring life,
(Sighed the old ram rod, dying of strangers),
Tidy and cursed in my dove cooed room
I lie down thin and hear the good bells jaw—
For, oh, my soul found a sunday wife
In the coal black sky and she bore angels!
Harpies around me out of her womb!
Chastity prays for me, piety sings,
Innocence sweetens my last black breath,
Modesty hides my thighs in her wings,
And all the deadly virtues plague my death!

A WINTER'S TALE

It is a winter's tale
That the snow blind twilight ferries over the lakes
And floating fields from the farm in the cup of the vales,
Gliding windless through the hand folded flakes,
The pale breath of cattle at the stealthy sail,

And the stars falling cold,
And the smell of hay in the snow, and the far owl
Warning among the folds, and the frozen hold
Flocked with the sheep white smoke of the farm house cowl
In the river wended vales where the tale was told.

Once when the world turned old
On a star of faith pure as the drifting bread,
As the food and flames of the snow, a man unrolled

The scrolls of fire that burned in his heart and head,
Torn and alone in a farm house in a fold

       Of fields. And burning then
In his firelit island ringed by the winged snow
And the dung hills white as wool and the hen
Roosts sleeping chill till the flame of the cock crow
Combs through the mantled yards and the morning men

       Stumble out with their spades,
The cattle stirring, the mousing cat stepping shy,
The puffed birds hopping and hunting, the milkmaids
Gentle in their clogs over the fallen sky,
And all the woken farm at its white trades,

       He knelt, he wept, he prayed,
By the spit and the black pot in the log bright light
And the cup and the cut bread in the dancing shade,
In the muffled house, in the quick of night,
At the point of love, forsaken and afraid.

       He knelt on the cold stones,
He wept from the crest of grief, he prayed to the veiled sky
May his hunger go howling on bare white bones
Past the statues of the stables and the sky roofed sties
And the duck pond glass and the blinding byres alone

       Into the home of prayers
And fires where he should prowl down the cloud
Of his snow blind love and rush in the white lairs.
His naked need struck him howling and bowed
Though no sound flowed down the hand folded air

       But only the wind strung
Hunger of birds in the fields of the bread of water, tossed
In high corn and the harvest melting on their tongues.
And his nameless need bound him burning and lost
When cold as snow he should run the wended vales among

        The rivers mouthed in night,
And drown in the drifts of his need, and lie curled caught
In the always desiring centre of the white
Inhuman cradle and the bride bed forever sought
By the believer lost and the hurled outcast of light.

        Deliver him, he cried,
By losing him all in love, and cast his need
Alone and naked in the engulfing bride,
Never to flourish in the fields of the white seed
Or flower under the time dying flesh astride.

        Listen. The minstrels sing
In the departed villages. The nightingale,
Dust in the buried wood, flies on the grains of her wings
And spells on the winds of the dead his winter's tale.
The voice of the dust of water from the withered spring

        Is telling. The wizened
Stream with bells and baying water bounds. The dew rings
On the gristed leaves and the long gone glistening
Parish of snow. The carved mouths in the rock are wind
    swept strings.
Time sings through the intricately dead snow drop. Listen.

        It was a hand or sound
In the long ago land that glided the dark door wide
And there outside on the bread of the ground
A she bird rose and rayed like a burning bride.
A she bird dawned, and her breast with snow and scarlet
    downed.

        Look. And the dancers move
On the departed, snow bushed green, wanton in moon light
As a dust of pigeons. Exulting, the grave hooved
Horses, centaur dead, turn and tread the drenched white
Paddocks in the farms of birds. The dead oak walks for love.

The carved limbs in the rock
Leap, as to trumpets. Calligraphy of the old
Leaves is dancing. Lines of age on the stones weave in a
    flock.
And the harp shaped voice of the water's dust plucks in a fold
Of fields. For love, the long ago she bird rises. Look.

    And the wild wings were raised
Above her folded head, and the soft feathered voice
Was flying through the house as though the she bird praised
And all the elements of the slow fall rejoiced
That a man knelt alone in the cup of the vales,

    In the mantle and calm,
By the spit and the black pot in the log bright light.
And the sky of birds in the plumed voice charmed
Him up and he ran like a wind after the kindling flight
Past the blind barns and byres of the windless farm.

    In the poles of the year
When black birds died like priests in the cloaked hedge row
And over the cloth of counties the far hills rode near,
Under the one leaved trees ran a scarecrow of snow
And fast through the drifts of the thickets antlered like deer,

    Rags and prayers down the knee-
Deep hillocks and loud on the numbed lakes,
All night lost and long wading in the wake of the she-
Bird through the times and lands and tribes of the slow flakes.
Listen and look where she sails the goose plucked sea,

    The sky, the bird, the bride,
The cloud, the need, the planted stars, the joy beyond
The fields of seed and the time dying flesh astride,
The heavens, the heaven, the grave, the burning font.
In the far ago land the door of his death glided wide,

And the bird descended.
On a bread white hill over the cupped farm
And the lakes and floating fields and the river wended
Vales where he prayed to come to the last harm
And the home of prayers and fires, the tale ended.

The dancing perishes
On the white, no longer growing green, and, minstrel dead,
The singing breaks in the snow shoed villages of wishes
That once cut the figures of birds on the deep bread
And over the glazed lakes skated the shapes of fishes

Flying. The rite is shorn
Of nightingale and centaur dead horse. The springs wither
Back. Lines of age sleep on the stones till trumpeting dawn.
Exultation lies down. Time buries the spring weather
That belled and bounded with the fossil and the dew reborn.

For the bird lay bedded
In a choir of wings, as though she slept or died,
And the wings glided wide and he was hymned and wedded,
And through the thighs of the engulfing bride,
The woman breasted and the heaven headed

Bird, he was brought low,
Burning in the bride bed of love, in the whirl-
Pool at the wanting centre, in the folds
Of paradise, in the spun bud of the world.
And she rose with him flowering in her melting snow.

lawrence durrell

A BALLAD OF THE GOOD LORD NELSON

The Good Lord Nelson had a swollen gland,
Little of the scripture did he understand
Till a woman led him to the promised land
     Aboard the Victory, Victory O.

Adam and Evil and a bushel of figs
Meant nothing to Nelson who was keeping pigs,
Till a woman showed him the various rigs
     Aboard the Victory, Victory O.

His heart was softer than a new-laid egg,
Too poor for loving and ashamed to beg,
Till Nelson was taken by the Dancing Leg
     Aboard the Victory, Victory O.

Now he up and did up his little tin trunk
And he took to the ocean on his English junk,
Turning like the hour-glass in his lonely bunk
     Aboard the Victory, Victory O.

The Frenchman saw him a-coming there
With the one-piece eye and the valentine hair,
With the safety-pin sleeve and occupied air
     Aboard the Victory, Victory O.

Now you all remember the message he sent
As an answer to Hamilton's discontent—
There were questions asked about it in the Parliament
     Aboard the Victory, Victory O.

Now the blacker the berry, the thicker comes the juice.
Think of Good Lord Nelson and avoid self-abuse,
For the empty sleeve was no mere excuse
    Aboard the Victory, Victory O.

"England Expects" was the motto he gave
When he thought of little Emma out on Biscay's wave,
And remembered working on her like a galley-slave
    Aboard the Victory, Victory O.

The first Great Lord in our English land
To honor the Freudian command,
For a cast in the bush is worth two in the hand
    Aboard the Victory, Victory O.

Now the Frenchman shot him there as he stood
In the rage of battle in a silk-lined hood
And he heard the whistle of his own hot blood
    Aboard the Victory, Victory O.

Now stiff on a pillar with a phallic air
Nelson stylites in Trafalgar Square
Reminds the British what once they were
    Aboard the Victory, Victory O.

If they'd treat their women in the Nelson way
There'd be fewer frigid husbands every day
And many more heroes on the Bay of Biscay
    Aboard the Victory, Victory O.

charles causley

RECRUITING DRIVE

Under the willow the willow
  I heard the butcher-bird sing,
Come out you fine young fellow
  From under your mother's wing.
I'll show you the magic garden
  That hangs in the beamy air,
The way of the lynx and the angry Sphinx
  And the fun of the freezing fair.

Lie down lie down with my daughter
  Beneath the Arabian tree,
Gaze on your face in the water
  Forget the scribbling sea.
Your pillow the nine bright shiners
  Your bed the spilling sand,
But the terrible toy of my lily-white boy
  Is the gun in his innocent hand.

You must take off your clothes for the doctor
  And stand as straight as a pin,
His hand of stone on your white breast-bone
  Where the bullets all go in.
They'll dress you in lawn and linen
  And fill you with Plymouth gin,
O the devil may wear a rose in his hair
  I'll wear my fine doe-skin.

My mother weeps as I leave her
  But I tell her it won't be long,
The murderers wail in Wandsworth Gaol
  But I shoot a more popular song.
Down in the enemy country
  Under the enemy tree

There lies a lad whose heart has gone bad
   Waiting for me, for me.

He says I have no culture
   And that when I've stormed the pass
I shall fall on the farm with a smoking arm
   And ravish his bonny lass.
Under the willow the willow
   Death spreads her dripping wings
And caught in the snare of the bleeding air
   The butcher-bird sings, sings, sings.

COWBOY SONG

I come from Salem County
   Where the silver melons grow,
Where the wheat is sweet as an angel's feet
   And the zithering zephyrs blow.
I walk the blue bone-orchard
   In the apple-blossom snow,
Where the teasy bees take their honeyed ease
   And the marmalade moon hangs low.

My maw sleeps prone on the prairie
   In a boulder eiderdown,
Where the pickled stars in their little jam-jars
   Hang in a hoop to town.
I haven't seen paw since a Sunday
   In eighteen seventy-three
When he packed his snap in a bitty mess-trap
   And said he'd be home by tea.

Fled is my fancy sister
   All weeping like the willow,
And dead is the brother I loved like no other
   Who once did share my pillow.
I fly the florid water
   Where run the seven geese round,

O the townsfolk talk to see me walk
  Six inches off the ground.

Across the map of midnight
  I trawl the turning sky,
In my green glass the salt fleets pass
  The moon her fire-float by.
The girls go gay in the valley
  When the boys come down from the farm,
Don't run, my joy, from a poor cowboy,
  I won't do you no harm.

The bread of my twentieth birthday
  I buttered with the sun,
Though I sharpen my eyes with lovers' lies
  I'll never see twenty-one.
Light is my shirt with lilies,
  And lined with lead my hood,
On my face as I pass is a plate of brass,
  And my suit is made of wood.

edwin honig

IN QUEST TO HAVE NOT

Always when I see Italian marble
and great burnished mahogany sitting quiet
and ruthless in the indulgence of five centuries,
always I ask whose is the skull
set in jewels grinning there in shadow
who thrust all this from him feverishly
as the white dove flew nimbly from the mouth
and the feathers made great onslaughts
against the mind, loosening, flattening himself
to dive into the eye of the needle.

THE GAZABOS

I saw them dancing,
the gazabos, apes of joy, swains of
their pocket mirrors, to each a world:
   a dancing, a gallumphing, a guzzling
     of themselves.

They yapped, they cooed,
they flapped their feet and winked grimaces
into grins. They rapped their knuckles on
   their teeth and bled and licked
     the blood like honey.

Turning the corner
to my street, I spat on each
gazabo as they came. They loved it,
   they could barely keep
     from following.

I had to beat
them off with barbed wire switches
ripped from neighbors' fences on
   the way. I escaped
     only when

they paused to smear
their bodies with their trickly wounds,
streaming welted faces ogle-
   laughing in the mirrors
     sideways.

Why is it now,
safe in my lacquered room, cradled
in my black, spoon-shaped easy
   chair, the whitest sheet
     of paper on

        my knees, I cannot
write a word? I read their eyes,
I taste their wounds. Do they live
    because they simply
        cannot die?

        Friends, multi-
tudes, oh lifelong shadows: are
you my filth, my worn out longings,
    my poems that dog me
        till I die?

david gascoyne

SEPTEMBER SUN: 1947

Magnificent strong sun! in these last days
So prodigally generous of pristine light
That's wasted only by men's sight who will not see
And by self-darkened spirits from whose night
Can rise no longer orison or praise:

Let us consume in fire unfed like yours
And may the quickened gold within me come
To mintage in due season, and not be
Transmuted to no better end than dumb
And self-efficient usury. These days and years

May bring the sudden call to harvesting,
When if the fields Man labours only yield
Glitter and husks, then with an angrier sun may He
Who first with His gold seed the sightless field
Of Chaos planted, all our trash to cinders bring.

john thompson, jr.

A LOVE FOR PATSY

See the little maunderer
Stretch out on the grass!
His heart is burst asun-
     der
The pieces cry Alas.

Upright, fat pink pieces
Of fluffy cloud float over-
     head.
The little facets of his eyes
Split by salty tears, so tired

Of seeing pieces of the
     world,
Close, and rustling grass,
Caws of an old unpleasant
     bird
Are sounds that say Alas;

They float like notes in the
     funny paper,
Round notes with sharp little
     tails.
Oh I'm blue, the supine
     moper
Says, I'm trapped in the toils

Of Patsy's black black hair.
Her hair is like the cool dry
     night

That waves through the
     window-bar
Where a moody jailbird sits
     apart

Shuffling his broken heart.
     I'm sad
As I can be. Her black
Black hair can never be com-
     pared
To dull dichotomic

Trees or prickly grass, in-
     flated
Clouds, even a great
One draped on the sun. Over-
     rated
Senseless things to stare at,

One here one there they're
     strewn,
Impinging pieces left out of
The world. Her eyes are
     green!
Oh oh, he says, I die of love.

See the weeping little wretch
He rolls in a frenzy!
In all the world no two things
     match
But the green eyes of Patsy.

robert lowell

MR. EDWARDS AND THE SPIDER

I saw the spiders marching through the air,
Swimming from tree to tree that mildewed day
  In latter August when the hay
   Came creaking to the barn. But where
    The wind is westerly,
Where gnarled November makes the spiders fly
Into the apparitions of the sky,
They purpose nothing but their ease and die
Urgently beating east to sunrise and the sea;

What are we in the hands of the great God?
It was in vain you set up thorn and briar
  In battle array against the fire
   And treason crackling in your blood;
    For the wild thorns grow tame
And will do nothing to oppose the flame;
Your lacerations tell the losing game
You play against a sickness past your cure.
How will the hands be strong? How will the heart endure?

A very little thing, a little worm,
Or hourglass-blazoned spider, it is said,
  Can kill a tiger. Will the dead
   Hold up his mirror and affirm
    To the four winds the smell
And flash of his authority? It's well
If God who holds you to the pit of hell,
Much as one holds a spider, will destroy,
Baffle and dissipate your soul. As a small boy

On Windsor Marsh, I saw the spider die
When thrown into the bowels of fierce fire:
  There's no long struggle, no desire
   To get up on its feet and fly—

It stretches out its feet
And dies. This is the sinner's last retreat;
Yes, and no strength exerted on the heat
Then sinews the abolished will, when sick
And full of burning, it will whistle on a brick.

But who can plumb the sinking of that soul?
Josiah Hawley, picture yourself cast
   Into a brick-kiln where the blast
   Fans your quick vitals to a coal—
     If measured by a glass,
How long would it seem burning! Let there pass
A minute, ten, ten trillion; but the blaze
Is infinite, eternal: this is death,
To die and know it. This is the Black Widow, death.

THE DEATH OF THE SHERIFF

"forsitan et Priami fuerint quae fata, requiras?"
Noli Me Tangere

We park and stare. A full sky of the stars
Wheels from the pumpkin setting of the moon
And sparks the windows of the yellow farm
Where the red-flannelled madmen look through bars
At windmills thrashing snowflakes by an arm
Of that Atlantic. Soon
The undertaker who collects antiques
Will let his motor idle at the door
And set his pine-box on the parlor floor.
Our homicidal sheriff howled for weeks;
We kiss. The State had reasons: on the whole,
It acted out of kindness when it locked
Its servant in this place and had him watched
Until an ordered darkness left his soul
A *tabula rasa;* when the Angel knocked
The sheriff laid his notched
Revolver on the table for the guest.
Night draws us closer in its bearskin wrap

And our loved sightless smother feels the tap
Of the blind stars descending to the west
To lay the Devil in the pit our hands
Are draining like a windmill. Who'll atone
For the unsearchable quicksilver heart
Where spiders stare their eyes out at their own
Spitting and knotted likeness? We must start:
Our aunt, his mother, stands
Singing *O Rock of Ages,* as the light
Wanderers show a man with a white cane
Who comes to take the coffin in his wain,
The thirsty Dipper on the arc of night.

WHERE THE RAINBOW ENDS

I saw the sky descending, black and white,
Not blue, on Boston where the winters wore
The skulls to jack-o'-lanterns on the slates,
And Hunger's skin-and-bone retrievers tore
The chickadee and shrike. The thorn tree waits
Its victim and tonight
The worms will eat the deadwood to the foot
Of Ararat: the scythers, Time and Death,
Helmed locusts, move upon the tree of breath;
The wild ingrated olive and the root

Are withered, and a winter drifts to where
The Pepperpot, ironic rainbow, spans
Charles River and its scales of scorched-earth miles
I saw my city in the Scales, the pans
Of judgment rising and descending. Piles
Of dead leaves char the air—
And I am a red arrow on this graph
Of Revelations. Every dove is sold.
The Chapel's sharp-shinned eagle shifts its hold
On serpent-Time, the rainbow's epitaph.

In Boston serpents whistle at the cold.
The victim climbs the altar steps and sings:
"Hosannah to the lion, lamb, and beast
Who fans the furnace-face of IS with wings:
I breathe the ether of my marriage feast."
At the high altar, gold
And a fair cloth. I kneel and the wings beat
My cheek. What can the dove of Jesus give
You now but wisdom, exile? Stand and live,
The dove has brought an olive branch to eat.

THE DRUNKEN FISHERMAN

Wallowing in this bloody sty,
I cast for fish that pleased my eye
(Truly Jehovah's bow suspends
No pots of gold to weight its ends);
Only the blood-mouthed rainbow trout
Rose to my bait. They flopped about
My canvas creel until the moth
Corrupted its unstable cloth.

A calendar to tell the day;
A handkerchief to wave away
The gnats; a couch unstuffed with storm
Pouching a bottle in one arm;
A whiskey bottle full of worms;
And bedroom slacks: are these fit terms
To mete the worm whose molten rage
Boils in the belly of old age?

Once fishing was a rabbit's foot—
O wind blow cold, O wind blow hot,
Let suns stay in or suns step out:
Life danced a jig on the sperm-whale's spout—
The fisher's fluent and obscene
Catches kept his conscience clean.

Children, the raging memory drools
Over the glory of past pools.

Now the hot river, ebbing, hauls
Its bloody waters into holes;
A grain of sand inside my shoe
Mimics the moon that might undo
Man and Creation too; remorse
Stinking, has puddled up its source;
Here tantrums thrash to a whale's rage.
This is the pot-hole of old age.

Is there no way to cast my hook
Out of this dynamited brook?
The Fisher's sons must cast about
When shallow waters peter out.
I will catch Christ with a greased worm,
And when the Prince of Darkness stalks
My bloodstream to its Stygian term . . .
On water the Man-Fisher walks.

dunstan thompson

LARGO

For William Abrahams

Of those whom I have known, the few and fatal friends,
All were ambiguous, deceitful, not to trust:
But like attracts its like, no doubt; and mirrors must
Be faithful to the image that they see. Light bends
   Only the spectrum in the glass:
   Prime colors are the ones which pass
   The less distorted. Friendship ends
In hatred or in love, ambivalence of lust:
Either, like Hamlet, haunted, doting on the least
Reflection of remorse; or else, like Richard, lost

In vanity. The frozen hands
That hold the mirror make demands;
And flexing fingers clutch the vision in a vise.
Each one betrays himself: the ghostly glazer understands
    Why he must work in ice.

All friends are false but you are true: the paradox
Is perfect tense in present time, whose parallel
Extends to meeting point; where, more than friends, we fel
Together on the other side of love; where clocks
    And mirrors were reversed to show
    Ourselves as only we could know;
    Where all the doors had secret locks
With double keys; and where the sliding panel, well
Concealed, gave us our exit through the palace wall.
There we have come and gone: twin kings, who roam at wil
    Behind the court, behind the backs
    Of consort queens, behind the racks
On which their favorites lie who told them what to do.
For every cupid with a garland round the throne still lack
    The look I give to you.

The goddess who presided at our birth was first
Of those in fancy clothes fate made us hate to fight:
The Greeks with gifts, good looks, so clever, so polite,
Like lovers quick to charm, disarming, too well versed
    In violence to wear weapons while
    They take a city for a smile.
    By doomed ancestral voices cursed
To wander from the womb, their claws plucked out our sight
Who nighttime thinking we are followed down the street
By blind men like ourselves, turn round again, and wait,
    Only to hear the steps go past
    Us standing lonely there, at last
Aware how we have failed; are now the Trojan fool
For all the arty Hellenistic tarts in plaster cast:
    The ones who always rule.

We are alone with every sailor lost at sea
Whose drowning is repeated day by day. The sound
Of bells from buoys mourning sunken ships rings round
Us, warning away the launch that journeys you and me
   On last Cytherean trips in spring.
   There the rocks are where sirens sing
   Like nightingales of death. But we,
Hearing excitements, music for the ear, have bound
Our voyage to find its ending where the sterile sand
Spends pearls and coral on a skull. The sailing wind
   Is with us now and then: blows high
   As halcyon clouds across the sky:
Falls fast to doldrums while the moon is also young,
Untided, half to harvest whole. See how our sirens die
     Before their song is sung.

What we have always wanted, never had, the ease,
The fame of athletes, such happy heroes at a game,
Beloved by every likely lad, is not the same
As what we have: these measured methods how to please
   An indolent and doubtful boy,
   Who plays at darts, breaks for a toy
   The sometime valued heart. Why seize
The moment in the garden, on the stair, to blame
Our nameless Eros for his daring? Too little time
Is left for love. When we come back, what welcome home
   Will he award our wounded eyes?
   What uniform be his disguise
In dreams, when sleeping sentries always march away
Once more to war? Now is our novelty: we may surprise
     The faun at end of day.

Make no mistake, my soldier. Listen: bugle calls
Revoke your leisure like a leave, invade your peace
With orders on the run, and, loud as bombs, police
Your life for death. The poet's blood-brick tower falls:
   Even his vanity is gone,
   Which leaves the loser all alone.

Not private poems, but public brawls
Demand his drumbeat history, the pulse that must increas
Until his heart is ransomed from its jewel. Revise
Your verse. Consider what king's killer did to those
   Who wrote their way between the shells
   That last delusive time. Farewells
Are folly to our serpent queen. She will not sign
Discharge of conscience for a masterpiece, but, hissing, tell
    Failure in every line.

We are the mountaineers who perish on the slopes
Of heaven high and perfect Himalayan peak:
Exhausted by the cold, we can no longer speak
To one another—only signal by the ropes.
   Those best before us have, alas,
   Plunged through a gentian-blue crevasse:
   The snow-blind flaw. Their glacial hopes
Shine as a stream of desperate stars, icebound, and bleak,
That mock their nimbused glory from a frigid lake.
Where we stand now, they stood much farther: climbing lik
   Legendary guides. But traps
   Were waiting for their last collapse:
Inviting visions from the moon world air—misplace
A step to follow, dance to death. They fell, so we, perhap
   May do as well with grace.

Now noble guests depart for good, wearing our loss
Like flowers. O Damon, decked with asphodel, who move
Among the shadow dwellers. But he shall hear the hoove
Of unicorns at gallop, see them, coursing, toss
   Their fluted horns above the cool
   Unpoisoned waters in love's pool,
   And, kneeling, lay their heads across
A beatific virgin's breast. The day approves
His passage: sunlight on the secret river gives
Bright benediction to his boat. Elysian waves
   Bear him, the hero, far from us
   To join the gods. Illustrious!

No words may worship him. The laurel is not all
That withers at the roots, since we, lamenting him, are thus
  Autumnal for his fall.

Armed, say you? Armed, my lord. So, likewise, you and I,
Who with the butchered ghost must stalk the battlements,
Shall watch—cold-comfort guards—how lonely lie the tents
Where strangers sleep together just before they die.
  Look where their banners in the air
  Are half-staff hung. The cockcrow dare
  Of dawn is mourning in the sky.
Our thoughts like bayonets blood time. What precedents
Of passion shall we use to brave the coward? Once
Bombs are as roses, will he kiss the black-heart prince?
  Honor, more heavy than the sea,
  May overwhelm both you and me
To give no quarter choice at all: gay boys, whom war
Won janizary; youths, who flung away their shields. So we
  Are *mort à Singapore.*

Narcissus, doubled in the melting mirror, smiles
To see himself outfaced by tears, and, sorrowing, hands
His ace of love to harlequin of hearts, who stands
The distant edge of laughter. Time's joker still compiles
  Trick score of triumph, trumps the queen
  To play his knave of emeralds. Green
  Gamester reflects the water guiles
Of palming, reads the gambled cards, and then demands
Another pack to shuffle. But the glass partner bends
The fate five fingers round a saint's stigmata, wounds
  By dealing diamonds from his nails.
  No marveled metaphor avails
To vantage this beloved impersonator twin,
Whose coronet, crown crystal, qualifies a peer. My voice fails.
  In your name poems begin.

ruth herschberger

THE LUMBERYARD

We watched our love burn with the lumberyard,
Bats in their wheeling showed our crazéd sense,
We stood in fields where weeds with chiggers scrambled,
And stood the heat flush in our face, immense.

Softly the crowd acclaimed the devastation,
And we, we smiled to see the embers twist,
Tottering towers and poles with flashing wires.
We shifted feet when shifting structures kissed.

Up in the sky the stars were red sparks shuttling,
Planes with a scouter's appetite hung by.
And at our backs the Negro huts were lit
With yellow mist, a ghostly gayety.

Sound above all: the cracking and the crocked,
As bones that, whetted by the warmer flames,
Edged into death, until the crimson glow
Vanquished the knotted amber boards, the names.

All banished, all decided, all cast in;
Far back beyond, the trees made silver white
By steaming flames, rose as cold piles of cloud
To cool this mirror of the blazing night.

And we beheld, we watched, as drunk as all,
And gladdened when the bursting peaked and sprung,
Rejoiced to see the threat of fire win,
And sang to see the worthy timbers wrung.

We watched our love burn with the lumberyard,
Magnificent the sight, the sin, the shame,
The vice profusely lavished; wheeled the bats
Silent as we, but crazed, crazed as the flame.

alex comfort

THE ATOLL IN THE MIND

Out of what calms and pools the cool shell grows
dumb teeth under clear waters, where no currents
fracture the coral's porous horn

Grows up the mind's stone tree, the honeycomb,
the plump brain coral breaking the pool's mirror,
the ebony antler, the cold sugared fan.

All these strange trees stand upward through the water,
the mind's grey candied points tend to the surface,
the greater part is out of sight below.

But when on the island's whaleback spring green blades
new land over water wavers, birds bring seeds
and tides plant slender trunks by the lagoon

I find the image of the mind's two trees, cast downward,
one tilting leaves to catch the sun's bright pennies,
one dark as water, rooted among the bones.

richard wilbur

JUGGLER

A ball will bounce, but less and less. It's not
A light-hearted thing, resents its own resilience.
Falling is what it loves, and the earth falls
So in our hearts from brilliance,
Settles and is forgot.
It takes a skyblue juggler with five red balls

To shake our gravity up. Whee, in the air
The balls roll round, wheel on his wheeling hands,
Learning the ways of lightness, alter to spheres

Grazing his finger ends,
Cling to their courses there,
Swinging a small heaven about his ears.

But a heaven is easier made of nothing at all
Than the earth regained, and still and sole within
The spin of worlds, with a gesture sure and noble
He reels that heaven in,
Landing it ball by ball,
And trades it all for a broom, a plate, a table.

[ ] back to juggler

Oh, on his toe the table is turning, the broom's
Balancing up on his nose, and the plate whirls
On the tip of the broom! Damn, what a show, we cry:
The boys stamp, and the girls   to
Shriek, and the drum booms   heaven
And all comes down, and he bows and says goodbye.

If the juggler is tired now, if the broom stands
In the dust again, if the table starts to drop
Through the daily dark again, and though the plate
Lies flat on the table top,
For him we batter our hands   we appreciate /) ✓ ✓
Who has won for once over the world's weight.   worth

BEASTS

Beasts in their major freedom
Slumber in peace tonight. The gull on his ledge
Dreams in the guts of himself the moon-plucked waves below,
And the sunfish leans on a stone, slept
By the lyric water;

In which the spotless feet
Of deer make dulcet splashes, and to which
The ripped mouse, safe in the owl's talon, cries

Concordance. Here there is no such harm
    And no such darkness

    As the selfsame moon observes
Where, warped in window-glass, it sponsors now
The werewolf's painful change. Turning his head away
    On the sweaty bolster, he tries to remember
        The mood of manhood,

    But lies at last, as always,
Letting it happen, the fierce fur soft to his face,
Hearing with sharper ears the wind's exciting minors,
    The leaves' panic, and the degradation
        Of the heavy streams.

    Meantime, at high windows
Far from thicket and pad-fall, suitors of excellence
Sigh and turn from their work to construe again the painful
    Beauty of heaven, the lucid moon
        And the risen hunter,

[handwritten annotations: → constellation → interfering w/ nature → once a beast, rose /. hunter]

    Making such dreams for men
As told will break their hearts as always, bringing
Monsters into the city, crows on the public statues,
    Navies fed to the fish in the dark
        Unbridled waters.

○

The idle dayseye, the laborious wheel,
The osprey's tours, the pointblank matin sun
Sanctified first the circle; thence for fun
Doctors deduced a shape, which some called real
(So all games spoil), a shape of spare appeal,
Cryptic and clean, and endlessly spinning unspun.

Now I go backward, filling by one and one
Circles with hickory spokes and rich soft shields
Of petalled dayseyes, with herehastening steel

Volleys of daylight, writhing white looks of sun;
And I toss circles skyward to be undone
By actual wings, for wanting this repeal
I should go whirling a thin Euclidean reel,
No hawk or hickory to true my run.

GRACE

"'The young lambs bound as to the tabor's sound.' They toss and toss; it is as if it were the earth that flung them, not themselves. It is the pitch of graceful agility when we think that."
G. M. HOPKINS, Notebooks

So active they seem passive, little sheep
Please, and Nijinsky's out-the-window leap
And marvelous midair pause please too
A taste for blithe brute reflex; flesh made word
Is grace's revenue.

One is tickled, again, by the dining-car waiter's absurd
Acrobacy—tipfingered tray like a wind-besting bird
Plumblines his swinging shoes, the sole things sure
In the shaken train; but this is all done for food,
Is habitude, if not pure

Hebetude. It is a graph of a theme that flings
The dancer kneeling on nothing into the wings,
And Nijinsky hadn't the words to make the laws
For learning to loiter in air; he "merely" said,
"I merely leap and pause."

Lambs are constrained to bound. Consider instead
The intricate neural grace in Hamlet's head;

A grace not barbarous implies a choice
Of courses, not in a lingo of leaps-in-air
But in such a waiting voice

As one would expect to hear in the talk of Flaubert.
Piety makes for awkwardness, and where
Balance is not urgent, what one utters
May be puzzled and perfect, and we respect
Some scholars' stutters.

Even fraction-of-a-second action is not wrecked
By a graceful still reserve. To be unchecked
Is needful then: choose, challenge, jump, poise, run. . . .
Nevertheless, the praiseful, graceful soldier
Shouldn't be fired by his gun.

A BLACK NOVEMBER TURKEY

Nine white chickens come
With haunchy walk and heads
Jabbing among the chips, the chaff, the stones
And the cornhusk-shreds,

And bit by bit infringe
A pond of dusty light,
Spectral in shadow until they bobbingly one
By one ignite.

Neither pale nor bright,
The turkey-cock parades
Through radiant squalors, darkly auspicious as
The ace of spades,

Himself his own cortège
And puffed with the pomp of death,
Rehearsing over and over with strangled râle
His latest breath.

The vast black body floats
Above the crossing knees
As a cloud over thrashed branches, a calm ship
        Over choppy seas,

Shuddering its fan and feathers
In fine soft clashes
With the cold sound that the wind makes, fondling
        Paper-ashes.

The pale-blue bony head
Set on its shepherd's-crook
Like a saint's death-mask, turns a vague, superb
        And timeless look

Upon these clocking hens
And the cocks that one by one,
Dawn after mortal dawn, with vulgar joy
        Acclaim the sun.

sidney keyes

THE ANTI-SYMBOLIST

If one could only be certain beyond all question
That nature revolves through a zodiac of symbols
Upon an axis of creative mind:
Then one might plan in expectation
Of enlightenment, a perfect revolution
Or at least repetition, and escape suspense.
But nothing seems related, incident or vision,
To any but an arbitrary thought:
The wind moving between the cypresses
Stirs only single leaf, stale wreath. To them
Fighting the roots and drowned beyond memory

Under the cypresses, there is no word for Wind,
And the wind never dies. The tall old woman
Eating her sandwiches on a pompous vault
And her dog who loves to play tag with tombstones,
Need never recur, yet link me with the drowned ones
Of earth, quite unforgettably.

We should not work that way. Anticipation
Is crooked thinking, for nature unobserved
Revolving never, remains its own reflection.
And time flows through us from its sources
Toward the unguessed waterfall, the desert
Of dry eternity; as old men in Greece
Saw dimly its current and our black Niagara.
Forward is not our business; but the higher
Reaches may at least be mapped
With some small boast of skill and application—
And enough science to arrive at morning
Without undue surprise or any fear
Before the estuary lashed with pain, the sharp
Lift of the bar, and feel the tide making westward.
Then only in that drowned man's paradise
Of Hy Brasil or currentless Sargasso,
May the dead and the wind and the old woman
And her dog and my over-curious mind
Meet neighbourly and mingle without question.

joseph bennett

TO ELIZA, DUCHESS OF DORSET

In the negro gardens negro birds
Plummet in the shadows, falling thirds.
Dorset in sable plumage comes.
A hawk! A raven in his tediums.

Daughter to that good Earl, once President
Of England's Council, and her Parliament,
Duchess, if that falling shadow strikes
And strikes no more, as Dorset softly likes,

And in your heart the spike its purple draws,
And on your coral neck the marble claws—
O Duchess feel the negro soil beneath
Your crushed mouth and your splintered teeth.

Eliza strangling on the lawn at Knole,
The flowers sinking toward the twilit Pole,
And walking, calling, Dorset now distends;
Dorset cock and cockatoo; and raven ends.

UPTOWN EXPRESS

A surfing party from the isle of task
    Drowned the leaden weight-marks of their eyes.
They did not come to swim, they came to bask,
    Filtering the unhappy sunlight from their skies.
    It was not their odor but their cries
Drove the warbling sappers from our shores.
    It was not the blackbirds but the flies
Attacked the bright circumference of their cores,
The wheels that run at large beneath the trembling railway
        floors.

Blind after blind the long-line subway flies,
    Timed to the writhing of its element.
Within, the public turns with calcined eyes,
    Spiralling at man's advértisement;
    Sign upon sign the itch incontinent
Spills at the holes in the eye of dazzling brain;
    So carrion shine in the gleam of excrement,
Lighting up the faces in a porcelain terrain,
And so condors drop upon a prey already slain.

Blind now a man, with stick's advértisement,
    Beats at the silence in the metal floor of cars.
Eyeless the blind, yet still incontinent,
    Forcing the doors, to cross these shifting bars,
    Shaking a cup that flame of mercy chars,
He seeks the milk and honey on these signs.
    No matter how the driving platform jars,
No matter where his requiem inclines,
He is the gray flamingo of these swift electric shrines.

Rage at the human flourishes in cars
    Where wrist to wrist the spirits breathe their last.
Rage burns, and turn of spirit chars.
    It is the crush of eagles standing fast.
    Wheel upon wheel the diving cars drive past.
O arks which bear the dense electric rays
    Staunching up the flow of human caste,
Your lamps have drenched the heads which stand ablaze,
Your galleries go plunging in the silt of flashing clays.

roy basler

EXODUS

Uranium cumulus mushrooms bursting sores
Upon empyrean lawns impressed Them there,
Beneath the wondrous tree; the poison spores
Of radiocirrus fungi spread fresh fare
For theoretic thought in triplicate.
In unison with single voice They spoke:
"Since Adam's day the sacrificial smoke
Has grown too lushy rank to tolerate;
Our primal verdict favoring industry
Took no account of this polluted air.
That notion of expanding space may be
The stretch of time to save Our triune neck;
Let's pick a spot of universe to spare,
Perhaps between the Great and Lesser Bear,
And out of here right quickly get the heck!"

daniel g. hoffman

THE SEALS IN PENOBSCOT BAY

hadn't heard of the atom bomb,
so I shouted a warning to them.

Our destroyer (on trial run) slid by
the rocks where they gamboled and played;

they must have misunderstood,
or perhaps not one of them heard

me over the engines and tides.
As I watched them over our wake

I saw their sleek skins in the sun
ripple, light-flecked, on the rock,

plunge, bubbling, into the brine,
and couple & laugh in the troughs

between the waves' whitecaps and froth.
Then the males clambered clumsily up

and lustily crowed like seacocks,
sure that their prowess held thrall

all the sharks, other seals, and seagulls.
And daintily flipped the females,

seawenches with musical tails;
each looked at the Atlantic as

though it were her looking-glass.
If my warning had ever been heard

it was sound none would now ever heed.
And I, while I watched those far seals

tasted honey that buzzed in my ears
and saw, out to windward, the sails

of an obsolete ship with banked oars
that swept like two combs through the spray

And I wished for a vacuum of wax
to ward away all those strange sounds,

yet I envied the sweet agony
of him who was tied to the mast,

when the boom, when the boom, when the boom
of guns punched dark holes in the sky

galway kinnell

TO CHRIST OUR LORD

The legs of the elk punctured the snow's crust
And wolves floated lightfooted on the land
Hunting Christmas elk living and frozen.
Indoors snow melted in a basin and a woman basted
A bird spread over coals by its wings and head.

Snow had sealed the windows; candles lit
The Christmas meal. The special grace chilled
The cooked bird, being long-winded and the room cold.
During the words a boy thought, is it fitting
To eat this creature killed on the wing?

For he had shot it himself, climbing out
Alone on snowshoes in the Christmas dawn,
The fallen snow swirling and the snowfall gone,

Heard its throat scream as the rifle shouted,
Watched it drop, and fished from the snow the dead.

He had not wanted to shoot. The sound
Of wings beating into the hushed morning
Had stirred his love, and the things
In his gloves froze, and he wondered,
Even famishing, could he fire? Then he fired.

Now the grace praised his wicked act. At its end
The bird on the plate
Stared at his stricken appetite.
There had been nothing to do but surrender,
To kill and to eat; he ate as he had killed, with wonder.

At night on snowshoes on the drifting field
He wondered again, for whom had love stirred?
The stars glittered on the snow and nothing answered.
Then the Swan spread her wings, cross of the cold north,
The pattern and mirror of the acts of earth.

richard selig

FROM THE SIXTEENTH FLOOR

Pardoning this borough for its evil,
I look past the tops of buildings, to where
The sky is. Remembering that man's malice,
This man's fate; the former's cunning,
The latter's jeopardy—seeing the sky,
Placid in spite of soot and heartache,
I am reminded to pray. Redemption,
Like our janitor, comes as we go home:
A stooped man turning out the lights.

howard nemerov

THE GOOSE FISH

On the long shore, lit by the moon
To show them properly alone,
Two lovers suddenly embraced
So that their shadows were as one.
The ordinary night was graced
For them by the swift tide of blood
That silently they took at flood,
And for a little time they prized
    Themselves emparadised.

Then, as if shaken by stage-fright
Beneath the hard moon's bony light,
They stood together on the sand
Embarrassed in each other's sight
But still conspiring hand in hand,
Until they saw, there underfoot,
As though the world had found them out,
The goose fish turning up, though dead,
    His hugely grinning head.

There in the china light he lay,
Most ancient and corrupt and grey.
They hesitated at his smile,
Wondering what it seemed to say
To lovers who a little while
Before had thought to understand,
By violence upon the sand,
The only way that could be known
    To make a world their own.

It was a wide and moony grin
Together peaceful and obscene;
They knew not what he would express,
So finished a comedian
He might mean failure or success,

But took it for an emblem of
Their sudden, new and guilty love
To be observed by, when they kissed,
    That rigid optimist.

So he became their patriarch,
Dreadfully mild in the half-dark.
His throat that the sand seemed to choke,
His picket teeth, these left their mark
But never did explain the joke
That so amused him, lying there
While the moon went down to disappear
Along the still and tilted track
    That bears the zodiac.

peter kane dufault

NOTES ON A GIRL

The half-moons of her calves eclipse
each other prettily as she walks,
and something photometric trips
the triggers of her heels whose clacks

acclaim each sweet occlusion. She
is vain, is vain. So much the worse
for us: Her swansthroat under-knee,
her thigh, torso—an 'ipse-verse'—

are hidden, but are all her thought,
as Carmelites, they say, in prayers
hold the far earth's meridians taut.
Her thought is vain, but so is theirs.

God knows we're doomed from that first peek
that makes us hunt the secret place,
Who wears such stars around His neck
and will not let us see His face.

anthony hecht

SAMUEL SEWALL

Samuel Sewall, in a world of wigs,
Flouted opinion in his personal hair;
For foppery he gave not any figs,
But in his right and honor took the air.

Thus in his naked style, though well attired,
He went forth in the city, or paid court
To Madam Winthrop, whom he much admired,
Most godly, but yet liberal with the port.

And all the town admired for two full years
His excellent address, his gifts of fruit,
Her gracious ways and delicate white ears,
And held the course of nature absolute.

But yet she bade him suffer a peruke,
"That One be not distinguished from the All";
Delivered of herself this stern rebuke
Framed in the resonant language of St. Paul.

"Madam," he answered her, "I have a Friend
Furnishes me with hair out of His strength,
And He requires only I attend
Unto His charity and to its length."

And all the town was witness to his trust:
On Monday he walked out with the Widow Gibbs,
A pious lady of charm and notable bust,
Whose heart beat tolerably beneath her ribs.

On Saturday he wrote proposing marriage,
And closed, imploring that she be not cruel,
"Your favorable answer will oblige,
Madam, your humble servant, Samuel Sewall."

philip larkin

NEXT, PLEASE

Always too eager for the future, we
Pick up bad habits of expectancy.
Something is always approaching; every day
Till then we say,

Watching from a bluff the tiny, clear
Sparkling armada of promises draw near.
How slow they are! And how much time they waste,
Refusing to make haste!

Yet still they leave us holding wretched stalks
Of disappointment, for, though nothing balks
Each big approach, leaning with brasswork prinked,
Each rope distinct,

Flagged, and the figurehead with golden tits
Arching our way, it never anchors; it's
No sooner present than it turns to past.
Right to the last

We think each one will heave to and unload
All good into our lives, all we are owed
For waiting so devoutly and so long.
But we are wrong:

Only one ship is seeking us, a black-
Sailed unfamiliar, towing at her back
A huge and birdless silence. In her wake
No waters breed or break.

william h. matchett

OLD INN ON THE EASTERN SHORE

On stifling summer days
While a listless peacock strays
Through the overgrown
    boxwood maze,
Scratching for insects and
    seeds
Among prehensile weeds,
The giant magnolia bleeds.
Each ravished ivory bud
Drops tarnished petals of
    blood
Whose heavy fragrance
    collects
In stagnant pools and infects
The pulsing air. No skill
Can protect the tainted will
From paralysis or death.
Merely to draw your breath
Is effort enough for the day,
As wilting lungs obey
The example of decay.
Brickdust drifts from the wall
In response to the crystal call
Of the oriole whose nest
Hangs from the loveliest
Branch of the oak like a shy
Tear on the cheek of the sky.
The afternoon creeps by
As slowly as the tide
Creeps into the cove to hide
The fetid mud where the
    sedge
Lines the channel's edge,
Bringing salt from the ocean

With imperceptible motion,
And bringing, at last, a breeze
That rummages through the
    trees,
Trails its fingers over the lawn
Stifles a heavy yawn
And curls at your feet and dies.
The silence magnifies
Each distant, diminutive
    sound—
The sturdy, steady pound
Of a pump across the river,
The spluttering of a flivver
On the county road, the drone
Of a sleepless locust, the
    groan
Of the sleeping spaniel—
    each noise
Accumulates and destroys
Any chance of comfort or
    rest.
A fitful nap is the best
You can wish for.

            Here is the end
Of all dreams. Here you sus-
    pend
Hope, pride, ambition,
In unclouded recognition.
Who would have thought
    that grace
Would seek out such a place?
Who would have suspected
    that light

Sufficient for second sight
Might linger here as a ghost,
Haunting the innermost
Heart of the boxwood maze,
Like the darkly shimmering
  rays
From a mythical pirate's
  cache,
Seeping out, not in a flash
Of insight, but slowly per-
  vading
The afternoon, slowly per-
  suading
Your eyes to turn inward and
  stare
At the emptiness honored
  there?
Caught, too weak to resist
The knowledge, too weak to
  insist
On turning your back, you
  must face
The evaded commonplace.
Your senses coalesce
In a multiple consciousness,
For your cognizance does not
  prevent
Awareness of sound and scent,
And this insight does not
  float
In an atmosphere vaguely
  remote
But anchors to here and now,
This place, the white oak
  bough,
The oriole's nest, the sweet
Sickly smell of magnolia, the
  heat

Reflected from red brick walls,
These, and the figure that
  sprawls
Uncomfortably in the shade,
You, and your wish to evade
The knowledge, that too is
  clear,
As is the mounting fear
Of your helplessness, hot and
  tired,
Lacking the will-power
  required.

It will pass. The insight
  will fade
With the sunset, and you will
  persuade
Yourself, as the evening
  grows cool,
That you have been playing
  the fool,
Allowing yourself to suppose
You had seen some truth in
  the throes
Of prostration, some horrible
  truth
Of deception & wasted youth,
The fantasies of a brain
Suffering under the strain
Of a long, hot, humid day,
Too exhausted to read or to
  play
The radio. You will rise
With the first of the fireflies
And, knowing yourself no
  sinner,
Will go in to bathe before
  dinner.

frank o'hara

TO THE HARBORMASTER

I wanted to be sure to reach you;
though my ship was on the way it got caught
in some moorings. I am always tying up
and then deciding to depart. In storms and
at sunset, with the metallic coils of the tide
around my fathomless arms, I am unable
to understand the forms of my vanity
or I am hard alee with my Polish rudder
in my hand and the sun sinking. To
you I offer my hull and the tattered cordage
of my will. The terrible channels where
the wind drives me against the brown lips
of the reeds are not all behind me. Yet
I trust the sanity of my vessel; and
if it sinks, it may well be in answer
to the reasoning of the eternal voices,
the waves which have kept me from reaching you.

POEM

The eager note on my door said "Call me,
call when you get in!" so I quickly threw
a few tangerines into my overnight bag,
straightened my eyelids and shoulders, and

headed straight for the door. It was autumn
by the time I got around the corner, oh all
unwilling to be either pertinent or bemused, but
the leaves were brighter than grass on the sidewalk!

Funny, I thought, that the lights are on this late
and the hall door open; still up at this hour, a
champion jai-alai player like himself? Oh fie!
for shame! What a host, so zealous! And he was

there in the hall, flat on a sheet of blood that
ran down the stairs. I did appreciate it. There are few
hosts who so thoroughly prepare to greet a guest
only casually invited, and that several months ago.

w. d. snodgrass

APRIL INVENTORY

The green catalpa tree has turned
All white; the cherry blooms once more.
In one whole year I haven't learned
A blessed thing they pay you for.
The blossoms snow down in my hair;
The trees and I will soon be bare.

The trees have more than I to spare.
The sleek, expensive girls I teach,
Younger and pinker every year,
Bloom gradually out of reach.
The pear tree lets its petals drop
Like dandruff on a tabletop.

The girls have grown so young by now
I have to nudge myself to stare.
This year they smile and mind me how
My teeth are falling with my hair.
In thirty years I may not get
Younger, shrewder, or out of debt.

The tenth time, just a year ago,
I made myself a little list
Of all the things I'd ought to know;
Then told my parents, analyst,
And everyone who's trusted me
I'd be substantial, presently.

I haven't read one book about
A book or memorized one plot.
Or found a mind I didn't doubt.
I learned one date. And then forgot.

And one by one the solid scholars
Get the degrees, the jobs, the dollars.

And smile above their starchy collars.
I taught my classes Whitehead's notions;
One lovely girl, a song of Mahler's.
Lacking a source-book or promotions,
I showed one child the colors of
A luna moth and how to love.

I taught myself to name my name,
To bark back, loosen love and crying;
To ease my woman so she came,
To ease an old man who was dying.
I have not learned how often I
Can win, can love, but choose to die.

I have not learned there is a lie
Love shall be blonder, slimmer, younger;
That my equivocating eye
Loves only by my body's hunger;
That I have poems, true to feel,
Or that the lovely world is real.

While scholars speak authority
And wear their ulcers on their sleeves,
My eyes in spectacles shall see
These trees procure and spend their leaves.
There is a value underneath
The gold and silver in my teeth.

Though trees turn bare and girls turn wives,
We shall afford our costly seasons;
There is a gentleness survives
That will outspeak and has its reasons.
There is a loveliness exists,
Preserves us. Not for specialists.

esther mathews

SONG

I can't be talkin' of love, dear,
I can't be talkin' of love.
If there be one thing I can't talk of
That one thing do be love.

But that's not sayin' that I'm not lovin'—
Still water, you know, runs deep,
An' I do be lovin' so deep, dear,
I be lovin' you in my sleep.

But I can't be talkin' of love, dear,
I can't be talkin' of love,
If there be one thing I can't talk of
That one thing do be love.

w. s. merwin

DECEMBER: OF APHRODITE

Whatever the books may say, or the plausible
Chroniclers intimate: that I was mad,
That an unsettling wind that season
Fretted my sign and fetched up violence
From the vagaries of dream, or even that pride
Is a broad road with few turnings, do not
Believe them. In her name I acted.

(Vidal once, the extravagant of heart,
For the love of a woman went mad, mad as a dog,
And the wolves ate him; Hercules, crazed
By that jealous goddess, murdered his children;
Samson, from a woman's lap, woke blinded,
Turning a mill in Gaza; Adam, our father,
Eating from his wife's hand, fell from the garden.)

Not that from heaven she twisted my tenderness
Into a hand of rage, nor because she delighted
In burnt offering, I in my five senses
Cut throats of friends, burned the white harvest, waged
Seven months' havoc even among
Her temples; but because she waited always
There in the elegant shell, asking for sweetness.

And though it was in her name the land was ravaged,
Spilled and dishonored, let it not be said
That by her wiles it was done, nor that she gave
That carnage her blessing. All arrogant demons
Pretending changelessness, who came first when she called,
Have faded and are spent, till out of the strong,
Without death, she conjured the honeycomb.

She sits at evening under a gray arch
Where many marvels fell, where all has fallen:
The blue over her dolphins, the poplar leaves,
The cold rain, all but the grave myrtle
And the rings of her ringdoves. The doge of one calendar
Would give her a name of winter, but where I stand
In the hazed gold of her eyes, the world is green.

DICTUM: FOR A MASQUE OF DELUGE

There will be the cough before the silence, then
Expectation; and the hush of portent
Must be welcomed by a diffident music
Lisping and dividing its renewals;
Shadows will lengthen and sway, and, casually
As in a latitude of diversion
Where growth is topiary, and the relaxed horizons
Are accustomed to the trespass of surprise,
One with a mask of Ignorance will appear
Musing on the wind's strange pregnancy.

And to him one must enter from the south
In a feigned haste, with disaster on his lips,
And tales of distended seas, continents
Submerged, worlds drowned, and of drownings
In mirrors; unto this foreboding
Let them add sidelong but increasing mention,
With darkening syllables, of shadows, as though
They stood and traded restlessness beneath
A gathering dark, until their figures seem
But a flutter of speech down an expense of wind.

So, with talk, like a blather of rain, begun,
Weather will break and the artful world will rush
Incontinent. There must be a vessel.
There must be rummage and shuffling for salvation
Till on that stage and violence, among
Curtains of tempest and shaking sea,
A covered basket, where a child might lie,
Timbered with osiers and floated on a shadow,
Glides adrift, as improbably sailing
As a lotus flower bearing a bull.

Hills are to be forgotten; the patter of speech
Must lilt upon flatness. The beasts will come;
And as they come, let one man, by the ark,
Drunken with desolation, his tongue
Rounding the full statement of the seasons,
Tremble and stare, his eyes seeming to chase
A final clatter of doomed crows, to seek
An affirmation, a mercy, an island,
Or hills crested with towns, and to find only
Cities of cloud already crumbling.

And these the beasts: the bull from the lotus flower
With wings at his shoulders; and a goat, winged;
A serpent undulating in the air;
A lion with wings like falling leaves;
These are to wheel on a winged wheel above

The sullen ark, while hare, swine, crocodile,
Camel and mouse come; and the sole man, always,
Lurches on childish limbs above the basket—
To his mere humanity seas shall not attain
With tempest, nor the obscure sky with torches.

(Why is it rumored that these beasts come in pairs
When the anatomies of their existence
Are wrought for singularity? They walk
Beside their shadows; their best motions are
Figments on the drapery of the air.
Their propagation is a redoubling
Merely of dark against the wall, a planetary
Leaning in the night unto their shadows
And stiffening to the moment of eclipse;
Shadows will be their lean progeny.)

At last the sigh of recession: the land
Wells from the water; the beasts depart; the man
Whose shocked speech must conjure a landscape
As of some country where the dead years keep
A circle of silence, a drying vista of ruin,
Musters himself, rises, and stumbling after
The dwindling beasts, under the all-colored
Paper rainbow, whose arc he sees as promise,
Moves in an amazement of resurrection,
Solitary, impoverished, renewed.

A falling frond may seem all trees. If so
We know the tone of falling. We shall find
Dictions for rising, words for departure;
And time will be sufficient before that revel
To teach an order and rehearse the days
Till the days are accomplished: so now the dove
Makes assignations with the olive tree,
Slurs with her voice the gestures of the time:
The day foundering, the dropping sun
Heavy, the wind a low portent of rain.

jon silkin

A SPACE IN THE AIR

The first day he had gone
I barely missed him. I was glad almost he had left
    Without a bark or flick of his tail,
        I was content he had slipped

Out into the world. I felt,
Without remarking, it was nearly a relief
    From his dirty habits. Then, the second
        Day I noticed the space

He left behind him. A hole
Cut out of the air. And I missed him suddenly,
    Missed him almost without knowing
        Why it was so. And I grew

Afraid he was dead, expecting death
As something I had grown used to. I was afraid
    The clumsy children in the street
        Had cut his tail off as

A souvenir of the living and
I did not know what to do. I was fearing
    Somebody had hurt him. I called his name
        But the hole in the air remained.

I have grown accustomed to death
Lately. But his absence made me sad,
    I do not know how he should do it
        But his absence frightened me.

It was not only his death I feared,
Not only his but as if all of those
    I loved, as if all those near me
        Should suddenly go

Into the hole in the light
And disappear. As if all of them should go
Without barking, without speaking,
Without noticing me there

But go; and going as if
The instrument of pain were a casual thing
To suffer, as if they should suffer so,
Casually and without greatness,

Without purpose even. But just go.
I should be afraid to lose all those friends like this.
I should fear to lose those loves. But mostly
I should fear to lose you.

If you should go
Without affliction, but even so, I should tear
The rent you would make in the air
And the bare howling

Streaming after your naked hair.
I should feel your going down more than my going down.
My own death I bear everyday
More or less

But your death would be something else,
Something else beyond me. It would not be
Your death or my death, love,
But our rose-linked dissolution.

So I feared his going,
His death, not our death, but a hint at our death. And I shall
always fear
The death of those we love as
The hint of your death, love.

ted hughes

THE MARTYRDOM OF BISHOP FARRAR

Burned in the reign of Mary Tudor at Caermarthon. *"If I flinch from the pain of burning, believe not the doctrine that I have preached."* (His words on being chained to the stake.)

Bloody Mary's venomous flames can curl;
They can shrivel sinew and char bone
Of foot, ankle, knee, and thigh, and boil
Bowels, and drop his heart a cinder down;
And her soldiers can cry, as they hurl
Logs in the red rush: "This is her sermon."

The sullen-jowled watching Welsh townspeople
Hear him crack in the fire's mouth; they see what
Black oozing twist of stuff bubbles the smell
That tars and retches their lungs: no pulpit
Of his ever held their eyes so still,
Never, as now his agony, his wit.

An ignorant means to establish ownership
Of his flock! Thus their shepherd she seized
And knotted him into this blazing shape
In their eyes, as if such could have cauterised
The trust they turned towards him, and branded on
Its stump her claim, to outlaw question.

So it might have been: seeing their exemplar
And teacher burned for his lessons to black bits,
Their silence might have disowned him to her,
And hung up what he had taught with their Welsh hats:
Who sees his blasphemous father struck by fire
From heaven, might well be heard to speak no oaths.

But the fire that struck here, come from Hell even,
Kindled little heavens in his words
As he fed his body to the flame alive.

Words which, before they will be dumbly spared,
Will burn their body and be tongued with fire
Make paltry folly of flesh and this world's air.

When they saw what annuities of hours
And comfortable blood he burned to get
His words a bare honouring in their ears,
The shrewd townsfolk pocketed them hot:
Stamp was not current but they rang and shone
As good gold as any queen's crown.

Gave all he had, and yet the bargain struck
To a merest farthing his whole agony,
His body's cold-kept miserdom of shrieks
He gave uncounted, while out of his eyes,
Out of his mouth, fire like a glory broke,
And smoke burned his sermons into the skies.

THE HAG

The old story went that the cajoling hag
Fattened the pretty princess within a fence
Of barbs the spiders poked their eight eyes out in
Even, the points were so close, fattened her
With pastry pies and would not let her incline
One inch toward the threshold from the table
Lest she slip off the hag's dish and exchange
The hag's narrow intestine for the wide world.
And this hag had to lie in a certain way
At night lest the horrible angular black hatred
Poke through her side and surprise the pretty princess
Who was well-deceived by this posture of love.

Now here is an old hag, as I see,
Has got this story direly drastically wrong,
Who has dragged her pretty daughter home from college,
Who has locked up her pretty eyes in a brick house
And has sworn her pretty mouth shall rot like fruit
Before the world shall make a jam of it

To spread on every palate. And so saving,
She must lie perforce at night in a certain way
Lest the heart break through her side and burst the walls
And surprise her daughter with an extravagance
Of tearful love, who finds it easier
To resign her hope of a world wide with love,
And even to rot in the dark, but easier under
Nine bolts of spite than on one leash of love.

THE THOUGHT-FOX

I imagine this midnight moment's forest:
Something else is alive
Beside the clock's loneliness
And this blank page where my fingers move.

Through the window I see no star:
Something more near
Though deeper within darkness
Is entering the loneliness:

Cold, delicately as the dark snow,
A fox's nose touches twig, leaf;
Two eyes serve a movement, that now
And again now, and now, and now

Sets neat prints into the snow
Between trees, and warily a lame
Shadow lags by stump and in hollow
Of a body that is bold to come

Across clearings, an eye,
A widening deepening greenness,
Brilliantly, concentratedly,
Coming about its own business

Till, with a sudden sharp hot stink of fox
It enters the dark hole of the head.
The window is starless still; the clock ticks,
The page is printed.

index of authors and titles

PUBLISHER'S NOTE

Mr. Williams chose the following poems by T. S. Eliot
for inclusion in *The Pocket Book of Modern Verse:*

> The Love Song of J. Alfred Prufrock
> Morning at the Window
> The Wind Sprang up at Four O'Clock
> The Waste Land
> Sweeney Among the Nightingales
> Journey of the Magi
> East Coker
> The Boston Evening Transcript
> Gerontion
> Whispers of Immortality

For these and other poems by Mr. Eliot the publisher
recommends the following books to the reader:

The Complete Poems and Plays of T. S. Eliot
published by Harcourt, Brace & Co. $6.00

The Collected Poems of T. S. Eliot
published by Harcourt, Brace & Co. $4.25

A Little Treasury of Modern Poetry
(College Edition), *edited by Oscar Williams*
published by Charles Scribner's Sons $3.75

Immortal Poems of the English Language
edited by Oscar Williams
published by Washington Square Press, Inc. 90c

F. T. Palgrave's *The Golden Treasury* (A Mentor Book)
revised and enlarged by Oscar Williams
published by The New American Library 95c

(See Editor's Note, Page 9)

ABOUT THE EDITOR

Oscar Williams (1900–1964), editor of this book, was himself a distinguished poet. The author of five books of poetry, including *That's All That Matters* and *Selected Poems*, he has been called "clever, disconcerting, rash" (Lionel Abel) and "a very real and important poet . . . (whose) powerful imagery and unique personal idiom will add a permanent page to American poetry" (Dylan Thomas).

Mr. Williams achieved literary distinction not only as a highly original and vigorous American poet, but also as one of the great poetry anthologists of his time. His most outstanding anthologies are "The Little Treasury Series," *The War Poets, Immortal Poems of the English Language, The Pocket Book of Modern Verse* and *The New Pocket Anthology of American Verse*, the latter three published by Washington Square Press, Inc. These are accepted as present-day classics in their fields and are in wide use in colleges and universities. Other anthologies include a revised edition of Palgrave's *The Golden Treasury, The Major British Poets, The Major American Poets*, and *The Silver Treasury of Light Verse*.

Mr. Williams' last and most ambitious anthology was *Master Poems of the English Language*, now also published by Washington Square Press, Inc. A huge work of over 1100 pages, illustrated with portraits of the poets and combining a comprehensive anthology with a broad sampling of critical writing, it is a superb contribution by the man Robert Lowell called "probably the best anthologist in America."